USES AND MISUSES OF DATA FOR EDUCATIONAL
ACCOUNTABILITY AND IMPROVEMENT

The *Yearbook of the National Society for the Study of Education* (ISSN 0077-5762, online ISSN 1744-7984) is published in April and June by Blackwell Publishing with offices at 350 Main St, Malden, MA 02148 USA; PO Box 1354, Garsington Rd, Oxford, OX4 2DQ, UK; and PO Box 378 Carlton South, 3053 Victoria, Australia.

Society and Membership Office:
The *Yearbook* is published on behalf of the National Society for the Study of Education, with offices at: University of Illinois at Chicago, College of Education (M/C 147) 1040 W. Harrison Street Chicago, IL 60607-7133. For membership information, please visit www.nsse-chicago.org.

Subscription Rates for Volume 104, 2005

	The Americas[†]	Rest of World[‡]
Institutional Standard Rate*	$125	£77
Institutional Premium Rate	$138	£85

*Includes print plus basic online access. [†]Customers in Canada should add 7% GST or provide evidence of entitlement to exemption.
[‡]Customers in the UK should add VAT at 5%; customers in the EU should also add VAT at 5%, or provide a VAT registration number or evidence of entitlement to exemption.
For more information about Blackwell Publishing journals, including online access information, terms and conditions, and other pricing options, please visit www.blackwellpublishing.com.
All orders must be paid by check, money order, or credit card. Checks should be made payable to Blackwell. Checks in US dollars must be drawn on a US bank. Checks in Sterling must be drawn on a UK bank.

Volume 104 is available from the publisher for $40 a copy. For earlier Volumes please contact Periodical Service Company, L. P., 11 Main Street, Germantown, NY 12526-5635 USA Tel: (+518) 537-4700, Fax: (+518) 537-5899, Email: Psc@backsets.com or http://www.backsets.com

For new orders, renewals, sample copy requests, claims, changes of address and all other subscription correspondences please contact the Journals Department at your nearest Blackwell office (address details listed above). US office phone 800-835-6770 or 781-388-8200, Fax 781-388-8232, Email subscrip@bos.blackwellpublishing.com; UK office phone +44 (0) 1865-778315, Fax +44 (0) 1865-471775, Email customerservices@oxon.blackwellpublishing.com; Asia office phone +61 3 9347 0300, Fax +61 3 9347 5001, Email subscriptions@blackwellpublishingasia.com.

The *Yearbook* is mailed Standard Rate. Mailing to rest of world by DHL Smart & Global Mail. Canadian mail is sent by Canadian publications mail agreement number 40573520.

Postmaster: Send all address changes to *Yearbook of the National Society for the Study of Education*, Blackwell Publishing Inc., Journals Subscription Department, 350 Main St., Malden, MA 02148-5020.

Blackwell
Synergy Sign up to receive Blackwell *Synergy* free e-mail alerts with complete *Yearbook* tables of contents and quick links to article abstracts from the most current issue. Simply go to www.blackwell-synergy.com, select the journal from the list of journals, and click on "Sign-up" for FREE email table of contents alerts.

Disclaimer: The Publisher, the National Society for the Study of Education and Editor(s) cannot be held responsible for errors or any consequences arising from the use of information contained in this journal; the views and opinions expressed do not necessarily reflect those of the Publisher, Society or Editor(s).

USES AND MISUSES OF DATA FOR EDUCATIONAL ACCOUNTABILITY AND IMPROVEMENT

104th Yearbook of the
National Society for the Study of Education

PART II

Edited by
JOAN L. HERMAN
EDWARD H. HAERTEL

20 NSSE 05

Distributed by BLACKWELL PUBLISHING MALDEN, MASSACHUSETTS

National Society for the Study of Education

The National Society for the Study of Education was founded in 1901 as successor to the National Herbart Society. It publishes an annual two-volume Yearbook, each volume dealing with a separate topic of concern to educators. The Society's yearbook series, now in its one hundred and fourth year, presents articles by scholars and practitioners who are noted for their significant work in critical areas of education.

The Society welcomes as members all individuals who wish to receive its publications and take part in Society activities. Current membership includes educators in the United States, Canada, and elsewhere throughout the world—professors and graduate students in colleges and universities; teachers, administrators, supervisors, and curriculum specialists in elementary and secondary schools; policymakers and researchers at all levels; and any others with an interest in teaching and learning.

Members of the Society elect a Board of Directors. The Board's responsibilities include reviewing proposals for Yearbooks and authorizing their preparation based on accepted proposals, along with guiding the other activities of the Society, including presentations and forums.

Current dues (for 2005) are a modest $40 ($35 for retired members and for students in their first year of membership; $45 for international membership). Members whose dues are paid for the current calendar year receive the Society's Yearbook and are eligible for election to the Board of Directors.

Each year the Society arranges for meetings to be held in conjunction with the annual conferences of one or more of the national educational organizations. All members are urged to attend these meetings, at which the current Yearbook is presented and critiqued. Members are encouraged to submit proposals for future Yearbooks.

Uses and Misuses of Data in Accountability Testing is part II of the 104th Yearbooks. Part I, published earlier, is titled *Media Literacy: Transforming Curriculum and Teaching*.

For further information, write to the Secretary, NSSE, University of Illinois at Chicago, College of Education M/C 147, 1040 W. Harrison St., Chicago, Illinois 60607-7133 or see http://www.nsse-chicago.org

v

DAVID ROGOSA, Stanford University
ELLE RUSTIQUE-FORRESTER, Stanford University
JEROME M. SHAW, University of California, Santa Cruz
KYO YAMASHIRO, Center for the Study of Evaluation/CRESST, University of California, Los Angeles
RAYMOND YEAGLEY, Rochester School Department, Rochester, New York

Reviewers of the Yearbook

CHARLES ACHILLES, Seton Hall, Eastern Michigan University
LORIN ANDERSON, University of South Carolina, Columbia
LINDA BEHAR-HORENSTEIN, University of Florida, Gainesville
WILLIAM L. BROWN, Michigan Educational Assessment Program, Michigan Department of Education
JOSEPH CIECHALSKI, East Carolina University
FAITH CRAMPTON, University of Wisconsin Milwaukee
GABRIEL DELLA-PIANA, National Science Foundation
PETER DEMYAN, San Jacinto School District, California Howard Everson, The College Board
WENDY DICKINSON, University of South Florida
R. TONY EICHELBERGER, University of Pittsburgh
HOWARD EVERSON, The College Board
JANET FAIRMAN, University of Maine
BRIAN GONG, The National Center for the Improvement of Educational Assessment
EDMUND HAMANN, Brown University
JANET HEDDESHEIMER, The George Washington University
MARGIE JORGENSEN, Harcourt Assessment
KATHERINE KASTEN, University of North Florida
LAKSHMI KRIPILANI, Seton Hall University
CHERIE PEIL, Victor Elementary School District, Victorville, California
RICK PHILLIPS, Eastern Washington University
JOHN SMITHSON, University of Wisconsin, Madison
SAMUEL STRINGFIELD, University of Louisville
SUSAN STUDER, California Baptist University
CINDY TANANIS, University of Pittsburgh
JAMES TAYLOR, American Institutes for Research
CHARLES VANOVER, University of Michigan
HARTGER WASSINK, Consultant, The Netherlands
JENNYLYNN WERNER, Six Sigma Performance, Tempe, Arizona
E. JANE WILLIAMS, The Ohio State University

Table of Contents

Part One
CHAPTER
Foundations

Part Two
Design and Analysis Issues

Part Three
Issues of Fairness and Consequences

Part Four
Moving to Better Practice

Preface

On January 8, 2002, President Bush signed into law the No Child Left Behind Act of 2001 (NCLB), making assessment and accountability the cornerstone of federal policies to promote educational opportunities for the disadvantaged—the economically poor, students of color, English learners, and students with disabilities—and to reduce the achievement gap between these students and their more advantaged peers. The statute insists that all children can and will achieve high standards and requires that schools show regular progress toward this goal on state-developed, standards-based tests. Every child in grades three through eight and at the high school level must be tested annually in reading and mathematics, and all districts and schools must show adequate yearly progress to enable all their students to achieve proficiency in the standards by the year 2014. Those districts and schools that fail to meet annual, state-established proficiency targets—deemed adequate yearly progress (AYP)—for every numerically significant subgroup are subject to progressive corrective actions, which over five years can result in reconstitution and takeover. Parents of students in schools that fail to meet their targets may request their children be transferred to another school and over time may enroll their children in private, supplementary services, all at district expense. With such sanctions, the law creates unprecedented pressure for districts and schools to improve test performance; moreover, for most districts and schools AYP targets mean improvement trajectories that have rarely, if ever, been seen (see Linn, 2003).

Now three years after the passage of the bill, assessment and accountability loom large on the educational agenda, enmeshed in political and technical controversy and assuring full employment for those with assessment and measurement expertise. There is a straightforward logic to current accountability policy: states establish standards, set goals, measure progress, and enforce expectations with sanctions. Educators and students are expected to focus teaching and learning on the standards and to use feedback from the tests to inform their efforts, to refine their educational programs and strategies, and to improve student learning.

However, while the policy logic may be appealingly simple, the reality of assessment and accountability surely are not, as the history of educational assessment well documents. Without even addressing the central problem of policy success—assuring effective instruction for all students—the technical challenges of accountability design and use are complicated. Complex decisions must be made about what should be assessed and whose values are represented, about what kinds of tests should be developed and how, about how various elements of the system are designed and analyzed. Perplexing questions of fairness and consequences arise, and while many lessons have been learned about improving and instantiating evidence-based practices, substantial quandaries remain. As the chapters of this volume demonstrate, the field has moved forward in its understanding of assessment and its role in accountability and educational improvement, but significant challenges remain.

The first set of chapters in the volume deal with foundational issues. Edward Haertel and Joan Herman start with "A Historical Perspective on Validity Arguments for Accountability Testing." In it, they explore the historical arguments that have been mounted as rationales for educational testing over the last century. Starting from the days of Edward Thorndike, the birth of educational measurement, and Ralph Tyler's groundbreaking vision of curriculum evaluation, they trace theories and themes that reverberate in today's accountability systems: the ideas that education should produce measurable results; that data on performance should be useful to educators and others in analyzing and improving their performance; that assessment data have both motivational and informational value; that devising assessments is a very complex endeavor and can never fully capture the complexity of human performance; and that fairness must be a continuing concern. The promise of testing and accountability for improving education has been advanced over and over again, each time clothed in the psychology of the time, with each generation applying ever more sophisticated knowledge to the shortcomings of its predecessors. The search continues.

Lorraine McDonnell, in "Assessment and Accountability from the Policymaker's Perspective," then explores the political roots of current accountability testing. Her analysis elaborates on the ways in which testing serves as a political accountability tool, playing a prominent role in the political oversight of public education and the democratic accountability of elected officials. The ideological and cultural debates that surround the definition of standards and what should be taught and tested are also, at base, political issues. McDonnell describes the various constituencies with an interest in educational assessment and probes how political incentives motivate and shape testing policy for policymakers and their constituents. The chapter concludes with a discussion of the implications of a political perspective on testing, focusing particularly on the likelihood that such a perspective can be reconciled with professional testing standards and the concerns of professional educators.

In "Goals for Learning and Assessment," Judith Ramaley continues the discussion of the goals and values that ultimately underlie accountability systems. She explores the changing definitions of scientific literacy and the role of science in today's world. She considers their implications for our conceptions of what it means to be educated and prepared for the challenges of adult life, work, and citizenship. She argues that narrow definitions of scientific literacy need to be expanded and that the question of what is worth knowing must be broadly considered. As she notes, "If we choose carefully what we test and if we hold ourselves accountable for measuring learning that matters, we will send strong signals about what we think it means to be well-educated and what knowledge and skills we value as a society."

Robert Linn, in "Issues in the Design of Accountability Systems", moves the volume to technical issues that are fundamental in the creation of systems that can contribute to improved teaching and student learning. Linn first considers fundamental questions of assessment quality—alignment, validity, and reliability. A second set of issues focus on how tests results are interpreted and used. For example, does the system focus on status, or on change in student performance, or both? Are results used to make decisions about individual students or only about schools? A final set of issues relates to decisions about how results are reported, for example, the setting and use of performance standards, the establishment of goals or targets, and the rules for disaggregating results.

Daniel Koretz, in "Alignment, High Stakes, and the Inflation of Test Scores," explores in greater depth the validity and alignment issues raised by Linn. As Koretz notes, the alignment of testing and instruction does not guarantee the validity of test results and indeed may contribute to score inflation. Based on the range of activities in which teachers might engage to align their instruction and prepare students for high-stakes tests, Koretz defines inappropriate preparation practices and discusses how such practices relate to the mechanisms of score inflation. He ends by considering two fundamental challenges that face policymakers in designing test-based accountability systems: evaluating the validity of gains and tuning the system to create the right mix of incentives to minimize score inflation. Among his recommendations are: regular evaluation of gains, attainable performance targets, the use of multiple measures, and the reestablishment of a role for professional judgment.

In "Exploring Models of School Performance: From Theory to Practice," Kilchan Choi, Pete Goldschmidt, and Kyo Yamashiro explore competing models for determining school performance and effectiveness. They consider as model building blocks important properties of assessment, a range of test metrics, and a variety of ways of summarizing student achievement and monitoring student achievement over time. They present a continuum of accountability models that ranges from simple calculations on the one end to complex statistical models on the other. They focus particularly on value-added models (VAM), which represent the upper end of the spectrum, comparing the results from VAM with inferences based on current federally mandated accountability models. They also present empirical evidence on the effects of adjusting accountability models for student characteristics. Their work clearly shows that choice of model matters. Schools that are identified as effective under one model may not be identified as effective under another.

David Rogosa closes the section with "Statistical Misunderstandings of the Properties of School Scores and School Accountability," which presents an overview of important statistical misconceptions that have arisen in current work on educational assessment and school accountability. The chapter presents a series of nine vignettes, starting with misunderstandings about the statistical uncertainty in a group summary (school-score) to the consequences of uncertainty for properties of accountability decisions to attempts to adjust accountability criteria for the effects of uncertainty. As Rogosa notes, "Accountability is not a bad thing, but it can be done badly." He clarifies statistical concepts that are central to good practice.

Moving to issues of fairness and consequences of accountability testing, Jamal Abedi focuses on the challenges of assuring valid assessments for English learners, in "Issues and Consequences for English Language Learners." He points to the importance of including English Language Learning (ELL) students in accountability systems to assure their educational needs are met and explores the dilemmas and challenges in doing so. The chapter is structured around six factors that potentially have a significant impact on equity and fairness for ELLs: ELL classification; inclusion/exclusion rules; the confounding of language with assessment; the use of native language assessment; the appropriateness, validity, and feasibility of accommodations; and cultural factors. As Abedi notes, "The greater the impact of these factors on ELL student performance, the more the fairness of the accountability system is compromised."

Diana Pullin similarly explores conundrums in the assessment of students with disabilities in "When One Size Does Not Fit All—The Special Challenges of Accountability Testing for Students with Disabilities." She examines the unique set of challenges for accountability testing that are complicated by the history of educating students with disabilities, the social and educational policy goals for these students, and the legal provisions for the education of these students. As Pullin observes, despite strong mandates, there is limited research available to inform assessment design or the validity of results. And as the stakes and visibility of current testing programs increase, the potential for misuse of data concerning these students becomes more significant.

In "Is the Glass Half Full or Mostly Empty? Ending Social Promotion in Chicago," Melissa Roderick, Jenny Nagoaka, and Elaine Allensworth explore the effects of high stakes testing in Chicago, where grade-to-grade promotion is contingent on test results. After describing the Chicago policy and its evaluation, Roderick and colleagues examine available evidence supporting pro and con claims about students', parents', and teachers' responses to the Chicago initiative and investigate the effects of the policy on students' test scores overall and on students who were retained. Results suggest a mixed and complex picture of program effects: while there is evidence of important benefits, results also suggest significant negative impact on the lowest performing and most vulnerable children in the system. The authors suggest the need for additional research on retention and on optimal strategies for serving the needs of students who are struggling. As they conclude, "the key is to move beyond the debates of retention versus social promotion, accountability versus capacity building, to begin to understand how we may better build accountability and incentive systems that combine the best of both worlds: that promote attention to students, motivate students to achieve, and make parents, teachers, and students partners in education, while at the same time pushing instruction in positive ways and building strong systems of supports for teachers and schools to mount effective strategies."

In his chapter on "High School Exit Examinations: When Do Learning Effects Generalize?" John Bishop examines the mixed results of research on the effects of high-stakes testing on student learning. He distinguishes minimum competency tests (MCTs) and standards-based exams (SBEs) from Curriculum-Based External Exit Exam Systems (CBEEESs), and further distinguishes between voluntary CBEEESs and universal CBEEESs. He argues that the distinguishing features of CBEEESs should make them more effective than MCTs or SBEs in motivating greater effort and achievement for both low-achieving and high-achieving students, and finds supporting evidence for his hypothesis in a variety of studies in the United States and around the world.

Linda Darling-Hammond and Elle Rustique-Forrester conclude the section with "The Consequences of Student Testing for Teaching and Teacher Quality," in which they analyze the consequences of accountability testing for the nature and quality of teaching and for the recruitment and retention of a high-quality teaching workforce. They find that the use of student assessment as a strategy for improving education has had positive consequences for teaching and teacher quality in some contexts, but that unintended negative consequences have also been found in systems that use limited measures and that emphasize sanctions without attention to improving school and teaching quality. They conclude with policy recommendations for assessment system design and use, including broader use of performance assessments; system designs that combine large-scale and classroom assessments; systematic investments in teacher knowledge and school capacity; incorporation of standards-based evaluation in licensing, certification, and ongoing evaluation; and incentives that support organizational learning rather than "gaming" the system.

The final section of the volume investigates current assessment practices and how they can be improved. In "Data Use and School Improvement: Challenges and Prospects," Margaret Heritage and Raymond Yeagley examine characteristics of effective data use, outline challenges in incorporating evidence-based practices in schools, and offer perspectives on how best practice in data use can become a widespread reality in schools. They consider basic questions that underlie school inquiry, the essential characteristics of data needed to guide school improvement, and key elements in integrating data into school practices. After laying out the stages of effective data use practices, they conclude by noting the considerable human capital and leadership challenges involved in making data use a reality in schools and caution that "the objective of assessment is to provide structure, rather than stricture, for professional practice."

In "Getting Things Right at the Classroom Level," Jerome Shaw discusses assessment from the perspective of the classroom, including in his purview both external, large-scale assessment and internal, curriculum-based assessment. His discussion is guided by two fundamental principles: assessment for learning and assessment for equity. Assess-

ment for learning addresses the extent to which "assessment contribute[s] to and does not impede student learning in *individual classrooms*."
The equity principle draws attention to current inequities in the American educational system for students who are nonwhite, nonnative
speakers of English, female, and/or poor, and implicates assessment as
a factor contributing to such inequity. The equity principle asks "To
what extent does assessment contribute to and not impede learning for
all individual students?" Shaw provides examples of how these principles can be incorporated into classroom practice by "integrating content
and cultural standards into assessment design, judiciously using accommodations during the delivery of assessments, and basing scoring decisions on knowledge of diverse students' culture and language."

Closing the volume, Eva Baker, in "Technology and Effective
Assessment Systems," observes that "It is time for rethinking assessment systems from design perspectives and the ways in which technology can improve their quality." Baker lays out critical features of
learning-based assessment development and describes the design components of a synchronized accountability system, which bases external
and classroom measures on the common benchmarks. In the system,
assessment is routinely used to monitor and improve instruction and
external assessments and measures of transfer are used to evaluate and
assure the validity of system results. The chapter emphasizes how technology could help with the design and implementation of such a system, support teacher capacity to engage in assessment, and improve
reports. Finally, Baker advocates for systematic evaluation of accountability and assessment systems, recommending as criteria for success,
in addition to feasibility: (1) observed increases in the sophistication of
teacher-made measures; (2) teachers' enhanced ability to identify and
assist students in the acquisition and application of skills and knowledge; (3) students' acquisition of knowledge and skill at faster rates; and
(4) students' ability to transfer learning (standards) in situations other
than the agreed-upon state test.

We believe that the accumulated chapters well illustrate the range
of factors that must be addressed in the design and appropriate use of
accountability systems that can serve educational improvement. Optimal designs require multiple lenses and perspectives—advanced technical expertise, sophisticated sociopolitical understandings, sensitivity
to diversity and equity, and strategic knowledge about the practicalities
of organizational change and effective educational strategies. Even with
the substantial and varied knowledge bases that have been assembled in
these areas, success remains elusive. We hope that this volume will serve

to document the current state of the art and contribute to continuing research and dialogue that fuels success.

We thank all the authors of the volume for their contributions. We are particularly grateful to Debra Miretzky at the National Society for the Study of Education (NSSE) for her patient prodding, thoughtful reviews, and very helpful editing. We are thankful as well for insightful reviews we received from the many anonymous NSSE members who reviewed earlier drafts.

Joan L. Herman
Edward H. Haertel
Editors

REFERENCES

Linn, R.L. (2003). Accountability: Responsibility and reasonable expectations. *Educational Researcher, 32*(7), 3–13.
No Child Left Behind Act of 2001, Pub. L. No. 107-110, 115 Stat. 1425 (2002).

Part One
FOUNDATIONS

CHAPTER 1

A Historical Perspective on Validity Arguments for Accountability Testing

EDWARD H. HAERTEL AND JOAN L. HERMAN

Using achievement tests to hold students and schools accountable seems an obvious idea. Students come to school to learn. Tests show which students, in which schools, are meeting learning standards and which are not. Those students and schools that are falling short should be held accountable. Of course, the rationales for accountability testing programs are much more complex than that, as are testing's effects, both intended and unintended. In this chapter, we describe various rationales for accountability testing programs over the past century. This history forms the backdrop for current test-driven reforms, including Public Law 107-110, the No Child Left Behind Act of 2001 (NCLB), which was signed into law in January 2002. Our goals are first, to illustrate the diversity of mechanisms whereby testing may affect educational practice and learning outcomes, and second, to show that while many

Edward Haertel is a Professor of Education in the School of Education at Stanford University. Joan Herman is the Co-director of the Center for Research on Evaluation, Standards, and Student Testing (CRESST) and the UCLA Center for the Study of Evaluation.

The work reported herein was supported under the Educational Research and Development Centers Program, PR/Award Number R305B960002, as administered by the Institute of Education Sciences (IES), and the U.S. Department of Education. The findings and opinions expressed in this report are those of the authors and do not necessarily reflect the positions or policies of the National Center for Education Research, the Institute of Education Sciences (IES), or the U.S. Department of Education.

of the same ideas have recurred over time in different forms and guises, accountability testing *has* become more sophisticated. We have a better understanding today than in the past of how to make accountability testing an effective policy tool, although it remains to be seen if we will make the best use of this understanding. The NCLB legislation incorporates various testing policy mechanisms. It relies on testing to focus attention on valued learning outcomes; to spur greater effort on the part of administrators, teachers, and students; to help parents become better informed about school quality; and to direct the allocation of educational resources, including within-school allocations of time and effort, toward groups of students that have lagged behind. Companion federal initiatives rely on testing to identify and to promote effective instructional programs. A look back may offer some insight into both the promise and the pitfalls of contemporary policies.

A theory of action for educational reform typically embodies one or more intended uses or interpretations of test scores. Testing is usually just one part of a more comprehensive reform strategy. For example, assessments might be expected to identify students requiring remedial assistance, focus attention on teachers whose students are doing especially well or poorly, identify schools where additional resources are needed, or draw attention to achievement disparities among demographic groups. Other elements of the reform strategy would address the delivery of the remedial assistance, reward or sanction deserving teachers, or allocate needed resources. Testing also may be expected to further reform goals in ways less directly tied to the information provided by the scores themselves. For example, a testing program may be expected to clarify learning objectives for teachers or to encourage them to focus on the (tested) basics instead of (untested) "frills," to induce students to work harder, or to focus public attention on issues of school quality and resources. These various mechanisms each imply some *interpretive argument* (Kane, 1992) that could be set forth by way of justification. Interpretive arguments are rationales, often implicit, that might explain exactly how accountability testing is expected to be beneficial. Obtaining and weighing evidence to support or refute the interpretive argument is the business of test validation.

More ominous interpretive arguments may also be formulated. Perhaps accountability testing merely offers the public some hollow assurance as to elected officials' commitment to education. After all, those who propose new testing programs are likely to see achievement gains in two or three years, right on schedule for the next election (Linn, 2000). Perhaps by reinforcing categories of success and failure, testing contributes to the reproduction of social inequality (Varenne & McDermott, 1999). Testing may subtly shift the blame for school failure from inadequate school resources, poor teacher preparation, or out-of-school factors to teachers and students who are "simply not working hard enough," and thereby divert attention from more costly, more needed reforms.

The next sections of this chapter describe testing during different periods, from the early 20th century to the present. Most of these periods are characterized by one or another predominant mode of test use in education. Where appropriate, we refer back to the earlier roots of testing applications characteristic of a given period.

The Turn of the 20th Century: The Birth of Educational Testing

Expectations for educational accountability and student assessment have come a long way since 1864, when the Reverend George Fisher of Greenwich Hospital School in England put forth, apparently to no avail, the idea of a "Scale-Book," which would

contain the numbers assigned to each degree of proficiency in the various subjects of examination: for instance, if it be required to determine the numerical equivalent corresponding to any specimen of "writing," a comparison is made with the various standard specimens, which are arranged in this book in order of merit; the highest being represented by the number 1, and the lowest by 5, and the intermediate values by affixing to these numbers the fractions 1/4, 1/2, or 3/4. (Cited in Ayres, 1918, p. 9)

The scale book in turn would be used to assign each student "a fixed standard of estimation that could be used in determining the sum total . . . or value of any given set of results" (cited in Ayres, 1918, p. 10, where it is attributed to E.B. Chadwick in *The Museum, a Quarterly Magazine of Education, Literature and Science*, Vol. II, 1864). It is long since 1894, as well, when Dr. J.M. Rice in the United States first proposed and was ridiculed for the idea of using an objective standard—in his case a test of 50 spelling words—to compare the relative effectiveness of methods used in different schools (as related by Ayres, pp. 9–15).

Fisher and Price were forbearers to what Ayres (1918) credits as "the real beginning of the scientific measurement of educational products" (p. 12), the publication of the Thorndike Scale for the Measurement of Merit in Handwriting in March, 1910, and E.L. Thorndike's subsequent persuasion on the necessity for measurement and the need to experiment with tests and scales (see, e.g., Thorndike, 1910, *The Contribution of Psychology to Education*). By 1916, Thorndike and his students had developed additional standardized tests in reading, language, arithmetic, spelling, and drawing (Office of Technology Assessment, 1992). From the beginning, Thorndike pushed concepts that have wide currency today—that education involves the measurement of complex endeavors with endless dimensions from which we must abstract concrete representations for measurement; that scale matters; that the validity of measures must be confirmed with empirical evidence; that reliability and accuracy are essential and require multiple measures—the use of single tasks or items is not sufficient—and that assuring fairness is a challenging concern (see Thorndike, 1918). With regard to the latter, Thorndike particularly advocated the need for and suggested methods "designed to free measurements from certain pernicious disturbing factors, notably unfair preparation for the test, inequities in interest and efforts, and inequalities in understanding what the task is" (Thorndike, 1918, p. 23).

Early attentive to today's concern with value-added methodologies, Thorndike (1918, p. 16) observed that "education is concerned with the changes in human beings," and its effectiveness could be judged by differences in student behavior—things made, words spoken, acts of performance, etc.—from one point to another. And he predicted the many users who could benefit from such measures—scientists, administrators, teachers, parents, students themselves; and the many uses to which measurement could be put, for example, determining the effects of different methods of teaching or of various features of schools, determining the achievement of total educational enterprises or systems, and even giving individual students information about their own achievement and improvement to serve both motivational and guidance purposes.

During this same period, city school systems, starting in 1911–12 with New York and moving soon after to Boston, Detroit, and other cities, began to incorporate tests in fledgling efforts to evaluate the results of public schools. It was during this time that educational testing and evaluation gained its first strong foothold. Early tests had a strongly norm-referenced character and were sometimes poorly aligned with learning objectives. But by the 1930s, power tests had begun to supplant speed tests, and an array of new tests became available to measure basic skills, reasoning, and application of knowledge (Findley, 1963). And in 1929, E.F. Lindquist, at the University of Iowa, initiated the first state-wide testing program, using the Iowa Tests of Basic Skills. These tests were soon made available outside the state of Iowa, and added impetus to the shift in testing away from sorting and selecting and back toward diagnosis and remediation (Office of Technology Assessment, 1992, pp. 122–124).

While Thorndike, at Columbia University, focused primarily on achievement testing, another testing movement was taking hold as well, largely led by L.M. Terman at Stanford University. Terman was among the psychologists who developed the Army Alpha and Beta examinations used to screen and classify recruits after the United States declared war on Germany in 1917. Following the war, Terman and others were eager to apply their new science of mental measurement to the improvement of education. In *The Intelligence of School Children*, Terman (1919, p. xiv) stated that the Army tests "demonstrated beyond question that the methods of mental measurement are capable of making a contribution of great value to army efficiency . . . That their universal use in the schoolroom is necessary to educational efficiency will doubtless soon be accepted as a matter of course." Terman's prediction proved accurate. In 1926, a national survey of urban schools found that over 85% of them used intelligence tests as one basis for classifying children into homogeneous classroom groupings (Chapman, 1979). Tracking students by ability fit well with the emphasis at the time on scientific management in education. And lower intelligence test scores among nonwhites and children of immigrants offered a comfortable explanation for achievement disparities. As students in lower tracks received less rigorous instruction, the predictions from the IQ test scores used for tracking became self-fulfilling prophesies. In his study of the intelligence testing movement in education, Chapman (1979) emphasized that tracking and other schemes for differentiating the curriculum offered to different children predated the intelligence testing movement. IQ testing did not give rise to tracking, but instead reinforced the practice by providing new classification methods and a stronger scientific rationale. The use of IQ tests for ability grouping persisted into the latter half of the 20th century.

Thus, two fundamental functions of measurement were evident from the beginning of educational testing. One function is sorting and selecting, comparing students with one another for purposes of placement or selection. The second is improving the quality of education. At times, these two categories overlap, as when tests are used both to determine which students merit a high school diploma and to spur greater student effort to meet the standard set. As will be seen, these two broad functions recur again and again.

New Functions for New Forms of Evaluation in the Eight-Year Study

In the 1930s, planning began for the Eight-Year Study, which was to investigate the effect of applying the ideals of progressive education to the high school curriculum. Dr. Ralph Tyler of the University of Chicago established a new objectives-based framework for testing and laid out a strong role for assessment in curriculum development and improvement. Formative assessment and continuous improvement models coined decades later have their roots in Tyler's framework. As he later articulated in *Basic Principles of Curriculum and Instruction* (Tyler, 1949), Tyler stressed four principles: define appropriate objectives; establish useful learning experiences; organize learning experiences to have maximum impact; and evaluate whether the objectives have been achieved, revising as necessary those aspects of learning that were not effective.

In addition to promoting the use of objectives-based assessments to judge program effectiveness, the Eight-Year Study was also significant in recognizing that radical changes could not be made to curriculum and instruction unless influential student evaluation methods were changed at the same time. Students from the 30 progressive high schools involved in the study were evaluated using specially designed "comprehensive evaluations," the term by which Tyler and his colleagues referred to their tests and examinations, and agreement was obtained from over 300 colleges to accept the evidence of these evaluations in lieu of more conventional transcripts and examination results (Madaus, Stufflebeam, & Scriven, 1983; Smith, Tyler, & the Evaluation Staff, 1942). As participating teachers and schools engaged in curriculum revision and instructional improvement, they also worked with study staff to develop new measures of their learning goals. These included not only such traditional academic concerns as the application of general science principles, but also scales of beliefs, interest indices, and responses to social problems. Information from these assessments, combined with teachers' observations and judgments, was used to develop comprehensive records of student performance that were to be used by colleges for admissions purposes. It is of interest to note that the records were to include *descriptions*—not scores—to characterize student accomplishment.

Acknowledging the common purposes of grading students, instructional grouping, and reports to parents, Smith et al. (1942, pp. 7–10) went on to discuss five additional, broader purposes these new evaluations would serve. The first three purposes were checking the effectiveness of educational institutions, checking the effectiveness of specific educational programs or school policies, and providing a basis for sound guidance of individual students. The fourth was "to provide a certain psychological security to the school staff, to the students, and to the parents" (p. 9). Especially in the context of an innovative educational program, these authors viewed a rigorous, comprehensive testing program as important in reassuring the participants that learning objectives were being met. They suggested that without a credible school-based testing program aligned to their progressive learning goals, external examinations like traditional scholarship tests or college entrance examinations might exert an undue influence on teachers' efforts, simply because they could provide some tangible evidence of success or failure. The fifth purpose was "to provide a sound basis for public relations" (p. 10). A strong testing program would reassure the community served by a school, providing "concrete evidence" of its accomplishments.

As the development of the comprehensive evaluations progressed, another purpose emerged:

As the evaluation committees carried out their work, it became clear that an evaluation program is also a potent method of continued teacher education. The recurring demand for the formulation and clarification of objectives, the continuing study of the reactions of students in terms of these objectives, and the persistent attempt to relate the results obtained from various sorts of measurement are all means for focusing the interests and efforts of teachers upon the most vital parts of the educational process. (Smith et al., 1942, p. 30)

In summary, the student assessments ("comprehensive evaluations") in the Eight-Year Study served to monitor student progress and guide instructional planning. They also afforded school-level accountability and were used in the evaluation of educational programs and policies. Much like performance assessments in the 1990s, these comprehensive evaluations in the 1930s also were intended to limit the influence of other forms of assessment (traditional scholarship tests or entrance examinations) that were viewed as less progressive and that could otherwise exert undue influence over curriculum and instruction. Again anticipating hopes expressed 50 years later for performance assessments, Tyler's comprehensive evaluations were intended to educate the public about new kinds of learning objectives and to clarify teachers' own understandings of their educational goals.

Measurement-Driven Instruction and Criterion-Referenced Testing

From the 1950s through the 1970s, the principal focus of theory and application in educational testing was measurement-driven instruction, a model that showed strong roots in the Tyler Rationale (e.g., Bloom, Hastings, & Madaus, 1971; Tyler, 1949). This educational testing model found its greatest application at the elementary school level, although curricula were designed along the same lines for learners of all ages, including adults. Material to be taught was analyzed into a series of narrow, carefully sequenced learning objectives (*learning units* or *frames*), each accompanied by a highly focused diagnostic test. These brief, frequent tests were used to guide instruction for individual learners; passing a test was required to proceed to the next unit or frame. The earliest program of this kind was probably the Winnetka Plan, described by one of its developers, Carleton W. Washburne (1925), in the Twenty-fourth NSSE Yearbook. Under this plan, students worked largely independently, using textbook lessons and mimeographed materials covering narrow learning objectives in a prescribed sequence. Self-tests could be used to monitor progress and to help students determine when they were prepared to take teacher-administered examinations. A record was kept of the date on which a pupil mastered each successive objective.

The 1950s brought a resurgence of interest in such fine-grained task analysis and individualized instructional management. There was considerable optimism at the time that individualized instruction using carefully designed curricula and associated tests could revolutionize schooling practices, as educational psychologists sought to apply principles from the behaviorist psychology of the time (Glaser, 1960). A new science of education was envisioned, with individualized instruction enabling virtually all children to succeed. The psychologist B.F. Skinner, and others, had shown that complex patterns of animal behavior could be shaped incrementally using carefully scheduled reinforcements (Skinner, 1953). Skinner drew implications for human learning from his work with animals, proposing a model for teaching in which the material to be learned was presented in a series of small steps, with probes to check understanding and immediate feedback on correctness. Borrowing from the language of computers, this teaching approach was called "programmed instruction." A critical feature, in the language of the time, was reinforcement of desired behaviors, in this case, correct responses to test questions. Programmed instruction could also be delivered by "teaching machines." Although histories trace development of teaching machines back to "a spelling machine patented in 1866" (Gotkin & McSweeney, 1967, p. 257), major figures in the development of these machines were Sidney L. Pressey, around 1914, and B.F. Skinner, from the 1940s into the 1960s. Early teaching machines were intended as adjuncts to teaching, but Skinner developed the notion of machines that could offer instruction with little human intervention (Gotkin & McSweeney, 1967; Skinner, 1960).

In 1956, Dr. Benjamin S. Bloom and colleagues at the University of Chicago published their *Taxonomy of Educational Objectives, Handbook 1: Cognitive Domain* (Bloom, Englehart, Furst, Hill, & Krathwohl, 1956). Bloom had been a student of Tyler's at the University of Chicago and shared Tyler's belief that the design of curriculum and instruction must begin with clearly stated objectives. The "Bloom Taxonomy" contributed substantially to the popularity of measurement-driven instructional approaches by showing how test items could be created to measure "higher-order thinking" (analysis, synthesis, evaluation) as well as "lower-order" learning outcomes like knowledge, comprehension, and application. The taxonomy also gave teachers and curriculum developers a common language to talk about different kinds of learning objectives. Along with Bloom's taxonomy, Robert Mager's (1962, 1975, 1984) *Preparing Instructional Objectives* helped popularize the idea of using tests for fine-grained instructional management, showing teachers how to formulate narrow learning objectives in measurable terms.

Using tests to inform fine-grained instructional decisions entailed a qualitatively different kind of test interpretation from testing for sorting or selection. Instead of interpreting students' scores with reference to the performance of a norm group, as with rankings or percentiles, the score of an individual student was compared with a fixed mastery criterion to determine whether that individual was ready to proceed. The idea of tests designed to show directly what an examinee was able to do, without reference to the performance of anyone else, was formalized by Glaser (1963) as "criterion-referenced testing." In this brief, seminal paper, Glaser articulated ideas that could be traced back to the Reverend George Fisher's proposed scale books. Measurement-driven instruction added the notion of a specific score level denoting "mastery" to this idea of a fixed, criterion-referenced measurement scale (Popham & Husek, 1969).

In the 1960s and 1970s, various models and curricular materials were developed that relied on criterion-referenced testing for individualized instructional management. Perhaps the best-known system of this kind was Bloom's (1968) "Mastery Learning" model. Under mastery learning, the material to be taught was divided into a series of units to be mastered sequentially, and mastery tests were created for each unit. End-of-unit tests indicated which students were ready to move on to the next learning unit and which were not. Those not yet demonstrating mastery were retaught, ideally using approaches different from the initial instruction, including peer tutoring. The goal was to enable virtually all students to attain mastery by assuring that each learner possessed all the prerequisite "cognitive entry behaviors" before embarking on the next unit of instruction. These test-driven instructional systems were a subject of the Sixty-sixth NSSE Yearbook (Lange, 1967). In the Sixty-eighth NSSE Yearbook, Lindvall and Cox (1969) described still other instructional programs designed along these lines, especially the Individually Prescribed Instruction (IPI) Mathematics Project, which they helped to develop at the Pittsburgh Learning Research and Development Center.

Theoretical development of measurement-driven instruction moved beyond the use of posttests to check students' readiness for the next unit in a fixed sequence. Branching was added to offer supplemental material for students who did not master a unit following the initial presentation. Pretests were introduced to guide the planning of instruction. Glaser and Nitko (1971, pp. 631–632) compared teaching without first making a "detailed diagnosis . . . of the initial state of the learner" with "prescribing medication for an illness without first examining the symptoms." The great hope, however, was that distinct kinds of instruction might eventually be offered, tailored to each individual student's own learning aptitudes. This was the vision of "aptitude–treatment interaction" (ATI) research set forth in Lee J. Cronbach's (1957) influential paper on "The Two Disciplines of Scientific Psychology" and later summarized in Cronbach and Snow's (1977) *Aptitudes and Instructional Methods*. Rather than forcing all students to adapt to a single mode of instruction and sorting them according to their degrees of success, instruction might instead be adapted to each student's needs, enabling nearly all to attain levels of success previously enjoyed by only a few. To fully realize this vision of adaptive instruction, not only the student's prior knowledge, but also their aptitudes were to be assessed, as explained by Glaser and Nitko (1971):

In terms of decisions to be made, the information required is that which answers the question, given that this student has been located at a particular point in the curriculum sequence, what is the instructional alternative that will best adapt to his individual requirements and thus maximize his attainment of the next instructionally relevant objective? . . . It is probably true that a single test of the conventional type now published and used in schools will not be able to provide all the data . . . required in an adaptive instructional system . . . The basic assumption underlying nonadaptive instruction is that not all pupils can learn a given instructional task to a specified degree of mastery. Adaptive instruction, on the other hand, seeks to design instruction that assures that a given level of mastery is attained by most students. (pp. 643–645)

The aptitude measures required would go far beyond the one-dimensional rankings provided by the IQ tests of decades before. The hope was for tests of specific abilities that could be used to prescribe the optimum form of instruction for each learner. Most scholarship at the time emphasized the need for research on task analysis, individual differences, and alternative modes of instruction. Gagné (1965) showed how complex behaviors could be analyzed into elaborate "learning hierarchies," but it is fair to say that the design of tests and instructional materials featuring "criterion-referenced testing" quickly outpaced the available research. As "Criterion-Referenced Testing" grew into a popular movement, its central principles were compromised. At the same time, it became clear that while the behaviorist principles of task analysis at the time might be suitable for beginning instruction in reading (e.g., letter-sound correspondences) and mathematical computation, they worked less well for more complex kinds of learning outcomes. And despite substantial research investments, stable aptitude–treatment interactions proved elusive, with few exceptions. Nonetheless, criterion-referenced interpretations of carefully designed tests have figured in more recent test-based reform initiatives, including performance assessment and standards-based reform.

Educational Testing for Program Evaluation

At the same time as narrow criterion-referenced tests were being used to guide day-to-day classroom instruction, there was increasing use of broader summative tests, often covering a year or more of instructional content, for program evaluation. The former Soviet Union's launch of Sputnik in 1957 prompted broad concern over the competitiveness of U.S. students and the quality of U.S. education. One outcome was the development of new curricula in mathematics and the sciences, under the auspices of the National Science Foundation. As new instructional materials like BSCS Biology, PSSC Physics, and CHEM Study chemistry came into widespread use, the National Science Foundation and other sponsors began to require evaluations of their effectiveness (Cronbach et al., 1980). A review of findings from over 20 such evaluations found that "groups studying from the innovative curriculum scored higher on virtually every test which favored the innovative curriculum, *but* groups studying from the *traditional* curric-

12 A HISTORICAL PERSPECTIVE

ulum scored higher on a substantial number of comparisons in which the test content more nearly resembled what *they* had studied" (Walker & Schaffarzick, 1974, p. 91, italics in original). Thus, the curricula that fared best in these evaluation studies were those that included new tests specifically aligned to new learning objectives.

Passage of the Elementary and Secondary Education Act of 1965 (ESEA), part of President Lyndon Johnson's "War on Poverty," greatly expanded the use of formal evaluations of educational programs. Under Title I of the ESEA, school districts received federal funds to provide extra academic support for children from low-income families. Extensive regulations were put in place to help assure that the money was spent appropriately. In addition, at Senator Robert Kennedy's insistence, an annual testing requirement was added for all children in Title I programs to determine whether the programs were meeting their objectives (Cross, 2003). The idea of evaluation was not new, but the mid-1960s brought federally funded educational evaluations of unprecedented size. This use of evaluation, in particular of objective test data, for program oversight fit well with the rational management practices pioneered in the military under the direction of Robert McNamara and then applied more widely under the Johnson administration (Lagemann, 1997).

Proponents of compensatory education hoped that evaluations documenting program effectiveness would build support for these social programs, but results were disappointing. Evaluations of ESEA, Head Start (aimed to preschool students), and Follow Through (providing continuing support to Head Start students as they progressed through school) failed to find evidence that the programs were effective. Madaus, Stufflebeam, and Scriven (1983) observed that one problem with these evaluations was the sorts of tests they employed. The standardized tests available at the time were designed and normed to provide accurate individual measurements and stable rankings of children of average ability for the grade tested. They measured broad abilities developed over years of schooling. As general ability tests, they were insensitive to short-term instructional effects. Also, they were sometimes too difficult for disadvantaged students, and were not aligned with learning objectives appropriate for Title I student populations.

Another major, federally commissioned study of the period was the Equality of Educational Opportunity Survey (EEOS), led by James Coleman (Coleman et al., 1966). This study was expected to demonstrate that profound achievement differences associated with social class and race were attributable to disparities in educational resources. Instead, the authors concluded that the quality of schooling had little effect independent of a child's family background and out-of-school environment. Rather than supporting increased outlays to redress inequalities in educational opportunity, the EEOS appeared to show that changes in school quality would likely have little effect.

Minimum Competency Testing

For many reasons, the 1970s brought growing discontent with public education. The apparent failure of compensatory education and the seeming intractability of achievement gaps were contributing factors. Another was a widely publicized, pervasive test score decline that began in the late 1960s and continued through the 1970s. Also, the problem of high levels of youth unemployment received much attention (e.g., National Research Council [NRC], 1983), and inadequate academic skills were viewed as contributing to the problem (Resnick, 1980). The media and alarmist reports from education reform panels fueled a popular perception that pupils were just being passed along from grade to grade, and a high school diploma no longer meant much of anything (Office of Technology Assessment, 1992). In response to disillusionment with educational reform policies focused on "inputs" (better resources, better curricula, new teaching methods), policymakers shifted attention to interventions that focused on outcomes. There was some experimentation with performance contracting (monetary incentives for teachers whose students reached specified benchmarks) and with accountability systems that tied state funding to school-level test scores, but these were short-lived (Cohen & Haney, 1980). The approach that caught on was minimum competency testing, an outgrowth of the "back to basics" movement of the 1970s. The minimum competency test (MCT) was a basic-skills test, usually in reading and mathematics. Typically, students were required to pass the MCT in order to receive a regular high school diploma, although MCTs could be used in other ways. Interpretation was criterion-referenced. That is, an absolute level of performance was required, represented by a passing score that was locally determined. The actual level of proficiency required was probably around the eighth grade level or lower in most cases. Indeed, some found that MCT reforms tended to be largely symbolic, in that expected proficiency levels were lowered so that politically unacceptable numbers of students would not fail, and the standard thus because so diluted that few systematic changes in instruction or learning occurred (Ellwein & Glass, 1986). Nonetheless, a national study found that students who did not pass their tests on the first try were more likely to drop out of school (Catterall, 1989).

Minimum competency testing began in a few school districts as early as 1962. By 1980, statewide minimum competency testing requirements had been implemented in 29 states, most having been initiated in 1975 or later. (In some states, the tests were used to place students in remedial programs or were required for grade promotion as opposed to high school graduation.) By 1985, although 33 states required students to take an MCT, only 11 still made passing the test a requirement for the high school diploma. Passing rates on MCTs in many states rose rapidly from year to year (Popham, Cruse, Rankin, Sandifer, & Williams, 1985). Despite these gains and positive trends on examinations like the National Assessment of Educational Progress (NAEP), there is little evidence that MCTs were the reason for improvements on other examinations; and the improvements in passing rates on MCTs themselves may have reflected little more than the effects of drill and practice narrowly focused on tested skills and possibly also the effect of increased dropout rates (Catterall, 1989; Shepard, 1991a). Over time, popular concern shifted from an emphasis on "basic skills" toward complex, "higher-order thinking" skills, and the MCT movement faded (Office of Technology Assessment, 1992, Chapter 2).

Performance Assessment and the Growth of the Standards Movement

As the 1980s dawned, the United States already was replete with standardized tests and data on student achievement. Results from annual tests stimulated by the 1965 Elementary and Secondary Education Act and its reauthorizations were routinely published in local newspapers; minimum competency testing was in full swing across the country; the federally funded National Assessment of Educational Progress (NAEP, now known as "The Nation's Report Card") had been reporting periodically on the performance of 9-, 13-, and 17-year-old students in reading, mathematics, writing, science, and additional content areas since its inception in 1969;[1] the College Board annually reported results of its Scholastic Aptitude Test (SAT); and international assessments were growing in popularity. However, as U.S. policymakers and the public looked at the data, they did not like what they saw. American business, furthermore, was concerned about international competitiveness and dissatisfied with the preparation of the entering workforce.

A Nation at Risk

Focusing particularly on NAEP, SAT, and international comparisons, a prominent national commission declared the country "A Nation at Risk" (National Commission on Excellence in Education [NCEE],

1983). At a time when the scientific and technical demands of the workforce and the citizenship were growing, the commission found student achievement in decline and urged that students be engaged in the rigorous curriculum they would need for future success. Among its five major recommendations, the commission advocated that "schools . . . adopt more rigorous and measurable standards, and higher expectations for academic performance and student conduct" (NCEE, 1983, p. 27). Making clear a strong public commitment to the twin goals of excellence and equity, to high expectations and to developing all individuals to their highest potential, the commission specifically recommended that:

Standardized tests of achievement (not to be confused with aptitude tests) should be administered at major transition points from one level of schooling to another and particularly from high school to college or work . . . [in order to]: (a) certify the student's credentials; (b) identify the need for remedial intervention; and (c) identify the opportunity for advanced or accelerated work. The tests should be administered as part of a nationwide (but not Federal) system of State and local standardized tests. This system should include other diagnostic procedures that assist teachers and students to evaluate student progress. (NCEE, 1983, p. 28)

Presaging today's standards-based accountability systems, the commission viewed standards and assessment as a major part of the solution in stemming the "rising tide of mediocrity" in American education (NCEE, 1983, p. 5) and gave rise to a number of complementary initiatives in the late 1980s and early 1990s. For example, President George H.W. Bush in 1989 convened the 50 governors in an Education Summit, resulting in agreement on six broad goals that American students should reach by the year 2000, as later reified in the creation of the federally funded National Education Goals Panel (National Education Goals Panel [NEGP], 1991). Two of the goals addressed expectations for student achievement and directly stimulated the development of standards and assessments; Goal 3 specified that:

American students will leave grades four, eight, and twelve having demonstrated competency in challenging subject matter, including English, mathematics, science, history, and geography; and every school in America will ensure that all students learn to use their minds well, so they may be prepared for responsible citizenship, further learning, and productive employment in our modern economy. (NEGP, 1991, p. 10)

Goal 4, in turn, insisted that American students become "first in the world in science and mathematics achievement" (NEGP, 1991, p. 16).

Moving to agree on what such competencies and achievement ought to be, national subject matter organizations, starting with the National Council of Teachers of Mathematics (1989), set about to define subject matter standards in their respective disciplines; the U.S. Secretary of Labor in 1990 appointed the Secretary's Commission on Achieving Necessary Skills (SCANS) to articulate the skills that students need for success in work, and in that same year, the Learning Research and Development Center, led by Lauren Resnick, and the National Center on Education and the Economy, led by Marc Tucker, established the New Standards Project to create a voluntary system of academic performance standards and assessments. Under President Clinton, in turn, the Goals 2000: Educate America Act (Public Law 103-227, 1994) established an initial framework and funding stream to support states and national entities to identify challenging academic content standards, develop measures of student progress, and link state and local reform efforts to enable students to meet the standards. The 1994 reauthorization of Title I, the Improving America's Schools Act (IASA), built on the Goals 2000 framework and required states to develop or adopt challenging content and performance standards that were to apply to all students, to develop assessments aligned with those standards, and to be accountable for student performance. Attention to inputs in Title I evaluation had waned; schools were to be accountable for performance outputs. Moreover, responding to growing interest in performance assessment, IASA also required that state tests address complex thinking skills and include multiple measures.

Assessment as a Reform Strategy

Content and performance standards represented a watershed in thinking about the role of assessment in reforming and improving schools. The problem with past approaches was becoming clear. With attention to traditional standardized, multiple choice test results on an upswing in the 1980s, so too was time devoted to testing and test preparation (Corbett & Wilson, 1991; Dorr-Bremme & Herman, 1986; Kellaghan & Madaus, 1991; Smith & Rottenberg, 1991). The net effect was a narrowing of the curriculum to the basic skills that were assessed, a neglect both of complex thinking skills and of subject areas that were not assessed, and a tendency for teachers to mimic the tests' multiple choice formats in their classroom curriculum (Haertel & Calfee, 1983). Critics saw existing testing—and thus prior iterations of measurement-driven instruction—as driving teaching and learning in the wrong direction, promoting outmoded behaviorist pedagogy that was unlikely to prepare students for success (Haertel, 1999; Herman, 1997; Herman & Golan, 1993; Resnick & Resnick, 1992; Shepard, 1991b). In the emerging view, if assessments were aligned with comprehensive content standards and if expected levels of attainment were codified in ambitious performance standards, then high-stakes testing could be transformed into a positive instrument of educational reform. The problem was not with testing, but was instead with using the wrong sorts of tests.

The New Standards Project and the performance assessment movement attempted to turn the negative into a positive. Cognizant of testing's role in communicating expectations, advocates sought to use performance assessment to broadcast a new vision of education and to promote a "thinking curriculum" (Gong & Reidy, 1996; Resnick & Resnick, 1992). If what you get is what you assess (WYGWYA, as the expression went then), then assessment needed to reflect the kind of teaching and learning activities that newer views of learning supported and be "tests worth teaching to" (Resnick & Resnick, 1992). Be they open-ended items that asked students to compose or explain their answers; inquiry-oriented research papers, experiments, or demonstrations; essays or artistic expressions; portfolios of varied work over the course of a semester or year; or any number of other options, the essence of performance assessments was that they asked students to *create* something of meaning, were intended to invoke authentic and real world applications, to tap complex thinking and/or problem solving, and were *not* multiple choice. Furthermore, because students typically were asked to construct unique answers, performance assessments usually required substantially more time than their multiple choice predecessors and needed to be scored by humans, exercising judgment, rather than by machines scanning graphite marks (Herman, Aschbacher, & Winters, 1992; Wiggins, 1992).

Validity and the Meaning of Assessment Quality

The performance assessment movement thus moved to create new standards for student learning by articulating what students ought to be able to do and framed these expectations in the context of *A Nation at Risk's* and the National Education Goals Panel's calls for rigorous curriculum. In so doing, the performance assessment movement highlighted some limitations of then current conceptions of test quality and created new challenges for educational measurement. Building on Samuel Messick's (1989) thinking on the central role of test use and consequences in validity research, Robert Linn and Eva Baker (1996) argued for an expanded vision of test validity that considered multiple internal and external criteria. Among the internal validity criteria they suggested were content quality, curricular importance, content coverage, cognitive complexity, linguistic appropriateness, ancillary skills, and meaningfulness of tasks for students; and among the external validity criteria were consequences for students and teachers, fairness, transfer and generalizability, comparability, and instructional sensitivity.

Research showing the fragility of student performance across ostensibly similar performance assessment tasks created special challenges for the generalizability and comparability criteria. That a student did well on one mathematics problem-solving task, for example, did not mean she/he would do well on a second such task. This variability meant that it would take a number of tasks to get an accurate estimate of student achievement in a particular knowledge domain. Then available research suggested that from 5 to 20 tasks were needed to obtain reliable individual estimates (Baker, 1994; Dunbar, Koretz, & Hoover, 1991; Shavelson, Baxter, & Gao, 1993) depending on the knowledge domain and the breadth of its specification. Even at the lower end, the time demands of typical performance assessment tasks challenged their feasibility for large-scale use. For example, the hours of testing time required to get adequate reliability on the free response sections of 21 Advanced Placement tests ranged from 1 hour 15 minutes (in physics) to 13 hours (in European History) (Linn & Baker, 1996, p. 97). Performance assessment, in short, brought tensions between traditional psychometric views of test quality and broader conceptions focused on consequences.

Challenges in Fairness and Equity

Performance assessment brought new tensions in assessment equity as well. Advocates believed that traditionally low-performing students would likely be more engaged and thus be better able to show what they knew on the authentic tasks of performance assessment, and they hoped that publicly articulating standards would raise expectations and promote richer educational opportunities for economically poor and culturally diverse students. As Baron and Wolf (1996) observed, performance assessment was the tool of choice for those from two distinct perspectives on American education. One view, emanating from *A Nation at Risk*, regarded American education as failing and promoted rigorous assessments as a means to establish consequences for individuals and schools, ultimately serving sorting functions. The second represented the vision of the egalitarian common school, where performance assessments were intended to make public higher expectations for students and to promote dialogue and action about who had the opportunity to attain those standards. At the same time, Gordon and Bonilla-Bowman (1996) questioned performance assessment's ability to bridge these two paradigms and affect the status quo, concerned that historically such innovations had been "redesigned in ways that continue to exclude those who have been historically underserved" (p. 35). They further raised issues of the adequacy of students' opportunity to learn; the potential for teacher bias in scoring performance assessments; and the possibility for conflicts between students' internal standards, which were likely to be culturally based and unique to each individual, and external standards, which were likely to be more technical and to reflect the power relationships of the dominant culture. They also noted possible collisions when assessment systems reflecting high standards met the reality of inequities in schooling. As they observed:

The choice cannot be between denial of opportunity [e.g., a diploma] or acceptance of lower standards. Failure to hold students of color to a common standard because of an acknowledgment of the inferior quality of their previous schooling is crippling, though perhaps not as destructive as exclusion from the opportunity for correction because of the failure to meet arbitrary standards. Obviously, the solution of this problem lies in the direction of more appropriate pedagogical intervention. (pp. 46–47)

Performance Assessment and the Improvement of Teaching

Others too saw great value in performance assessment for promoting pedagogical improvement, echoing some of the thoughts of Tyler and his colleagues 60 years earlier. Beyond communicating higher expectations and modeling meaningful instructional activities, advocates noted the professional development benefits of involving teachers in developing and scoring performance assessments (Goldberg & Rosewell, 2000; Resnick & Resnick, 1992), and the special value of involving teachers in learning communities where, in the context of appraising student work, they could develop common expectations, derive insights on students' thinking and understanding, share successful strategies for improving students' learning opportunities, and get support for changing teaching practices (Darling-Hammond & Ancess, 1996; LeMahieu & Eresh, 1996). For indeed, performance assessment represented a radical change in the epistemology for teaching. Echoing the hopes for Mastery Learning and similar measurement-driven instructional approaches a generation before, performance assessment was tied to new, developmental views of learning in which support and effort could enable most students to attain high expectations. Proponents hoped it would bring broad acceptance of new definitions of what it meant to know and understand (Baron & Wolf, 1996; Wolf & Reardon, 1996). Grounded in constructivism, new pedagogical theory brought new ideas about the role of assessment in and for learning (Stiggins, 2002) and increasing attention to students' self-assessment, ideas that also ground today's interest in classroom and formative assessment (see Shepard, 2000; and section below)

The Current Accountability Context

Today's accountability and assessment context features many of these same ideas about the role of standards and assessment in improving student learning, ideas advanced by the 2001 No Child Left Behind mandates. NCLB strengthened the accountability requirements of the 1994 reauthorization by insisting that states implement statewide accountability systems covering *all* public schools and students based on challenging academic content standards in reading and mathematics; annually assess all students in grades 3–8, plus one high school grade, relative to established standards;[2] and create annual statewide performance targets for schools to assure that all students reach proficiency in both subjects by the year 2014. In the interests of encouraging schools to address the needs of all their students and of reducing the achievement gap, NCLB requires not only that all schools meet their states' annual performance targets in terms of the percentage of students scoring "proficient"—deemed adequate yearly progress (AYP)— but that schools meet them for every numerically significant subgroup at the school, as defined by race or ethnicity, language status, poverty, and disability status. Schools and school districts that fail to meet their achievement targets over time are designated "in need of improvement," and are subject to corrective action leading up to restructuring or reconstitution, with all these actions presumably aimed at getting them back on track relative to AYP targets. Parents at such schools are given options for sending their children to other schools or for special supplementary services, funded by their local school district. Ironically, while NCLB attempts to focus on the rigorous academic standards that were the hallmark of performance assessment reforms in the previous decade, the cost and feasibility of annual state testing at so many grade levels has probably discouraged the use of extended performance assessments (General Accounting Office, 2003). Even in the face of NCLB requirements for multiple measures and for a range of evidence to support the validity of state tests, state assessments have retreated to the predominant use of multiple choice items, once again raising the worries of the last decade about attention to the complex thinking and problem-solving skills that underlie truly rigorous academic standards. According to the annual "Quality Counts" report by *Education Week*, in 2004–05 virtually all states employed multiple-choice tests, and all but four (five with the District of Columbia) used extended response questions in English/Language Arts. Roughly two-thirds of the states employed short-answer questions, but only one used portfolios as part of its state accountability system, and performance assessments were not even listed as a category (Skinner, 2005, p. 87).

The NCLB Theory of Action

Nonetheless, NCLB firmly continues the policy assumption that being explicit about standards for student performance and measuring student progress toward them, coupled with sanctions and incentives, will leverage the improvement of student learning. The intent is to provide a technical assessment system that can not only measure performance and provide feedback to support improvement, but perhaps more importantly, can serve motivational and symbolic purposes. The system establishes the target for reform efforts, communicates to educators, administrators, and parents what is expected, and provides incentives and/or sanctions for actions, thereby stimulating all levels of the education system to focus on achieving the NCLB goals for AYP and ostensibly assuring that all children will be proficient by the year 2014.

Figure 1 shows one view of how accountability is supposed to work, focusing particularly on the quality of classroom teaching and learning necessary to enable students to reach intended standards (Herman, 2004). While the full and coordinated support of all levels and resources of the educational system may be needed to achieve policy goals, it seems axiomatic that students cannot be expected to become proficient unless and until the content and process of their classroom instruction well prepares them to do so. As the figure shows, standards are the basis for accountability assessments and likewise are the targets of classroom teaching and learning. Feedback from the assessment is used to improve learning opportunities for students and to increase their attainment of standards. Because every subgroup of students within the school must attain the AYP targets, schools and teachers must hold high expectations and provide appropriate opportunities to learn to *all* students, including whatever augmented programs and special services traditionally low-achieving students may need to attain success. Although Figure 1 focuses on the impact of assessments at the classroom level, schools and districts also are expected to use the feedback from state assessments to

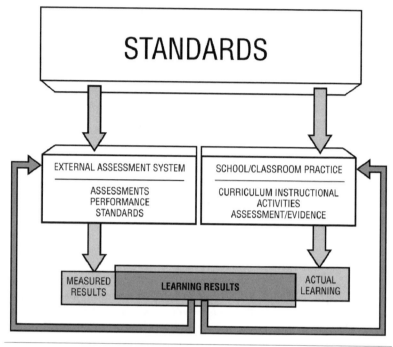

FIGURE 1
An ideal model for standards-based accountability.

gauge their strengths and weaknesses, to identify students who may need special help, and to be strategic in taking action and coordinating available resources to improve student performance.

What should be apparent from Figure 1 is the importance of several technical features of the system. First, the alignment of standards, assessments, and classroom instruction is critical to the validity of the system. It is only when the contents and processes of teaching and learning correspond to the standards that students indeed have the opportunity to learn what they need to be successful. And it is only when assessment is aligned with both standards and classroom instruction that assessment results can provide sound information about both how well students are doing and how well schools and classroom teaching are doing in helping students to attain the standards. Because of the centrality of alignment to current policy logic, researchers over the last decade have worked to develop methodologies for assessing it, looking particularly at the match between content and cognitive demand (see, e.g., Porter, 2002; Rothman, Slattery, Vranek, & Resnick, 2002; Webb, 1997, 2002). Their work shows an uneven match between standards and state assessments.

However, even with tight alignment, Figure 1 tries to make it clear that all tests are fallible and can only measure a part of what students are learning. Tests can only assess that which can be measured in the finite time allotted for testing and through the particular formats employed in the tests—meaning that it is impossible for tests to assess everything that is important. Furthermore, all measures also contain error and thus provide only an imperfect *estimate* of student performance. With the advent of standards-based tests, these imperfect estimates must then be converted into proficiency classifications—based on one of a number of standard-setting methods that have been developed over the last four decades, a process that brings significant technical challenges (Haertel & Lorié, 2004). Based on AYP requirements, percentages of students scoring at or above proficient must be determined for each numerically significant subgroup within a school or district, raising thorny questions about the minimum size needed to achieve sufficient stability of subgroup estimates and creating tensions between technical concerns about the quality of the data and consequences relative to assuring attention to subgroup needs.

Figure 1 also attempts to make clear that state assessments are not the only assessments of importance in the system. The continuous improvement model that accountability envisions means that educators must keep their eyes on student learning, conduct regular assessments *of* and *for* student learning to see how students are doing relative to standards, use the information to understand what students need, and take appropriate, meaningful action based on learning evidence—just as Tyler and his colleagues envisioned seven decades ago. We expand later in this chapter on current theory about formative classroom assessment *for* learning (Black, Harrison, Lee, Bethan, & Wiliam, 2004; Stiggins, 2002).

In Figure 1, standards guide curriculum and instruction as well as assessment, and all students are given access to the entire content of the agreed-upon standards. While this may represent an optimal view of standards-based reform, but Figure 2 may better represent the current reality. Research cited earlier strongly suggests that educators, particularly in schools that are under the greatest pressure to show improvement, are teaching to the test, not the standards (Pedulla et al., 2003; Stecher et al., 1998, 2000). Accountability tests thus are the lens through which the standards are interpreted and serve to define the standards. Standards in subjects not tested and standards that are not

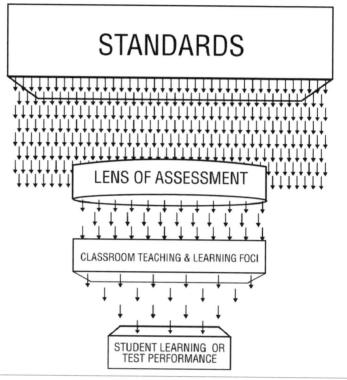

FIGURE 2
Potential effect of accountability testing on student learning.

included in subject matter tests seem to get at most weak treatment in classroom teaching and learning.

As Figure 2 highlights, a focus on tests rather than standards has serious consequences for students. Rather than being exposed to the full breadth of knowledge and skills that society has determined are important for future success, students have the opportunity to learn only a relatively narrow, test-based curriculum. Traditionally low performing students—the economically disadvantaged, language minority, and students of color, students with disabilities—are most likely to be negatively affected, since their instruction is most likely to focus intensely on reaching proficiency based on state assessment results (see Darling-Hammond & Rustique-Forrester, chapter 12, this volume). There is the danger of a dual curriculum evolving for these versus more advantaged students and of serious equity problems.

Moreover, with the specifics of the test—rather than the essentials of the discipline or meaningful learning—as a primary focus, there also is growing danger of test score inflation. Students may be learning only what is tested, and increases in test scores may not generalize to other situations (see Koretz, chapter 5, this volume). Potential mismatches between tests and standards can lead educators and policymakers to misinterpret test results and fail to address genuine needs.

These same issues and basic theories of action are relevant to high school exit examinations that are growing in popularity across the country. Harkening back to the minimum competency testing reforms of the 1970s and 1980s, and responding to similar concerns from U.S. business and universities about students' preparation, the idea is that high school exit examinations will reflect the standards that students must reach for future success. There is an expectation that students will be motivated to learn this material and schools and teachers will be motivated to teach it if passing the test is required for high school graduation. By the year 2003, 19 states required exit examinations and five were scheduled to phase them in over the next few years (Center on Education Policy, 2003, p. 5). Echoing as well the concerns around earlier MCT, the business community worries that current tests are not sufficiently rigorous to assure adequate student preparation (Achieve Inc., 2004). At the same time, there is pushback from parents and communities when unacceptable numbers of students fail to pass the tests. Similarly, the tests raise serious equity concerns, given the disproportionality of passing rates for economically poor students and students of color, and data suggesting a relationship between high school proficiency requirements and students dropping out. Exit examinations may reduce graduation rates especially for African American and Latino students, English language learners, and students with disabilities (Darling-Hammond, Rustique-Forrester, & Pechesne, 2005; see also Bishop, chapter 11, this volume).

Formative Assessment for Student Learning

Ultimately, students' needs must be addressed in the teaching and learning opportunities provided for them in classrooms, schools, and/ or other settings, and as noted above, any reasonable theory of action linking assessment with student learning would hold an important place for classroom assessment. Just as Ralph Tyler (1949) advocated for the use of assessment to improve curriculum and Benjamin Bloom (1968) argued for the central role of ongoing assessment in mastery learning, so too is feedback on student learning seen as essential in today's classroom teaching and learning (Sadler, 1989). Indeed Black and Wiliam's (1998a, 1998b) historic meta-analysis found that formative assessment—the use of assessment to provide feedback to teachers and students to modify instruction and enhance learning—produces significant student learning gains beyond those of other available interventions and that it helps to narrow the achievement gap between low and high achievers. Their work presents a landmark in burgeoning interest in classroom and formative assessment as a strategy for improving student learning.

Wiliam (2004) notes that assessments for accountability and assessments for learning differ not so much in source—external versus classroom—but more importantly in design impetus and use. Assessments designed to serve learning purposes provide feedback for students and teachers that can be used to modify the teaching and learning activities in which they are engaged; such assessments become formative when the feedback is actually used to improve learning (Wiliam, 2004). In terms of designing assessments for learning, the National Research Council (NRC) report, *Knowing What Students Know* (NRC, 2001), insists that such assessments start with a model of student cognition, with assessment tasks designed and interpreted to inform inferences about students' learning and appropriate next steps, and that assessment design be consistent with modern views of effective pedagogy.

In modern conceptions, moreover, assessment becomes part and parcel of the teaching and learning process. Contemporary cognitive psychology recognizes that knowledge is always actively constructed by learners (NRC, 2000, 2001). A situative perspective reminds us that knowing is a verb before it is a noun—what is acquired through schooling is a set of capabilities for meaningful participation in activity structures; all knowing has a social component (Gipps, 1999). In earlier behaviorist models, assessment served to monitor students' status with regard to relatively static learning goals, so that someone or something could make adjustments as instruction was imparted. In modern conceptions, assessment provides opportunities for students to display their thinking and to engage with feedback that can help them to extend, refine, and deepen their understandings and reach more sophisticated levels of expertise. Portfolio assessments present one example of such assessments, in which students may engage in various types of writing to explore personal or content ideas, may be encouraged to include drafts to show their writing process, and may reflect on their own performance and progress (Calfee & Perfumo, 1996). Teachers' informal questioning during the course of class discussions presents another example, where questions are used to elicit students' understandings and alternate conceptions. Feedback is used to encourage students to confront their misconceptions and to move to higher levels of understanding (Gitomer & Duschl, 1995).

Conclusion

The past century's history of educational testing in the United States shows the varied ways in which assessment has been expected to support educational quality and the improvement of students' learning. This chapter has described widespread, popular movements as well as a few pivotal studies that have shaped popular perceptions of education and influenced educational policy. The story told is scarcely one of steady progress toward some inevitable ideal. Again and again, testing movements that seemed unstoppable have fallen short of expectations and faded away, only to be replaced by some new approach. Nonetheless, each new testing initiative has left its traces, and the theories, hopes, and expectations of the past reverberate in present testing policies and practices.

The stated goal of today's standards-based accountability is to help all children reach the same ambitious academic content standards. This is in striking contrast to the use of IQ tests during the first half of the 20th century to determine which children should be provided an academically rigorous curriculum and which would find such a curriculum beyond their abilities. Aptitude testing, the use of cognitive tests of different kinds to determine students' capabilities and limitations, evolved from the broad use of IQ tests for sorting students along a continuum toward testing of narrower abilities to predict the forms of instruction best suited to individual learners. Today, while some tests of "learning styles" are still in use, testing of individual abilities is largely limited to diagnosis and placement of children with specific cognitive disabilities.

Even though routine IQ testing of all children has largely disappeared, the use of tests for sorting and selecting has continued. Today, however, the sorting function relies on achievement tests rather than aptitude tests. Even the redoubtable Scholastic Aptitude Test, first designed to identify native talent wherever it might be found, has dropped "Aptitude" as its middle name and is instead described as a broad test of achievement and of reasoning *skills* that can be learned and practiced. Minimum competency tests and more recently high school exit examinations sort examinees into broad categories of passing and failing, although the stated goal of these tests is to assure that all meet the standard, not to penalize those who fall short. This shift from aptitude toward achievement testing is consistent with the aspiration that all students master a rigorous academic curriculum. Unlike some important learning aptitudes, achievement can be increased through individual effort.

From Washburne's Winnetka Plan through the periods of aptitude–treatment interaction research, teaching machines, and criterion-referenced testing, testing was used to guide instructional decision making for individual learners. Fine-grained tests closely tied to narrow learning objectives dictated the pacing of instruction and provided feedback to students and their teachers. These methods were bound up with a conception of curriculum and instruction that has grown less popular, although some highly scripted, basic-skills curricula are still widely used and have strong adherents.

As the goals of education have shifted away from acquiring factual knowledge toward "higher-order thinking," the limitations of narrow paper-and-pencil measures have become clear. Although multiple-choice tests are still used to measure many valued learning outcomes, it is recognized today that they are poor measures of some of the most important goals of education. For a short time, it appeared that portfolio-based assessments and performance assessments might hold the key to rapid instructional improvement and the closing of historic achievement gaps that have separated underserved from more advantaged learners. Echoing the hopes of Tyler's Eight-Year Study for new forms of tests to support new forms of learning, performance assessments were adopted uncritically in the 1990s as a tool of educational reform. Disillusionment with high costs, low reliability, and poor student performance on these examinations, coupled with the dramatic increase in amount of testing required under NCLB, have brought a shift back to heavy reliance on multiple-choice tests; the promise and potential of performance assessment remain unfulfilled.

One constant in this changing picture has been the idea that education should produce measurable results. Again and again, policymakers have advanced accountability testing as a means for improving education, each generation responding to the failings of the previous. From the days of Joseph Rice and the school testing programs of the early 1900s, through the Head Start program evaluations of the 1960s, and up to the increasingly prescriptive testing requirements of successive ESEA reauthorizations culminating in NCLB, policymakers have used tests in an attempt to discover which schools and districts are fulfilling their responsibilities and which are falling short. NCLB responds to the perceived failings of previous accountability testing programs in various ways. Because improvement seemed to come too slowly under state accountability systems, "adequate yearly progress" has been defined in a way intended to bring all children to "proficient" by 2014. Because achievement gaps have persisted, student subgroups must be tracked separately and each must meet the same annual measurable objectives for a school to demonstrate AYP. Because it matters what is tested, states must use tests aligned with rigorous academic content standards. Because multiple-choice tests alone are poor measures of complex learning outcomes, NCLB calls for the use of multiple measures. These are promising innovations, but history shows that testing alone, in itself, is unlikely to bring about major educational improvement. It remains to be seen how effective today's accountability testing will prove to be in supporting genuine, comprehensive educational reform.

NOTES

1. Since the mid-1980s, NAEP has reported results for grades 4, 8, and 12, rather than for student cohorts defined by chronological age.

2. Science standards and assessment must be implemented at selected grade levels by the year 2007.

REFERENCES

Achieve, Inc. (2004). *The expectations gap: A 50-state review of high school graduation require-ments*. Washington, DC: Achieve, Inc. Retrieved January 12, 2005 from http://www.achieve.org

Ayres, L.P. (1918). History and present status of educational measurements. In G.M. Whipple (Ed.), *The measurement of educational products. The seventeenth yearbook of the National Society for the Study of Education*, Part II (pp. 9–15). Bloomington, IL: Public School Publishing Company.

Baker, E.L. (1994). Researchers and assessment policy development—A cautionary tale. *American Journal of Education, 102*, 450–477.

Baron, J.N., & Wolf, D.P. (1996). Editor's preface. In J.N. Baron & D.P. Wolf (Eds.), *Performance-based student assessment: Challenges and possibilities. The ninety-fifth yearbook of the National Society for the Study of Education*, Part I (pp. ix–xiii). Chicago: National Society for the Study of Education.

Black, P., Harrison, C., Lee, C., Bethan, M., & Wiliam, D. (2004). Working inside the black box: Assessment for learning in the classroom. *Phi Delta Kappan, 86*(1), 8–21.

Black, P., & Wiliam, D. (1998a). Assessment and classroom learning. *Assessment in Education, 5*, 7–74.

Black, P., & Wiliam, D. (1998b). Inside the black box: Raising standards through class-room assessment. *Phi Delta Kappan, 80*(2), 46–48.

Bloom, B.S. (1968). Learning for mastery. *Evaluation Comment, 1*(2), 1–12. (Available from the ERIC Document Reproduction Service, ED 053419.)

Bloom, B.S., Englehart, M.D., Furst, E.J., Hill, W.H., & Krathwohl, D.R. (1956). *Tax-onomy of educational objectives: The classification of educational goals, handbook I: Cognitive domain*. New York: Longmans, Green.

Bloom, B.S., Hastings, J.T., & Madaus, G.F. (1971). *Handbook on formative and summative evaluation of student learning*. New York: McGraw-Hill.

Calfee, R., & Perfumo, P. (Eds.). (1996). *Writing portfolios in the classroom: Policy and practice, promise and peril*. Mahwah, NJ: Lawrence Erlbaum Associates.

Catterall, J.S. (1989). Standards and school dropouts: A national study of tests required for high school graduation. *American Journal of Education, 98*, 1–34.

Center on Education Policy. (2003). *State high school exit exams: Put to the test*. Washington, DC: Author.

Chapman, D.P. (1979). *Schools as sorters: Lewis M. Terman and the intelligence testing movement, 1890–1930*. Unpublished doctoral dissertation, Stanford University.

Cohen, D.K., & Haney, W. (1980). Minimums, competency testing, and social policy. In R.M. Jaeger & C.K. Tittle (Eds.), *Minimum competency achievement testing* (pp. 5–22). Berkeley, CA: McCutchan.

Coleman, J.S., Campbell, E.Q., Hobson, C.J., McPartland, J., Mood, A.M., Weinfeld, F.D., & York, R.L. (1966). *Equality of educational opportunity*. Washington, DC: U.S. Government Printing Office.

Corbett, H.D., & Wilson, B.L. (1991). *Testing, reform, and rebellion*. Norwood, NJ: Ablex Publishing.

Cronbach, L.J. (1957). The two disciplines of scientific psychology. *American Psychologist, 12*, 671–684.

Cronbach, L.J., Ambron, S.R., Dornbusch, S.M., Hess, R.D., Hornik, R.C., Phillips, D.C., Walker, D.F., & Weiner, S.S. (1980). *Toward reform of program evaluation*. San Francisco: Jossey-Bass.

Cronbach, L.J., & Snow, R.E. (1977). *Aptitudes and instructional methods*. New York: Halsted Press.

Cross, C. (2003). *Political education: National policy comes of age*. New York: Teachers College Press.

Darling-Hammond, L., & Ancess, J. (1996). Authentic assessment and school develop-ment. In J.N. Baron & D.P. Wolf (Eds.), *Performance-based student assessment: Chal-*

lenges and possibilities. The ninety-fifth yearbook of the National Society for the Study of Education, Part I (pp. 52–83). Chicago: National Society for the Study of Education.

Darling-Hammond, L., Rustique-Forrester, E., & Pecheone, R. (2005). *Multiple measures approaches to high school graduation*. Palo Alto, CA: School Redesign Network at Stanford University.

Dorr-Bremme, D., & Herman, J. (1986). *Assessing student achievement: A profile of classroom practices* (CSE Monograph Series in Evaluation 11). Los Angeles: University of California, Center for the Study of Evaluation.

Dunbar, S., Koretz, D., & Hoover, H.D. (1991). Quality control in the use of performance assessment. *Applied Measurement in Education, 4,* 289–303.

Elementary and Secondary Education Act of 1965 (ESEA), Pub. L. 89-10, 79 Stat. 27 (1965).

Ellwein, M.C., & Glass, G.V. (1986). *Standards of competence: A multi-site case study of school reform* (CSE Technical Report 263). Los Angeles: Center for the Study of Evaluation, University of California at Los Angeles. (Available from the ERIC Document Reproduction Service, ED293883.)

Findley, W.G. (1963). Purposes of school testing programs and their efficient development. In W.G. Findley (Ed.), *The impact and improvement of school testing programs. The sixty-second yearbook of the National Society for the Study of Education*, Part II (pp. 1–27). Chicago: National Society for the Study of Education.

Gagné, R.M. (1965). *The conditions of learning*. New York: Rinehart & Winston.

General Accounting Office. (2003, May). *Characteristics of tests may influence expenses; information sharing may help states realize efficiencies* (GAO 03-389). Retrieved February 10, 2005, from http://www.gao.gov/cgi-bin/getrpt?GAO-03-389. (Available from ERIC Document Reproduction Service, ERIC document ED477361.)

Gipps, C. (1999). Socio-cultural aspects of assessment. *Review of Research in Education, 24,* 355–392.

Gitomer, D.H., & Duschl, R. (1995). Moving toward a portfolio culture in science education. In S.M. Glynn & R. Duit (Eds.), *Learning science in the schools: Research reforming practice* (pp. 299–325). Mahwah, NJ: Lawrence Erlbaum Associates.

Glaser, R. (1960). Christmas past, present, and future: A review and preview. In A.A. Lumsdaine & R. Glaser (Eds.), *Teaching machines and programmed learning: A source book* (pp. 23–31). Washington, DC: National Education Association.

Glaser, R. (1963). Instructional technology and the measurement of learning outcomes: Some questions. *American Psychologist, 18,* 519–521.

Glaser, R., & Nitko, A.J. (1971). Measurement in learning and instruction. In R.M. Thorndike (Ed.), *Educational measurement* (2nd ed., pp. 625–670). Washington DC: American Council on Education.

Goals 2000: Educate America Act of 1994, Pub. L. 103-227, 108 Stat. 125 (1994).

Goldberg, G.L., & Rosewell, B.S. (2000). From perception to practice: The impact of teachers' scoring experience on performance based instruction and classroom practice. *Educational Assessment, 6,* 257–290.

Gong, B., & Reidy, E. (1996). Assessment and accountability in Kentucky's school reform. In J.N. Baron & D.P. Wolf (Eds.), *Performance-based student assessment: Challenges and possibilities. The ninety-fifth yearbook of the National Society for the Study of Education*, Part I (pp. 215–233). Chicago: National Society for the Study of Education.

Gordon, E.W., & Bonilla-Bowman, C. (1996). Can performance-based assessments contribute to the achievement of educational equity? In J.N. Baron & D.P. Wolf (Eds.), *Performance-based student assessment: Challenges and possibilities. The ninety-fifth yearbook of the National Society for the Study of Education*, Part I (pp. 32–51). Chicago: National Society for the Study of Education.

Gotkin, L.G., & McSweeney, J.F. (1967). Learning from teaching machines. In P.C. Lange (Ed.), *Programmed instruction. The sixty-sixth yearbook of the National Society for*

32   A HISTORICAL PERSPECTIVE

the *Study of Education*, Part II (pp. 255–283). Chicago: The National Society for the Study of Education.

Haertel, E.H. (1999). Performance assessment and education reform. *Phi Delta Kappan*, *80*, 662–666.

Haertel, E.H., & Calfee, R.C. (1983). School achievement: Thinking about what to test. *Journal of Educational Measurement*, *20*, 119–132.

Haertel, E.H., & Lorié, W.A. (2004). Validating standards-based test score interpretations. *Measurement: Interdisciplinary Research and Perspectives*, *2*, 61–103.

Herman, J.L. (1997). Large-scale assessment in support of school reform: Lessons learned in the search for alternative measures. *International Journal of Educational Research*, *27*, 395–413.

Herman, J.L. (2004). The effects of testing on instruction. In S. Fuhrman & R. Elmore (Eds.), *Redesigning accountability* (pp. 141–166). New York: Teachers College Press.

Herman, J.L., Aschbacher, P.R., & Winters, L. (1992). *A practical guide to alternative assessment*. Alexandria, VA: Association for Supervision and Curriculum Development.

Herman, J.L., & Golan, S. (1993). Effects of standardized testing on teaching and schools. *Educational Measurement: Issues and Practice*, *12*(4), 20–25, 41–42.

Improving America's Schools Act of 1994 (IASA), Pub. L. No. 103-382, 108 Stat. 4056 (1994).

Kane, M. (1992). An argument-based approach to validation. *Psychological Bulletin*, *112*, 527–535.

Kellaghan, T., & Madaus, G. (1991). National testing: Lessons for America from Europe. *Educational Leadership*, *49*(3), 87–93.

Lagemann, E.C. (1997). Contested terrain: A history of education in the United States, 1890–1990. *Educational Researcher*, *26*(9), 5–17.

Lange, P.C. (Ed.). (1967). *Programmed instruction. The sixty-sixth yearbook of the National Society for the Study of Education*, Part II. Chicago: National Society for the Study of Education.

LeMahieu, P.G., & Eresh, J.T. (1996). Coherence, comprehensiveness, and capacity in assessment systems: The Pittsburgh experience. In J.N. Baron & D.P. Wolf (Eds.), *Performance-based student assessment: Challenges and possibilities. The ninety-fifth yearbook of the National Society for the Study of Education*, Part I (pp. 125–142). Chicago: National Society for the Study of Education.

Lindvall, C.M., & Cox, R.C. (1969). The role of evaluation in programs for individualized instruction. In R.W. Tyler (Ed.), *Educational evaluation: New roles, new means. The sixty-eighth yearbook of the National Society for the Study of Education*, Part II (pp. 156–188). Chicago: National Society for the Study of Education.

Linn, R.L. (2000). Assessments and accountability. *Educational Researcher*, *29*(2), 4–16.

Linn, R.L., & Baker, E.L. (1996). Can performance-based student assessments be psychometrically sound? In J.N. Baron & D.P. Wolf (Eds.), *Performance-based student assessment: Challenges and possibilities. The ninety-fifth yearbook of the National Society for the Study of Education*, Part I (pp. 84–103). Chicago: National Society for the Study of Education.

Madaus, G.F., Stufflebeam, D., & Scriven, M.S. (1983). Program evaluation: An historical overview. In G.F. Madaus, M.S. Scriven, & D. Stufflebeam (Eds.), *Evaluation models: Viewpoints on educational and human services evaluation* (pp. 3–22). Norwell, MA: Kluwer Academic Publishers.

Mager, R.F. (1962). *Preparing instructional objectives*. Palo Alto, CA: Fearon Publishers.

Mager, R.F. (1975). *Preparing instructional objectives* (2nd ed.). Belmont, CA: Fearon Publishers.

Mager, R.F. (1984). *Preparing instructional objectives* (rev. 2nd ed.). Belmont, CA: Pitman Management and Training.

Messick, S. (1989). Validity. In R.L. Linn (Ed.), *Educational measurement* (3rd ed., pp. 13–103). New York: American Council on Education and Macmillan.

National Commission on Excellence in Education (NCEE). (1983). *A nation at risk: The imperative for educational reform.* Washington, DC: U.S. Government Printing Office.

National Council of Teachers of Mathematics. (1989). *Curriculum and evaluation standards for school mathematics.* Reston, VA: Author.

National Education Goals Panel (NEGP). (1991). *The National Education Goals Report: Building a nation of learners.* Washington, DC: National Education Goals Panel. (For sale by the US. Government Printing Office, Superintendent of Documents).

National Research Council (NRC). (1983). *Education for tomorrow's jobs.* Committee on Vocational Education and Economic Development in Depressed Areas (S.W. Sherman, Ed.). Washington, DC: National Academies Press.

National Research Council (NRC). (2000). *How people learn: Brain, mind, experience, and school* (expanded edition). Committee on Developments in the Science of Learning (J.D. Bransford, A.L. Brown, & R.R. Cocking, Eds.). Washington, DC: National Academies Press.

National Research Council (NRC). (2001). *Knowing what students know: The science and design of educational assessment.* Committee on the Foundations of Assessment (J.W. Pellegrino, N. Chudowsky, & R. Glaser, Eds.). Washington, DC: National Academies Press.

No Child Left Behind Act of 2001, Pub. L. No. 107-110, 115 Stat. 1425 (2002).

Office of Technology Assessment. (1992). *Testing in American schools: Asking the right questions* (OTA-SET-519). Washington, DC: U.S. Government Printing Office.

Pedulla, J., Abrams, L., Madaus, G., Russell, M., Ramos, M., & Miao, J. (2003). *Perceived effects of state mandated testing programs on teaching and learning.* Boston: National Board on Educational Testing and Public Policy.

Popham, W.J., Cruse, K.L., Rankin, S.C., Sandifer, P.D., & Williams, R.L. (1985). Measurement-driven instruction: It's on the road. *Phi Delta Kappan, 66,* 628–634.

Popham, W.J., & Husek, T.R. (1969). Implications of criterion-referenced measurement. *Journal of Educational Measurement, 6,* 1–9.

Porter, A.C. (2002). Measuring the content of instruction: Uses in research and practice. *Educational Researcher, 31*(7), 3–14.

Resnick, D. (1980). Minimum competency testing historically considered. *Review of Research in Education, 8,* 3–29.

Resnick, L.B., & Resnick, D.P. (1992). Assessing the thinking curriculum: New tools for educational reform. In B.G. Gifford & M.C. O'Conner (Eds.), *Changing assessments: Alternative views of aptitude, achievement and instruction* (pp. 37–75). Boston: Kluwer Academic Publishers.

Rothman, R., Slattery, J.B., Vranek, J.L., & Resnick, L.B. (2002). *Benchmarking and alignment of standards and testing* (CSE Technical Report 566). Los Angeles: University of California, National Center for Research on Evaluation, Standards, and Student Testing (CRESST).

Sadler, D.R. (1989). Formative assessment and the design of instructional systems. *Instructional Science, 18,* 119–144.

Shavelson, R.J., Baxter, G.P., & Gao, X.H. (1993). Sampling variability of performance assessments. *Journal of Educational Measurement, 30,* 215–232.

Shepard, L.A. (1991a). *Will national tests improve student learning?* Paper presented at the American Educational Research Association Public Interest Invitational Conference, Accountability as a State Reform Instrument: Impact on Teaching, Learning, and Minority Issues and Incentives for Improvement, Washington, DC, June 5, 1991. Available as CSE Technical Report 342, National Center for Research on Evaluation, Standards, and Student Testing, Center for the Study of Evaluation, UCLA. UCLA: CRESST.

Shepard, L.A. (1991b). Psychometricians' beliefs about learning. *Educational Researcher, 20,* 2–16.

34   A HISTORICAL PERSPECTIVE

Shepard, L.A. (2000). The role of assessment in a learning culture. *Educational Researcher,* 29(7), 4–14.

Skinner, B.F. (1953). *Science and human behavior.* New York: Macmillan.

Skinner, B.F. (1960). Teaching machines. In A.A. Lumsdaine & R. Glaser (Eds.), *Teaching machines and programmed learning* (pp. 137–158). Washington, DC: National Education Association.

Skinner, R.A. (2005, January 6). State of the states. *Education Week, 24*(17), 77–106.

Smith, M.L., & Rottenberg, C. (1991). Unintended consequences of external testing in elementary schools. *Educational Measurement: Issues and Practice, 10*(4), 7–11.

Smith, E.R., Tyler, R.W., & the Evaluation Staff. (1942). *Appraising and recording student progress* (The Adventure in American Education Series, Vol. III). New York: Harper & Bros.

Stecher, B.M., Barron, S.L., Chun, T., & Ross, K. (2000). *The effects of the Washington state education reform on schools and classroom* (CSE Technical Report 525). Los Angeles: National Center for Research on Evaluation, Standards, and Student Testing, University of California.

Stecher, B.M., Barron, S.L., Kaganoff, T., & Goodwin, J. (1998). *The effects of standards-based assessment on classroom practices: Results of the 1996–1997 RAND survey of Kentucky teachers of mathematics and writing* (CSE Technical Report 482). Los Angeles: National Center for Research on Evaluation, Standards, and Student Testing, University of California.

Stiggins, R.J. (2002). Assessment crisis: The absence of assessment FOR learning. *Phi Delta Kappan, 83*(10), 758–765.

Terman, L.M. (1919). *The intelligence of school children.* Boston: Houghton-Mifflin.

Thorndike, E.L. (1910). The contribution of psychology to education. *Journal of Educational Psychology, 1,* 5–12.

Thorndike, E.L. (1918). The nature, purposes, and general methods of measurements of educational products. In G.M. Whipple (Ed.), *The measurement of educational products. The seventeenth yearbook of the National Society for the Study of Education,* Part II (pp. 16–24). Bloomington, IL: Public School Publishing Company.

Tyler, R.W. (1949). *Basic principles of curriculum and instruction.* Chicago: University of Chicago Press.

Varenne, H., & McDermott, R. (1999). *Successful failure: The school America builds.* Boulder, CO: Westview Press.

Walker, D.F., & Schaffarzick, J. (1974). Comparing curricula. *Review of Educational Research, 44,* 83–111.

Washburne, C.W. (1925). A program of individualization. In C.W. Washburne (Chairman), *Adapting the schools to individual differences. The twenty-fourth yearbook of the National Society for the Study of Education,* Part II (pp. 257–272). Bloomington, IL: Public School Publishing Company.

Webb, N.L. (1997). *Criteria for alignment of expectations and assessments in mathematics and science education.* Madison, WI: National Institute for Science Education and Council of Chief State School Officers.

Webb, N.L. (2002, April). *An analysis of the alignment between mathematics standards and assessments for three states.* Paper presented at the meeting of the American Educational Research Association, New Orleans, LA.

Wiggins, G. (1992). Creating tests worth taking. *Educational Leadership, 49*(8), 26–33.

Wiliam, D. (2004). *Assessing instructional and assessment practice: What makes a lesson formative?* Presentation at 2004 annual conference of the National Center for Research on Evaluation, Standards, and Student Testing (CRESST), Los Angeles, CA.

Wolf, D.P., & Reardon, S.F. (1996). Access to excellence through new forms of student assessment. In J.N. Baron & D.P. Wolf (Eds.), *Performance-based student assessment: Challenges and possibilities. The ninety-fifth yearbook of the National Society for the Study of Education,* Part I (pp. 1–31). Chicago: National Society for the Study of Education.

CHAPTER 2

Assessment and Accountability from the Policymaker's Perspective

LORRAINE M. MCDONNELL

To a large extent, recent assessment policies represent a political solution to an educational problem.[1] Not only has the impetus for the movement come from politicians, the business community, and others outside the education establishment, but the definition of the problem to which standards and assessment are the solution has a decidedly political cast. At the heart of the problem, as policymakers and others have defined it, is inadequate and unequal educational achievement; all students need to achieve at higher levels, particularly those who have been hampered by low expectations and insufficient opportunities to learn. But linked to this education-focused definition is an assumption that at least part of the problem can be attributed to the schools' lack of accountability to parents and other taxpayers who fund public education and give it legitimacy (Gormley & Weimer, 1999; McDonnell, 2004; Peterson & West, 2003).

Consequently, standards and assessment policies embody both educational and political elements. The education portion of the solution focuses on the articulation of clear academic content and performance standards to guide teaching and learning, and the alignment of classroom instruction with those standards. Testing is certainly part of the educational dimension of this policy—as ways of measuring overall progress in meeting the standards and aiding in instructional decisions about individual students. But testing is even more central to the political dimensions of the standards movement, for which it primarily serves as an accountability mechanism.

However, few analyses have examined what testing's political status means for how those outside the education establishment view exter-

Lorraine M. McDonnell is a Professor in the Department of Political Science at the University of California, Santa Barbara.

nally mandated tests and what they expect them to accomplish. This chapter provides such an analysis by first elaborating on the notion that testing and accountability have become political issues. It then describes the various constituencies with an interest in educational assessment and examines how the political incentives that motivate policymakers and their constituents shape testing policy.[2] The chapter concludes with a discussion of the implications of a political perspective on testing, focusing particularly on the likelihood that such a perspective can be reconciled with professional testing standards and also be responsive to the concerns of professional educators.

Before proceeding, two caveats are in order. First, this chapter can only lay out the issues that a political perspective on testing raises. Because of the lack of systematic studies on the topic, it cannot evaluate either the impact of politics on test design or what happens when tests are used to advance policy or political purposes. Second, readers need to keep in mind that political claims to speak and act authoritatively on educational testing differ from the claims of educators or testing and measurement experts. Educators speak with legitimacy derived from norms of professional practice, and testing and measurement experts have recourse to research and professional standards. In contrast, politicians' claims to legitimacy come from their legal authority as elected representatives of the citizenry that funds public schools. The relative weight accorded each of these different sources of authority in discussions of test design and use is a normative exercise that will be decided differently in different places and circumstances. But it is certainly the case that claims based on professional expertise, research, and political authority each have sufficient legitimacy to be considered seriously, and that the design of testing policies is likely to be more successful if efforts are made to reconcile these claims when they are at odds with one another.

The Political Foundations of Assessment Policy

Researchers examining a range of federal and state assessment policies have found that the use of student testing as a political accountability tool is typically premised on three assumptions:

- As public institutions, schools should be held accountable to citizens and their elected representatives for their effective operation and especially for student learning (Gruber, 1987).
- However, because educators know a lot more about what occurs in schools than do either politicians or the public, this serious

information asymmetry often has hindered efforts to hold schools accountable (Gormley & Weimer, 1999; McDonnell, 2004).

• Consequently, some kind of externally imposed, standardized instrument is needed to provide comparable data on schools and students, so as to equalize the information available to everyone with a stake in the educational system (Heubert & Hauser, 1999; U.S. Congress, Office of Technology Assessment, 1992).

Thus standardized testing has come to play a prominent role in the political oversight of public education.

Standardized tests are used in two different ways that represent fundamentally different perspectives on how they can serve as instruments of public accountability. For uses that have come to be called *low-stakes tests*, no significant, tangible, or direct consequences are attached to the assessment results. In these instances, it is assumed that a standardized test can reliably and validly measure student achievement; that politicians, educators, parents, and the public will then act on the information generated by the test; and that their actions will improve educational quality and student achievement. In effect, information is assumed to be a sufficient incentive for these various groups to take action to improve the quality of schooling. *High-stakes* uses of tests, in contrast, are based on the assumption that information alone is insufficient to motivate educators to teach well and students to learn to high standards. Instead, the promise of rewards or the threat of sanctions is needed to ensure change. Rewards in the form of monetary bonuses may be given to schools or teachers; sanctions may be imposed through external oversight or takeover by higher-level officials. For individual students, high stakes include the use of tests in decisions about their promotion and graduation (Heubert & Hauser, 1999).

Holding educators and their students to account is not the only way that testing functions as an accountability mechanism. Theories of democratic accountability also assume that citizens can and should hold their elected officials accountable for the performance of public schools (Gruber, 1987). Hence voters may factor in educational quality concerns when they judge politicians' past job performance as part of their voting decisions, and test data can serve as an important source of information in making such evaluations.

In addition to their accountability dimension, standards and assessment are also political issues because their content often touches on ideological and cultural debates at the heart of politics. State assessments are typically designed to measure performance on academic content standards, and as such, reflect value choices about what is most important for students to learn and what constitutes mastery of that knowledge. In the process of making those decisions, abiding philosophical issues, such as which educational decisions should be the prerogative of the state and which should remain within the purview of the family, have been linked with practical questions about when students should use calculators and what role phonics, spelling, and grammar should play in an inquiry-oriented curriculum. The political arena has thus become a primary venue for deciding what should be taught and tested (McDonnell, 2004).

The Multiple Constituents of Assessment Policy

In looking across the landscape of constituencies with an interest in educational testing, three characteristics stand out. The first is the number and diversity of the groups involved. They range from well-organized national organizations such as the Business Roundtable and the National Education Association to small local groups such as Parents Against Proficiency Testing in Ohio and the Parents Coalition to Stop High Stakes Testing in New York. In between are organizations that represent elected officials, test publishers, school administrators, education researchers, students with special needs, and those pressing for equal learning opportunities for all students.

These groups all subscribe to the same general goal of improving student learning, but they disagree about the means to achieve it and the role of testing in education reform strategies. In most cases, organizational positions on test-related issues are motivated both by their material interests (e.g., whether members stand to gain financially or could be sanctioned as a result of a particular test) and by their beliefs about the proper role of testing (e.g., it is one of the few ways to ensure that the education system takes responsibility for poor students; tests are less reliable and valid measures of student learning than other instruments).

A second feature is that groups with similar purposes and constituents do not always hold comparable positions on testing issues, and positions can shift, depending on the particular issue. For example, both the American Federation of Teachers (AFT) and the National Education Association (NEA) have argued strongly in favor of using other indicators in addition to a single test score in making high-stakes decisions about individual students. However, the AFT has been more supportive of the high-stakes use of tests in making promotion and graduation decisions than the NEA, which voted to support any legislation that allows parents to opt their children out of standardized testing requirements (Heubert & Hauser, 1999; "Teachers Vote," 2001). Similarly, a number of civil rights organizations such as the National Association for the Advancement of Colored People (NAACP) and the Mexican American Legal Defense and Educational Fund have strongly opposed the high-stakes use of standardized tests, especially when they are the sole criterion in making decisions about students' promotion and graduation. In contrast, the Education Trust, an organization that promotes high standards for disadvantaged students, supports increased testing as part of a strategy to close the achievement gap between affluent and poor students and between white students and students of color.

A third feature is the extent to which student testing has become a highly visible issue, characterized by a politics similar to that of other high-profile policies. Throughout the 1990s, organized groups with an interest in assessment policy focused their attention on the states as the major arena in which decisions about test content and use were made. However, the passage of the federal No Child Left Behind Act (NCLB)[3] in 2002 nationalized debate over student testing and made it the target of interest group activity at all three governmental levels. As a result of both federal and state policies, then, the lobbying strategies and efforts to shape public opinion common to large interest groups are now evident on testing issues. For example, the Business Roundtable, a strong supporter of standards and assessment, issued a booklet designed to assist its members and other advocates in addressing the "testing backlash" occurring in some states and local communities (Business Roundtable, 2001). As criticism of NCLB has mounted, the Business Roundtable also joined with other business groups in a letter to the Speaker of the House of Representatives reiterating their strong support for the legislation and urging Congress to give NCLB the time it needs to work. Similarly, the Education Trust organized more than 100 superintendents and other education leaders to send a joint letter to Congress urging lawmakers to resist pressure to scale back the accountability provisions in NCLB (Gewertz, 2003).

On the other side of the issue, during the deliberations leading to NCLB's passage, most of the organizations representing the education establishment, such as the teacher unions, the school administrator organization, and the school boards association, mobilized to press for modifications in those testing provisions that could adversely affect their members (Brownstein, 2001). Over the first two years of NCLB's implementation, members of these same groups have pressed the U.S. Department of Education for modifications in program regulations and lobbied Congress for changes that require revisions in the law (Schemo, 2004). They have been joined by various state officials, concerned both about the number of schools in their states that will be designated as "needing improvement" and about what they see as an inadequately funded mandate that disrupts ongoing state education reform and accountability initiatives (Becker & Helderman, 2004; Center on Education Policy, 2004).

But not all the politics of testing has revolved around the lobbying strategies of national organizations. Much of what has come to be called the "testing backlash" has been the result of grassroots organizing by suburban, middle-class parents. Examples include the boycott of New York's eighth grade test organized by a group of mothers at a Scarsdale middle school (Zernike, 2001), the petition drive organized by parents in six suburban legislative districts in opposition to Massachusetts' Comprehensive Assessment System (MCAS) (Greenberger, 2000), and a variety of rallies held in about a dozen states with the number of participants ranging from as few as a dozen in Detroit to 1,500 in Albany (Manzo, 2001). Reasons for parental opposition vary, but the most common stem from concerns that extensive test preparation is hindering classroom innovation; that the standards being tested are vague or inappropriate; that reliance on tests disadvantages children who either have not had the opportunity to learn the material being tested or are poor test takers; and that the tests consume too much time and are a source of stress, particularly for younger students (Schrag, 2000).

It is too early to tell whether these grassroots protest activities will spread and come to represent a national movement in opposition to the high-stakes use of tests. At this point, however, the backlash is limited to suburban communities within a few states. Somewhat ironically, the parents of those students who are least likely to feel the adverse effects of high-stakes testing are the ones who have organized thus far. Whether testing opponents will be successful in mobilizing a broad spectrum of parents and the public will largely depend on how urban, minority, and working class parents react if and when sanctions are imposed on large numbers of their children.[4]

Political Incentives and Testing Policy

Elected officials' interest in testing is typically motivated by genuine concern about students and their educational achievement. However, the electoral incentive plays a large role in that motivation, not only because of politicians' self-interest in getting reelected, but also because they cannot accomplish their policy goals unless they are returned to office. The relationship between the politics of testing and electoral politics is especially tight in those cases where politicians such as President George W. Bush have made student testing a centerpiece of their policy agendas. Electoral incentives lead politicians to prefer policies that (1) are responsive to public opinion; (2) produce at least some effects quickly; and (3) may also accomplish purposes only tangentially related to testing (Downs, 1957; Kingdon, 1993; Moe, 2000).

What Policymakers Can Deduce from Public Opinion about Testing and Accountability

Because it can be volatile and not well informed on some issues, public opinion, as measured by surveys, does not always provide a clear and unambiguous measure of public sentiment. In addition, politicians typically use public opinion polls as only one basis for making decisions, weighing them against their own policy preferences and those of constituency groups already mobilized around an issue. Nevertheless, public opinion can play an important legitimating function either in support of or in opposition to particular policy choices. In the case of testing, public opinion has traditionally been a source of diffuse support for those committed to an activist policy stance.

A variety of poll data indicate strong support for standardized testing and its high-stakes uses, with the public also seeming to acknowledge its shortcomings and potential consequences. At the same time, responses to some survey items suggest that the public may not be particularly well informed on aspects of student testing. Across a variety of state and national polls, a majority of respondents support the high-stakes use of tests (Fuller, Hayward, & Kirst, 1998; Immerwahr, 1997; Johnson & Immerwahr, 1994; Mass Insight, 1997; Rose & Gallup, 2001). For example, in the 2001 Phi Delta Kappa/Gallup poll, 53% of respondents supported requiring students in their local communities to pass standardized tests for promotion from one grade to another, with a similar proportion (57%) favoring such tests as a condition for receiving a high school diploma. However, that approval level has declined somewhat from the two-thirds of respondents who supported these high-stakes uses the previous five times between 1978 and 2000 that Gallup asked the question (Hochschild & Scott, 1998). A nationally representative survey of parents conducted by Public Agenda in 2000, several months after the first reports of a parental testing backlash, obtained much the same results as earlier polls. Only 11% of those surveyed felt that their children were required to take too many standardized tests, and 67% strongly agreed with policies that impose higher academic standards even if their own child has to attend summer school before being promoted to the next grade (Public Agenda, 2000).[5]

There is also some evidence that the public understands the limitations of testing. For example, in the National Public Radio/Kaiser Family Foundation/Kennedy School national poll released in September 1999, 69% of those polled said that standardized tests should be used to determine whether students are promoted or graduate (with no differences between parents and nonparents). But only 12% said that they were "very confident" that "test scores on standardized tests are an accurate indicator of a student's progress and abilities," although an additional 56% said that they were "somewhat confident" (NPR Online, 1999). More recent polls also suggest that the admonitions of testing experts and various professional groups about the dangers of decisions based on a single test score have filtered through to the public. In the 2000 Phi Delta Kappa/Gallup poll, only 13% of those surveyed believed that a single standardized test is the best way to measure student achievement, with 85% saying that standardized tests should be combined with either a teacher-designed test or a portfolio of student work (Rose & Gallup, 2000). Similarly, 79% of the parents surveyed by Public Agenda strongly or somewhat agreed with the statement, "It's wrong to use the results of just one test to decide whether a student gets promoted or graduates" (Public Agenda, 2000).

Looking across all the available poll data on public attitudes toward standardized testing collected over the past two decades, it appears that the public is more broadly supportive of high-stakes testing than the education and civil rights groups that have taken a position on the topic. But there is also evidence that public opinion may not be particularly well informed on this and other education policy issues. We know, for example, that on general knowledge questions about education policy, public perceptions are often mistaken.[6] With regard to testing, 51% of the parents surveyed in the Public Agenda poll reported that they did not know whether the standardized tests that their children take ask fair questions that students should be able to answer (Public Agenda, 2000). It is important to note that for this item, parents' lack of knowledge is at least partly due to test security procedures that minimize public release of test items. However, that and other reasons suggest that most parents and members of the public are unaware of the full range of consequences related to high-stakes testing and the limits on the information that tests can provide.

Recent surveys that ask respondents specifically about NCLB indicate that even though awareness is growing, a significant proportion of the public lacks knowledge about the legislation. When the Phi Delta Kappa/Gallup poll asked respondents in May and June 2004 how much they knew about NCLB, 28% of the nationally representative sample (and 24% of parents in the sample) reported knowing "nothing at all," with an additional 40% (38% of parents) knowing "very little" (Rose & Gallup, 2004). Given these relatively low information levels, it is too early to tell whether opinion about NCLB will mirror the public's past approval of high-stakes testing, or whether it will weaken that support. Nevertheless, there is some indication that NCLB may undermine the stable, high approval ratings of the past. In a poll conducted for the Educational Testing Service, Hart and Teeter (2004) found that when NCLB was explained to a nationally representative sample of respondents, the proportion with a favorable opinion (39%) equaled those with an unfavorable opinion (38%), with 23% still having no opinion. Perhaps more telling are the 2003 Phi Delta Kappa/ Gallup poll findings that two-thirds of respondents felt student performance on a single statewide test will not provide a fair picture of whether a school needs improvement, with a similar proportion saying that the current emphasis on standardized tests will encourage teachers "to teach to the test" and indicating that as a "bad thing" (Rose & Gallup, 2003).

Although the public may have only vague ideas about student testing, its support of the concept has traditionally provided political cover for politicians interested in high-stakes testing, particularly when pursuing an agenda opposed by key interest groups. Whether NCLB will change that dynamic remains an unanswered question. In the short term, however, the overwhelming majority of the public (80%) continues to believe that schools need greater accountability, and a sizable proportion (34%) define greater accountability as higher standards for students combined with testing to ensure those standards are being met (Hart & Teeter, 2004).[7] Consequently, the public is likely to maintain its support for policies that promote external accountability through testing or other mechanisms.

Producing Policy Effects Quickly

Two- and four-year electoral cycles mean that politicians find it very difficult to sell patience to an electorate that expects quick results. This constraint makes education reforms with testing at their core particularly appealing, because they seemingly alter what happens in individual classrooms within a very short period.

Close to 30 years of research on policy implementation have shown that policymakers at the federal and state levels often cannot "mandate what matters" (McLaughlin, 1987, p. 172). For education policy, this limitation has meant that reforms designed to alter classroom instruction have had only a limited impact because few top-down mandates or incentives are sufficient to overcome a lack of local will or capacity. However, externally mandated assessments are the one top-down policy lever that seems consistently to change local behavior. Although the impact of such assessments varies—depending on the type of test, the grade levels being tested, students' socioeconomic status, and the uses to which the test is put—a growing body of research indicates that school and classroom practices do change in response to these tests (e.g., Cohen & Hill, 2001; Firestone, Mayrowetz, & Fairman, 1998; McDonnell, 2004; Mehrens, 1998; Stecher, Barron, Kaganoff, & Goodwin, 1998; Wolf, Borko, Elliott, & McIver, 2000). Clearly, the effects of mandated assessments have not always been beneficial for students or what policymakers intended. Nevertheless, given the limited array of strategies available to them, politicians have viewed standardized testing as too powerful a lever not to use it. From their perspective, assessment policies also produce results quickly because test scores typically increase during the first few years after a new test is introduced. The validity of such score gains has long been questioned by researchers (Koretz, McCaffrey, & Hamilton, 2001; Linn, 2000), but most policymakers remain convinced that something real occurs if only because the tests shine a public spotlight on educators who must then respond.

The desire to produce some results within the constraints of the electoral cycle does not necessarily mean that policymakers expect all or most of the effects of a testing policy to be generated quickly. For example, Kentucky's education reform legislation gives schools 20 years to move all their students to the "proficient" level of mastery of the state standards, and NCLB gives schools 12 years to move all students to the "proficient" level, as defined by state standards. In these and similar cases, however, policymakers expect testing policies to produce steady, incremental progress, thus indicating to the public that schools are improving and moving in a direction consistent with the long-term goals of the policy.

Testing as a Route to Achieving Other Policy Goals

In trying to balance competing constituent interests, elected officials may use testing policies to satisfy demands not directly related to the ostensible purposes of testing and assessment, or to diffuse efforts to adopt controversial policies. For example, advocates for students with disabilities have lobbied federal and state officials to include them in whatever standards and accountability systems are established, as a way of requiring schools to be more explicitly and publicly accountable for those students (McDonnell, McLaughlin, & Morison, 1997). As a result, testing accommodations for students with disabilities have increased over the past few years, raising the question of whether or not those students' test scores should be "flagged" to indicate their different testing conditions. Although this question is of interest to psychometricians and others concerned about valid interpretations of long-term trends in test score data, it is of considerably less significance to policymakers and special education interest groups who see the participation of students with disabilities in a state testing system to be of greater importance than whatever data are produced.

For policymakers concerned about preserving the vitality of the public school system in the face of moves to implement vouchers, standards and assessment policies have become a way to show that public education can be rigorous, responsive, and accountable. In fact, one could argue that the standards and assessment movement is currently the only "big idea" serving as a counterpoint to vouchers. Alternatively, the failure of standards policies, as evidenced by a steady stream of low test scores or negative consequences imposed on many students, may increase public and elite support for vouchers and greater school choice.

Implications of a Political Perspective for the Purposes and Uses of Tests

A review of current assessment policies indicates that policymakers expect them to accomplish one or more of seven different purposes:

- Provide information about the status of the education system
- Aid in instructional decisions about individual students
- Bring greater curricular coherence to the system
- Motivate students to perform better and parents to demand higher performance

- Act as a lever to change instructional content and strategies
- Hold schools and educators accountable for student performance
- Certify individual students as having attained specified levels of achievement or mastery. (Heubert & Hauser, 1999; McDonnell, 1994)

Assessment policies have varied in purpose and use over time as more states have moved away from low-stakes tests that primarily served informational purposes to high-stakes tests designed to hold schools and students accountable through the imposition of rewards and sanctions, to change classroom instruction, and to certify individual students for promotion and graduation. The shift from low- to high-stakes uses has also been accompanied by a move on the part of a growing number of states and some large urban school districts to use the same test for multiple purposes. So, for example, a state assessment tied to state curriculum standards might be used to provide information on the status of the system, to influence classroom instruction in a particular direction, to reward and sanction schools, and to decide about student promotion and graduation.

In using the same test for multiple high-stakes purposes, policymakers are at odds with the professional standards of the testing and measurement community. Those standards stress the need to base high-stakes decisions on more than a single test; validate tests for each separate intended use; and provide adequate resources for students to learn the content being tested, among other principles (American Educational Research Association, 2000). In disregarding these standards, policymakers are using assessments in ways that exceed the limits of current testing technology. As the National Research Council's report on *High Stakes* noted:

Policy and public expectations of testing generally exceed the technological capacity of the tests themselves. One of the most common reasons for this gap is that policymakers, under constituent pressure to improve schools, often decide to use existing tests for purposes for which they were neither intended nor sufficiently validated. So, for example, tests designed to produce valid measures of performance only at the aggregate level—for schools and classrooms—are used to report on and make decisions about individual students. In such instances, serious consequences (such as retention in grade) may be unfairly imposed on individual students. (Heubert & Hauser, 1999, p. 30)

Although there are a number of reasons for this disjuncture between standards of good testing practice and policymakers' actions, three are especially notable. The first has already been mentioned: policymakers often decide to rely on existing tests because they perceive a fleeting political opportunity to act, thus necessitating that they move quickly while they have an open policy window, or they believe that, even with imperfect tests, more good than harm will result. Policymakers often acknowledge that critics of current testing systems are making valid points. However, from their perspective, the technical constraints identified by testing experts are problems that should be remedied to the extent possible, but in an iterative fashion simultaneous with the implementation of test-based policy (McDonnell, 1994). Basically, elected officials are people of action who cannot wait for the perfect test, and are willing to settle for less than an optimal one on the assumption that it can be improved over time and that in the interim, students will benefit from focused attention on their learning.

A second reason is that policymakers, testing experts, and educators operate in very different worlds, with each group having only a limited understanding of the others' incentives, constraints, and day-to-day work. For many politicians, this lack of understanding means that they are crafting policies with limited knowledge of the nature of teaching and learning and the role of tests in measuring the effects of those processes. This factor was noted during the congressional debate over NCLB. Members of Congress with close ties to the education system or who themselves had been teachers were skeptical of how much Congress could accomplish with additional testing requirements, while those without firsthand experience in schools argued that it is critical to be able to measure what students are learning, and that annual tests are the way to accomplish that purpose and improve educational quality (Nather, 2001).

Finally, the relatively low cost of testing and the levels of investment that policymakers are willing to make in education reforms have also accelerated the multiple uses of tests. Although most assessment policies are part of larger reform strategies that often include funding for student remediation, curriculum and test development, and professional preparation of teachers, those funds are typically insufficient to meet the demands of new standards and testing systems. Because the cost of the tests themselves are relatively low (ranging from $3 to $35 per student) and seem to produce a lot of "bang for the buck," policymakers often underestimate the full costs of preparing teachers to convey the requisite curriculum effectively and of giving students adequate opportunities to learn it. The problem of underinvestment is compounded by the tight timelines under which these systems typically have to be implemented and show results. The potential effects of even reasonably adequate funding are likely to be diminished if the time frame is unreasonable. These funding and time pressures, then, work against the development of separate tests for different purposes.

In their desire to move quickly and to use tests that are readily available, policymakers have not been entirely unresponsive to the concerns of testing experts and educators. Whether in response to the criticisms of experts, the threat of lawsuits, or potential parental and teacher backlash, some states, for example, have delayed full implementation of high school exit examinations or have lowered the score required to pass them.[8] However, anyone surveying the current terrain of testing policy has to be struck by what appears to be a widespread resolve by politicians at all three governmental levels to stay the course on standards and assessment.

Conclusions

Simply by virtue of the different worlds in which they work, a cultural divide will always exist between policymakers and the testing and measurement community, but even if that divide can never be bridged entirely, it could be narrowed. However, over the past decade, the two communities seemed to have moved farther apart in their views about student testing and its uses.

Reconciling professional testing standards and political imperatives would require changes in the actions and worldviews of both groups. Policymakers would have to consider the full costs of the testing systems they are implementing. The most important of these costs is the need to provide every student subject to high-stakes testing with adequate and appropriate opportunities to learn the content being tested. A realistic assessment of the human resource, financial, and time investments necessary before most students can be justly expected to have mastered the requisite content will likely slow the current rate at which high-stakes tests are being implemented.

Commensurate with this stocktaking, policymakers would need to persuade their constituents to be more patient in their judgments about public education, especially the two-thirds of voters who have no school-age children and little firsthand knowledge of schools. Part of selling patience to the public requires providing evidence that schools are indeed responsive to public expectations. However, another part is also convincing citizens that accountability is a two-way street: schools cannot perform to community standards unless the community also meets its obligations to support the schools adequately. Arguing against quick policy "fixes" is always difficult. However, this kind of message

has been more successfully communicated in other policy areas—
ranging from the environment to medical research—suggesting that a
much better job can be done in education, and also that the American
public is sophisticated enough to hear such a message.

Above all, narrowing the gap between testing standards and political
imperatives would require policymakers to be more accepting of the
limitations of tests and their potential uses. Like most myths in public
policy, the belief that assessments can provide unbiased and comprehensive data about student achievement is an influential one (De
Neufville & Barton, 1987). Policymakers and their constituents want
to believe that judgments about local schools and individual students
are based on information that it is technically sound and free of bias.
These assumptions about objectivity and lack of bias are even more
critical when some schools and students are being rewarded and others
are being sanctioned. When winners and losers are created through
policy, decisions need to be justified on what appear to be objective
grounds. Therefore, even if policymakers were to be more accepting of
the limits of testing, they would still need to replace the myth of the
objective test with an equally powerful one, because policymaking is
about persuasion, and myths persuade. Whether such a replacement
myth can even be found and whatever it might be, it would have to
serve the same public function—namely, facilitating the political
accountability of schools and allocating scarce resources in a seemingly
fair and impartial way.

This summary of how policymakers would need to change if the
divide between politics and professional standards were to be narrowed
also defines what the testing and measurement community would need
to do. Currently, it is primarily a voice of caution, identifying the
shortcomings of current systems by noting what is not working as it
should and indicating where harmful or unintended consequences are
likely to occur (e.g., Heubert & Hauser, 1999; Koretz & Barron, 1998;
Linn, Baker, & Betebenner, 2002; Rhoades & Madaus, 2003). The role
of critic is an honorable and appropriate one for scholars, but the events
of the past decade suggest that if testing experts want their admonitions
to be heeded, they may have to change their strategies. Above all, they
need to provide policymakers with alternatives to current testing
regimes that are feasible and that address the public's desire to have
more accountable, responsive, and effective schools. As with policymakers' greater acceptance of the limits of testing, moving from critic to
system builder will be a difficult change for many members of the
testing and measurement community. Without compromising their
own research-based principles, they will need to accept that in a democ-

50   FROM   THE   POLICYMAKER'S   PERSPECTIVE

racy, authority for deciding on the contours of testing systems rests with elected officials, and that accountability to the electorate is at least as equally legitimate a claim as scientific knowledge. In the short term, the most effective strategy would probably be for testing experts to identify what changes could be made within the basic contours of existing assessment systems to make them reasonably consistent with standards of good testing practice. In doing so, testing experts would need to take into account the political incentives that press for information about students and schools that is valid, comparable, and understandable to the public; that can be used to leverage and motivate educators' and students' behavior; and that can produce tangible and credible results within a reasonable time frame.

None of these changes would be straightforward or easy to accomplish. However, one way to begin the process would be to combine the political and professional oversight of testing and assessment systems. Often in state systems, these functions are separate: expert panels evaluate and advise on the technical aspects of a particular test, while decisions about its uses are made independently, frequently by state legislators. More closely integrating these two functions would allow each group to understand better the other's values and concerns, and to deliberate about ways to accommodate their differing perspectives. If viewing testing through a political lens tells us anything, it is that political and professional perspectives must be reconciled if students are to benefit from the hopes and expectations of each group.

NOTES

1. This chapter is a revised and updated version of McDonnell (2002). It is used with RAND's permission.

2. Political incentives refer to those factors that motivate politicians, interest group representatives, and other citizens to act in the political arena. These motivations can include the desire of politicians to get reelected, their interest in enacting particular kinds of policies, and interest groups' and citizens' interest in promoting specific policy goals. As with most domestic policy, the political incentives that motivate testing policy are diverse and vary over time and across political venues at the federal, state, and local levels.

3. NCLB, signed by President G.W. Bush in early 2002, amends the Elementary and Secondary Education Act (ESEA) and requires for the first time that all students in grades 3 through 8 be tested annually in mathematics and reading as a condition for states receiving ESEA Title I funds. NCLB also requires that states develop measurable objectives for improved achievement for all students, with consequences for schools that fail to meet progress targets, including required improvement plans, student transfer options, and even major restructuring. To ensure that schools work to improve the achievement of all students, they are required to disaggregate and report test scores by demographic and educational subgroups such as specific ethnic groups, economically disadvantaged students, and those with limited English proficiency. At the time of its enactment, NCLB, endorsed by huge majorities in both houses of Congress, represented a remarkable

consensus between the two national political parties, and reflected President Bush's campaign pledge to "leave no child behind."

4. Much of the media attention on the politics of testing has focused on lobbying aimed at the executive and legislative branches of the federal and state governments. However, civil rights groups in several states have also tried to use the courts to stop or modify high-stakes testing programs. Thus far, all have been unsuccessful. The most notable was the GI Forum case in Texas in which the federal district court ruled that although the Texas Assessment of Academic Skills (TAAS) had a disparate impact on minority students, the test and its uses are not unconstitutional, and that the plaintiffs failed to prove that the disparate impact was more significant than the concomitant positive impact (*GI Forum et al. v. Texas Education Agency, et al.*, 2000).

5. An additional 19% of the sample said that they somewhat approved of such a policy even if their child has to attend summer school. When asked if they approved of the policy even if their child were held back in grade, 46% strongly approved and an additional 21% approved somewhat.

6. For example, the 1996 Phi Delta Kappa/Gallup poll found that although the high school dropout rate has steadily declined, 64% of those surveyed thought that it had increased over the past 25 years. In the same survey, only 26% could accurately estimate the proportion of students receiving special education services (Elam, Rose, & Gallup, 1996). In a more recent *Washington Post*/Kaiser Family Foundation/Kennedy School poll, only 29% of the registered voters surveyed knew that the federal government provides less than a quarter of the funding for the nation's public schools (*The Washington Post*, 2000).

7. In the Hart and Teeter (2004) poll, respondents were asked which of three phrases comes closest to what they mean by "we need greater accountability." In addition to the 34% who chose a standards and assessment definition, 32% defined it as "tighter controls on how education dollars are spent, and less waste," and 30% as "teachers and administrators who listen to parents and follow through to ensure that their concerns are addressed." As evidence of differences between the public and policymakers, in a separate sample of 304 education policymakers, 45% defined "greater accountability" as standards and assessment, 22% as fiscal controls, and 19% as responsive teachers and administrators.

8. For example, Arizona delayed requirements to withhold diplomas, while California postponed the effective date of its exit exam from 2004 to 2006 and Maryland will phase in its exit examination in 2008 rather than 2007. After only 36% of students taking the mathematics portion of Nevada's exit examination passed after the first attempt, the state temporarily lowered the cut score on the test from 304 to 290 (Center on Education Policy, 2003).

REFERENCES

American Educational Research Association. (2000). Position statement of the American Educational Research Association concerning high-stakes testing in preK-12 education. *Educational Researcher, 29*(8), 24–25.

Becker, J., & Helderman, R.S. (2004, January 24). Va. delegates denounce Bush education law. *The Washington Post,* pp. A1, A14.

Brownstein, R. (2001, July 24). Belatedly, a front is forming to fight education legislation. *The Los Angeles Times,* p. A14.

Business Roundtable. (2001). *Assessing and addressing the "testing backlash."* Washington, DC: Author.

Center on Education Policy. (2003). *State high school exit exams put to the test.* Washington, DC: Author.

Center on Education Policy. (2004). *From the capital to the classroom.* Washington, DC: Author.

Cohen, D.K., & Hill, H.C. (2001). *Learning policy.* New Haven, CT: Yale University Press.

De Neufville, J.I., & Barton, S.E. (1987). Myths and the definition of policy problems. *Policy Sciences, 20,* 181–206.

Downs, A. (1957). *An economic theory of democracy.* New York: Harper and Row.

Elam, S.M., Rose, L.C., & Gallup, A.M. (1996). The 28th Annual Phi Delta Kappa/ Gallup poll of the public's attitudes toward the public schools. *Phi Delta Kappan, 78*(1), 41–59.

Firestone, W.A., Mayrowetz, D., & Fairman, J. (1998). Performance-based assessment and instructional change: The effects of testing in Maine and Maryland. *Educational Evaluation and Policy Analysis, 20*(2), 95–113.

Fuller, B., Hayward, G., & Kirst, M. (1998). *Californians speak on education and reform options.* Berkeley: Policy Analysis for California Education.

Gewertz, C. (2003, November 26). Educators endorse rules on accountability. *Education Week, 23*(13), 16.

GI Forum et al. v. Texas Education Agency et al., 87 F. Supp. 2d 667 (W.D. Tex. 2000).

Gormley, W.T., Jr., & Weimer, D.L. (1999). *Organizational report cards.* Cambridge, MA: Harvard University Press.

Greenberger, S.S. (2000, October 24). Critics intensify MCAS battle ballot questions, association vote are focus of effort. *Boston Globe,* p. B1.

Gruber, J.E. (1987). *Controlling bureaucracies: Dilemmas in democratic governance.* Berkeley: University of California Press.

Hart, P.D., & Teeter, R.M. (2004, July). Equity and adequacy: Americans speak on public school funding: A national public opinion survey conducted for the Educational Testing Service. Retrieved August 24, 2004, from http://www.tc.columbia.edu/Hechinger.

Heubert, J.P., & Hauser, R.M. (Eds.). (1999). *High stakes: Testing for tracking, promotion, and graduation.* Washington, DC: National Academies Press.

Hochschild, J., & Scott, B. (1998). Trends: Governance and reform of public education in the United States. *Public Opinion Quarterly, 62*(1), 79–120.

Immerwahr, J. (1997). *What our children need: South Carolinians look at public education.* New York: Public Agenda.

Johnson, J., & Immerwahr, J. (1994). *First things first: What Americans expect from the public schools.* New York: Public Agenda.

Kingdon, J.W. (1993). Politicians, self-interest, and ideas. In G.E. Marcus & R.L. Hanson (Eds.), *Reconsidering the democratic public* (pp. 73–89). College Station: Pennsylvania State University Press.

Koretz, D.M., & Barron, S.J. (1998). *The validity of gains in scores on the Kentucky Instructional Results Information System (KIRIS).* Santa Monica, CA: RAND.

Koretz, D.M., McCaffrey, D.F., & Hamilton, L.S. (2001, April). *Toward a framework for validating gains under high-stakes conditions*. Paper presented at the annual meeting of the National Council on Measurement in Education, Seattle, April.

Linn, R.L. (2000). Assessments and accountability. *Educational Researcher, 29*(2), 4–16.

Linn, R.L., Baker, E.L., & Betebenner, D.W. (2002). Accountability systems: Implications of requirements of the No Child Left Behind Act of 2001. *Educational Researcher, 31*(6), 3–16.

Manzo, K.K. (2001, May 16). Protests over state testing widespread. *Education Week, 20*(36), 1, 26.

Mass Insight. (1997). *Education reform: The public's view of standards and tests*. Cambridge, MA: Author.

McDonnell, L.M. (1994). *Policymakers' views of student assessment*. Santa Monica, CA: RAND.

McDonnell, L.M. (2002). Accountability as seen through a political lens. In L.S. Hamilton, B.M. Stecher, & S.P. Klein (Eds.), *Making sense of test-based accountability in education* (pp. 101–120). Santa Monica, CA: RAND.

McDonnell, L.M. (2004). *Politics, persuasion, and educational testing*. Cambridge, MA: Harvard University Press.

McDonnell, L.M., McLaughlin, M.J., & Morison, P. (Eds.). (1997). *Educating one and all: Students with disabilities and standards-based reform*. Washington, DC: National Academy Press.

McLaughlin, M.W. (1987). Learning from experience: Lessons from policy implementation. *Educational Evaluation and Policy Analysis, 9*(2), 171–178.

Mehrens, W.A. (1998). Consequences of assessment: What is the evidence? *Education Policy Analysis Archives, 6*(13). Retrieved May 13, 2002, from http//ericae.net/ericdc/EJ582965.htm

Moe, T.M. (2000). The two democratic purposes of public education. In L.M. McDonnell, P.M. Timpane, & R. Benjamin (Eds.), *Rediscovering the democratic purposes of education* (pp. 127–147). Lawrence: University Press of Kansas.

Nather, D. (2001). Student-testing drive marks an attitude shift in Congress. *CQ Weekly*, June 30, 1560–1566.

No Child Left Behind Act of 2001, Pub. L. No. 107-110, 115 Stat. 1425 (2002).

NPR Online. (1999). *NPR/Kaiser/Kennedy School education survey*. Retrieved May 10, 2002, from http://www.npr.org/programs/specials/poll/education/education.results.html

Peterson, P.E., & West, M.R. (Eds.). (2003). *No child left behind? The politics and practice of school accountability*. Washington, DC: Brookings Institution Press.

Public Agenda. (2000). Survey finds little sign of backlash against academic standards or standardized tests. Retrieved June 19, 2001, from http://www.publicagenda.org/issues/pcc_detail

Rhoades, K., & Madaus, G. (2003). *Errors in standardized tests: A systemic problem*. Boston, MA: National Board on Educational Testing and Public Policy, Boston College.

Rose, L.C., & Gallup, A.M. (2000). The 32nd annual Phi Delta Kappa/Gallup poll of the public's attitudes toward the public schools. *Phi Delta Kappan, 82*(1), 41–57.

Rose, L.C., & Gallup, A.M. (2001). The 33rd annual Phi Delta Kappa/Gallup poll of the public's attitudes toward the public schools. *Phi Delta Kappan, 83*(1), 41–48.

Rose, L.C., & Gallup, A.M. (2003). The 35th annual Phi Delta Kappa/Gallup poll of the public's attitudes toward the public schools. *Phi Delta Kappan, 85*(1), 41–56.

Rose, L.C., & Gallup, A.M. (2004). The 36th annual Phi Delta Kappa/Gallup poll of the public's attitudes toward the public schools. *Phi Delta Kappan, 86*(1), 41–52.

Schemo, D.J. (2004, March 25). 14 states ask U.S. to revise some education law rules. *The New York Times*, p. A14.

Schrag, P. (2000, August). High stakes are for tomatoes. *The Atlantic Monthly, 286*(2), 19–21.

Stecher, B.M., Barron, S., Kaganoff, T., & Goodwin, J. (1998). *The effects of standards-based assessment on classroom practices: Results of the 1996–1997 RAND survey of Kentucky teachers of mathematics and writing.* CSE Technical Report 482. Los Angeles: National Center for Research on Evaluation, Standards, and Student Testing, University of California.

Teachers vote to let parents decide on tests. (2001, July 8). *The New York Times*, p. A15.

U.S. Congress, Office of Technology Assessment. (1992). *Testing in American schools: Asking the right questions.* Washington, DC: U.S. Government Printing Office.

Washington Post. (2000). Washington Post/Kaiser Family Foundation/Harvard University. Issues I: Education. Retrieved May 10, 2002, from http://www.washingtonpost.com/wp-srv/politics/polls/vault/stories/data061800.htm

Wolf, S.A., Borko, H., Elliott, R.L., & McIver, M.C. (2000). That dog won't hunt! Exemplary school change efforts within the Kentucky reform. *American Educational Research Journal, 37*(2), 349–393.

Zernike, K. (2001, May 4). Suburban mothers succeed in their boycott of an 8th-grade test. *The New York Times*, p. A19.

CHAPTER 3

Goals for Learning and Assessment

JUDITH A. RAMALEY

Why Do We Keep Trying to Reform Our Educational System?

To understand what we Americans want from our schools and why we never seem to be happy with what our schools are accomplishing, it is helpful to think about the role of schooling in American life. We have traditionally considered our schools as a mechanism for social improvement (Graham, 1995), as a way to guarantee a better society (Tyack & Cuban, 1995), and as a way to enable all of us to seek "the good life" (Nel Noddings via Glenda Lappan, personal communication). As Patricia Graham puts it, "What the society has felt either unable or unwilling to undertake with its adults, it has expected the schools to accomplish with its children" (p. 4).

Graham (1995) goes on to say that schools remain the mainstay of our public aspirations for bringing up our children. As she sees it, our schools are like the Battleships of World War II:

Large, powerful, cumbersome, with enormous crews, these giants of the ocean go where they are told to go by some distant authority, which presumably understands better than anyone on the ship, including the captain, where and why they should go. Maneuverability is not their strength. When ordered to change course they do so, but there are significant delays between the time of course direction orders and the ship going in a different direction. (p. 3)

These cumbersome ships are not well equipped to serve the many needs of our children. As Graham puts it, our young people need a fleet of more maneuverable vessels, not a cumbersome battleship. We need to pay attention to what is going on in the school and how schools interact with communities as well. In simple terms, we all share a

Judith A. Ramaley is Professor of Biomedical Sciences and Fellow of the Margaret Chase Smith Center for Public Policy at the University of Maine-Orono.

responsibility for the quality of education. Furthermore, the value of education is best examined in the context of its use, not just in our schools, but in all aspects of daily life.

If we take as our premise that schools have always been asked to serve larger, often conflicting societal ends, the shifts in expectations and the different urgencies that have driven our efforts at education reform in the past century become clearer. As a nation, we have gone through many painful changes driven by waves of immigration and by societal disruptions caused by the introduction of new technologies. The new expectations generated by these experiences often conflicted radically with what the schools had been asked to do in an earlier era, and inevitably dictated changes in the curriculum. As we will see, the concerns of one era sound strangely like the concerns of another, but the approach we take to science education, in particular, with each wave of educational reform reflects the technologies that were troubling then as well as the impact of scientific knowledge on society (Bybee, 1997).

I will quote from David Tyack and Larry Cuban (1995) to set the stage for an exploration of the changing definitions of the role of science in the curriculum and our approach to the concept of "scientific literacy." According to them, "For over a century and a half, Americans have translated their cultural anxieties and hopes into dramatic demands for school reform" (p. 1). As we move quickly from one period of reform to the next, starting with the controversies that shaped education at the close of the 19th century, we will see a return again and again to a core set of problems that are as urgent today as they were 100 years ago. Even a casual study of the different eras of reform reflects a set of common challenges: (1) how to assimilate new people into our society; (2) how to raise our children to be citizens, sharing common values and expectations about what it means to be an adult living in a democracy and possessing the knowledge and skill to participate in democratic life; (3) how to prepare our young people to enter a workforce that is being radically shaped by the social and economic impacts of new technologies; and (4) how to promote equality of opportunity and a better quality of life for everyone. This last theme links up in an interesting way to emerging ideas about human and social capital, concepts that we will return to shortly. All of these objectives have implications for how science is taught and what we think our students ought to know and be able to do with the science that they know, as well as with their understanding of "the nature of science" and how scientific knowledge progresses.

In moving from one era to another we will see different answers to what it means to be educated and how we should teach. We will swing back and forth between two schools of thought whose contrasting claims we have not resolved even today. These controversies shape the context for accountability and assessment. What should we measure in order to decide if our aspirations for our young people have been realized? What does it mean to know something and what does it take to be able to use what we know effectively? In the complex world of today, how do scientific facts, ideas, and ways of knowing fit into the other important aspects of our experience and understanding, including our aesthetic, political, economic, and moral debates (Latour, 2004)?

We will find ourselves contemplating the gulf between those who believe that the mark of an educated person is the amount of facts they know (*educational traditionalists*) and those who consider the goal of education to be the production of creative, responsible, productive citizens who are capable of informed decision making (*educational progressives*). I must admit that when I am asked which is more important, *cultural literacy* or *critical thinking and effective citizenship*, I usually say "yes." We need both. If only it were that simple! Unfortunately, the former is much easier to measure than the later.

The Debate of Traditionalists and Progressives: Is It More Important to Learn Something or to Learn How to Learn Something?

Educational traditionalists define explicit goals of learning and employ discipline and order in the classroom, a teacher-led curriculum, and regular testing to assess student progress. According to Tom Loveless (2001), traditionalists "are skeptical that children naturally discover knowledge or will come to know much if left to their own devices" (p. 2). They believe that "pupils should be presented with facts, principles and rules of action which are to be learned, remembered and then applied" (Bruner, 1977, p. 55). This view has a certain appeal since it makes very clear and uncontestable what is to be learned, and standards for assessing learning can be developed easily. The immediate implications of traditionalism for assessment are obvious. Students need to know "the facts" and be able to use the vocabulary of science to read about science. Assessment in this mode consists "largely of discussions of the key concepts and methods that students should know" (Eisenhart, Finkel, & Marion, 1996, p. 266).

Educational progressives/constructivists, according to Loveless (2001), consider a school to be a community of learners. Learning is the making of meaning, an active construction guided by the teacher but built on the interests and understandings of the students. The teacher's challenge is to understand what a child knows—how she or he thinks and arrives at what she or he believes. Children, like adults, are seen as constructing a model of the world as an aid to interpreting their experiences. Science is one element of that world. If this world has some connection to their daily lives, it will make sense. If, on the other hand, they are asked to suspend belief and enter a different world in the classroom from the one they experience elsewhere, it is very likely that students will lose interest in science (Eisenhart et al., 1996). For progressives, knowledge is what is shared through discourse and truths are the product of evidence, argument, and construction rather than authority, either textual or pedagogic (Bruner, 1996).

Those who prefer the traditionalist view would describe the thinking of constructivists as "fuzzy," "without standards, rules, or hierarchies of skill." They would claim that this perspective is responsible for teacher education programs that downplay content, teachers who know very little about the subjects they will teach, and students who know very little about their own heritage. Those who espouse contemporary aspects of educational reform would argue that simple knowledge of facts and the faithful use of algorithms are functions that computers can perform; that the basic skills required for successful entry into the workforce and reasonable professional progress are more demanding than they were even a decade ago and cannot easily be met by our current curriculum. In *The New Division of Labor: How Computers are Creating the Next Job Market*, Frank Levy and Richard Murnane (2004) argue that computers are a better option than people when the problems can be described with rules-based logic, a step-by-step manual that provides a procedure for any imaginable contingency. What a rules-based system cannot do, however, is deal with new problems that come up, problems unanticipated by the program of rules. Furthermore, computers cannot capture the remarkable store of how-to or tacit knowledge that we all use daily but would have a lot of trouble articulating (Levy & Murnane, 2004, pp. 18–19). As Levy and Murnane put it: "In the absence of predictability, the number of contingencies explodes as does the knowledge required to deal with them. The required rules are very hard to write" (p. 20). One wonders, in fact, if rules underlying creativity and innovation can be written at all.

What human beings *can* do is seek patterns and make conceptual connections between a new unfamiliar context or challenge and more familiar ones. We use "case-based reasoning" to see similarities between a new problem and some relevant past experiences (Levy & Murnane, 2004, p. 23). These elements—cognitive flexibility, creativity, knowledge transfers, and adaptability—are the new basic skills of an educated generation and represent the capacities that are required in today's workplace. Even the new basic skills that should be acquired in K-12, as Murnane and Levy (1996) talk about them, require a solid knowledge of mathematics and reading skills, the ability to work in groups and to make effective oral and written presentations, and the ability to use computers to carry out simple tasks. The Business-Higher Education Forum (2003), in its recent report *Building a Nation of Learners*, explores the "widening 'skills gap' between traditional training and the skills actually needed in today's jobs and those of tomorrow" (p. 9) and urges higher education to adopt new approaches to learning that offer more engaging and relevant content and experiences targeted to individual learning styles and needs. In an earlier report, the Forum identified nine key attributes necessary for today's workplace: leadership, teamwork, problem solving, time management, self-management, adaptability, analytical thinking, global consciousness, and strong communication skills (listening, speaking, reading, and writing).

The challenge for educational constructivists[1] is that their "vision of a scientifically literate citizenry in which many and diverse people act in socially compassionate and democratically responsible ways" (Eisenhart et al., 1996, p. 266) is only loosely coupled at best with the actual curriculum. Their often wonderfully nuanced views of what it means to be scientifically literate run counter to current curricular standards that specify exactly what facts, concepts, and methods are to be learned and mastered and then assessed. We will have to develop better and more complex measures to understand what our students know, what they can do with what they know, and what they can learn as they explore issues of importance to themselves and to society at large.

What Kind of Education Should We Provide?

Over the past century, we have argued back and forth about the role of schooling and what kind of education we should provide for our young people. In the closing years of the 19th century, schools were expected to make social equality a reality by giving all students an equal chance to develop their mental powers to the fullest (Ravitch, 2000). It was more important to nurture intelligence and virtue than to learn a trade. The aim of the common school was clear in those days: "to promote sufficient learning and self-discipline so that people in a democratic society could be good citizens, read the newspapers, get a job, make their way in an individualistic and competitive society, and contribute to their community's well-being" (Ravitch, 2000, p. 25).

Schools at the end of the 19th century were expected to absorb the rapidly rising population of young people, many of them immigrants or the sons and daughters of immigrants. Society was troubled by social and economic change, rapid industrialization, the influx of foreigners, and increasing urbanization (Ravitch, 2000, p. 26). Social reformers sought to combat the ill effects of these changes and to usher in a new progressive era. The schools were a major tool for social reform.

Arguably, two of the most influential educators in the late 1890s were Charles W. Eliot, president of Harvard, and William Torrey Harris, U.S. Commissioner of Education. Both were tireless proponents of liberal education. They believed that the primary purpose of education was to improve the intelligence of all young people. What Eliot sought was mental power, the power to think, reason, observe, and describe, a suite of qualities we might now pack into the phrase *critical thinking*. For him, at that time, the goal of education was the training of the mind, regardless of the subject matter used for that purpose. Harris, in contrast, believed that certain subjects were essential to a liberal education. He sought to replace the classical traditions (Latin, Greek, and mathematics) with modern subjects (modern science, modern literature, and modern history). He was a crusader for universal education, built on a liberal arts core. Only later in his career did Eliot turn away from this broad conception and embrace the idea of social efficiency and vocational education tailored to the work that different people were "destined" to perform. From this shift sprang the idea of providing a liberal arts education for the elite who would go on to college to study the learned professions and a vocational education for everyone else, including most women, minorities, and members of the lower classes.

As the 20th century began, schooling was facing a critical choice. Were we to continue to provide a common curriculum for all students as Harris and Eliot had sought, or should the college-bound be educated differently from young people who were not going to college? In the 1890s, there was a great debate about what ought to be taught, to whom, at what age, for how long, and by what means. What subjects should be required for admission to college? Should high schools offer manual training and commercial subjects for those who were not going on to college? What was the purpose of education?

At the turn of the century, proponents of social reform sought to improve the living conditions of the urban poor, to introduce equitable taxation, to reform municipal politics, and to regulate monopolies. They also sought to make the schools instruments of social reform. The nation was making a transition from a rural and agricultural economy to an urban and suburban one. As this demographic shift took place, we began to attend to the problem of the poor and the socially disadvantaged and to explore what our young people would need to be successful in the workplace of a changing economy. Despite their efforts, the advocates of academics for everyone were overwhelmed by the proponents of educational efficiency, men like E.L. Thorndike, Lewis M. Terman, and Ellwood P. Cubberley, who sought to "dethrone the academic curriculum," and the doctrine of mental discipline, the belief that the goal of education was "to 'train' the mind and 'discipline' the will," as Ravitch (2000, p. 61) put it. The old curriculum was to be replaced by a differentiated curriculum, tailored to the needs of different segments of society and guided by scientific principles and intelligence testing. In this curriculum, very few students would need to study academic fields.

Many critics of this era, including Diane Ravitch (2000), describe this period with justifiable scorn: "In the reality of American public education, students in a course in laundry work were not gaining 'understanding and illumination' and were not learning about 'social facts and relationships.' They were simply learning to wash and press clothes" (p. 59).

World War II "brought America into an age dominated by science and technology" (Bybee, 1997, p. 2). As the war ended, educators again turned their attention to reform. The Harvard Redbook, entitled *General Education in a Free Society*, captured the gist of the problem, a set of expectations that we are still considering today:

Science education in general education should be characterized mainly by broad integrative elements—the comparison of scientific with other modes of thought, the comparison and contrast of the individual sciences with one another, the relations of science with its own past and with general human history, and of science with problems of human society . . . Unfortunately, these areas are slighted most often in modern teaching. [Note: they still are!] (Harvard Committee, 1945, p. 155)

The 1950s were watershed years for education as our nation tried to come to grips with the demands of a technological age and the barriers created by inequity and social privilege. Again, the schools were called to be mechanisms for responding to socioeconomic change; in this case, to deal with inequities in access to a quality education for all children. As Bybee (1997) points out, after World War II, education became a primary vehicle for social change and larger societal issues such as civil rights played out across the face of our schools and campuses. In 1954, in the case of *Brown v. Board of Education*, the U.S. Supreme Court ordered an end to school segregation at "all deliberate speed." The landmark decision overturned a high court ruling six decades earlier that black children could receive a "separate but equal" education (*Plessy v. Ferguson*, 1896). The reality, of course, was that schools for blacks were only separate, not equal. Fifty years later, while legal barriers no longer block minority students from obtaining the same education as whites, other hurdles do. We still have unacceptable achievement gaps in such vital subjects as math and science, and we are still trying to understand why.

In the immediate postwar period, many schools embraced the progressive ideas from the turn of the century about life adjustment and social education. School was to ensure that students were well adjusted and able to live according to society's norms (Bybee, 1997). This period ended abruptly in 1957, when the former Soviet Union launched Sputnik. While we trained our telescopes on the sky, we also turned our attention to the performance of our schools and were unhappy with what we saw. In September 1959, a group of scientists, scholars, and educators gathered at Woods Hole on Cape Cod to talk about how the teaching of science in our nation's schools might be improved. The results were captured by Jerome Bruner (1960/1977) in his book *The Process of Education*. It is a strange experience to read Bruner's account of the discussions that took place in 1959. It is as though the ink has not yet dried on the pages. The discussants at the Woods Hole Conference were worrying about how to facilitate a closer working relationship between scientists in the colleges and teachers in the schools. They were talking about a crisis in national security, "a crisis whose resolution will depend upon a well-educated citizenry" (Bruner, 1977, p. 1). They worried about what we should teach and to what end. They were concerned that we would lose our place in the world order if we did not produce enough scientists. Concepts of scientific literacy shifted from a concern about equal opportunity and the development of individual potential to a concern about attracting more students to the study of science and how a strong scientific community could secure a dominant place in the world order for our nation. In the wake of Sputnik, reform turned to making a classroom into a semblance of a research laboratory, and students into junior scientists (Bybee).

To see how fresh this is, consider a quote from *Road Map for National Security: Imperative for Change*, sometimes called the Hart-Rudman Report, released in January 2001 (Hart-Rudman Report, 2001):

> Our systems of basic science research and education are in serious crisis, while other countries are redoubling their efforts. In the next quarter century, we will see ourselves surpassed, and in relative decline, unless we make a conscious national commitment to maintain our edge. (p. 12)

Another surge of concern arose with the publication of *A Nation at Risk* in 1983. Many regard the document to be the starting point for the latest wave of educational reform and the basis for our current approach to science assessment. Many would also argue that we have yet to realize the vision expressed in the report. First, what did it say? The report stated its conclusions in dramatic terms:

> If an unfriendly power had attempted to impose on America the mediocre educational performance that exists today, we might well have viewed it as an act of war. As it stands, we have allowed this to happen to ourselves. We have even squandered the gains in achievement made in the wake of the Sputnik challenge. Moreover, we have dismantled essential support systems that helped make those gains possible. We have, in effect, been committing an act of unthinking, unilateral educational disarmament. (p. 5)

A National Risk advanced a short set of recommendations which basically took us back to that same fork in the road, at the turn of the 20th century, when we chose to separate the college-bound from those who were preparing to go immediately to work. It advised the road less traveled—toward academic excellence for all. Among its recommendations, all of which applied to all students whatever their life goals and experiences, were the following:

- Graduation requirements should be strengthened so that all students establish a foundation in five *new* basics: English, mathematics, science, social studies, and computer science.
- Schools and colleges should adopt higher and measurable standards for academic performance.
- The amount of time students spend engaged in learning should be significantly increased.
- The teaching profession should be strengthened through higher standards for preparation and professional growth.

Today, knowledge production and the effective use of that knowledge are essential for individual and organizational success, both in the for-profit and nonprofit sectors. This is a contemporary version of the industrialization that shaped life at the turn of the 20th century, except that the industrial age has now given way to the information age. We stand at the threshold of yet another technological revolution as more and more of our learning and our interactions take place in cyberspace. Responsible citizenship also increasingly requires an appreciation of the influence of technology on society and deeper understandings of cultural differences, the impact of humans on the environment, and the contributions of science and mathematics to our ability to understand each other and the world around us.

As we move into the 21st century, there are many challenges ahead. Social stratification in this country has become increasingly linked to our system of education, especially postsecondary education. Whether or not a person enrolls in postsecondary education, the type of school he or she attends and the amount of education he or she receives will have a profound effect on occupational status, access to further career advancement, and quality of life. A key component of that education must be science education (Ramaley, 2002).

These realities have significant implications for our approach to K-12 education. We must rethink yet again what learning means, who our students are, how to close the gap in participation and educational achievement among various sectors of our society, and how to support the continuous learning that modern society demands. This exploration must be explicit since it shapes what we choose to measure and how we choose to measure it.

What Should We Measure?

In designing a curriculum and the assessment tools that go with it, we need to examine the difference between the acquisition of *information* and the generation of *knowledge*, which is linked to the difference between what Norris and Phillips (2002) would call *fundamental* literacy and *derived* literacy. For them, fundamental literacy is the ability to decode a text, whether in written or in representational form (e.g., graphs, tables, images). Figuring out what the text means, however, is more complex than decoding and involves the ability to comprehend an argument and the case made for the claims in that argument. This derived literacy underlies our ability to make sense of what we read about science and how we interpret the meaning of scientific advances.

As John Seely Brown put it, "Learning . . . requires immersion in a community of practice, enculturation in its ways of seeing, interpreting and acting" (2000, p. 15). Memorizing does not. Is learning the mastery of content by memorization and practice or is learning the making of meaning in a community of other learners?

Sadly, we are still arguing about whether education is "the steady supply of facts and information" (Brown & Duguid, 2000, p. 135) and accurate computation, or the thoughtful development of understanding and knowledge in the company of a community of fellow learners, often with the goal of making collective decisions about matters that affect not only our own lives but the lives of our neighbors or the lives of people we may never meet who live far away from us. We are still caught between these competing ideas about education even today. The design of good assessment tools depends on a clear vision of what it means to "know" something—familiarity with facts and information, or good decision making when confronted with unscripted or partially defined problems, or both.

An Approach to Assessment in the 21st Century: What Does It Mean to Be Educated?

Armed with compelling educational visions that draw upon their own institutional histories, missions, and conditions, educational leaders and their communities can decide what they want to measure and can then select ways to conduct those measurements that will guide them in evaluating how well they and their students are accomplishing the goals they have set. Do the assessments make educational sense? Will the information they provide help the institution achieve its educational goals? With an educational compass in hand, the institution and its leadership will be less likely to become distracted or drift off course or earnestly measure the wrong things or attach inappropriate meanings to what they *can* measure.

Strong educational purpose can guide any institution, whatever its mission, through troubling times. What follows is my own approach to thinking about education in the 21st century. This vision is based on a remarkable conversation that took place at the National Science Foundation (NSF) in April 2004. The ideas, however, are my own reflections on what I heard and do not represent any official view of NSF or of the participants, for that matter. My purpose in providing this information is to show how a school or a college or a university can approach its educational mission by defining and then following the dictates and expectations of a shared vision of what it means to be educated. After each element of this vision I will comment on its relevance to assessment.

Demonstrating the Qualities of an Educated Person

A key attribute of an educated person is an ongoing love of learning and a curiosity about the world. A love of learning can develop in many ways and at different times, stimulated by an inspiring teacher, by a sense of purpose and personal responsibility, by the experience of generating new knowledge—in short, by any means that offers the opportunity to be taken seriously by people we respect.

Application to assessment. The underlying motivation to learn is central to an effective educational process and is at least as important as the particular things we know. However, we rarely try to test for it or examine how a love of learning can be fostered during schooling. As Eisenhart et al. (1996) point out, our schools are being asked to solve four very large and complex problems. First, the schools must deal with the low level of scientific knowledge in our country. Second, they must deal with the poor teaching that many believe helps to explain our poor performance on international assessments of science and mathematics. Third, they must find a way to address the painful gaps in both participation and achievement that cause the percentages of women and minorities who pursue science, technology, engineering, and mathematics (STEM) study to remain unacceptably low. Finally, our schools must prepare our citizens to use scientific knowledge to make important decisions in their lives and to engage in responsible action in their communities. Our current educational strategies and assessments address the first two challenges but rarely include the other two.

A key problem is that science, as it is often presented in the classroom, fails to engage the interests and passions of students, especially those for whom traditional forms of scientific discourse are unfamiliar and frightening. In fact, there often are no clear connections or strategies that would allow students to discover that science can have socially interesting and useful applications and that it can be used in socially responsible ways. Somehow, we expect our students to learn how to use science in their daily lives without practicing those skills. Instead we ask them to learn scientific facts and concepts and experience "real hands-on science" in the classroom. This is what we usually test. Important as this knowledge is for understanding science and how science is done, it can be argued that facts, concepts, and an understanding of the nature of science gained from hands-on learning are not sufficient for understanding what science is really all about. Students do not in their daily educational experiences encounter the complex social networks that define the domains of science and what is judged to be known and knowable.

Eisenhart et al. (1996) report on a conversation in a kindergarten classroom that illustrates the problem. By insisting on "talking like a scientist" the teacher in this example "writes over" what the student is saying and invalidates the child's own experience and what he cares about. The child, named Danny, wants to talk about a piece of lava that his mother gave him on a trip to Mount Vesuvius. He says he has kept it very carefully and that he has never dropped it. The teacher wants him to characterize it. Is it rough or smooth, light or heavy? All of Danny's personal meaning and his real interest in his lump of lava get lost as the teacher insists on "teaching." Over the course of time, students can, *if their interest can be sparked*, acquire the language and thought patterns of science and mathematics. If we accept Vygotsky's (1978) argument that knowledge is socially constructed through the use of language, then growing competence in science does require the acquisition of a specialized vocabulary. Beyond that there is what Richards (as cited in Moschkovich, 1996) calls a *register*, a set of argumentation rules and styles, values and beliefs that are part of the traditions of a field.

Learning science and mathematics are not just exercises in vocabulary training, though, any more than learning to communicate in a second language is accomplished by memorizing words. As Moschkovich (1996, p. 247) argues, "Learning to participate in mathematics discourse is not merely or primarily a matter of learning vocabulary definitions. Instead, it involves learning how to use language while solving and discussing problems in different contexts." When should the emphasis on talking about concepts in such a way actually begin? As Project 2061 (American Association for the Advancement of Science [AAAS], 1993) clearly recognizes in its approach to a scientific curriculum:

For students in the early grades, the emphasis should overwhelmingly be on gaining experience with natural and social phenomena and on enjoying science. Abstractions of all kinds can gradually make their appearance as students mature and develop an ability to handle explanations that are complex and abstract. This phasing-in certainly applies to generalizations about the scientific worldview, scientific inquiry, and the scientific enterprise. (p. 2)

What is going on between Danny and his teacher is a premature privileging of one kind of language and thought—the scientific—over making connections between science and other important things in Danny's life. As the authors put it, "Success in school work depends on children's ability to suspend their knowledge of reality outside of school" (Eisenhart et al., 1996). No wonder many young people and adults do not find any science around them in the real world; they left it behind in the classroom. They did not see any way to bring this knowledge into their daily lives and perhaps had little or no inclination to try. In fact, one reason for the lack of women and minorities in advanced science and engineering programs is that students who care about societal needs, who want to apply science and engineering skill to solving societal problems, and who want to be of service are systematically weeded out of programs such as engineering (Downey, Hegg, & Lucena, 1993).

Educated people can find creative and adaptive solutions to newly emerging problems as well as old ones that are ever with us. To prepare our students for life and work in the 21st century, we must provide opportunities for them to learn in the same way that professionals and "experts" learn. This can be fostered by exploring fields of study in the same way that these fields are actually advanced through discovery, integration, interpretation, and application of knowledge. Education must look beyond the classroom to the challenges of the community, the complexities of the workplace, and the major issues in the world (Zinser, 2004).

Application to assessment. Efforts to change a curriculum and to assess learning must be approached with a broader vision of the world beyond the classroom. On campus and in the schools, concepts of education must be assessed not only from the perspective of individual departments and disciplines but also as a way to support shared responsibilities for education, scholarship, and community engagement. Lee and Roth (2003) and Roth and Desautels (2004) have explored how science can play a role in citizen-initiated efforts to clean up a stream, a watershed, and ground water quality. They discuss how citizens and scientific experts can interact productively in public discussions and problem solving at a community level. The implications for both what we do in our schools and how we assess learning are not hard to find.

Lee and Roth (2003) point out that most recent efforts to define a scientific curriculum for grades K-12 suggest that a good science education should contribute to the development of compassionate human beings who lead responsible, productive, and creative lives. They further note that the various standards and curricula tend to present lists of scientific topics that children need to study and know before they can be considered scientifically literate, and that the resulting science education is based on "helping students learn the 'habits of mind' that practicing scientists supposedly possess" (p. 404). What is generally absent from these reports is any pathway between the facts and habits of mind and the actual practice of good citizenship, or any expression of what competent application of science to the demands of citizenship would require, let alone how to assess this competence.

Recent critics of our current scientific curriculum point out that turning all students into "little scientists" may be missing the point. Some argue that true scientific or mathematical thinking of the kind that advances knowledge is a rare gift. Mathematician Norman Levitt (1999) claims, "Science is an elitist calling—demanding raw intelligence and special skills that far exceed what is to be expected of the average person" (p. 4). He concludes that the culture of democracy (i.e., the view that science is for everyone) may well be incompatible with the actual culture and pursuit of science. Morris Shamos (1995) makes a similar case and concludes that true scientific literacy, which he describes as "a complex understanding of theorization, experimentation, and scientific reasoning," is "beyond the reach of most of us" (p. 42).

In an essay on undergraduate science education, Michael Flowers (2000) takes on these arguments and explores what we have been learning about the nature of science itself from the fairly new field of science studies. Is it something everyone can know and do, or is it not? If science is indeed knowable by the ordinary person, what *ought* we to know about the scientific enterprise? If one goal of science education is to understand what science is all about and how knowledge is produced, then what is to be understood? He references John Durant (1993), who argued that there are three ways to approach science literacy. One can (a) know a lot about science or (b) know how people like to think science works or (c) know how science really works. Durant argues that the scientific community is simply a special case of a social network maintained by complex social capital systems that generate, validate, and disseminate knowledge. He suggests that the public needs to be familiar with more than merely factual knowledge or idealistic images of "the scientific method" or the "scientific mindset." What we all need is "a feel for the way that the social system of science actually works to deliver what is usually reliable knowledge about the world" (Durant, cited in Flowers, 2000, p. 41).

Beyond that, a study of science by itself and a knowledge of facts, concepts, and principles will not help us gain a "keen appreciation of the places where science and technology articulate smoothly with one's experience of life, of moments at which to turn to science for help or to look elsewhere, and of the trustworthiness of expert claims and institutions" (Flowers, 2000, p. 41).

There are a number of practical applications of this ability to integrate science with the rest of what one knows. Lee and Roth (2003) studied the municipality of Oceanside, a community located in coastal British Columbia. They explored how science is enmeshed with the personal and public issues of our times (Restivo, 1988). They concluded from their two years of engaging as participant observers in the community, as it struggled with problems of water quality:

It may not be necessary that all citizens have acquired the same stock of scientific knowledge but rather that all citizens have the competence to enter whatever knowledge they have into the public (political) discourse. It is only when science can participate in such conditions where other knowledge forms are equally considered that science has become truly democratic. (Roth & Desautels, 2004, p. 2)

For them, science is a necessary ingredient in the development of an informed and engaged citizenry, but it cannot stand alone when it is to be employed in the process of public problem solving (Rich, 2002) that characterizes a deliberative democracy, nor should it be accorded a privileged position in that discourse. These ideas will surely not sit well with the scientific community, but they do lead to important questions about what we ought to be testing. It does not do much good to *know* something if we cannot use it responsibly to address issues of significance. How can we build in experience with using scientific information and arguments in association with other perspectives derived from other academic fields, common sense, and life experience? Then how do we test whether our students have learned to do that?

Educated people understand how we know what we know and how to construct a warranted foundation for the claims we make about what is true. To create environments where authentic learning can occur that develops in the same way that our understanding of disciplines and intellectual challenges develops, we must set up new contexts that are not bounded by disciplinary or institutional imperatives, where the scholarly interests of faculty and students are integrated with the realities and urgencies of society, and where learning can have consequences for both students and the community (i.e., engaged learning) and/or the fields they study (i.e., undergraduate experiences of research and discovery).

Application to assessment. The case for changes in assessment and plans for implementing change must be held to the same standards as any other form of scholarly work, and the key assumptions and arguments for a particular course of action must be spelled out clearly. Beyond trying to do science in the classroom the way science is "done," what we really need is to help our students get a better feel for the warrants for scientific claims. As Flowers (2000) puts it, "When one does science, one also does society" (p. 44). Our assessment strategies need to capture that. How do students match up arguments from science, culture, law, economics, or ethics? Do these perspectives "smoothly articulate" or do they clash? Are some points of view rejected as unfamiliar or unreal?

Borrowing from concepts developed by Norris and Phillips (2002), it is possible to tell how students read scientific material or listen to scientific arguments or expert opinions. Do they assume that scientific argument is a trump card (a deferential stance), or that their own beliefs and experiences are more valid than a scientific argument (a dominant stance), or that what they hear or read needs to be held up to careful scrutiny and tested (a critical stance)? From the perspective of the study of literacy, "what a text means always must be inferred from what it says plus other extra textual information. There is no alternative when reading but to bring to the text thoughts from outside of it" (Norris & Phillips, 2002, p. 231). At its best, neither reader nor text is supreme. Understanding is a *negotiation* between them. So, how do we capture that in an assessment? How do we figure out what the reader or participant brings to an argument?

Norris and Phillips (2002) tell the story of how students, both in high school and in a college-level course, read and interpreted a news article about the Jovian moon, Europa, where they learned that "beneath the moon's frozen crust an ocean surges" (p. 234). Elsewhere in the report there were pictures of the surface of Europa, showing jumbled icebergs and cracks that looked like ice fields on earth. The expectation was that the students would realize that the statement about a surging ocean was not a fact, but rather an interpretation. They were asked to indicate whether the surging ocean statement was true, likely to be true, likely to be false, or false, or if they were uncertain of the truth status (the right answer, of course). Only 19% of the students judged that the statement was uncertain, while 25% thought it was true,

52% thought it was likely to be true, 2% thought it was likely to be false, and a trailing 1% thought it was false. Over 80% of the students were not able to decipher the conceptual framework woven into the text or ask probing questions about what they read. Why not? What else can we learn about the thinking process that these students used? They all said the text was easy to read, and yet most of them missed the point. At one level these students are scientifically literate because they could "read" and understand the words. At another, more important level, they were not.

Education carries with it the expectation that educated people use their knowledge and acquire new understanding in a responsible way, mindful of the effects of their actions on others. They have a moral imagination.[2] Engaged learning exposes students to essential dimensions of the responsible use of power that comes from the generation and application of knowledge. This can prepare students to live and work in a complex and changing world characterized by many different cultural spaces and many significant challenges and uncertainties.

The qualities of liberal education are important for everyone whether they pursue studies in an arts and sciences discipline or a professional field and whether they are going after an undergraduate degree or an associate degree or a certificate (American Association of Colleges and Universities, 2002). Liberal education is best thought about as a way of developing the human imagination and cultivating habits of the mind and heart that lead to new understanding, rather than a specific set of arts and sciences disciplines. Martha Nussbaum calls this "the moral imagination," "the capacity to transcend divisions created by distance, cultural difference and mistrust" (Nussbaum, 2004, p. 42). These are capacities much needed today. We all know that knowledge has consequences. An approach to learning and teaching at any age that can foster both moral imagination and the development of a deep sense of responsibility for living a life of compassion, respect, and concern for the lives and truths of others can situate those consequences more appropriately.

Application to assessment. Educational institutions are themselves microcosms of the complexity of life beyond their boundaries. We do not, however, often attempt to understand these external influences or use community assets effectively as a learning environment for our students. As new approaches to community-based scientific literacy catch on, we will need new assessment tools to measure what students learn, how the experience affects them and their teachers, and the value and impact on the community itself of the work they do. Such assessment strategies already exist for higher education and are being used to guide further development of institutional engagement and curricular reform (Holland, 2001; Holland & Ramaley, 1998).

Summary

There are many ways to describe the qualities of an educated person. The important point is that we should take time to do so, since science education must fit into the broader picture of what it means to have the human and social capital necessary to live well and virtuously in a complex age. Both concepts are derivatives of economic theory that attempts to understand how value is created and exchanged (Lin, Cook, & Burt, 2001). Human capital refers to what individuals know and the skills they possess. Social capital, while still developing as a theoretical construct, can be thought of as "resources embedded in social structures and networks, rather than in individuals" (Lin et al., 2001, p. vii). Social capital can be formed and then used through a complex interaction of the political economy, society at large, the community, and organizations within communities, including educational institutions. If we think about science education in the context of such networks, it becomes clear that we cannot be truly scientifically literate all by ourselves. It is important that, as educated citizens, we learn to tap into these networks, learn from them, contribute to them, and exert influence knowledgably and responsively. Part of scientific literacy rests on our ability to function as parts of social networks and to use these networks to obtain information, enhance our own social credentials and influence, exert influence on decision makers, and reinforce our own identity as learners and educated people (Lin et al., 2001, p. 6).

What can we do now about both our approach to the science curriculum and the assessment of learning as we enter the next generation of reform? According to Jerome Bruner (1996) and those who have followed him, including John Seely Brown (2000), Paul Feltovich, Richard Coulson, and Rand Spiro (2001), and Joe Novak (1998):

1. We need fresh ways to engage our young people in the exploration of knowledge that is growing at such a rapid rate (Bruner, 1996). We can do this by involving them in the thinking and exploration that generates that knowledge.
2. We should "talk physics" or "talk math," with students rather than talk *about* these subjects with them (Bruner, 1977).

3. We should build a *spiral curriculum*. In such a model, we can make knowledge and problem solving accessible by starting where a student is; that is, by building on what they already know and how they think (Bruner, 1977) and then gradually adding elements and dimensions as the student progresses toward more sophisticated understanding.

4. The kinds of concepts that are both difficult to learn and resistant to correction when misunderstood are just the kind of things we most need to know and understand in our complex and changing world. There are ways to help students learn this material. To do so, we need to create opportunities for teachers to work together and explore ways to approach the topics that students find the hardest to understand. Through teacher collaboration, we can continue to develop teaching as a true profession, a community of professional practice.

5. The notion that children must learn by repetition and rote must be replaced with a rich concept of young people as thinkers in their own right, who can learn best in a context that is meaningful to them. This is not a new idea. John Dewey wanted to create a context in which what a child learns was incorporated into his or her experiences in a way that "allows educators to draw upon natural interests in the hope of building genuine curiosity about intellectual matters" (Boisvert, 1998, p. 103). All of us, in fact, are better able to learn if we are helped to become makers of meaning in collaborative settings where we can draw upon a rich cultural tradition of shared learning. The transmission of information, which is free of any context or of a particular person or situation and can be facilitated by information technology, is less important than the generation and sharing of knowledge, which *do* have contexts and require working relationships (Brown, 2000).

6. We need to rethink the relationship between academic knowledge and civic involvement. As we continue to find ways to integrate public engagement into our teaching and into the scholarly work of higher education, we will need new ways to think about science and its relationship to other forms of knowledge. As Rice (2003) put it, "the way issues are framed and key words defined can fundamentally shape public understanding" (p. 1). Science needs to be accessible to the public and useful in public discourse. Our students need to learn to talk about science without necessarily sounding like scientists.

Today, we are expected to achieve high standards of learning for all students as we face the rapid changes brought about by the technologies and social challenges of our own age. However, our expectations of what our schools can do are really still an expression of our cultural anxieties. In a basic way, these challenges are the same as they were at the turn of the 20th century. As we seek new ways to define the goals of an educational experience and new tools for measuring what our students know and can do with what they know, we will add much needed depth to the way we approach both teaching and learning. We will then be able to prepare our students more effectively for the 21st century.

NOTES

1. Constructivists are also called progressives in Tom Loveless's (2001) taxonomy, although this term is also used by other educational historians to signify the reformers who sought to replace an academic curriculum with vocational studies.

2. The concept of *moral imagination* comes from the work of Martha Nussbaum (2004). It refers to the capacity "to view with sympathy the situation of people who live at a distance or who look different from ourselves" (p. 42). It allows us to take seriously the lives of other people and to be concerned about their well-being.

REFERENCES

American Association for the Advancement of Science (AAAS). (1993). *Benchmarks for Scientific Literacy Project 2061*. New York: Oxford University Press. Retrieved July 12, 2004, from http://www.project2061.org/tools/benchol/ch1/ch1.htm

American Association of Colleges and Universities. (2002). *Greater expectations: A new vision for learning as a nation goes to college*. National panel report. Washington, DC: Author.

A Nation at Risk. (1983). Retrieved December 2, 2004, from http://www.ed.gov/pubs/NatAtRisk/risk.html

Boisvert, R.D. (1998). *John Dewey: Rethinking our time*. Albany: State University of New York Press.

Brown, J.S. (2000, March/April). Growing up digital: How the web changes work, education, and the ways people learn. *Change*, 11–20. Retrieved from http://www.aahe.org/change/digital.pdf

Brown, J.S., & Duguid, P. (2000). *The social life of information*. Boston: Harvard Business School Press.

Brown v. Board of Education. 347 U.S. 483 (1954).

Bruner, J. (1960/1977). *The process of education*. Cambridge, MA: Harvard University Press.

Bruner, J. (1996). *The culture of education*. Cambridge, MA: Harvard University Press.

Business-Higher Education Forum. (1999, September). *Spanning the chasm: A blueprint for taking action*. Washington, DC: American Council on Education and National Alliance of Business.

Business-Higher Education Forum. (2003). *Building a nation of learners: The need for changes in teaching and learning to meet global challenges*. Retrieved November 13, 2004, from http://www.acenet.edu/bookstore/pdf/2003_build_nation.pdf

Bybee, R.W. (1997). *Achieving scientific literacy: From purposes to practices*. Portsmouth, NH: Heinemann.

Downey, G., Hegg, S., & Lucena, J. (1993, June). *Weeded out: Critical reflection in engineering education*. Paper presented at the American Anthropological Association, Washington, DC.

Eisenhart, M., Finkel, E., & Marion, S.F. (1996). Creating the conditions for scientific literacy: A re-examination. *American Educational Research Journal, 33*(2), 261–295.

Feltovich, P.J., Coulson, R.L., & Spiro, R.J. (2001). Learners' (mis)understanding of important and difficult concepts. In K.D. Forbes & P.J. Feltovich (Eds.), *Smart machines in education: The coming revolution in educational technology AAAI* (pp. 349–375). Menlo Park, CA: MIT Press.

Flowers, M. (2000, Summer). Unsettling science literacy. *Liberal Education, 86*(3), 36–45.

Graham, P.A. (1995). Assimilation, adjustment and access: An antiquarian view of American education. In D. Ravitch & M.A. Vinovskis (Eds.), *Learning from the past* (pp. 3–24). Baltimore, MD: Johns Hopkins University Press.

Hart-Rudman Report. (2001). The Phase III Report of the U.S. Commission on National Security/21st Century. Retrieved August 25, 2004, from http://www.rense.com/general10/roadmap.htm

Harvard Committee. (1945). *General education in a free society*. Cambridge, MA: Harvard University Press.

Holland, B.A. (2001). Toward a definition and characterization of the engaged campus: Six cases. *Metropolitan Universities, 12*(3), 20–29.

Holland, B.A., & Ramaley, J.A. (1998). *What partnership models work to link education and community building?* Proceedings of the Joint Forum of U.S. Department of Education and U.S. Department of Housing and Urban Development.

Holton, G. (2003, April 25). An insider's view of "A Nation at Risk" and why it still matters. *The Chronicle of Higher Education*, pp. B13–15.

Latour, B. (2004). *Politics of nature: How to bring the sciences into democracy*. Cambridge, MA: Harvard University Press.

Lee, S., & Roth, W. (2003). Science and the "good citizen": Community-based scientific literacy. *Science, Technology and Human Values, 28*(3), 403–424.

Levitt, N. (1999). *Prometheus bedeviled: Science and the contradictions of contemporary culture*. New Brunswick, NJ: Rutgers University Press.

Levy, F., & Murnane, R.J. (2004). *The new division of labor: How computers are creating the next job market*. Princeton, NJ: Princeton University Press.

Lin, N.K., Cook, K., & Burt, R.J. (2001). *Social Capital: Theory and research*. New York: Aldine de Gruyter.

Loveless, T. (2001). *The great curriculum debate: How should we teach reading and math*. Washington, DC: The Brookings Institution Press.

Moschkovich, J.N. (1996). Moving up and getting steeper: Negotiating shared descriptions of linear graphs. *The Journal of the Learning Sciences, 5*(3), 239–277.

Murnane, R.J., & Levy, F. (1996). *Teaching the new basic skills: Principles for educating children to thrive in a changing economy*. New York: The Free Press.

Norris, S.P., & Phillips, L.M. (2002). How literacy in its fundamental sense is central to scientific literacy. *Science Education, 87*(2), 224–241.

Novak, J. (1998). *The pursuit of a dream: Education can be improved. Teaching science for understanding: A human constructivist view*. San Diego, CA: Academic Press.

Nussbaum, M. (2004, Winter). Liberal education and global community. *Liberal Education, 90*(1), 42–47.

Plessy v. Ferguson. 163 U.S. 537 (1896).

Ramaley, J.A. (2002). *Meeting the needs of the market*. Universities Project Final Report, Salzburg, Austria: Salzburg Seminar.

Ravitch, D. (2000). *Left back: A century of battles over school reform*. New York: Simon and Schuster.

Restivo, S. (1988). Modern science as a social problem. *Social Problems, 35*, 206–225.

Rice, R.E. (2003, Fall). Rethinking scholarship and engagement: The struggle for new meanings. *Campus Compact Reader*, 1–9.

Rich, R.F. (2002). *Social science information and public policy making*. New Brunswick, NJ: Transaction Publishers.

Roth, W., & Desautels, J. (2004). Educating for citizenship: Reappraising the role of science education. *Canadian Journal of Science, Mathematics and Technology, 4*(2), 149–169.

Shamos, M.H. (1995). *The myth of scientific literacy*. New Brunswick, NJ: Rutgers University Press.

Tyack, D., & Cuban, L. (1995). *Tinkering toward utopia: A century of public school reform*. Cambridge, MA: Harvard University Press.

Vygotsky, L.S. (1978). *Mind in society: The development of higher psychological processes*. Cambridge, MA: Harvard University Press.

Zinser, E. (2004, Winter). Making the case for liberal education. *Change, 90*(1), 38–41.

Part Two
DESIGN AND ANALYSIS ISSUES

CHAPTER 4

Issues in the Design of Accountability Systems

ROBERT L. LINN

Student achievement test results are the coin of the realm in educational accountability systems in the United States. For a number of years, both states and the federal government have relied heavily on tests to judge the quality of schools. The exact characteristics of the accountability systems have evolved over the years and vary a good deal from one state to another, as do the state and federal accountability systems. Nonetheless, the systems share, at least implicitly, some underlying beliefs and goals, including:

- The quality of education is not as good as it should be.
- Student learning needs to be improved.
- Student outcomes rather than process or resource measures should be used to judge school quality.
- Content standards and associated assessments will make it clear what teachers are expected to teach and students are expected to learn.

    Robert L. Linn is Professor of Education at the University of Colorado at Boulder and Co-director at the UCLA National Center for Research on Evaluation, Standards, and Student Testing (CRESST).
    The work reported herein was supported under the Educational Research and Development Centers Program, PR/Award Number R305B960002, as administered by the Institute of Education Sciences (IES) and the U.S. Department of Education. The findings and opinions expressed in this report are those of the author and do not necessarily reflect the positions or policies of the National Center for Education Research, the Institute of Education Sciences (IES), or the U.S. Department of Education.

- Schools should be held accountable for the learning of all their students.
- Holding schools accountable for student achievement will motivate greater effort on the part of educators and students.
- Information provided by the accountability system can contribute to improved teaching and student learning.

Despite the shared beliefs and goals, there is considerable variation in the accountability systems that have been put in place by different states. There are differences in state testing practices, such as the grades and subjects tested,[1] and differences in the stakes that are attached to results (e.g., rewards and sanctions for schools, requiring students to pass the tests for graduation from high school or promotion to the next grade). There has been a general trend to add high stakes to assessment policies that merely exhort teachers and students to do better (McDonnell, 2004). When high stakes are attached to results, however, states vary as to whether these stakes affect individual students as well as schools.

Some of the differences in assessment and accountability systems are the result of specific legislation while others are simply the result of administrative decisions and traditions that evolved over time in ways that vary from state to state. Some of the differences are also the result of purposeful system design decisions that are intended to meet particular goals.

There are many issues that need to be addressed in the design of an educational accountability system. The purpose of this chapter is to identify and clarify design issues that are critical in the creation of an accountability system that can contribute to improved teaching and student learning. Since student achievement is at the heart of the current accountability movement, a number of issues that are discussed are concerned with how student achievement is assessed. Other important issues are concerned with the uses that are made of student test results. For example, is the focus on status, or on change, or both? Are results used to make decisions about individual students, or only about schools? Issues also arise in decisions about the reporting of results (e.g., the setting and use of performance standards and rules for disaggregated reports of results).

A Brief History of Accountability Systems

There are two related but separate tracks in the development of the school accountability systems that are now in place in the United States. Federal legislation, starting with the Elementary and Secondary Edu-

cation Act (ESEA) of 1965 and continuing with successive reauthorizations of ESEA, including the most recent, the No Child Left Behind
(NCLB) Act of 2001, provides one track. The second track is comprised
of state testing and accountability policies and legislation and is therefore more variable.

State Accountability Systems

During the 1970s many states introduced minimum-competency
testing requirements for high school graduation and/or grade-to-grade
promotion. As the name suggests, the tests generally required only low-
level knowledge and skills. Other forms of testing were in most cases
left to school districts. In the 1980s, however, many states introduced
statewide testing programs. The 1980s was "a decade characterized by
deep concern over what was perceived to be poor performance on the
part of American students" (Hamilton, 2003, p. 27). Testing was viewed
as a useful tool to both monitor and stimulate educational reform
efforts. In many states the tests that were used were published standardized tests; however, some states contracted with test publishers to have
tests developed that were intended to be a better match to state curriculum guidelines. School-level rewards and/or sanctions were introduced by some states.

By the 1990s there was a shift away from the low-level requirements
of the minimum-competency days. States began to introduce ambitious
content standards and assessments that were geared to measure the
higher-level understanding and skills called for in the standards. States
also began reporting assessment results in terms of student performance
standards, for example, the percentage of students at the proficient level
or above.

Federal Requirements

The Elementary and Secondary Education Act was the largest and
most enduring of the federal efforts to provide compensatory educational programs for children from low-income families. Title I of ESEA
included requirements for testing children receiving Title I services.
Initially results for Title I students were reported using grade equivalent
(GE) scores obtained from the administration of norm-referenced tests.
The GE scores were found to lack any comparability across test publishers or across subjects for a single publisher. In response to this lack
of comparability, the Title I Evaluation and Reporting System (TIERS)
was introduced. TIERS required the use of norm-referenced tests and
the reporting of the results on a new scale, the normal curve equivalent

(NCE) scale. NCEs assume a normal distribution of achievement and assign scores from 1 to 99 in a way that makes NCEs of 1, 50, and 99 coincide with the national percentile ranks of 1, 50, and 99, respectively.

By 1994, when the Improving America's Schools Act (IASA) reauthorizing ESEA was enacted, there was widespread recognition that the reporting of results in terms of NCE scores only for Title I students had major weaknesses. The separate testing of Title I students was often out of sync with the testing of other students and with the content standards that some states had adopted. IASA required all states to adopt content standards and student performance standards for reporting results on assessments that were supposed to be consistent with the content standards. It also required that states use the same assessments for Title I students as were used by other students in the state. The most recent reauthorization of ESEA is, of course, NCLB, which will be discussed in more detail below.

Assessment of Student Achievement

What is to be assessed often is only specified in the most general terms in legislation. NCLB, for example, requires the assessment of students in mathematics and reading or English language arts in grades 3 through 8 and in one high school grade by 2005–06. By 2007–08 states will have to assess students in science at least once in each of three grade spans—3 through 5, 6 through 9, and 10 through 12. NCLB also requires states to set challenging academic content standards and stipulates that the assessments must be aligned with the state's content standards. Legislation in many states has similar requirements. Such requirements leave a great deal of flexibility in the definition of content standards, the setting of performance standards, and the design of assessments, however. There is also flexibility with regard to a number of specifics in meeting the requirements of NCLB, such as the setting of the minimum number of students needed for reporting results for any subgroup for determining whether specified adequate yearly progress (AYP) targets have been met by a school or district.

Standards-Based Assessments

Every state except Iowa has established content standards in mathematics and reading or English language arts. The content standards vary substantially in their rigor and specificity, and in some states do not cover all grades (see, e.g., Cross, Rebarber, & Torres, 2004; Education Week, 2004). Specificity of content standards is critical if standards are to provide a clear blueprint for the development of assess-ments. Alignment of assessments with academic content standards is not only called for in legislation, it is essential if assessments are to guide instruction in ways that are intended by the standards.

There is a good deal of evidence that high-stakes assessments influ-ence what teachers teach (see, e.g., Hamilton, 2003; Linn, 2003; McDonnell, 2004; Stecher & Hamilton, 2002). Assessments, especially high-stakes assessments, are likely to have more of an impact than content standards on what teachers emphasize. Thus, when content standards and assessments are not aligned, the assessments are likely to distort the intent of the content standards.

Alignment between tests and assessments and content standards is important for reinforcing the intent of the standards. This important role of alignment led the American Educational Research Association (AERA) to include the following comment in its published position statement on high-stakes testing.

Both the content of the test and the cognitive processes engaged in taking the test should adequately represent the curriculum. High-stakes tests should not be limited to that portion of the relevant curriculum that is easiest to measure. When testing is for school accountability or to influence the curriculum, the test should be aligned with the curriculum as set forth in standards documents representing intended goals of instruction. (American Educational Research Association [AERA], 2000, p. 2).

Evaluating Alignment

Although it is widely agreed that alignment of assessments and content standards is important, there is much less agreement about how alignment should be evaluated. Bhola, Impara, and Budkendahl (2003) reviewed several different approaches that have been used in recent years to evaluate alignment. The approaches differ in complexity. The least complex approach merely matches the content covered by test items to the content categories of the standards. More complex approaches add consideration of cognitive processes (e.g., Porter, 2002). The evaluation of alignment with respect to cognitive processes is important, because assessments that align well with content standards in terms of coverage of content may do so by overemphasizing factual knowledge and the use of routine procedures, rather than conceptual understanding and problem-solving skills that are often emphasized in content standards. As was stressed in the AERA statement referenced above, assessing only what is easiest to measure is not sufficient. Assessing only factual recall when the content standards stress understanding and problem solving, for example, leads to an assessment target that is poorly aligned with the content standards and is likely to undermine the intent of the standards.

Further complexity may be added to the evaluation of alignment by considering characteristics such as content match, relative emphasis, and depth (similar to cognitive complexity) (see, e.g., La Marca, Redfield, Winter, Bailey, & Despriet, 2000; Webb, 1999). Linguistic criteria (e.g., Herman, Webb, & Zuniga, 2002) may also be important to consider along with content and cognitive processes, especially in the assessment of the content knowledge and understanding of English language learners. With any of the approaches, the evaluation of the degree of alignment of assessments and standards is dependent on the level of specificity of the content standards.

Baker (in press) discussed different approaches to alignment in terms of four metaphors: correspondence (the extent of agreement between assessments and standards); bridge (the connections between assessments and standards); gravitational pull (generalized processes such as problem solving that cut across content areas); and congruence. The congruence metaphor corresponds most closely to the way in which alignment is generally evaluated. Complete congruence would require that all instructional goals be clearly specified in the content standards and that each goal be validly measured. Although such complete congruence is unrealistic, the goal in studies of alignment is to evaluate the degree to which it is approximated.

Despite the varied approaches that have been taken, the question of alignment has been given much more attention in recent years than it has received in the past. Moreover, alignment is clearly an issue that peer reviewers of state responses to NCLB have been attending to and will continue to attend to, thereby assuring continued attention to the topic.

Valid and Reliable Assessments

Legislation mandating assessments and accountability typically include statements that the assessments and/or the accountability judgments must be valid and reliable. As is true of alignment, however, validity and reliability are not all-or-none characteristics. Rather, they are matters of degree. Validity also depends on the specific inferences that are made from assessment results and the uses that are made of the results. For example, an inference that the assessment results reflect the degree to which students have mastered the content standards will depend on the degree to which the assessment is aligned with the standards and therefore has an adequate degree of content validity.

The validity of a conclusion that improvement in assessment results for a school reflects better achievement of the content standards from one year to the next depends on the degree of alignment, but it also depends on a number of other considerations. For example, it depends on the assumption that the assessment is equally novel for the students taking the assessment in different years. If the same form of a test is used year after year, or if there is substantial, say, 40% or more, overlap of the items from one year to the next, then an increase may be due to differences in familiarity with the specific test content, and therefore may not generalize to the broader domain of achievement the test is intended to represent. Certainly, the lack of generalization of gains shown on states' assessments to gains on other measures of achievement has led to questions about the validity of the gains (see, e.g., Hamilton, 2003; Klein, Hamilton, McCaffrey, & Stecher, 2000; Koretz & Barron, 1998).

Interpretive problems caused by the reuse of tests became evident in the 1980s when most states were reporting upward trends in test scores based on repeated use of the same tests year after year. Indeed, Cannell (1987) reported that almost all states were reporting results above the national average. This "Lake Wobegon effect" (Koretz, 1988; see also Koretz, chapter 5, this volume) was shown to be the result of inflated scores due to the continual reuse of a single form of a test. When a new test was introduced in a state, there was usually a precipitous drop in the performance on the new test in comparison with that obtained with the old test. Furthermore, the gains found on state tests lacked generalizability to other measures such as the National Assessment of Educational Progress (NAEP) (see, e.g., Hamilton, 2003; Linn, 2000; Linn, Graue, & Sanders, 1990).

Prior to the enactment of NCLB, most states had moved away from complete reliance on off-the-shelf, norm-referenced tests and had introduced assessments that were designed with the intent of being aligned with the state's content standards. Along with this shift, states are more frequently introducing new items each year. In some cases, however, the core of the assessment still consists of a norm-referenced test that is supplemented with items written specifically for the state in an effort to better align with the content standards. In such cases, there is a need to alternate forms of the core norm-referenced test to avoid excessive year-to-year overlap.

Some items of an assessment have to be repeated from one year to the next in order to equate assessment forms so results in one year can

be compared with those of earlier years. This is true whether or not a
norm-referenced test is a component of the assessment. A balance is
needed between having enough items for dependable year-to-year
equating and having so many common items that score gains may be
artificially inflated. An overlap of something in the range of a fifth to a
quarter of the items will generally be sufficient for equating purposes
without substantially undermining the ability to generalize from
observed gains to the larger domain of achievement that the assessment
is intended to measure.

As is true of validity, reliability also needs to be evaluated in relation
to the uses and interpretations of assessment results. For school
accountability uses the reliability of individual scores, while of concern
for appropriate interpretations of student scores, is not the main issue.
Rather, the primary concern is with the consistency of results used to
make judgments about schools. Thus, when NCLB requires that AYP
be defined in a manner that is statistically reliable (§ 1111(b)(2)(C)(ii–
iii)), it should be interpreted to mean that schools should be consistently
classified as meeting or failing to meet AYP targets. Consistency of
classification of schools in terms of AYP status depends on the number
of students in the schools. Small schools will be less reliably classified
than large schools (Hill & DePascale, 2003; Linn & Haug, 2002).
Because schools can fail to meet the AYP target when any single subgroup for which disaggregated results must be reported fails to meet
the target, it is also the case that schools with many subgroups of
students of sufficient size to be reported will also be classified less
reliably than schools with a more homogeneous student body (Hill &
DePascale, 2003; Kane, Staiger, & Geppert, 2002).

Accountability Uses of Student Assessment Results

Student assessment results are used in several different ways by
systems that have been put in place by states as part of their state-
mandated accountability efforts or in response to NCLB. Student
assessment results for particular grades and subjects aggregated at the
school level may be compared with a performance target. The emphasis
may be on current status or on improvement. Improvement may be
judged by comparing the performance of successive cohorts of students
(e.g., fourth-grade students in 2004 compared with fourth-grade students in 2003), or it may be judged by tracking student performance
longitudinally (e.g., the comparison of the performance of the same
students as fifth graders in 2004 with their performance as fourth

graders in 2003). Some systems focus on each content area assessed, while other systems rely on composite results across content areas. State systems may focus only on results for the school as a whole or, as is required by NCLB, may also set requirements for subgroups of students defined by race/ethnicity, socioeconomic status, disability status, and English language proficiency.

Status Measures

Reporting results for a school in terms of current status (e.g., the percentage of students at the proficient level, or an index score determined by the percentage of students in each of several performance categories) is part of almost all state accountability systems and is required by NCLB. Reliance on current status measures only, however, raises a number of issues of fairness to schools. Current status is "contaminated by factors other than school performance, in particular, the average level of achievement prior to entering first grade—average effects of student, family, and community characteristics on student achievement growth from first grade through the grade in which students are tested" (Meyers, 2000, p. 2).

On the other hand, current status indicators have the perceived advantage that they hold all students and schools to the same standards of performance. They obviously also provide information about where students and schools stand at a given point in time, and when current status is compared with performance targets, how far there is to go.

The No Child Left Behind Act holds schools accountable for meeting AYP targets, which are called annual measurable objectives (AMOs). Despite the fact that the "P" in AYP stands for progress, in any given year, it is only current status compared with the AMOs that determines whether or not a school has met AYP requirements.[2] Because current status measures place schools serving poor and/or initially low-achieving students at a disadvantage in comparison with schools serving more affluent and/or initially high-achieving students, most state accountability systems consider improvement in some form in addition to current status.

Improvement Measures

Successive cohorts. The most common approach to measuring improvement is to compare the performance of successive cohorts of students in the same school. The successive cohort approach to measuring improvement has the advantage of simplicity; it does not require the tracking of individual students from one year to the next. This approach has its limitations, however. It does not account for changes in student characteristics from one year to the next. The performance of students who transfer into a school shortly before the date that assessments are administered cannot reasonably be attributed to instruction provided by the school, but they will help determine school gains or losses unless they are explicitly excluded in the calculation of year-to-year change. Change or difference scores are also less reliable than the individual scores that are used to compute the difference. Consequently, schools that show minimal gains or even losses in one change cycle will frequently have large gains in the next change cycle. Conversely, schools with outstanding gains in one change cycle will often show only small gains, or may even have losses, in the next change cycle (see, e.g., Haney, 2002; Linn & Haug, 2002).

Longitudinal measures of change. Tracking individual students from year to year allows each student to serve as his or her own control. Longitudinal measures of student growth are appealing to schools and teachers, in part, because they generally hold the school accountable only for students that are enrolled in the school for at least a year. On the other hand, exclusion of mobile students is viewed as a disadvantage by those who want all students included in the accountability system.

Student growth may be monitored over a pair of years (e.g., fourth to fifth grade) or over multiple years (e.g., third, fourth, and fifth grades). Simple difference scores or complex statistical analyses may be used to estimate growth. In either case, the scores at one grade level need to be comparable to those in other grade levels included in the analysis for the use of gain scores.

Because a test appropriate for, say, sixth-grade students contains more challenging content than one appropriate for fourth-grade students, simple scores such as the number of correct responses are not comparable for tests used at different grade levels. Typically scores at different grade levels are made comparable by constructing a vertical scale, that is, a scale that places scores on tests used at different grade levels on a common numerical scale. A vertical scale is usually created by including a common set of anchor items on assessments administered at adjacent grades. The assessment items that are unique to each adjacent grade are placed on a common vertical scale by fixing the statistics for the common anchor items.

Mathematics assessments at grades 3 and 8 obviously have dramatically different content and require quite different skills. It is implicitly assumed, however, that a vertical scale that spans grades 3 through 8 measures a common construct. In fact, however, the construct changes over grade levels. For example, the factual and procedural knowledge required to add and subtract and recognize geometric figures at the third grade level may differ substantially from the conceptual under-standing and prealgebra problem-solving skills required at the eighth grade level. Such changes in the complexity of the construct that is measured make difference scores across a wide span of grade levels difficult to interpret (see, e.g., Reckase, 2004). On the other hand, difference scores on a vertical scale for adjacent grades or a small span of, say, three grade levels are easier to interpret because of the greater similarity of test content and the cognitive processes required of stu-dents by assessments designed for use at adjacent grades.

In addition to the need to attend to shifts in the construct measured across grade levels, it is important to understand the statistical proper-ties of vertical scales. It is particularly important to attend to the relative size of the variance in vertical scale scores from one grade to the next. Vertical scales have on occasion had variances that decreased with grade level, had variances that were approximately equal, or had variances that increased with grade level. Gain scores, for example, the difference between the vertical scale scores obtained by sixth-grade students in 2004 and the scores they obtained as fourth-grade students in 2002, clearly would have different interpretations depending on whether vari-ability decreases, increases, or remains constant across grade levels.

Issues raised by changes in the construct measured and changes in the variability of scores over grades are most evident in the interpreta-tion of simple difference scores. These issues, however, need careful consideration regardless of whether simple difference scores or more sophisticated statistical models are used to estimate growth in student achievement.

Analyses of longitudinal data. There has been considerable interest in recent years in using complex statistical models to analyze longitudinal student achievement test data collected over several years to estimate school and teacher contributions to student gains in achievement. The most prominent example of this type of analysis is the Tennessee Value Added Assessment System (TVAAS) (Sanders & Horn, 1998). The "value added" terminology is used to convey the notion that the esti-mated teacher and/or school effects represent the contributions made by either a teacher or a school to student gains on achievement tests beyond that expected based on student performance for the past three years. The analytic models employed by Sanders have attracted a great deal of attention across the country. The widespread interest is due, in part, to findings reported by Sanders and his colleagues that purport to show that teacher contributions to student learning are quite large compared with other factors (Wright, Horn, & Sanders, 1997) and that teacher effects accumulate over time (Sanders & Rivers, 1996).

The interest in value-added models has mushroomed since the approach was introduced on a large scale in Tennessee a decade ago. As noted by Wainer (2004) in his introduction to the special issue of the *Journal of Educational and Behavioral Statistics* on value-added models, several states in addition to Tennessee already use some form of longitudinal measurement, and several more either are exploring or have already mandated the use of value-added models with longitudinal data. "Enthusiasm for this approach stems in large part from the belief that it can remove the effects of factors not under the control of the school, such as prior performance and socioeconomic status, and thereby provides a more accurate indicator of school or teacher effectiveness than is possible when these factors are not controlled" (McCaffrey, Lockwood, Koretz, Louis, & Hamilton, 2004, p. 68; for a more extended discussion see Choi, Goldschmitt, & Yamashiro, chapter 6, this volume; McCaffrey, Lockwood, Koretz, & Hamilton, 2003).

Statements regarding the "effectiveness" of teachers or schools based on results of value-added analyses are basically causal claims. Rubin, Stuart, and Zanutto (2004) have argued, however, that value-added analyses "should not be seen as estimating causal effects of teachers or schools, but rather as descriptive measures" (p. 113). In a similar vein, Raudenbush (2004) cautions that although value-added analyses "when combined with other information have potential to stimulate discussions about how to improve practice . . . they should not be taken as direct evidence of the effects of instructional practice" (p. 128). Ballou (2004) provides a different perspective in his rejoinder to the arguments made by Raudenbush and by Rubin et al., arguing that the estimates, done properly, will not necessarily be biased and noting that all models are subject to criticism.

Reporting and Interpreting Results

A defensible and useful educational accountability system based on student achievement requires valid and reliable measurement of the intended content domain. It also requires well-defined, systematic procedures for analyzing student achievement data to make inferences about the performance of schools. As has been discussed in previous sections of this chapter, there are many considerations that enter into the choice of measurement procedures and into the choice of statistical procedures used to estimate overall school performance. In addition to the measurement and analytic considerations, the validity and utility of the accountability results depend on the ways in which the results are reported and interpreted.

Performance Standards

Approaches to reporting achievement test results that were used in the past, such as national percentile ranks, scale, grade equivalent, or normal curve equivalent scores, fell into disfavor in the last decade. Such reporting has generally been replaced by standards-based score reports that present results in terms of percentages of students in performance categories, for example, below basic, basic, proficient, and advanced. Alternatively, or in addition, percentages of students who score above a given level (e.g., proficient or above) may be reported. The switch to performance standards as a reporting mechanism was motivated by the desire to go beyond normative statements about performance to answer the question: how good is good enough?

The interest in performance standards developed fairly rapidly at the national level and in a number of states. The Goals 2000: Educate America Act of 1994 and the Improving America's Schools Act of 1994 called for performance standards that were intended to specify the level of achievement that should be considered good enough—typically referred to as proficient. Performance standards, referred to as achievement levels, were set for NAEP by the National Assessment Governing Board. A number of states also set performance standards, often modeled after NAEP, for their state assessments.

These performance standards had several common properties. They were absolute rather than normative. They were set in a context that called for ambitious, "world-class" standards and they divided the range of student achievement on an assessment into a relatively small number (typically four) of categories. Finally, they were expected to apply to all, or nearly all, students.

The No Child Left Behind Act of 2001 requires states to set "challenging student academic achievement standards" (§ 1111(b)(1)(A)) for their state assessments in mathematics and reading/English language arts. States must set at least three performance standards for their assessments to comply with NCLB requirements. Two of the standards (proficient and advanced) are supposed to correspond to high levels of achievement and the third standard (basic) is intended to provide a means of monitoring progress toward proficient achievement. Most states had already set performance standards for their reading and mathematics assessments before NCLB was signed into law in January 2002, although not necessarily at all the grade levels that must be assessed by 2005–06. Since that time the remaining states have set performance standards for their assessments and, in a few instances, states that had already set standards have revised or renamed their standards and taken steps to set them at grades where they did not have assessments that will be required under NCLB. It is notable that the state standards vary greatly in stringency and that standards set by states after NCLB became law tend to be less stringent than standards set before 2002, presumably because of the sanctions imposed by NCLB for schools where the percentage of students meeting standards falls below established annual targets.

Status and Improvement Targets

As was noted previously, the context in which performance standards were set in the 1990s on NAEP and on state assessments was one in which there was considerable discussion of high, world-class performance expectations. Not surprisingly, the standards tended to be set at quite high levels (see, e.g., Shepard, Glaser, Linn, & Bohrnstedt, 1993). It is also worth noting that the NAEP performance standards and standards on many state assessments served only hortatory purposes and had no real consequences for students or schools prior to the enactment of NCLB.

NCLB and state expectations. More recent state uses of performance standards have had consequences for schools and/or students, and there certainly are consequences for schools and districts under NCLB. NCLB specifies procedures that states are to use to set AMOs, based on the percentage of students performing at the proficient level or above, that are to be used to determine if schools, districts, and states make AYP. The AYP targets must be set such that all students will be at the proficient level or above by 2014. Sanctions are imposed on schools not meeting their AYP targets two years in a row and the sanctions become increasingly severe for schools not meeting targets for a third, fourth, and fifth year in a row.

If the NCLB requirement that states set standards at challenging levels is followed and the proficient standard is set at a high level, then the mandate that all students perform at the proficient level or higher by 2014 will be completely unrealistic. Using trends on NAEP as a benchmark, Linn (2003, 2004) has shown that the rate of improvement in student achievement would have to be many times faster for the next decade than it has been for any comparable period of time in the last 40 years. Unless the AYP targets assuming the achievement of the 100% proficient or above goal by 2014 are changed, nearly all schools will fail to meet their AYP targets within the next few years.

Ambitious but realistic expectations. Ambitious expectations are desirable to encourage concentrated effort on the part of educators and students. In order for the expectations to be met, educators and students must have the capacity to meet the targets that are set. Effort alone is insufficient if teachers lack the knowledge they need to meet expectations. Exhortation may increase motivation, but is no substitute for capacity building. Even added resources, capacity building, and increased effort, however, cannot lead to the accomplishment of goals that are set at unrealistically high levels. Thus, it is critical that expectations be set at ambitious but realistic levels.

One way to ensure that performance goals are both ambitious and realistic is to base the goals on the accomplishments of schools displaying the most rapid gains in achievement over a period of several years. If the rates of improvement that the top, say, 10% of schools have achieved over the past five years were set as expectations for all schools, for example, the goals would certainly be ambitious for the vast majority of schools, but they would also be more realistic than expectations such as those set by NCLB that take no account of what has been achieved in the past by exemplary schools. Note that by focusing on *sustained improvement* rather than status, schools that are successful in teaching students living in poverty, not just schools serving upper middle-class students who perform at high levels in a given year, could be the ones that set the growth targets for other schools.

Subgroup performance. One of the important features of the NCLB accountability system is the requirement to report results separately for students with disabilities, economically disadvantaged students, and students with limited English proficiency, and by race/ethnicity. Such disaggregated reporting of results was already required by the accountability systems in a few states, but with the enactment of NCLB is now required in all states. Reporting performance for the subgroups specified by NCLB is important for ensuring that attention be given to the achievement of groups of students that have too often been ignored in the past. It is also critical for monitoring the degree to which achievement has been reduced.

Although it is highly desirable that disaggregated reporting of student achievement results required under NCLB be continued, there is a problem caused by this requirement that needs to be addressed. Since schools can fail to meet AYP in many different ways, but can meet it in only one way, it turns out that schools with a sufficient number of students in each of several targeted groups to be reported are less likely to meet AYP targets than schools of the same size and similar performance but with a homogeneous student body (e.g., nearly all students who belong to one racial/ethnic group).

The most straightforward way of avoiding the overidentification of schools with multiple subgroups as failing to make AYP would be to modify the safe harbor provision of NCLB. This provision allows schools, when a subgroup of students falls short of the AYP target, to still meet AYP if (1) the percentage of students in that subgroup who score below the proficient level is decreased by 10% from the year before; and (2) there is improvement for that subgroup on other indicators.

Because the 10% reduction in students scoring below the proficient level is a very high bar, very few schools that would not otherwise make AYP do so because of the safe harbor provision. Only a tiny fraction of schools actually meet AYP through the safe harbor provision because it is so extreme. Changing the safe harbor provision from a 10% reduction in below proficient to, say, a 3–4% reduction would go a long way toward solving the problems caused by the multiple hurdles created by subgroup reporting while assuring improvement in performance of all subgroups.

Value-Added Reporting

Value-added models yield measures of individual student gains in achievement, and when those gains are linked to the students' schools and teachers, those gains are converted into estimates of school effects and teacher effects. Gains may be expressed in a variety of metrics, including scale scores or comparisons with national norms.

Schools. TVAAS reports estimates of school gains in comparison with state and national gains. Mean gains are reported for a school by grade level and subject area (reading, mathematics, language, science, and social studies). Those mean gains are compared with gains statewide and gains from one grade to the next in national norms. Cumulative percents of national norm gains are also reported. A cumulative percent of national norm of 110, for example, indicates that the school is gaining at a rate that is faster than the national norm. Although the analyses that yield the estimates of gain for a school are complex, the descriptive statement that the gain exceeds the national norms gain is straightforward and not subject to much, if any, controversy.

It is the interpretation of the gains as an indication of school effectiveness that is controversial. As was discussed above, such an interpretation is fundamentally a causal claim, and strong and questionable assumptions must be satisfied to make causal inferences about school or program effectiveness from the results of value-added analyses. Detailed explanations for this conclusion about the inability of value-added analyses to support causal inferences are provided by Raudenbush (2004) and by Rubin et al. (2004), but see also Ballou (2004), who noted that the specification of any model may be questioned. He also suggested that, by making allowances for students' starting level, value-added models are better than the approach of NCLB, which makes no such allowances.

Teachers. Not all applications of value-added models include estimates of teacher "effects." Indeed, some state mandates, for example, Ohio's, are, by design, limited to the school with no intention of estimating gains associated with individual teachers. Individual estimates of "teacher effects" are produced by TVAAS but they are intended for use by the teacher and are not included in public reports. The estimated "[t]eacher effects are deviations from the district average" within a given year (Ballou, Sanders, & Wright, 2004, p. 40). As in the case of estimated "school effects," causal interpretations of "teacher effects" can be justified only if strong, unverifiable assumptions are met.

Students. Measures of student gains in achievement obtained from value-added analyses are far less controversial than the measures obtained for either teachers or schools. This is so because the gains are treated as descriptive information without any causal attributions. The goal is usually to determine if a student has made a year's worth of growth in a year or to indicate that the rate of growth is sufficient to achieve some target such as achievement at the proficient or advanced level by some specified grade.

Summary and Conclusion

External assessments of student achievement have been used for purposes of school accountability for more than half a century. The specific ways that assessments have been used have expanded and changed over the years. As McDonnell (2004) noted, "assessment has become a critical accountability tool" (p. 9). There are several reasons for the appeal of assessment-based accountability (see, e.g., Linn, 2000; McDonnell, 2004).

Assessments, unlike changes in instructional practices, can be mandated at the state level and there is reasonable assurance that they will be implemented in ways that are generally consistent with adopted policies. Compared with other alternative policies intended to improve student achievement, such as reducing class size or adding tutors, assessments are also relatively inexpensive. Assessments can be implemented in a relatively short period of time and the results are visible. In addition to their hortatory value, it is relatively easy to increase the stakes associated with assessment results by adding rewards and sanctions.

Despite the clear appeal of assessment-based accountability and the widespread use of this approach, the development of assessments that are aligned with content standards and for which there is solid evidence of validity and reliability is a challenging endeavor. Alignment of an assessment with the content standards that it is intended to measure is critical if the assessment is to buttress rather than undermine the standards. Too little attention has been given to the evaluation of alignment of assessments and standards.

Evaluations of alignment can provide support to validity claims regarding content, but other types of evidence are needed to support the myriad interpretations of assessments within an accountability system. The conclusion that improved performance on an assessment implies better learning of the content domain, for example, requires evidence that the gains generalize to other indicators of achievement in the content domain.

Moving from assessment results for individual students that may have good validity as measures of student achievement in a content area to aggregate results to draw inferences about the quality of schools poses additional validity questions. Although the finding that a large percentage of students score at the proficient level or above may provide an accurate indication of the achievement of students within a school, it cannot simply be converted to a conclusion that the high achievement is the result of good instruction or that the school is of high quality. The high achievement may reflect prior achievement and other characteristics of the student body, as much or more than it does the quality of instruction in a given year.

Similarly, gains in achievement for successive cohorts of students in a school may be due to improved instruction, but they may also be due to a variety of other factors such as changes in the mix of students or a narrow focus on the specific assessment. Longitudinal student data can rule out the possibility that gains are due to changes in the mix of students from one year to the next. The use of sophisticated value-added analyses can eliminate some of the possible interpretations of gains; however, as was discussed above, causal claims that the gains are due to school or teacher effects can still be challenged.

Performance standards were introduced as a means of reporting results, in part because it was thought they would make results easier to interpret, and in part to set expectations for acceptable levels of achievement. Because of the huge variability in the stringency of performance standards from state to state, it is not clear that standards-based reporting has made results more readily interpretable.

The high level of performance standards that is encouraged by NCLB and that has been put in place on assessments in a number of states, together with the NCLB mandate that all students be at the proficient level or above by 2014, has resulted in expectations that are quite unrealistic. Something will have to give. Either the expectations will be made more realistic or nearly all schools will fall short of AYP targets within the next few years.

Several characteristics of accountability systems are important if the system is going to have its intended positive effects on teaching and student learning. Assessments need to be aligned with content standards, which in turn need to provide clear indications of the content to be taught and the cognitive processes that students are expected to use in demonstrating understanding and solving problems. Both status and improvement should be considered in the accountability system. Attention needs to be given to the performance of subgroups of students who have lagged behind their better off peers in the past. The jury is still out on what combination of rewards and sanctions is most effective. It is clear, however, that teachers in schools that are not performing well need assistance and sustained professional development so that they can better do the job that they almost all would like to do—more effectively facilitating the learning of every student.

NOTES

1. Federal testing requirements under NCLB have introduced some common requirements regarding grades and subjects tested, but states are free to test additional subjects or grades.

2. NCLB does have a safe harbor provision that allows a school that would not otherwise meet AYP to still be classified as meeting AYP if (1) the percentage of students who score below the proficient level is decreased by at least 10% from the year before; and (2) there is improvement for the subgroup on other indicators. In practice, however, few schools are "saved" by the safe harbor provision because the bar is set so high.

REFERENCES

American Educational Research Association (AERA). (2000). *AERA position statement concerning high-stakes testing in preK-12 education.* Retrieved from http://www.aera.net/about/policy/stakes.htm

Baker, E.L. (in press). Aligning curriculum, standards, and assessments: Fulfilling the promise of school reform. In C.A. Dwyer (Ed.), *Measurement and research in the accountability era.* Mahwah, NJ: Lawrence Erlbaum Associates.

Ballou, D. (2004). Rejoinder. *Journal of Educational and Behavioral Statistics, 29*(1), 131–134.

Ballou, D., Sanders, W., & Wright, P. (2004). Controlling for student background in value-added assessment of teachers. *Journal of Educational and Behavioral Statistics, 29*(1), 37–65.

Bhola, D.S., Impara, J.C., & Buckendahl, W. (2003). Aligning tests with states' content standards: Methods and issues. *Educational Measurement: Issues and Practice, 22*(3), 21–29.

Cannell, J.J. (1987). *Nationally normed elementary achievement testing in America's public schools: How all 50 states are above the national average* (2nd ed.). Daniel, WV: Friends of Education.

Cross, R.W., Rebarber, T., & Torres, J. (Eds.). (2004). *Grading the systems: The guide to state standards, tests, and accountability policies.* Washington, DC: The Fordham Foundation and Accountability Works. Retrieved from http://www.edexcellence.net/foundation/publication.cfm?id=328

Education Week. (2004, January 8). Quality Counts 2004, *33*(17).

Elementary and Secondary Education Act of 1965 (ESEA), Pub. L. 89-10, 79 Stat. 27 (1965).

Goals 2000: Educate America Act of 1994, Pub. L. 103-227, 108 Stat. 125 (1994).

Hamilton, L. (2003). Assessment as a policy tool. *Review of Research in Education, 27*, 25–68.

Haney, W. (2002, May 6). Lake Woebeguaranteed: Misuse of test scores in Massachusetts, Part I. *Education Policy Analysis Archives, 10*(24), 1–41.

Herman, J.L., Webb, N., & Zuniga, S. (2002). *Alignment and college admissions: The match of expectations, assessments, and educator perspectives.* Paper presented at the annual meeting of the American Educational Research Association, New Orleans, LA.

Hill, R.K., & DePascale, C.A. (2003, April). *Adequate yearly progress under NCLB: Reliability considerations.* Paper presented at the 2003 annual meeting of the National Council on Measurement in Education, Chicago. Retrieved October 15, 2004, from http://www.nciea.org/

Improving America's Schools Act of 1994 (IASA), Pub. L. No. 103-382, 108 Stat. 4056 (1994).

Kane, T.J., Staiger, D.O., & Geppert, J. (2002). *Randomly accountable.* Retrieved September 29, 2004, from http://www.educationnext.org/20021/56.html

Klein, S.P., Hamilton, L.S., McCaffrey, D.F., & Stecher, B.M. (2000). *What do test scores in Texas tell us?* Santa Monica, CA: RAND.

Koretz, D. (1988). Arriving at Lake Wobegon: Are standardized tests exaggerating achievement and distorting instruction? *American Educator, 12*(2), 8–15, 46–52.

Koretz, D.M., & Barron, S.I. (1998). *The validity of gains in score on the Kentucky Instructional Results Information System (KIRIS).* Santa Monica, CA: RAND.

La Marca, P., Redfield, D., Winter, P., Bailey, A., & Despriet, L. (2000). *State standards and state assessment systems: A guide to alignment.* Washington, DC: Council of Chief State School Officers.

Linn, R.L. (2000). Assessments and accountability. *Educational Researcher, 29*(2), 4–14.

Linn, R.L. (2003). Accountability: Responsibility and reasonable expectations. *Educational Researcher, 32*(7), 3–13.

Linn, R.L. (2004). *Rethinking the No Child Left Behind Accountability System*. Washington, DC: Center on Education Policy.

Linn, R.L., Graue, M.E., & Sanders, N.M. (1990). Comparing state and district results to national norms: The validity of the claims that "everyone is above average." *Educational Measurement: Issues and Practice, 9*(3), 5–14.

Linn, R.L., & Haug, C. (2002). Stability of school building scores and gains. *Educational Evaluation and Policy Analysis, 24*(1), 27–36.

McCaffrey, E.F., Lockwood, J.R., Koretz, D.M., & Hamilton, L.S. (2003). *Evaluating value-added models for teacher accountability*. Santa Monica, CA: RAND.

McCaffrey, E.F., Lockwood, J.R., Koretz, D.M., Louis, T.A., & Hamilton, L.S. (2004). Models for value-added modeling of teacher effects. *Journal of Educational and Behavioral Statistics, 29*(1), 67–101.

McDonnell, L.M. (2004). *Politics, persuasion, and educational testing*. Cambridge, MA: Harvard University Press.

Meyers, R.H. (2000). Value-added indicators: A powerful tool for evaluating science and mathematics programs and policies. *NISE Brief, 3*, No. 3. Madison: National Center for Improving Science Education, University of Wisconsin-Madison.

No Child Left Behind Act of 2001, Pub. L. No. 107-110, 115 Stat. 1425 (2002).

Porter, A.C. (2002). Measuring the content of instruction: Uses in research and practice. *Educational Researcher, 31*(7), 3–14.

Raudenbush, S.W. (2004). What are value-added models estimating and what does this imply for statistical practice? *Journal of Educational and Behavioral Statistics, 29*(1), 121–129.

Reckase, M.D. (2004). The real world is more complicated than we would like it to be. *Journal of Educational and Behavioral Statistics, 29*(1), 117–120.

Rubin, D.B., Stuart, E.A., & Zanutto, E.L. (2004). A potential outcomes view of value-added assessment. *Journal of Educational and Behavioral Statistics, 29*(1), 103–116.

Sanders, W., & Horn, S. (1998). Research findings from the Tennessee value added assessment system (TVAAS) database: Implications for educational evaluation and research. *Journal of Personnel Evaluation in Education, 12*(3), 247–256.

Sanders, W.L., & Rivers, J.C. (1996). *Cumulative and residual effects of teachers on future student academic achievement*. Research Progress Report. Knoxville, TN: University of Tennessee Value-Added Research and Assessment Center.

Shepard, L., Glaser, R., Linn, R., & Bohrnstedt, G. (1993). *Setting performance standards for student achievement*. Stanford, CA: National Academy of Education.

Stecher, B.M., & Hamilton, L.S. (2002). Putting theory to the test: Systems of "educational accountability should be held accountable." *Rand Review, 26*(1), 16–23.

Wainer, H. (2004). Introduction to a special issue of the *Journal of Educational and Behavioral Statistics* on value-added assessment. *Journal of Educational and Behavioral Statistics, 29*(1), 1–3.

Webb, N.L. (1999). *Alignment of science and mathematics standards and assessments in four states*. Research Monograph 18. Madison, WI: National Institute for Science Education.

Wright, S.P., Horn, S.P., & Sanders, W.L. (1997). Teacher and classroom context effects on student achievement: Implications for teacher evaluation. *Journal of Personnel Evaluation in Education, 11*, 57–67.

CHAPTER 5

Alignment, High Stakes, and the Inflation of Test Scores

DANIEL KORETZ

For several decades, some measurement experts have warned that high-stakes testing could lead to inappropriate forms of test preparation and score inflation, which we define as a gain in scores that substantially overstates the improvement in learning it implies (e.g., Koretz, 1988; Linn & Dunbar, 1990; Madaus, 1988; Shepard, 1988). This issue has been a concern in the public debate about education reform at least since the "Lake Wobegon" reports of the 1980s (Cannell, 1987; Koretz, 1988; Linn, Graue, & Sanders, 1990), which discussed the implausibly large proportion of states and districts claiming to be above average in student achievement.

One common response to this problem has been to seek "tests worth teaching to." The search for such tests has led reformers in several directions over the years, but currently, many argue that tests well aligned with standards meet this criterion. If tests are aligned with standards, the argument runs, they test material deemed important, and teaching to the test therefore teaches what is important. If students are being taught what is important, how can the resulting score gains be misleading?

Daniel Koretz is a Professor of Education at Harvard's Graduate School of Education and an Associate Director of the Center for Research on Evaluation, Standards, and Student Testing (CRESST).

The work reported herein was supported under the Educational Research and Development Centers Program, PR/Award Number R305B960002, as administered by the Institute of Education Sciences (IES) and the U.S. Department of Education. The findings and opinions expressed in this report are those of the author and do not necessarily reflect the positions or policies of the National Center for Education Research, the Institute of Education Sciences (IES), or the U.S. Department of Education.

The material in the section with the heading "Inappropriate Test Preparation and 'Tests Worth Teaching To'" (pp. 100–104) is copyrighted by the author and is reprinted here with his permission.

No one can dispute that tests should measure important content, and for many (but not all) purposes, tests should be aligned with curricular goals. Thus in many cases, alignment is clearly better than the alternative, and nothing that follows here argues otherwise. Unfortunately, however, this does not imply that alignment is sufficient protection against score inflation. Inflation does not require that a test assess unimportant material, and focusing the test on important material—for example, through alignment—is not necessarily sufficient to prevent inflation.

The purpose of this chapter is to explain the relationship between alignment and score inflation. The first sections clarify what is meant by inappropriate test preparation and provide a concrete, hypothetical example that illustrates a process by which scores become inflated. These are followed by a more complete discussion of the mechanisms of score inflation and their link to teachers' responses to high-stakes testing. A final section discusses some implications.

Inappropriate Test Preparation and "Tests Worth Teaching To"

The problem of inappropriate test preparation has two related aspects. The first, already noted, is inflation of test scores. The second is undesirable pedagogy. This can take numerous forms, such as boring drill and practice focused on test content or the elimination of important content not emphasized by the test. The two are obviously closely intertwined: undesirable forms of instruction are among the primary factors that cause inflation of scores.

These two aspects of inappropriate test preparation, undesirable pedagogy and score inflation, do not entirely overlap, however, and solutions to one of them will not necessarily solve the other. Instruction that creates meaningful gains in scores could be undesirable in other respects. An example might be successful but very stressful drill that is so aversive that students develop an abiding dislike of the subject or of formal schooling. Similarly, instructional changes that are desirable in other respects may nonetheless contribute to score inflation.

Therefore, it is important to be clear what is meant by "tests worth teaching to." Some people use the term to refer to tests that encourage meaningful improvements in student performance, while others use it to refer to those that encourage desirable changes in instruction, such as an increase in the amount of writing across the curriculum or the inclusion of larger, more complex problems in mathematics instruction. Still others seem to use the term to refer to both of these at once, incorrectly assuming that if you accomplish one, you necessarily accomplish the second.

In this chapter, our focus is on validity and score inflation. We do not discuss systematically the research that has shown both positive and negative effects of test-based accountability on instruction (see, e.g., Stecher, 2002). We discuss the incentives to change instruction created by test-based accountability primarily because of their link to validity and inflation.

Tests as Samples of Performance: A Concrete Example

A hypothetical, concrete example can illustrate the principles that underlie score inflation, as well as many other important issues in measurement. Assume that you confront the following challenge. You produce a journal, and you are going to hire several people newly graduated from college to work on it. You find that you have a large number of applicants and need a procedure for selecting from among them. Assume that you have decided that among the factors you will consider in making your choices is the strength of the applicants' vocabularies. It is not essential for this example that vocabulary be the basis for selection because the same principles apply to other cognitive skills and knowledge. However, vocabulary provides a particularly clear and uncontroversial illustration.

The sheer size of the applicants' vocabularies would be an impediment to evaluating them. Several studies suggest that the typical graduate of a four-year college has a vocabulary of approximately 17,000 root words (Biemiller, 2001). Therefore, the only practical option is to test the students on a small sample of words that they might know. This is precisely how vocabulary tests are constructed. One can obtain a serviceable estimate of the relative strength of the applicants' vocabularies using a small sample of words. Let's assume 40 words for this example.

To evaluate individuals' vocabularies on the basis of 40 words, it is essential to select the words carefully. Suppose that you were given three lists from which to choose words for the test. Table 1 shows the

TABLE 1

THREE WORDS FROM EACH OF THREE HYPOTHETICAL WORD LISTS

A	B	C
siliculose	bath	feckless
vilipend	travel	disparage
epimysium	carpet	miniscule

first three words from each of these three lists. On each list, the words not shown are roughly similar in difficulty to those shown. It is obvious that one would learn nothing useful from lists A and B. List A comprises highly unusual, specialized words that few if any of the applicants are likely to know. Therefore, all of the applicants would do extremely poorly on a test made up of List A words, and one would learn essentially nothing about the relative strength of their vocabularies. Conversely, List B is made up of easy, extremely simple words that all college graduates would know, so they too would provide no useful information. So one would choose list C: words that are middling in difficulty, such that some students would know each word and others would not. Only the use of such words would allow one to differentiate between the applicants with stronger and weaker vocabularies. (For certain other purposes, one might select test content without regard to difficulty, but that is beyond the scope of this chapter.)

Taken this far, the example illustrates a fundamental principle that could be called the *sampling principle of testing*. In most achievement testing, one is interested in reaching conclusions about students' proficiency in a broad *domain* of achievement. In this case, the domain is vocabulary; in a more common case, it might be reading or eighth-grade mathematics. In most cases, one cannot measure these proficiencies exhaustively, or even close to exhaustively, because the domains of interest are so large. Instead, one creates a small sample of a given domain and measures students' proficiency in that small sample. One must then *generalize* from performance in the small sample to the mostly unmeasured performance in the larger domain about which one draws conclusions.

Thus, any useful conclusion based on scores requires that one draw an inference about proficiency in the domain from proficiency in the small sample. The quality of that inference—the degree to which the inference is supported by performance on the test—is what is meant by *validity*. This is why experts in measurement say that validity is an attribute of an inference, not an attribute of the test itself. Even a test that provides very good support for one given inference may provide inadequate support for another, so it is misleading to talk about a "valid test."

Returning to the hypothetical example, suppose that someone intercepted each of your applicants on the way to your testing session and taught them all of the words on your vocabulary test. Let's examine what would happen to the validity of several of the most important inferences one might draw from the scores.

In the problem as given, the primary inference is one about *relative* performance: identifying which applicants have relatively strong vocabularies. Clearly, this form of teaching to the test would render the scores useless for supporting this inference. As a result of this test preparation, all of the students would receive perfect or nearly perfect scores. The applicants would become indistinguishable in terms of this particular basis for selection.

The same problem usually arises when the user of scores is not interested in ranking but instead wants to draw inferences about the *absolute* level of performance or about the size of a gain in performance. This is particularly important at present because of the emphasis on evaluating whether students meet performance standards. In the case of our example, such inferences might be of the form "all applicants showed very strong vocabularies" or "applicants showed large gains in their vocabularies." Note that these conclusions do not rely on comparisons with the performance of other students.

The teaching to the test in this example would undermine the validity of these absolute inferences as well. It is true that many of the students would have learned additional words, and let's assume that they will remember them. We tested 40 words, and we chose words that were moderate in difficulty, so let's say that the typical applicant knew 20 of them and learned the other 20. So this intervention—teaching to the test in a very direct way—would have increased their vocabularies by roughly a tenth of 1%. This is trivial. By the same token, it would be misleading to conclude that all students had very strong vocabularies. If one constructed another test from a similar sample of words, one would find that many of the students would do much less well on it, because in fact their vocabularies would remain the same as they had been before.

There is one case in which teaching the examinees the specific 40 words would not cause inflation—that is, when the inference based on scores refers to the 40 tested words, not to a larger domain from which they are drawn. That is, this form of test preparation is not problematic when the sampling principle of testing does not apply. One can find examples of this—for example, one could test knowledge of the rules of English punctuation exhaustively—but they are generally not important in current achievement testing. Put differently, the important inferences based on scores on large-scale assessments almost all depend on the sampling principle, that is, on generalizing from the tested sample to the domain from which items are sampled.

Thus, this intervention would have created score inflation. All students would score perfectly or nearly perfectly on the test, but this sharp increase would reflect at best a trivial improvement in vocabulary. In addition, it would have eliminated the gap between high and low performers, but this seemingly dramatic accomplishment would be entirely illusory. To put this in terms of the sampling principle of testing, this intervention would have made the tested sample of words unrepresentative of the domain of words about which inferences are to be drawn. By doing so, it made score-based inferences, both inferences about levels of proficiency and inferences about gains, invalid.

Note that this score inflation did not require that the tested words be unimportant. Score inflation arises when performance on the tested sample increases substantially more than proficiency in the domain about which inferences are drawn, even if the tested sample comprises important content. It is for this reason that alignment is insufficient to guard against inflation. We will return to this after showing some real examples of score inflation.

Real Examples of Score Inflation

Although the hypothetical example above is contrived, it accurately represents some of the ways in which test-based accountability can lead to deceptively large gains in scores. Only a handful of empirical studies have evaluated the validity of score gains under high-stakes conditions, but they have usually found severe inflation.

The first study to evaluate score inflation empirically (Koretz, Linn, Dunbar, & Shepard, 1991) looked at a district testing program in the 1980s that used commercial, off-the-shelf, multiple-choice achievement tests. By the standards of the day, the program was moderately high-stakes, although by the standards of 2004, it was quite low-stakes. The system entailed pressure and publicity but no concrete sanctions or rewards for test scores.

Through 1986, the district used one of the major tests of this type, indicated by the diamond for 1986 and labeled "first district test" in Figure 1. During the years before 1986, not shown in Figure 1, scores on this test had risen substantially. By 1986, the average mathematics score of third graders in the district had reached a grade equivalent (GE) of 4.3. GEs show performance in terms of the point in schooling at which a score is typical, measured in academic years and months (with 10 months per academic year). These students were tested in the seventh month of third grade, so if they had achieved at the typical level for students at their point in schooling, they would have attained an

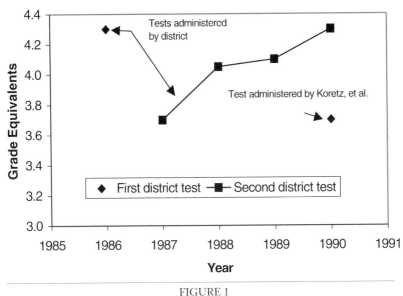

FIGURE 1

An example of score inflation on a moderate-stakes multiple-choice test.

average GE of 3.7. Instead, they achieved an average score equivalent to that reached by the typical (median) student in the third month of fourth grade nationwide. In other words, their scores made them appear to be half an academic year above average—a good showing, given that the district enrolled many poor and minority students.

In 1987, the district switched to a competing test, and scores dropped by half an academic year. Now their average GE was 3.7, exactly typical of the nation as a whole. Over the next three years, the district's average score on the new test rapidly climbed, reaching in 1990 the same level observed on the old test in 1986. This trend is shown by the squares in Figure 1 and is labeled "second district test." This "sawtooth" pattern—a large drop in scores when a new test is introduced, followed by rapid gains to a level similar to that before the change—is common and well documented (e.g., Linn, 2000; Linn et al., 1990).

In the Koretz et al. (1991) study, randomly selected classrooms were administered one of a variety of other tests in addition to the district's current test in 1990. The largest sample of classrooms was administered exactly the same test that had been used by the district through 1986.

The scores of this set of classrooms—randomly selected and therefore representative of the entire district—are shown by the diamond labeled with "test administered by Koretz et al." in Figure 1. The performance of students on this test had dropped by half an academic year since the district had switched tests and was essentially identical to the performance students had shown on the second test when it was first administered in 1987.

Regardless of the test used, students scored half a year lower on a test that was unexpected than on a test for which teachers had time to prepare. It does not seem that the second test was harder, or that it contained new material and that student performance improved as students mastered this additional material. Rather, what appears to have happened is that students and teachers *substituted* mastery of material emphasized on the second test for mastery of material emphasized on the first test. Achievement was *transferred* among material sampled from the domain for the two tests. Unless one could argue that the material given more emphasis was much more important than that which was deemphasized, this represents score inflation.

Similar patterns have been shown by a number of other studies (e.g., Jacob, 2002; Klein, Hamilton, McCaffrey, & Stecher, 2000; Koretz & Barron, 1998). Typically, gains on high-stakes tests have been three to five times as large as gains on other tests (such as the National Assessment of Educational Progress) with low (or lower) stakes, and in numerous cases, large gains on high-stakes tests have been accompanied by no gains whatever on lower-stakes tests. Moreover, the problem is not confined to commercial, off-the-shelf, multiple-choice tests. It has appeared as well with standards-based tests and with tests using no multiple-choice items.

Score Inflation, Teacher Behavior, and Alignment

Although the vocabulary example above illustrates a mechanism of score inflation, it oversimplifies the problem. A more detailed framework is needed to show the several ways in which scores can become inflated, to link these to teachers' responses to testing, and to clarify what must be done to avoid inflation, even when tests are aligned with standards.[1]

To evaluate the validity of score gains obtained under high-stakes conditions, one needs to examine the specific sources of gains in scores and compare these to the improvements that users of scores infer from the gains. To the extent that improvements reflected in the test score signify commensurate improvements in the aspects of performance about which inferences are drawn, the inferences are valid. In the above example, the sources of gains were the specific words, fewer than 40 in total, that students learned as a result of the intervention. The intended inference, however, referenced 17,000 words, not 40, and the gains in scores would have justified an inference about improved vocabulary only if they signaled a broad increase.

To put this more formally, Koretz, McCaffrey, and Hamilton (2001) suggested thinking of both scores and the inferences based on them in terms of *performance elements*. This term refers to all of the aspects of performance that underlie both performance on a test and inferences based on it. Some of these performance elements are substantive and are intended to represent the domain about which inferences are drawn. An example would be the specific words you decided to include on your vocabulary test. Others are not substantively important but may none-theless have a substantial impact on performance. For example, the choice of item format or scoring rubric may influence performance, even when those choices are not dictated by the test's intended inferences. Decisions of format may go far beyond the choice between multiple-choice and constructed response. For example, one might present an algebra problem verbally, algebraically, graphically, or even pictorially (see Figure 2). In some cases, the choice among these presentations may be substantive, in the sense of being tied to the intended inferences, but in many cases it will not be, and it may influence scores regardless.

Any test will assign weights—that is, relative importance—to these performance elements. For example, the more items on a test that measure a given element, the more impact performance on that element will have on a student's test score. However, these weights may not be entirely intentional, and they may not entirely reflect the emphases in state standards, even when the test is well designed. One reason is that a given test item may require various knowledge and skills to solve. A clear example arose some years ago when the author and several col-leagues were asked to review a pilot form of a state's new ninth-grade mathematics test. A sizable percentage of items required facility with coordinate geometry, even though this was not specifically mentioned in the state's standards. The test developers had not misread the stan-dards. Coordinate geometry can be a good way to present topics in basic algebra that were emphasized by the state's standards. The developers had made use of this fact and, in so doing, had inadvertently given a very high weight to coordinate geometry. This sort of inadvertent emphasis can be a key to score inflation.

Use the balance scales below to answer the question below.

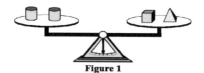

Figure 1

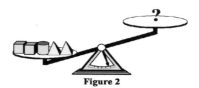

Figure 2

How many cylinders must be placed on the empty side of the second scale to make that scale balance?

A. 5   B. 2   C. 3   D. 4

FIGURE 2

An eighth-grade question from the Massachusetts MCAS test (Massachusetts Department of Education, 2000).

Similarly, users assign weights to performance elements in drawing inferences from test scores, even though these weights are typically not explicit. For example, in reading that tenth-grade scores in mathematics improved, many users will infer that this represents improvement in secondary-school material, such as algebra, but not in very basic elementary-school material, such as subtraction.

The validity of gains can be expressed in these terms. Users will infer from an increase in scores some weighted improvement in performance on a collection of elements, many of which will not be included in the test—just as most words were not included in the vocabulary test used as an example earlier. To the extent that the increase in performance on tested elements warrants this inference, it is valid. But if the increases on tested elements do not signify an increase in performance on many elements given substantial weight by the users of scores—as was the case in the example above—then the inference about improvement is not warranted, and scores have become inflated.

Forms of Test Preparation

To understand how these considerations play out in actual practice and how they relate to alignment, we will consider a variety of ways in which teachers may prepare students for a high-stakes test. Note that in this discussion, we deliberately avoid some common ways of categorizing these responses. The term "test preparation" is often used pejoratively to refer to inappropriate forms of test preparation. However, in this discussion, the term has only its literal meaning: all of the methods (whether desirable or undesirable) that teachers use to prepare students for a test. In this discussion, we also avoid the common distinction between "teaching to the test" and "teaching the test," where the latter refers to teaching the exact items on the test and the former refers to desirable forms of test preparation. We find this usage more confusing than helpful because it mischaracterizes as a dichotomy a continuum of behaviors, many of which, beyond teaching the actual items, have the potential to inflate scores.

A number of forms of test preparation may produce unambiguous, meaningful gains in performance. Teachers may work harder, for example, or they may find ways to teach more effectively. They may also teach more, for example, by providing remedial instruction outside of regular school hours. These are the sorts of responses that proponents of test-based accountability envision.

At the other extreme, teachers (or students) may cheat. For example, teachers may provide students with advance access to test items, provide inappropriate assistance during the testing session, or even change incorrect answers after the fact. Whatever the form and whatever the motivation, cheating by its very nature cannot produce meaningful gains in scores.

More interesting and more problematic is the gray area between these two extremes. The responses in this gray area might produce meaningful gains, score inflation, or both. Therefore, these responses are the most difficult to address and warrant the most careful attention. Following Koretz et al. (2001), we distinguish between three types of responses that fall into this gray zone: *reallocation*, *alignment*, and *coaching*.

Reallocation. Reallocation refers to shifts in instructional resources among the elements of performance. Research has shown that when scores on a test are important to teachers, many of them will reallocate their instructional time to focus more on the material emphasized by the test (e.g., Koretz, Barron, Mitchell, & Stecher, 1996; Shepard & Dougherty, 1991). The resources that are reallocated are not necessarily limited to instructional time. They include all of the resources that parents, students, teachers, and administrators can allocate among elements of performance. Many observers believe that reallocation is among the most important factors causing the sawtooth pattern shown in Figure 1.

Reallocation *transfers* achievement among elements of performance. These transfers can have a variety of effects on scores and on the validity of inferences about gains, depending on both the characteristics of the test and the nature of the performance elements that receive both increased and decreased emphasis in instruction. Clearly, if the test leads educators to stress material that is not important for the main intended inferences (as might happen if the test were poorly aligned), an increase in scores is likely to represent score inflation. However, reallocation can lead to inflation even if the test and the resulting instruction focus on important material. For example, suppose that teachers increase emphasis on tested elements but do not change their emphasis on other elements that are important for inferences but are given little or no weight by the test. In such a case, real achievement would increase, but far less than scores would, because the increase on the tested elements would overstate the increase across the whole domain. This would be analogous to our vocabulary example. More likely, given the time constraints confronting teachers, is that an increase in emphasis on the tested elements would lead to a decrease in emphasis on other, untested elements. If some of these untested elements are important for the intended inferences, then the increase in scores could mask either no change or an actual decrease in mastery of the domain the test is supposed to represent. This sort of reallocation could account for the results of the experiment shown in Figure 1.

When reallocation inflates scores, it does so by making the score created from the tested elements unrepresentative of the domain about which inferences are drawn. However, it does not bias a student's performance on the individual elements. Their improved performance on those particular elements is real, but just like the improved performance of students on the words included in our hypothetical vocabulary test, this does not indicate a similar improvement of mastery of the entire domain.

Alignment. Content and performance standards comprise material—performance elements, in the terminology used here—that someone (not necessarily the ultimate user of scores) has decided are important. If material is emphasized in the standards, that implies that users should give this material substantial weight in the inferences they draw about student performance. Alignment gives this same material high weights in the test as well.

Alignment between tests and standards affects scores when teachers in turn align their instruction with the test. This alignment of instruction with the test is simply a special case of reallocation, and the conditions under which it will cause meaningful gains or score inflation are the same as in any other case of reallocation. That is, the issue is not merely the importance of the elements that receive greater instructional emphasis as a result of alignment. It is also essential to consider the material that receives either constant or decreased emphasis. No matter how well aligned, most tests can cover only a sample of the material implied by the standards and important for inferences based on scores. Therefore, alignment of instruction with the test is likely to produce incomplete alignment of instruction with the standards, even if the test is aligned with the standards. If performance on the elements omitted from or deemphasized by the test stagnates or deteriorates while performance on the emphasized elements improves, scores will become inflated. That is, scores will increase more than actual mastery of the content standards.

Coaching. The term "coaching" is used in a variety of different ways in writings about test preparation. Here it is used to refer to two specific, related types of test preparation, called substantive and non-substantive coaching.

Substantive coaching is an emphasis on narrow, substantive aspects of a test that capitalizes on the particular style or emphasis of test items. The aspects of the test that are emphasized may be either intended or unintended by the test designers. For example, in one study of the author's, a teacher noted that the state's test always used regular polygons in test items and suggested that teachers should focus solely on those and ignore irregular polygons. The intended inferences, however, were about polygons, not specifically regular polygons.

Substantive coaching shades into both reallocation and cheating. Several years ago, an article in the *Washington Post* reported the following example of test preparation provided by the district office in Montgomery County, Maryland, a wealthy and high-achieving district outside of Washington:

The question on the review sheet for Montgomery County's algebra exam [provided by district officials] reads in part: "The average amount that each band member must raise is a function of the number of band members, b, with the rule f(b) = 12,000/b." The question on the actual test reads in part: "The average amount each cheerleader must pay is a function of the number of cheerleaders, n, with the rule f(n) = 420/n." (Strauss, 2001, p. A09)

One might reasonably argue whether this is substantive coaching, as defined here, or simple cheating, but in either case, any resulting increase in scores was almost certainly inflated.

Nonsubstantive coaching refers to the same process when focused on nonsubstantive aspects of a test, such as characteristics of distractors (incorrect answers to multiple-choice items), substantively unimportant aspects of scoring rubrics, and so on. Teaching test-taking tricks (process of elimination, plug-in, etc.) can also be seen as nonsubstantive coaching. In some cases—for example, when first introducing young children to the op-scan answer sheets used with multiple-choice tests— a modest amount of certain types of nonsubstantive coaching can increase scores and improve validity by removing irrelevant barriers to performance. In most cases, however, it either wastes time or inflates scores.

Coaching differs from reallocation and alignment in the mechanism of score inflation. Recall that reallocation and alignment inflate scores by making the tested elements unrepresentative of the domain as a whole, without biasing estimates of performance on individual elements. In contrast, coaching does bias performance on individual elements.

Conclusion

Despite its benefits, alignment is not a guarantee of validity under high-stakes conditions. Even with superb alignment, the unavoidable incompleteness of tests makes them vulnerable to the inflationary effects of reallocation, of which alignment is a special case. Moreover, alignment offers no protection against the corrupting effects of coaching.

These facts are neither an argument against alignment nor justification for throwing one's hands up in despair. Rather, they indicate that regardless of alignment, policymakers designing test-based educational accountability systems face two fundamental challenges:

- evaluating the validity of observed score gains; and
- tuning the system to create the right mix of incentives and thereby minimize score inflation.

Evaluating the Validity of Score Gains

Research to date makes clear that score gains achieved under high-stakes conditions should not be accepted at face value. The same is true of apparent improvements in historic achievement gaps between groups, such as racial/ethnic groups. The sawtooth pattern widely observed when new tests are introduced—even tests without very high stakes—casts doubt on the meaningfulness of the large initial gains that often accompany the implementation of new testing programs. Investigations of score gains under high-stakes conditions, although as yet few in number, consistently show large inflation, in some cases dwarfing the meaningful, generalizable improvements in student performance. This inflation creates an illusion of overall progress and can be misleading in other ways as well. For example, variations in the amount of inflation can incorrectly suggest that some programs or schools are more effective than others.

In response to this uncertainty, policymakers should institute regular monitoring and evaluation of the validity of score gains achieved in high-stakes systems and should resist the temptation to take score increases at face value. This can be done by means of a combination of redesign of tests (e.g., by deliberately adding items that are sufficiently novel to thwart coaching) and occasional larger-scale evaluations. This monitoring and evaluation is the only way to provide the public, policymakers, and educators with trustworthy information about the condition of education. While this would be a fundamental and somewhat burdensome change in practice, it would merely bring educational policy into line with practice in numerous other areas of public policy. In many other areas—for example, the evaluation of the safety and efficacy of drugs—it is widely taken as a given that the public is owed a rigorous evaluation of policies and activities that have potentially serious effects on its well-being. Given the power of high-stakes testing, the students, parents, and educators who are subject to it deserve the same.

Generating the Best Incentives

In many quarters, enthusiasm for test-based accountability appears to rest on a very simple model of incentives. If the system measures what is valuable (hence the importance of alignment) and rewards and punishes educators and sometimes students for their degree of success in producing it, students and teachers will be motivated to produce.

It now seems clear that this model is too simple and that merely holding teachers accountable for increases in scores runs the risk of creating the wrong mix of incentives (Koretz, 2003). The fact of score inflation is one indication of this. In addition, a number of studies have documented a variety of undesirable responses to test-based accountability (for a brief review, see Stecher, 2002). Thus, even in a well-aligned system, policymakers still face the challenge of designing educational accountability systems that create the right mix of incentives—incentives that will maximize real gains in student performance, minimize score inflation, and generate other desirable changes in educational practice.

This is a challenge in part because of a shortage of relevant experience and research. The nation has been so confident in simple test-based accountability—more specifically, so certain that it would work as desired if we could only find a "test worth teaching to"—that more complex and potentially more successful models have not been widely tried or evaluated. Thus, policymakers embarking on an effort to create a more effective system less prone to the drawbacks of simple test-based accountability must face uncertainty about how well alternatives will function in practice and should be prepared for a period of evaluation and mid-course correction.

With that caveat, however, several steps seem potentially helpful.

Evaluating Gains

In addition to its other benefits, evaluating score gains may be one of the most practical ways to improve the incentives created by test-based accountability. By identifying particularly severe score inflation, evaluation of gains would lessen the incentives to engage in the forms of test preparation most likely to produce it. Moreover, it might generate a more productive debate among educators and policymakers about the appropriate ways to respond to accountability.

Redesigning External Tests

Currently, the design of the tests used in accountability systems is guided by both traditional psychometric concerns, such as reliability and freedom from apparent bias, as well as the desire for alignment. The risk of undesired responses to testing might be lessened if the factors that facilitate both coaching and undesirable reallocation were also explicitly considered in designing tests. For example, developers should be alert to unnecessary recurrent patterns in content or presentation, to inadvertent overweighting of performance elements, and to omissions of elements with substantial importance to users' inferences. If teachers and test-preparation companies can find these patterns, so can test developers and the policymakers who hire them. The goal of these additional steps in design would be to change the way teachers evaluate and respond to the test. For example, rather than seizing on something that had recurred as a basis for narrowing the curriculum, teachers might wonder whether something omitted in the past might replace something else that had appeared for several years. The financial and practical costs of these changes may be appreciable, particularly in an era when the capacity of the testing industry is badly stretched. In addition, this approach poses technical issues in maintaining comparability over time. Nonetheless, this may prove to be an essential step in combating unwanted narrowing of the curriculum and score inflation.

Setting Attainable Performance Targets

Currently, the establishment of performance targets is arbitrary. States set their "Proficient" standard by whatever means they choose, and the rate of increase required of schools is then set formulaically by law. Rarely is there any consideration of research or historical evidence about the magnitude or rate of improvement that is reasonable to expect. Moreover, the rate of improvement can vary over time only within limits established by law. In some cases, this results in targets that are simply unrealistic.

Research has yet to clarify how variations in the performance targets set for schools affect the incentives faced by teachers and the resulting validity of score gains. One argument is that there is no harm in setting targets that are too high; the reasoning is that in striving for these unreachable targets, teachers will effect smaller but nonetheless important improvements. The counterargument is that because teachers can take shortcuts and create large gains in scores without improving student performance, excessively high targets will only increase the incentives to do so. In terms of research, the jury is still out, but the accumulating evidence on teachers' responses to test-based accountability (Stecher, 2002) and on the validity of score gains on high-stakes tests suggests that there may be serious risks in setting targets too high.

Relying on Multiple Measures

It is axiomatic in the field of measurement, if often ignored in practice, that important decisions should not be based on a single test score. The traditional reason for avoiding reliance on a single measure is the risk of incorrect decisions stemming from measurement error and the unavoidable incompleteness of any test. In the present context, however, there is an additional reason: relying on a single measure can exacerbate undesirable incentives (Koretz, 2003) and hence exacerbate score inflation.

Federal and state policies are beginning to reflect this axiom in calling for the use of multiple measures, but efforts to do so to date are generally limited, for example, adding one or a few measures of dropout and retention rates to a system that places primary emphasis on test scores. Again reflecting a lack of experience, the field can offer only limited guidance about how best to make more ambitious and effective use of multiple measures. However, this is an area of potentially great promise, and innovative efforts, coupled with rigorous evaluation, are warranted.

Reestablishing a Role for Professional Judgment

The test-based accountability systems of today are designed to be judgment-free. The systems produce a set of numbers by which anyone, including people with no knowledge of the nature or context of a given school, can supposedly judge a school to be sufficiently effective or not. Some observers attribute this design to a distrust of the educational establishment among many policymakers, but even absent such distrust, many observers would prefer to base a system on objective measures of performance than on more easily distorted and often more expensive subjective measures.

Economists, however, have long recognized that the choice between objective and subjective measures is a complex one. Derek Neal, in a recent paper that considers how accountability systems might be designed to respond to the problem of inflated test scores, noted "straightforward incentive systems based on objective standards are often problematic because objective performance standards are often easy to game" (Neal, 2002, p. 36). The inflation of scores discussed here is just one example of this gaming. Neal argued that for this reason, professionals in fields other than education rarely face incentives based on "simple formulae tied to an objective performance standard" (Neal, 2002, p. 37). But he also noted a difficulty in relying instead on subjective measures in public employment: in the public sector, the managers responsible for the evaluations lack any financial stake in the evaluation and therefore may feel freer to bias the evaluation for inappropriate reasons.

Despite this tension, policymakers may find in the end that they have little choice but to add measures based on expert judgment back into the mix for evaluating schools. These measures may be needed not only to avoid gaming the system but also to focus attention on the many critically important aspects of educational quality that cannot be captured by standardized tests, in order both to provide a better appraisal of schools and to give teachers a better mix of incentives to improve practice. Here again, however, policymakers must be prepared for a difficult period of experimentation, evaluation, and mid-course correction.

In sum, the design of an effective test-based accountability system that minimizes score inflation while maximizing beneficial changes in instruction and increases in student achievement remains a difficult challenge. Extant research is sufficient to suggest that the current, very simple approach is unlikely to meet its proponents' goals, but developing more effective alternatives will take us beyond what is well established and will require innovation, experimentation, and rigorous evaluation. Alignment, while important for many purposes, does not solve this problem for us.

NOTE

1. For a more detailed discussion of the framework described in this section see Koretz et al., 2001.

REFERENCES

Biemiller, A. (2001). Teaching vocabulary: Early, direct, and sequential. *American Educator*, *25*(1), 24–28, 47.

Cannell, J.J. (1987). *Nationally normed elementary achievement testing in America's public schools: How all fifty states are above the national average*. Daniels, WV: Friends for Education.

Jacob, B. (2002, May). *Accountability, incentives and behavior: The impact of high-stakes testing in the Chicago public schools*. Working paper W8968. Cambridge, MA: National Bureau of Economic Research.

Klein, S.P., Hamilton, L.S., McCaffrey, D.F., & Stecher, B.M. (2000). *What do test scores in Texas tell us?* Issue Paper IP-202. Santa Monica, CA: RAND. Available at http://www.rand.org/publications/IP/IP202/

Koretz, D.M. (1988). Arriving in Lake Wobegon: Are standardized tests exaggerating achievement and distorting instruction? *American Educator*, *12*(2), 8–15, 46–52.

Koretz, D. (2003). Using multiple measures to address perverse incentives and score inflation. *Educational Measurement: Issues and Practice*, *22*(2), 18–26.

Koretz, D., & Barron, S.I. (1998). The validity of gains on the Kentucky Instructional Results Information System (KIRIS). Report No. MR-1014-EDU. Santa Monica, CA: RAND.

Koretz, D., Barron, S., Mitchell, K., & Stecher, B. (1996). The perceived effects of the Kentucky Instructional Results Information System (KIRIS) (Report NO. MR-792-PCT/FF). Santa Monica, CA: RAND.

Koretz, D., Linn, R.L., Dunbar, S.B., & Shepard, L.A. (1991, April). The effects of high-stakes testing: Preliminary evidence about generalization across tests. In R.L. Linn (Chair) (Ed.), *The effects of high stakes testing*, symposium presented at the annual meetings of the American Educational Research Association and the National Council on Measurement in Education, Chicago.

Koretz, D., McCaffrey, D., & Hamilton, L. (2001). *Toward a framework for validating gains under high-stakes conditions*. CSE Technical Report 551. Los Angeles: Center for the Study of Evaluation, University of California.

Linn, R.L. (2000). Assessments and accountability. *Educational Researcher*, *29*(2), 4–16.

Linn, R.L., & Dunbar, S.B. (1990). The nation's report card goes home: Good news and bad about trends in achievement. *Phi Delta Kappan*, *72*(2), 127–133.

Linn, R.L., Graue, M.E., & Sanders, N.M. (1990). Comparing state and district test results to national norms: The validity of the claims that "Everyone is above average." *Educational Measurement: Issues and Practice*, *9*(3), 5–14.

Madaus, G. (1988). The influence of testing on the curriculum. In L. Tanner (Ed.), *Critical issues in curriculum. The eighty-seventh yearbook of the National Society for the Study of Education*, Part I (pp. 83–121). Chicago: National Society for the Study of Education.

Massachusetts Department of Education. (2000). Massachusetts Comprehensive Assessment System: Release of spring 2000 test items. Malden, MA: Author. Retrieved January 15, 2005, from http://www.doe.mass.edu/mcas/2000/release_na/98math_na.pdf

Neal, D. (2002). How would vouchers change the market for education? *Journal of Economic Perspectives*, *16*(4), 25–44.

Shepard, L.A. (1988, April). *The harm of measurement-driven instruction*. Paper presented at the annual meeting of the American Educational Research Association, Washington, DC.

Shepard, L.A., & Dougherty, K.C. (1991, April). Effects of high-stakes testing on instruction. In R.L. Linn (Chair) (Ed.), *The effects of high-stakes testing*, symposium presented at the annual meetings of the American Educational Research Association and the National Council on Measurement in Education, Chicago.

Stecher, B.M. (2002). Consequences of large-scale, high-stakes testing on school and classroom practices. In L.S. Hamilton, B.M. Stecher, & S.P. Klein (Eds.), *Making sense of test-based accountability in education* (pp. 79–100). Santa Monica, CA: RAND.

Strauss, V. (2001, July 10). Review tests go too far, critics say. *The Washington Post*, p. A09.

CHAPTER 6

Exploring Models of School Performance: From Theory to Practice

KILCHAN CHOI, PETE GOLDSCHMIDT, AND KYO YAMASHIRO

Our purpose in this chapter is to present and discuss competing accountability approaches, or models, designed to systematically indicate how a school's students are performing academically. Within the framework of the current federally mandated accountability legislation, increased interest in models measuring school performance has caused educational policymakers to consider several key issues. These issues include whether results from different accountability models yield different inferences about a school's performance, what assumptions underlie each of the models, how different models are implemented, and ultimately which model is best suited for a particular context.

We address these issues by building a framework for accountability models and then explicitly comparing and contrasting these competing models. In order to accomplish this, we first need to examine two distinct pieces of the larger puzzle. With the first piece, we briefly summarize previous research on school performance. This is done in order to ground all of the accountability models and provide some reference for considering how an accountability model might be con-

Kilchan Choi is a Senior Researcher and Project Director at the UCLA National Center for Research on Evaluation, Standards, and Student Testing (CRESST). Pete Goldschmidt is a Senior Researcher and Project Director at the UCLA National Center for Research on Evaluation, Standards, and Student Testing (CRESST). Kyo Yamashiro is a Research Analyst at the UCLA National Center for Research on Evaluation, Standards, and Student Testing (CRESST).

The work reported herein was supported under the Educational Research and Development Centers Program, PR/Award Number R305B960002, as administered by the Institute of Education Sciences (IES), and the U.S. Department of Education. The findings and opinions expressed in this report are those of the authors and do not necessarily reflect the positions or policies of the National Center for Education Research, the Institute of Education Sciences (IES), or the U.S. Department of Education.

structed. With the second piece, we present building blocks for accountability models. These building blocks include (1) important properties of assessments; (2) test metrics; (3) ways of summarizing student achievement; and (4) options for monitoring achievement growth over time, all of which need to be considered before they are incorporated into an accountability model.

Once we have the foundation and building blocks in place we can examine the continuum of accountability models, each of which results in a performance indicator. We consider the choice of model as lying on a continuum because accountability models range from simple calculations on the one end to complex statistical models on the other. At the complex end of the spectrum is a set of accountability models known as value-added models (VAMs), which we compare separately. We also compare inferences based on one of these VAMs against inferences based on current federally mandated accountability models.

Examining competing accountability models and linking them back to the foundations and building blocks lead to both theoretical and practical implications that are central in considering which model is most appropriate for a given physical or political context. One fundamental concern is whether the accountability model can accurately capture the academic progress of underprivileged students (e.g., low socioeconomic status [SES]), and by extension, underprivileged schools. Further, questions arise as to whether these students and schools can be compared fairly to more affluent students and schools. Based on this framework, we present empirical evidence on the effects of adjusting accountability models for student and school characteristics.

The chapter concludes with a brief summary and discussion of the salient issues surrounding accountability models.

A Framework for Accountability

Building a framework for accountability models requires us to briefly examine previous research on school performance. Divergent views persist on both what research methods and what research foci best capture school performance. Competing methods can be broadly categorized as qualitative and quantitative, while competing foci can be classified as emphasizing either school inputs or school outcomes. Inputs are factors such as the quality of teachers, the curriculum, and school policies and practices. Outcomes are often simply student assessment results. Both research methods and foci have implications for how an accountability model ought to be constructed. Part of the larger movement to align state policy and practice around high-quality content standards, the new accountability systems focus attention away from inputs and compliance to emphasize outcomes, or student performance on statewide standards-based assessments (Fuhrman & Elmore, 2004). From the beginning of the standards-based movement, many have argued that if assessments, professional development, and curriculum were all aligned to rigorous academic content standards, there would be more hope for equity in schools (Goals 2000; IASA, 1994; O'Day & Smith, 1993). Increasingly, large-scale test results have become the primary indicator for measuring the condition of public education and have become the symbol of the new accountability era (Elmore, Abelmann, & Fuhrman, 1996; Linn, 2000).

Not everyone agrees with this shift from inputs to outcomes. Many educators struggle against the reduction of their efforts into a single outcome indicator, contending that standardized tests cannot adequately or accurately measure school performance and arguing for multiple outcome measures. Some researchers strongly advocate for school accountability models that encompass a broader spectrum of indicators than just large-scale assessment results. Researchers argue for the need to monitor the quality and rigor of the academic curriculum, the safety and cleanliness of school facilities, and the equitable distribution of other resources, such as qualified teachers (Darling-Hammond, 2000; Oakes, 1989; Porter, 1988).

Despite the continued lack of consensus, current federal accountability legislation, as enacted by the No Child Left Behind (NCLB) Act of 2001, emphasizes a quantitative accountability model focusing on student outcomes. In this reauthorization of education funding for low-income children (Title I), the federal accountability legislation holds schools accountable for improving performance, as measured by their success in making adequate yearly progress (AYP) toward 100% proficiency by 2013–14 on standards-based assessment results in reading and mathematics. NCLB requires states to incorporate into their accountability systems specific testing requirements that include annually testing at least 95% of students in each numerically significant demographic subgroup in grades 3 through 8 and once between grades 10 and 12. Based on 2002–03 baseline data, states set specific annual targets that culminate in 100% proficiency by 2013–14. These intermediate targets vary from state to state. Meeting these annual targets, or making AYP, thus becomes the defacto accountability model for each state. Current NCLB legislation provides only one exception for schools that do not meet their annual AYP target, but demonstrate at least a 10%

gain in proficiency. These schools are considered compliant under the "Safe Harbor" provision.

The AYP accountability model is a high-stakes system that has several intended and unintended consequences. Novak and Fuller (2003) underline a statistical artifact of the construction of AYP, in that schools that are more diverse and serve greater numbers of disadvantaged students are penalized because they have a greater likelihood of failing to make AYP. Other researchers have criticized accountability-based test scores as highly susceptible to corruption when stakes are attached. This occurs through score inflation from familiarity with the test and a narrowing of the instructional focus by teaching to the test (Koretz, 1996; McNeil, 2000). In addition, calls have emerged from national education and civil rights groups to modify AYP to incorporate growth measures (Alliance for Fair and Effective Accountability, 2004; National Conference of State Legislatures, 2004). Many would like to explore alternative accountability models measuring school performance. This would be done either to validate results from the AYP model, as an alternative to the AYP model, or to more extensively and specifically explore aspects of performance that are otherwise not addressed by AYP (Council of Chief State School Officers, 2004). Questions currently raised regarding AYP point to the most salient issue with respect to all accountability models—do the results yield valid inferences concerning school performance?

Given that the current federal accountability model is based on quantitative evaluation of student outcomes, we focus our discussion on elements that should be considered in quantitative outcomes-based accountability models. By taking this route, we admittedly give qualitative methods short shrift. We do not, however, eliminate inputs from our discussion. In order to hold schools accountable for student performance, there is an implicit assumption that it is possible to isolate a school's effect from all other factors that might influence achievement (e.g., student background or inputs outside of a school's control). Without reliable and valid measures of both outcomes and inputs, attempts to estimate school performance will be limited and the inferences could be misleading.

Much of the school performance literature draws upon educational production function or school productivity traditions (Hanushek, 1979; Meyer, 1996). Underlying many of the models used in this type of research is the basic assumption that causal claims can be made about school performance. In other words, by evaluating school performance, we assume that it is possible to measure a school's quality or effectiveness—the causal effect of a school's practice on a student's achievement.

Results from accountability models are based on natural, quasi-experimental designs, yet these designs often suffer from confounded explanations for observed results. Some argue that we would actually need to randomly assign *schools* to various *practices or policies*, in order to adequately measure the causal effect of school policies and practices on achievement (Raudenbush, 2004b). This type of design would help to rule out rival hypotheses generated by potential confounding factors, such as the selection bias that might be present because certain kinds of students and teachers choose to attend or work in some schools over others (Campbell & Stanley, 1963). Still, there is some debate regarding experimental design and causal effects in education research; for example, whether random assignment is necessary and whether the design is appropriate to the research questions of interest and fitting the appropriate design to the questions of interest (Raudenbush, 2004a; Rubin, Stuart, & Zanutto, 2004; Shavelson & Towne, 2004).

Unlike some research on program effectiveness where experimental design is often controllable, large-scale school accountability evaluates school performance given the existing grouping of students and teachers in schools; hence, in this context, random assignment designs are, for the most part, moot. The approach since the late 1970s has been to use a regression-based analysis within a quasi-experimental framework in an attempt to disentangle student effects from school effects. In general, the idea is to relate current student achievement to the accumulated effects of student and family background factors, the accumulated effects of school inputs (e.g., class size, number of qualified teachers, percent of students qualifying for free lunch), and the student's innate ability prior to schooling effects (Hanushek, 1979). This approach is theoretically viable but empirically difficult because we would ultimately need an innate ability measure that is uncorrelated with schooling inputs (Griliches & Mason, 1972), which requires measuring ability before any schooling begins. These data are generally unavailable, since testing at early ages is not common and is not a popular concept with early childhood educators. Further, measuring the impact of the *accumulation* of student and family background, schooling, and other factors to a given time point is thought to be a highly imprecise endeavor.

The framework for accountability models implies that performance indicators must accurately reflect the school's ability to facilitate student learning through specific actions rather than merely reflecting the aggregated effects of student background. Previous research has identified specific student and school inputs that need to be considered, as well as limitations to causal claims that need to be heeded. This framework allows us to next consider specific building blocks of accountability models.

Understanding the School Performance Indicator Landscape

Many methodologists have written extensively about the relative strengths and weaknesses of various school quality indicators (Koretz, 1996; Meyer, 1996; Raudenbush & Wilms, 1995). We build on these arguments below to lay out the landscape of school performance—the proper measures, scales, summary statistics, and standards used to measure and judge school quality. Several preliminary criteria need to be taken into account with regard to test construction and inferences made from the test before adequate school accountability models can be developed:

- Does the test measure what it is supposed to measure (i.e., are inferences based on the test results *valid*)? How accurately, consistently, or precisely does the test measure the concept we believe is important (i.e., is the assessment *reliable* in measuring student learning)?
- Can results from the assessment be meaningfully aggregated from students to schools (i.e., if the test measures student learning, do aggregations to the school level reliably and validly measure *school performance or school quality*)?
- How are changes in performance over time measured? If the accountability system intends to measure performance or quality over time, do changes in school performance over time, as measured with results from this assessment, have meaning (i.e., do changes indicate *increases or decreases in school quality*, or do they merely represent changes in enrollment or in the scale of the test from year to year or grade to grade)?
- Should performance standards be set by some absolute or relative criteria or both?

These concerns will be discussed briefly below, though a complete treatment of these issues is beyond the scope of this chapter.

Test Construction and Metric Matter

Regardless of the perspective one takes on school performance, in a high-stakes accountability setting it is crucial that valid inferences about school quality can be made. Valid inferences from the results of any school accountability model depend on the data that go into the model. School accountability criteria are most commonly based on student scores on state-mandated assessments. Test results are considered *reliable* when the test in question repeatedly yields consistent results. Test results are considered *valid* when they measure what we think they are supposed to be measuring.

If results from a particular assessment are not reliable and do not generate results from which valid inferences about student achievement can be made, results will, at best, be misleading. In other words, an accountability model that is premised on standards, but selects an assessment that is not adequately aligned to standards or measures an uneven selection of standards, could falsely identify schools for doing a good or bad job of facilitating student learning toward that set of standards.

From this point forward, our discussion assumes that the selected test demonstrates reliable and valid results. Selection of such an assessment is an essential starting point for any accountability system. There are many metrics and scales to choose from when reporting assessment results: raw scores, percent correct, national percentile ranks, normal curve equivalents, and scale scores. Many of these metrics have very different qualities—qualities that impact our ability to average across students or to draw valid inferences about school performance. Further, accountability models that attempt to make inferences regarding student achievement growth over time must ensure that assessment results are meaningfully related across grades, so that the growth is also meaningful. Below we discuss the trade-offs of using some of the most common scales on which test results are reported for school accountability purposes.

Percentiles or National Percentile Ranks

Percentiles or National Percentile Ranks (NPR) perhaps represent one of the more familiar scales used in testing, since they are used in reporting on many of the national testing and certification programs such as the Scholastic Achievement Test (SAT) and the Graduate Record Examination (GRE). Percentiles measure a student's rank, or how well a student performed relative to a national population. A score placing a student in the 85th percentile, for example, indicates that he or she performed better than 85% of the students in the norming population; this provides that student with a ranking. One drawback often cited about percentile ranks is that they are not measured on an equal interval scale—meaning that changes at each point on the possible range do not represent equal changes in performance. In other words, a change from the 90th to the 91st percentile may be more significant (and more meaningful) than a change from the 50th to the 51st. Conducting calculations such as averages on percentile ranks across students in a classroom or school is considered inaccurate and inappropriate, because aggregating ordinal ranks is not a meaningful concept (Russell, 2000).

Normal Curve Equivalents

Averaging normal curve equivalents (NCEs) is more appropriate for school accountability purposes. This metric represents an equal interval scale, so that a change of one increment in one segment of the score range is just as meaningful or significant as a change in another segment. This allows for arithmetic calculations such as averaging to be more appropriate. Much like percentile ranks, NCEs are useful for making relative comparisons among students or schools. If the accountability system is designed to measure absolute changes in individual students' performance, however, NCEs are inappropriate because they are norm-referenced, which means they describe a relative position compared with a norming population.

Scale Scores

Scale scores are a conversion of raw scores placed on a scale that allows for averaging across students. If the focus of the accountability model is on ranking schools, NCEs and scale score results will be virtually identical (Goldschmidt, Choi, & Martinez-Fernandez, 2003). Scale scores, however, enable comparisons over time at the same grade level. So, for example, a 650 in the third grade this year is comparable to a 650 in the third grade the following year. This enables us to draw conclusions about whether a school's performance in the third grade is improving. We cannot unequivocally say, however, whether the results are due to the third-grade staff and instructional practices, or to the second-grade staff the year before, or to the fact that the group of students in the third grade came in more or less prepared than in previous years. One important caveat: a scale score is not necessarily scaled across different grade levels. This means that a five-point increase in scale scores on the third-grade test is not the same as a five-point increase on the fourth-grade test.

Ultimately, the optimal metric to use when examining change is a vertically equated Item Response Theory (IRT)-based scale score because it is on an interval scale and is comparable across grade levels and across time (Hambleton & Swaminathan, 1987). Thus, a change on a vertically equated scale score from one year to the next is an absolute measure of academic progress, irrespective of grade. Examining student achievement growth over spans longer than one grade level, however, can be difficult because equating is generally designed to compare contiguous grade pairs (Yen, 1986).

Despite the usefulness of scale scores, and the optimal qualities of vertically equated IRT-based scale scores, these metrics are far less prevalent than others mentioned here and are often not available to those who might benefit the most—school personnel. Assuming these types of metrics were made available for accountability systems by test publishers, however, one of the most important questions still remains: Can valid inferences concerning school performance be drawn from summaries of our measure of student performance? This can, in part, depend on how scores will be aggregated or statistically modeled. If the metric and test issues outlined above have not been adequately addressed, however, the methods discussed below for aggregating or modeling achievement will be extremely constrained.

Summarizing Achievement at the School Level

The next step is to define the model for aggregating or summarizing student-level test score information at the school level. We begin with two simple models of school performance summaries, both of which capture a snapshot of performance, are simple to compute, and are intuitively understood by the public: the percent proficient criteria and the average school achievement score. We highlight why these measures may be inadequate for measuring school performance. Following these models, we progress to statistical models that measure change in achievement over time, or VAMs.

Percent Proficient

Adequate yearly progress models of school performance across the country are based upon the percent proficient in a school, which essentially reflects the percent of students who have scored at or above a particular proficiency score. Though simple and intuitive, a percent proficient indicator is, in many ways, one of the weakest indicators of performance. Percent proficient is a status indicator, and primarily measures movement around a proficiency cut score. For example, if a student must score 680 on a test to be considered proficient, a percent proficient indicator is mostly measuring movement around that 680 score. Thus, students at the very bottom of the scale who improved from a 400 to a 600 would not count in this measure. Similarly, those students who fell from an 800 to 690 would not count in this model either. The percent proficient model misses a great deal of movement (both progress and regress) at other ends of the range, and is, for this reason, very limited. In addition, percent proficient scores—as with average or mean scores discussed below—are considered "contaminated" by prior performance and other confounding factors (e.g., student and family background characteristics, selection, etc.). This means that we have no way of separating out whether or not the high percentage of proficient students in a given year is due to the teaching and learning that happened in that year or to an influx of new, better-prepared students.

Average or Mean Performance

The school average (or mean) achievement level is another often-used measure of school performance. Similar to percent proficient scores, averages suffer from loss of information due to aggregation. In addition, averages tend to be contaminated by student background characteristics (e.g., disadvantaging schools with large populations of poor students; see Aitkin & Longford, 1986; Hanushek, 1979; Raudenbush, 2004b). As Table 1 indicates, based on correlations between school means from one year to the next, means are quite stable over time. However, it is important to note that a middle school's sixth grade average reading score is heavily influenced by how all of those students fared in their fifth grade classes the year before and/or whether those students came from families who read frequently at home. Back-

TABLE 1

CORRELATIONS OF MEAN SCHOOL PERFORMANCE BY YEAR

	Math 1994	Math 1995	Math 1996	Math 1997	Math 1998	Math 1999	Math 2000	Math 2001	Math 2002
Math 1993	0.96	0.91	0.89	0.87	0.90	0.90	0.88	0.88	0.87
Math 1994		0.94	0.92	0.90	0.92	0.91	0.90	0.89	0.89
Math 1995			0.93	0.90	0.91	0.90	0.88	0.87	0.88
Math 1996				0.96	0.93	0.90	0.90	0.87	0.89
Math 1997					0.94	0.92	0.91	0.89	0.89
Math 1998						0.97	0.95	0.94	0.93
Math 1999							0.97	0.95	0.94
Math 2000								0.96	0.95
Math 2001									0.96

ground characteristics may artificially inflate the year-to-year correlations and may have more to do with the stability of school populations than the quality of the school.

Aggregated, single-point-in-time status indicators that are not adjusted for confounding factors share a common weakness: changes in results from these models may have little to do with changes in school performance, per se, but may have more to do with changes in student populations. Adjusted (or conditional) means are a more precise model for summarizing school performance, but require statistical modeling in order to compare schools with similar conditions. Adjusted or conditional models of performance will be discussed further in the next section. Once a summary statistic is selected (e.g., adjusted means), questions still remain about how changes in these summary statistics will be measured and reported over time.

Tracking Changes in Performance Over Time

Assuming we agree on the test, the metric, and the summary statistic, those designing an accountability system must carefully consider how changes in performance over time will be taken into account. Detecting changes in school performance over time requires yet another set of considerations. Users of performance accountability information must first determine whether they believe that judgments about school performance should be based solely on a school's *status*—the level at which students are currently performing—or based on a school's *growth*—the improvements in students' performance over time—or based on a combination of both status and growth. For instance, the simplest model for tracking changes in performance over time has historically been to track a series of *status* indicators (e.g., school averages or percent proficient across multiple years). This type of "time series" data allows for trend data (from year to year) to be reported, but does not represent student growth, because individual students are not linked over time. Many of the concerns raised above still apply because the summary statistic chosen (e.g., unadjusted averages) is confounded by factors other than school performance. Time series data using adjusted averages would also be an option for tracking change over time.

However, other more sophisticated models use "panel data," which links individual students from year to year. This panel data enables longitudinal studies of student growth over time. Models that use growth based on individual student changes represent more appropriate ways of measuring change over time, and can control for individual differences over time as well. There are several ways of combining status and growth measures in one accountability system, though the intricacies of including both kinds of information is still a work in progress.[1] AYP is one such way, setting annual growth targets toward an absolute benchmark of 100% proficiency. It is important to note that although AYP tracks changes over time by setting intermediate targets, it is not a model that can accurately measure growth because changes are not based on the same individuals over time. In essence, AYP employs growth targets within a *time series* framework, carrying with it many of the drawbacks discussed.

Comparing Performance Standards

In order to make qualitative judgments about observed changes in performance, policymakers and practitioners must make clear choices about the standards they set for performance. Whether performance is measured based upon attainment at a single point in time or multiple time points, criteria for success (the performance standard) must be set. Should a school's performance be judged against an *absolute* standard of performance (100% proficient or, for example, a gain of 30 points or more), or based on a *relative* standard of performance (highest score among schools starting out in first decile)? Figure 1 compares many of the performance standards alluded to thus far. School A would be considered the top performer from an absolute *status* standard of performance, as well as relative to the rest of the sample, while School B would be the top performer from an absolute *growth* standard of performance, as well as relative to the rest of the sample. School C demonstrates the effect different standards have on judging school performance as it has relatively low status but relatively high gain. We would argue that *both* absolute and relative criteria are essential components to measuring and judging performance.

The kind of growth that we suggest is more appropriate for high-stakes accountability settings requires statistical models and falls under the general framework of VAMs.

Value-Added Models: Measuring Growth

Value-added models represent a specific subset of accountability models that provide estimates of students' progress over time. Student gains can simply be measured with *actual* gains between two time points on a given measure (e.g., student A's score in Year 2 minus his or her score in Year 1).[2] However, when student gains are summarized to the school level for estimates of school growth, this *actual gain* can be an

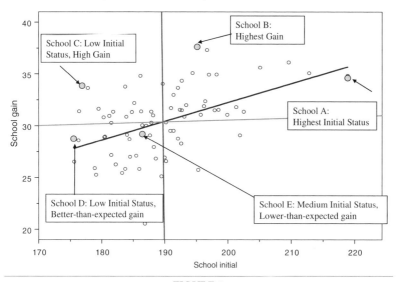

FIGURE 1

Effect of different criteria for determining school performance: school rank by different criteria.

1. Status (*x*-axis): A > B > E > C > D
2. Gain (*y*-axis): B > C > A > E > D
3. Conditional gain (regression line): B > C > D > E > A

Note that the vertical line and the horizontal line represent district average initial status and district average gain, respectively.

incomplete measure of school change because it ignores the nested structure of students within classrooms and classrooms within schools. For this reason, we define *school value-added models* to be regression-based models, *estimating* school gains between at least two time points, typically using multilevel models.[3]

Most VAMs either implicitly or explicitly compare a school's gain against other like, or similar, schools. Comparing "like with like" can mean that schools are compared with other schools that started out at similar levels of performance (e.g., those that start in the lowest 10%), or that serve similar populations of students (e.g., 85% English language learners). Many would argue that comparing "like with like" makes as much sense philosophically as it does methodologically (Goldstein & Spiegelhalter, 1996; Rumberger & Palardy, 2004). Researchers and educators alike acknowledge that adjusted models may be necessary to level the playing field (e.g., Good, Biddle, & Brody, 1975; Linn & Slinde, 1977; Thum, 2003a). To not use these adjustments in high-stakes accountability settings may risk exacerbating teacher and principal distribution issues. That is, highly qualified teachers and principals may stay away from "difficult" schools, knowing that they will not be adequately acknowledged for the difficult situation they are tackling. Further, the implicit assumption for all VAMs is that anything not explicitly accounted for in the model (e.g., background characteristics) will be absorbed in what is left over, which constitutes the value-added estimate. Leaving these characteristics unadjusted for would, in effect, "contaminate" the value-added estimate.

As an example of what we mean by comparing similar schools, if a given school's gain is higher than expected (e.g., higher than the average gain for all schools starting out at that same level), the school can be said to have added value, as exemplified by School C in Figure 1. Note under this criteria that School A is no longer a top performer. The concept that schools make gains but do not add value is not intuitive. We emphasize that schools add value when their gains are greater than a set criterion that can be either absolute or relative. Absolute criteria are those developed a priori, such as an external target; while relative criteria are data driven, such as the district average (the horizontal line in Figure 2) or regression-based expected gains (the fitted regression line in Figure 2). Without an external absolute standard for school gains and value-added estimates, deciding whether a gain is *sufficient* is difficult. More research on value-added standards setting is needed.

The simplest VAM—gain score—is defined below, with specific examples of more complex VAMs following.

Gain Scores or Adjusted Gains

We have defined VAMs to encompass those models that estimate gains through statistical modeling; this includes gain score and adjusted gain models. Both approaches model the outcome as a function of a set of inputs, which might include student or school background characteristics (if they are adjusted gains). Unlike a typical regression model where the outcome of interest is a score from a particular year, in gain score models, the outcome of interest is the change in scores from one time point to the next (Y_2-Y_1). Adjusted gains models are motivated by the aforementioned notion of comparing like with like and, as a result, the results provide a relative measure of gain, conditioned by the set of variables chosen for the model, such as student or school background variables or initial starting points.

Many believe—and studies have often shown—that there can be an important relationship between where a student starts out and how much he or she grows (see Choi & Seltzer, 2004; Muthen & Curran, 1997; Raudenbush & Bryk, 2002, chapter 11; Seltzer, Choi, & Thum, 2003). To address this relationship, some use the initial starting point as a predictor in the gains model. Using the starting point as a predictor raises some concerns, however, since Year 1 scores contain measurement error[4] and ignoring the measurement error leads to attenuated estimates of gains. This measurement error can be addressed through the modeling process.[5] Gain score models are perhaps the most common type of VAM. More complex modeling processes have also been employed in some high-profile settings in recent years; examples of such models are discussed below.

Examples of Current Value-Added Models

We present some of the strengths and weaknesses of commonly used VAMs and present empirical results from some of our own work in this area. Though the models below are more similar to each other than they are to, say, an AYP model, each has a slightly different focus and takes a slightly different approach to: what to adjust for and how; scaling issues and measurement error; assumptions about (linear) growth patterns; treating school effects as varying across schools or fixed; and how to represent cumulative effects of schools over time. We examine the following models and their approaches to addressing these modeling issues:

- Sanders's teacher effectiveness model (Tennessee Value-Added Model);
- McCaffrey's more general version of Sanders's model (RAND model);
- Chicago Public School Productivity model (CPSP);
- CRESST Student Growth Distribution model (CRESST Model).

Sanders's Model

This model—often referred to as the TVAAS, the Tennessee Value-Added Assessment System (Sanders, Saxton, & Horn, 1997)—incorporates multiple content measures as well as multiple cohorts and panel data (linked student data over time). It does not assume simple linear growth, and it implicitly adjusts for prior achievement by using the gain score method. That is, prior years' achievement is layered onto each subsequent year's achievement. As such, this model assumes that the effect of prior years' achievement remains stable as time goes by. Sanders's approach does not attempt to model the interaction between where a school starts and how much it grows. The model does not adjust for student background characteristics, though an extension of the model proposed by Ballou, Sanders, and Wright (2004) uses a two-stage procedure to adjust for differences in student and school background characteristics. Some of the challenges of the model are its tremendous requirements for data and computing capacity and its cost. Further, because the estimation procedures are proprietary, broader applications of this model are not currently possible.

McCaffrey et al.'s RAND Model

This model specifies a more general form of Sanders's model, that is, a multivariate, longitudinal mixed model that incorporates the complex nesting structure of student longitudinal data linked to teachers (McCaffrey, Lockwood, Koretz, Louis, & Hamilton, 2004). This model allows one to include adjustments for student and school characteristics. In addition, it does not assume that prior teacher effects are persistent or static (an assumption of Sanders's model), which allows us to test whether prior teacher effects differ from current teacher effects on current student outcomes and to what degree teacher effects fade with time. One of the shortcomings both in this model and in Sanders's model is that ranking teachers using this model is likely to be a challenge, because obtaining precise estimates of teacher effects requires a large data set (Ballou et al., 2004; also see Lockwood, Louis, & McCaffrey, 2002). The RAND study found that both McCaffrey's and Sanders's model identified only one-fourth to one-third of the teachers as distinct from the mean. This problem is, in part, due to the fact that the two approaches are modeling teacher effects, not school effects, and are therefore hampered by smaller sample sizes per classroom. The implication of these findings is that making distinctions between teachers based on their value-added estimates could be challenging. This model also does not address the interaction of where a school starts and how much it grows. In addition, wider application of this model could be limited by the complex estimation procedure used, model convergence problems, available software, and extensive computing time.

Chicago Public School Productivity Model

This model uses a "productivity profile" for the Chicago Public Schools, in which initial status trends (input trends) and gain trends (learning gain trends), as well as output trends (adding input and learning gain together), are estimated for each grade level (Bryk, Thum, Easton, & Luppescu, 1998). Productivity is judged by both the learning gain trend and the output trend, to address situations where gains are up but inputs and outputs are down (gap is spreading). One of the key strengths of the Chicago model is that the system is designed around a well-designed testing system (e.g., vertically equated test scores). This model does estimate both initial status as well as the gain, and can be applied to multiple subject areas and multiple cohort data. The model also explicitly takes measurement error into account. It is possible to adjust for student- and school-level characteristics. The model can be fitted using an accessible and well-known software program (HLM6; Raudenbush, Bryk, Cheong, & Congdon, 2004). However, this model does not specify modeling gain trends as a function of initial status trends.

CRESST Student Growth Distribution Model

The CRESST model uses latent variable regression in a hierarchical modeling framework (Choi, Seltzer, Herman, & Yamashiro, 2004; see also Choi & Seltzer, 2004; Seltzer et al., 2003). The key strengths of this model are that it estimates average school growth as well as the distribution of student growth within a school by explicitly modeling student growth as a function of a student's initial status. Modeling this relationship between where a student starts out and how much he or she grows allows us to provide complementary information about how equitably student growth is distributed within a school for particular performance subgroups (e.g., above or below average performers). Like the CPSP model, the CRESST model explicitly takes measurement error into account where standard errors of measurement are available. Similar to the other models here, the CRESST model can be extended to incorporate multiple measures and multiple cohorts; it is possible to adjust for observed student- and school-level covariates; and it is possible to adjust for student and school initial differences. Computation limitation with very large data sets might be a shortcoming of this model.

Two Empirical Studies

Below we present empirical results that address some of the more salient modeling and philosophical issues discussed above. The first study explores a comparison of results from status versus gains models, comparing performance classifications based on AYP results with those based on results from a VAM. The second study compares school performance results from an array of VAMs using different types of adjustments for background characteristics.

Comparing Performance Classifications Based on Status and Gain

We illustrate how results based on AYP and VAMs can differ based on an alternative way of measuring progress using the CRESST VAM as described in the previous section. We do so through analyses of a longitudinal data set from an urban school district in the Pacific Northwest. The outcomes of interest in this analysis are Iowa Test of Basic Skills (ITBS) reading scores for third graders in 2001 and those same students' fifth-grade scores in 2003. We examine what these growth patterns tell us about schools that meet their AYP targets and those that do not.

Our focus is to compare the state's AYP classifications (e.g., met or did not meet AYP) against the results that we obtained by fitting each school's data to the expected gains for each of the three different levels of initial status (i.e., expected gain for students 15 points below the school mean, expected school mean gain, and expected gain for students 15 points above the school mean). First, as can be seen in Figure 2, 15 schools among 51 schools meeting AYP (AYP schools) have an estimated gain that is smaller than the district average gain. Furthermore, among the remaining 36 schools, only 12 have gains that are statistically greater than the district mean gain. In contrast, almost half of the schools not meeting AYP (Non-AYP schools) (in Figure 3) have gains that are higher than the district average. Among those, we have two exceptionally well-performing schools. Schools 23 and 55 have gains that are higher than the district mean gain by approximately 5–10 points and are statistically greater than the district average gain. As such, we clearly see that there are remarkably large numbers of Non-AYP schools making sizable (and close to district average) gains.

Next, we compare AYP schools and Non-AYP schools based on the magnitude of the expected gain for students 15 points below and 15 points above the school average. Analyzing growth patterns among these subgroups allows us to note another trend, one that involves the closing or widening of achievement gaps. As can be seen in Figure 4, Type I schools show growth trajectories for the three performance subgroups that are parallel, meaning that all subgroups are growing at the same, upward rate. Type II and Type III schools show growth trajectories that either converge or diverge.

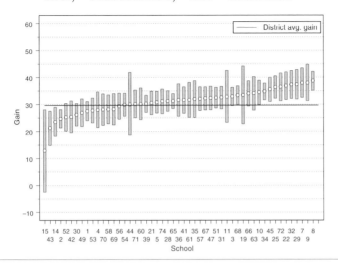

FIGURE 2

Expected mean gain in ITBS reading scores for AYP schools. The horizontal line represents the district average gain for our sampled 72 schools. The top line, middle circle, and bottom line of each bar represent the 95% confidence interval around the expected mean gain for a given school.

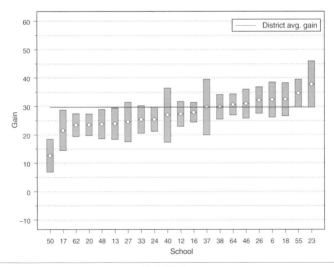

FIGURE 3

Expected mean gain in ITBS reading scores for Non-AYP schools. The horizontal line represents the district average gain for our sampled 72 schools. The top line, middle circle, and bottom line of each bar represent the 95% confidence interval around the expected mean gain for a given school.

In Type II schools, the initial gap between above-average and below-average students in the school closes over time, while the initial gap gets magnified in Type III schools. While this phrase is most often used to refer to the racial gap in achievement that exists in many schools, Type II schools in our sample are making progress in closing the gap between an important pair of subgroups—those who start out below average and those who start out above average. When evaluating a school's effectiveness or quality, however, it is difficult from an ethical point of view to choose the better of Type II or Type III schools. From a policy point of view, more resources and sanctions (e.g., through Title I, NCLB) are often targeted toward helping the lowest-performing students improve. Thus, it could be argued that those schools succeed-

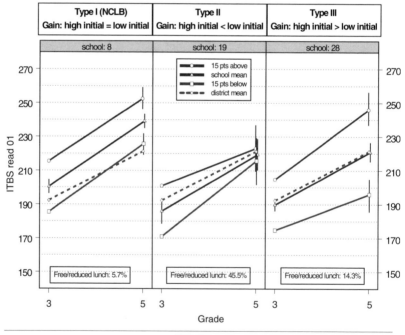

FIGURE 4

Distribution of student gain: Type I school: NCLB school with a substantial gain of more than 30 points across *all* performance subgroups. Type II school: Low adequate gain (less than 30 points) for students initially starting 15 points above the average, while substantial gain (larger than 30 points) for students initially starting 15 point below the average. Type III school: Low adequate gain (less than 30 points) for students initially starting 15 points below the average, while substantial gain (larger than 30 points) for students initially starting 15 points above the average.

ing with below-average groups (e.g., the Type II schools) are more successfully addressing the spirit of those legislative initiatives. Models like the CRESST model, which analyze different performance subgroups' growth, might be more effective in stimulating discussion among teachers and administrators to identify a school's success or weakness in addressing the needs of struggling students so that appropriate interventions can be taken (Seltzer et al., 2003).

Adjusting for Background Characteristics in Value-Added Models

We return to the issue of omitted variables and their effect on interpreting model results. Methodologists and education policy researchers continue to search for and debate the most appropriate ways to adjust for background characteristics. Some researchers describe the type of school effect measured in a multilevel setting in terms of adjustments made for school-level or student-level background characteristics (Raudenbush & Wilms, 1995; Wilms & Raudenbush, 1989).

We examined adjustment practices through a series of models, comparing the school performance results from each (Choi, Yamashiro, Seltzer, & Herman, 2004). The models included:

1. Three-level unconditional gains (no adjustment)
2. Adjusting for student initial status
3. Adjusting for student SES
4. Adjusting for student initial status + student SES
5. Adjusting for student initial status + student SES + school mean initial status
6. Adjusting for student initial status + student SES + school mean initial status + school mean SES.

Each model represents a step in adjusting for background characteristics. Models 2 through 4 are adjusting for only student background characteristics. In contrast, Models 5 and 6 are adjusting for not only student background characteristics but also for school contextual effects. Schools were ranked according to the gain estimated from each model and correlations were calculated across these rankings (see Table 2). The first model (Model 1, with no adjustments) serves as a reference point.

The correlations demonstrate several important findings about adjusting for student- and school-level background characteristics. First, adding in an adjustment for student SES (as measured by eligibility for free- or reduced-price lunch) adds very little once a student's initial status is controlled. The rank orderings from these two models

(Models 2 and 4) are perfectly correlated (1.00). This indicates that student initial status captures many of the effects that SES is attempting to measure. In other words, by controlling for initial status, the model already captures the preceding effects that SES might have on students. Once school-level contextual effects are added into the model (mean initial status and mean SES, as measured by percent qualifying for free- and reduced-price lunch), the rank ordering of schools in terms of their estimated gains differs significantly. After adjusting for the student-level characteristics (student initial status and SES), the school contextual effect of school mean initial status turns out to be insignificant, while the contextual effect of mean SES is significant. The correlations in Table 2 demonstrate this, as the results from adding in school mean initial status correlate highly (0.97) with results from the model without school mean initial status (Models 4 and 5); whereas, the results from the addition of school mean SES and initial status are not as highly correlated with the model with no school-level effects included (Models 4 and 6). Some researchers caution that adding in school mean SES may be overadjusting and removing some of the school policy and practice effects we are attempting to estimate (Raudenbush, 2004a). In summary, our data show that the choice of model matters. Results are sensitive to the type of school and student background characteristics adjusted for in the model and to how these adjustments are made.

TABLE 2

CORRELATION VALUE-ADDED ESTIMATES FOR DIFFERENT LEVELS OF ADJUSTMENTS

Model	1 No Adjustment	2 Student IS	3 Student SES	4 Student IS+SES	5 Student IS+SES & School IS	6 Student IS+SES & School IS+SES
No Adjustment	1					
Student IS	0.97	1				
Student SES	0.99	0.98	1			
Student IS+SES	0.95	1.00	0.97	1		
Student IS+SES & School IS	0.87	0.95	0.92	0.98	1	
Student IS+SES & School IS+SES	0.78	0.87	0.85	0.91	0.96	1

IS, initial status (initial starting point); SES, socioeconomic status.

Conclusions

In the current high stakes accountability environment, attention should be paid to the fact that, no matter what accountability model is chosen, performance indicators are merely *estimates* of true school performance. Using raw data to estimate school performance without adjustment produces misleading results. Estimates such as means, percent proficient, or raw year-to-year gain are unduly influenced by movement around the proficiency cut score or average, and can be attributed to chance or changes in enrollment, rather than true student achievement growth or school performance.

Within the context of a large-scale accountability setting, we believe that VAMs provide both the most informative and the most valid picture of school performance. Information gleaned from growth patterns based on individual students is more conducive to principal, teacher, or student use as formative and diagnostic tools about progress being made. Results of VAMs potentially lead to more valid inferences because they can account for differences in student initial academic status or other known achievement-moderating factors such as SES or language proficiency.

Despite the potential benefits of VAMs, there are still political and logistical obstacles to implementing these models. The most prominent political obstacle to value-added and longitudinal growth models is the NCLB emphasis on measuring school performance with a percent proficient indicator. Except for the Safe Harbor provision, the AYP model is not a true growth model, as it entails making a series of yearly static comparisons of actual to targeted proficiency levels.

The logistical obstacle is that most state assessment data systems are not currently designed to enable longitudinal analyses. Key features required to be in place, at a minimum, would be unique student identifiers to track students longitudinally; testing in multiple (if not all) grades per school level (elementary, middle, high school); vertically equated test scores (to compare scores across grades as well as over time); and consistency in testing from year to year (no changes in tests) and across grade and subject areas (no alternating between reading in grade 3 and math in grade 4). Although state assessment systems have not typically incorporated the key features needed to conduct longitudinal growth analyses based on individual gains, NCLB testing requirements will go a long way in bolstering state assessment systems in this regard.

Until the logistical challenges posed by the structure of state assessment systems and technical issues with regard to test construction are resolved, we suggest that models of school performance using adjustment factors outside a school's control (e.g., student background are preferable to models without adjustments. However, state and other advocacy groups should continue to insist that alongside status indicators, measures of growth (gains) should be incorporated into future accountability models. Combining or weighing results from different performance models (e.g., status versus gains) is no easy task. In addition, more work must be done on the development of performance standards, both absolute and relative. Policymakers and methodologists will need to work together to answer some of the technical and philosophical questions behind many of the questions raised in this paper, basing their conclusions on sound theory and a clearly defined purpose.

The technical differences between VAMs are important and may impact our judgments of school quality. The technical differences between VAMs are important, and may impact our judgments of school quality. However, these differences, and indeed the models themselves, can be confusing for policymakers and practitioners to understand and may turn them away from the many advantages these models have to offer. It is important to note, however, that the differences between these VAMs are much smaller than the differences between all VAMs and AYP models.

Making judgments about a school's quality should be done with much reserve and with great attention to how confident we feel about the measures, metrics, and models we have chosen to represent school quality. No single model will be able to address every possible concern; rather, judicious use of results from performance models allows us to look at what is surely a multidimensional construct—school quality—through a multidimensional perspective.

NOTES

1. Other methods involve statistical models that measure a school's or student's distance to target and calculate the probability of meeting the absolute target, given their growth to date (see Izumi & Doran, 2004; Thum, 2003b).

2. These actual gains are often described as the "unbiased estimate" of a student's gain in achievement (Bryk & Weisberg, 1976; Rogosa, 1995; Rogosa, Brandt, & Zimowski, 1982).

3. Multilevel decomposition of variance within and between schools is considered state-of-the-art by many researchers, given that it recognizes the nonrandom sampling within schools—that students in a particular classroom or school are more like each other than students in any other school in the sample.

4. Measurement error is the degree of uncertainty or variation we are likely to find in any measurement we take; test scores are no exception, since they represent an approximation of the skill or concept they are attempting to measure.

5. Some researchers do this through latent variable modeling, where the initial starting point is a latent variable, estimated within the model.

REFERENCES

Aitkin, M., & Longford, N. (1986). Statistical modeling issues in school effectiveness studies. *Journal of the Royal Statistical Society, 149*(1), 1–43.

Alliance for Fair and Effective Accountability. (2004, October 21). *Joint Organizational Statement on No Child Left Behind (NCLB) Act*. Message posted to http://www. childrensdefense.org/education/NCLB_joint_statement.pdf

Ballou, D., Sanders, W., & Wright, P. (2004). Controlling for student background in value-added assessment of teachers. *Journal of Educational and Behavioral Statistics, 29*(1), 37–65.

Bryk, A.S., & Weisberg, H. I. (1976). Value-added analysis: A dynamic approach to the estimation of treatment effects. *Journal of Educational Statistics, 1*, 127–155.

Bryk, A.S., Thum, Y.M., Easton, J.Q., & Luppescu, S. (1998). Assessing school academic productivity: The case of Chicago school reform. *Social Psychology of Education, 2*, 103–142.

Campbell, D.T., & Stanley, J.C. (1963). *Experimental and quasi-experimental designs for research*. Chicago: Rand McNally.

Choi, K., & Seltzer, M. (2004). Modeling heterogeneity in relationships between initial status and rates of change: Treating latent variable regression coefficients as random coefficients in a three-level hierarchical model. *Manuscript submitted for publication*.

Choi, K., Seltzer, M., Herman, J., & Yamashiro, K. (2004). Children left behind in AYP and non-AYP schools: Using student progress and the distribution of student gains to validate AYP. *CSE Technical Report*. Los Angeles: Center for Research on Evaluation, Standards, and Student Testing, University of California Los Angeles.

Choi, K., Yamashiro, K., Seltzer, M., & Herman, J. (2004, September). *Comparing like with like: The role of student and school characteristics in value-added models*. Paper presented at the Center for Research on Evaluation, Standards, and Student Testing (CRESST) Annual Conference, Los Angeles, CA.

Council of Chief State School Officers. (2004, November). *Brain trust on value added growth models*. Washington, DC, Author.

Darling-Hammond, L. (2000, January). Teacher quality and student achievement: A review of state policy evidence. *Education Policy Analysis Archives, 8(1)*. Retrieved October 10, 2004, from http://olam.ed.asu.edu/epaa/v8n1/

Elmore, R.F., Abelmann, C.H., & Fuhrman, S.H. (1996). The new accountability in state education reform: From process to performance. In H.F. Ladd (Ed.), *Holding schools accountable: Performance-based reform in education* (pp. 65–98). Washington, DC: The Brookings Institution.

Fuhrman, S.H., & Elmore, R.F. (Eds.) (2004). *Redesigning accountability systems for education*. New York: Teacher's College Press.

Goals 2000: Educate America Act of 1994, Pub. L. 103-227, 108 Stat. 125 (1994).

Goldschmidt, P., Choi, K., & Martinez-Fernandez, F. (2003). Using hierarchical growth models to monitor school performance over time: Comparing NCE to scale score results. *CSE Technical Report*. Los Angeles: Center for the Research on Evaluation, Standards, and Student Testing, University of California Los Angeles.

Goldstein, H., & Spiegelhalter, D. J. (1996). League tables and their limitations: Statistical issues in comparisons of institutional performance. *Journal of the Royal Statistical Society Series A, 159*, 384–443.

Good, T.L., Biddle, B.J., & Brody, J.E. (1975). *Teachers make a difference*. Lanham, MD: University Press of America.

Griliches, Z., & Mason, W. (1972). Education, income, and ability. *Journal of Political Economy, 80*(3), Part 2 (May–June), S74–S103.

Hambleton, R. K., & Swaminathan, H. (1987). *Item response theory: Principles and applications*. Boston: Kluwer.

Hanushek, E.A. (1979). Conceptual and empirical issues in the estimation of education production functions. *Journal of Human Resources, 14*(3), 351–388.

Improving America's Schools Act of 1994 (IASA), Pub. L. No. 103-382, 108 Stat. 4056 (1994).

Izumi, L., & Doran, H. (2004). *Putting education to the test: A value-added model for California*. San Francisco: Pacific Research Institute.

Koretz, D. (1996). Using student assessments for educational accountability. In E.A. Hanushek & D.W. Jorgenson (Eds.), *Improving America's schools: The role of incentives* (pp. 171–195). Washington, DC: National Academies Press.

Linn, R.L. (2000). Assessments and accountability. *Educational Researcher, 29*(2).

Linn, R.L., & Slinde, J.A. (1977). The determination of the significance of change between pre- and post-periods. *Review of Educational Research, 47*, 121–150.

Lockwood, J.R., Lewis, T.A., McCaffrey, D. (2002). Uncertainty in rank estimation: Implications for value-added modeling accountability systems. *Journal of Educational and Behavioral Statistics, 27*, 255–270.

McCaffrey, D., Lockwood, J.R., Koretz, D., Louis, T., & Hamilton, L. (2004). Models for value-added modeling of teacher effects. *Journal of Educational and Behavioral Statistics, 29*(1), 67–101.

McNeil, L.M. (2000). *Contradictions of school reform: Educational costs of standardized testing*. New York: Routledge.

Meyer, R.H. (1996). Value-added indicators of school performance. In E.A. Hanushek & D.W. Jorgenson (Eds.), *Improving America's schools: The role of incentives* (pp. 197–223). Washington, DC: National Academies Press.

Muthen, B., & Curran, P. (1997). General longitudinal modeling of individual differences in experimental designs: A latent variable framework for analysis and power. *Psychological Methods, 2*, 371–402.

National Conference of State Legislatures. (2004). NCLB Task Force Meeting, Portland, Oregon, October 10–11.

No Child Left Behind Act of 2001, Pub. L. No. 107-110, 115 Stat. 1425 (2002).

Novak, J., & Fuller, B. (2003). *Penalizing diverse schools? Similar test scores, but different students, bring federal sanction*. PACE policy brief. Berkeley: Policy Analysis for California Education.

Oakes, J. (1989, Summer). What educational indicators? The case for assessing the school context. *Educational Evaluation and Policy Analysis, 11*(2), 181–199.

O'Day, J., & Smith, M. (1993). Systemic reform and educational opportunity. In S. Fuhrman (Ed.), *Designing coherent education policy: Improving the system* (pp. 250–312). New York: Jossey-Bass.

Porter, A. (1988, March). Indicators: Objective data or political tool? *Phi Delta Kappan, 69*(7), 503–508.

Raudenbush, S.W. (2004a). What are value-added models estimating and what does this imply for statistical practice? *Journal of Educational and Behavioral Statistics, 29*(1), 121–129.

Raudenbush, S.W. (2004b). *School, statistics, and poverty: Can we measure school improvement?* Princeton, NJ: Educational Testing Service, Policy Evaluation and Research Center.

Raudenbush, S.W., & Bryk, A.S. (2002). *Hierarchical linear models: Applications and data analysis methods* (2nd ed.). Newbury Park, CA: Sage Press.

Raudenbush, S., Bryk, A., Cheong, Y., & Congdon, R. (2004). *HLM6: Hierarchical linear and non-linear modeling*. Homewood, IL: Scientific Software International.

Raudenbush, S.W., & Wilms, J.D. (1995). The estimation of school effects. *Journal of Educational and Behavioral Statistics, 20*, 307–335.

Rogosa, D.R. (1995). Myths and methods: Myths about longitudinal research, plus supplemental questions. In J.M. Gottman (Ed.), *The analysis of change* (pp. 3–65). Hillsdale, NJ: Lawrence Erlbaum Associates.

Rogosa, D.R., Brandt, D., & Zimowski, M. (1982). A growth curve approach to the measurement of change. *Psychological Bulletin, 92*, 726–774.

Rubin, D., Stuart, E., & Zanutto, E. (2004). A potential outcomes view of value-added assessment in education. *Journal of Educational and Behavioral Statistics*, 29(1), 103–116.

Rumberger, R.W., & Palardy, G.J. (2004). Multilevel models for school effectiveness research. In D. Kaplan (Ed.), *Handbook of quantitative methodology for the social sciences* (pp. 235–258). Thousand Oaks, CA: Sage Publications.

Russell, M. (2000). Summarizing change in test scores: Shortcomings of three common methods. *Practical Assessment, Research & Evaluation*, 7(5). Available at http://pareonline.net/getvn.asp?v=7&n=1

Sanders, W.L., Saxton, A.M., & Horn, S.P. (1997). The Tennessee Value-Added Assessment System: A quantitative, outcomes-based approach to educational assessment. In J. Millman (Ed.), *Grading teachers, grading schools. Is student achievement a valid evaluation measure?* (pp. 137–162). Thousand Oaks, CA: Corwin.

Seltzer, M., Choi, K., & Thum, Y.M. (2003). Examining relationships between where students start and how rapidly they progress: Implications for conducting analyses that help illuminate the distribution of achievement within schools. *Educational Evaluation and Policy Analysis*, 25(3), 263–286.

Shavelson, R.J., & Towne, L. (2004). What drives scientific research in education? *American Psychological Society*, 17(4), 27–30.

Thum, Y.M. (2003a). Measuring progress toward a goal: Estimating teacher productivity using a multivariate multilevel model for value-added analysis. *Sociological Methods and Research*, 32(2), 153–207.

Thum, Y.M. (2003b). No Child Left Behind: Methodological challenges and recommendations for measuring adequate yearly progress. *CSE Technical Report*. Los Angeles: Center for the Research on Evaluation, Standards, and Student Testing, University of California Los Angeles.

Wilms, J.D., & Raudenbush, S.W. (1989). A longitudinal hierarchical linear model for estimating school effects and their stability. *Journal of Educational Measurement*, 26(3), 209–232.

Yen, W.M. (1986). The choice of scale for educational measurement: An IRT perspective. *Journal of Educational Measurement*, 23(4), 299–325.

CHAPTER 7

Statistical Misunderstandings of the Properties of School Scores and School Accountability

DAVID ROGOSA

In public policy settings, statisticians constantly urge that the statistical uncertainty in relevant measures be reported and incorporated into decision making. Current work in educational assessment and school accountability provides a vivid instance of "be careful what you wish for" as, unfortunately, educational researchers' attempts to consider statistical uncertainty have caused serious missteps in the design and presentation of school accountability systems, in particular, the federal No Child Left Behind Act of 2001 (NCLB).

This chapter provides an overview of statistical issues arising in work on educational assessment and school accountability, organized around some of the most consequential misunderstandings. What are good descriptions of statistical properties (e.g., uncertainty) of school and subgroup scores? What are the consequences of the statistical uncertainty for school accountability systems? Solid answers to these questions would seem critical for sound and credible educational policy. Accountability is not a bad thing, but it can be done badly. A real threat to the viability of school accountability is the poor quality of technical work in educational research on the design and properties of accountability systems.

David Rogosa is Associate Professor, School of Education, Department of Statistics (by courtesy), and Department of Health Research and Policy, Division of Biostatistics (by courtesy) at Stanford University. Current statistical research activities include longitudinal research and educational assessment.

The work reported herein was supported under the Educational Research and Development Centers Program, PR/Award Number R305B960002, as administered by the Institute of Education Sciences (IES), U.S. Department of Education. The findings and opinions expressed in this report are those of the author and do not necessarily reflect the positions or policies of the National Center for Education Research, the Institute of Education Sciences (IES), or the U.S. Department of Education.

The chapter proceeds via a series of nine vignettes describing misunderstandings of statistical uncertainty in educational assessment and school accountability. The flow of the exposition is from assessments of the statistical uncertainty in a group summary (school-score) to the consequences of uncertainty for properties of accountability decisions to attempts to adjust accountability criteria for the effects of uncertainty. The first two vignettes describe misunderstandings of the accuracy of scores. The next three vignettes depict the consequences of statistical uncertainty for properties of accountability systems (including wayward claims of a substantial "diversity penalty" and "small school advantage"). The next set of three vignettes concentrates on the often-cited "margin of error" and its misapplication to accountability, as in the NCLB confidence intervals. The final vignette describes the frequent misinterpretation of correlation coefficients to indicate the strength of the relation between student demographics and educational performance.

Vignette 1. Volatility Scam, Part 1: Precision versus Reliability of a Group Score

An obvious starting point for properties of a school accountability system is the properties of a single-year school score. The school summary score constructed from the test results from the school's students can have a variety of forms: a composite such as the California Academic Performance Index (API) (ranging from 200 to 1000), the proportion of students scoring proficient or above that is used in NCLB, or an average national percentile rank as often reported for standardized tests. Each of these school scores (as with any measurement) contain statistical uncertainty, and one general message is that the accuracy of a measure should be judged by reference to the purposes to which the data are put, a common mistake being to ask too much of the data.

Claims of "volatility" in the school-level scores from testing programs by Kane and Staiger (2002) (also Linn & Haug, 2002, among others) represent a serious threat to defensible policy uses of test scores in school accountability systems. That is, if the volatility claims were true, then accountability decisions would not be credible. However, the misunderstandings of reliability versus precision for school scores render Kane–Staiger methodology and conclusions of no value (see Rogosa, 2002b, 2003a). Kane and Staiger use North Carolina and California data to demonstrate their volatility claims, with representative assertions:

We would infer that 14 to 15 percent of the variation in fourth-grade math and reading test scores was due to sampling variation. (p. 241)

We estimate that the confidence interval for the average fourth-grade reading or math score in a school with sixty-eight students per grade level would extend from roughly the 25th to the 75th percentile among schools of that size. Such volatility can wreak havoc in school accountability systems. (p. 236)

In reality, Kane–Staiger volatility is a disguised form of the reliability coefficient:

Kane–Staiger proportion of variance in group summary due to error
= 1 − reliability coefficient (of group summary).

Even using the Kane–Staiger criteria, the California data show little volatility. In terms of the California API using 1999 data, reliability coefficients for a population of schools of a specified size are given in Table 1 (c.f., calculations in Rogosa, 2002b, Section 1, 2002d). For median-size elementary or high schools less than 1% of the between-school variance in API scores is attributable to error. Moreover, for the single-grade results (and California does not report API scores by grade for reasons such as insufficient precision) that have relatively poor accuracy, little Kane–Staiger volatility would be seen, as the single-grade reliability coefficient is very high.

Further results reveal that Kane–Staiger methods and results err in both directions: Kane–Staiger methods find high volatility even when accuracy is very good, and Kane–Staiger methods determine the absence of volatility even when accuracy is moderate to poor. The primary misunderstanding is a confusion between the accuracy or precision of a school score (relevant to accountability) and relative standing measures such as reliability, which are irrelevant.

Technical Caricature

An artificial, analytic demonstration of the deficient properties of Kane–Staiger volatility methodology is taken from the caricatures in

TABLE 1
CALIFORNIA API RELIABILITY COEFFICIENTS

Elementary Schools		Grade 4		High Schools	
n	Reliability	n	Reliability	n	Reliability
150	0.982	68	0.965	500	0.991
350	0.992	79	0.970	1000	0.996
500	0.994	103	0.976	1500	0.997

Rogosa (2002b, 2003a). Start with a single year cross-section of perfectly measured school scores; "perfectly measured" indicates school scores with no statistical uncertainty, for example, schools composed of an infinite number of students with student test scores obtained from very long tests. For the population of schools, the distribution of true measurements for the collection of schools is specified to be Discrete Uniform [498, 502], that is, mass 1/5 at 498, . . . , 502. Thus, under perfect measurement the school scores would have mean 500, variance 2. The error process obscuring the perfectly measured score is specified to be the same for each school (assumption for simplicity; think of all schools being the same finite size). The error process is Discrete Uniform [−2, 2]; that is, this error process has mass 1/5 at −2, −1, 0, 1, 2, and thus the mean is 0 and error variance is 2 points. Consequently, in this caricature the standard error for a school score is 1.41, which appears small compared to the magnitude of the school score of 500. Another way of expressing the accuracy of the school score is in terms of a hit-rate: P{observed school score is no more than 1 point different from the perfectly measured score} = 0.6. (Note: the discrete distribution of the observed school scores for this population of schools has support on [496, 504] with distribution: Pr{school score = $500 + i$} = $(5 - |i|)/25$.) By these criteria a score for an individual school appears to be quite accurate.

However, the Kane–Staiger assignations of volatility use different criteria than accuracy of a school score. Over this collection of schools, the observed school scores have mean 500 and variance 4, and the reliability coefficient for the population of school scores is 2/4. Thus Kane–Staiger methodology would determine 50% of the observed variance to be due to error and would pronounce the school scores to be highly volatile. Furthermore, the Kane–Staiger explanatory vehicle of a confidence interval for the average school score would extend from the 15th to 85th percentiles of the score distribution (using interpolation, probability score 497 or less, probability score 503 or more both equal 0.12). (Note: Rogosa, 2002b, shows how this Kane–Staiger confidence interval is also expressed as a function of the score reliability coefficient.)

Vignette 2. Volatility Scam, Part 2: Consistency of Year-to-Year Improvement

Other venues for claims of volatility in school scores are year-to-year improvement and consistency of year-to-year improvement. As with the single-year school scores in the first vignette, the claims from the educational research literature of volatility in year-to-year improvement result from methodological misunderstandings: here, as simple as a failure to understand a basic property of the correlation coefficient, invariance under translation. The misattributions of volatility in year-to-year improvement are consequential for accountability because these misunderstandings have influenced NCLB discussions. In particular, the Council of Chief State School Officers (CCSSO; 2002) adequate yearly progress (AYP) report dismisses year-to-year improvement as an accountability criterion (see their Figure 4) because of "wide variability and lack of reliability (Kane & Staiger, 2002; Linn & Haug, 2002)" (p. 33) and "lack of technical merit" (p. 34). And recently many states have made unsuccessful initiatives for year-to-year improvement criteria in NCLB (c.f., O'Connell, 2004).

Linn and Haug (2002) present a correlational methodology for determining the "stability" or "volatility" of year-to-year improvement, and apply that methodology to school-level scores (successive fourth graders) from four years (1997–2000) of Colorado assessment data (CSAP). Linn and Haug heavily cite and build upon similar methodology and assertions of year-to-year volatility contained in Kane and Staiger (2002). A sampling of the assertions in Linn and Haug:

Year-to-year changes in scores for successive groups of students have a great deal of volatility. (p. 29).

It was found that the year-to-year changes are quite unstable. (p. 29)

The estimates of improvement, however, are quite volatile. This volatility results in some schools being recognized as outstanding and other schools identified as in need of improvement simply as the result of random fluctuations. (p. 35)

Similarly, the assertions of volatility in Kane and Staiger (2002) would seem to indicate a ubiquitous lack of consistency in improvement. In California, almost all improvement is found to be transient or "fleeting:"

Although the California schools tend to be larger, the data reveal slightly more volatility in the California Academic Performance Index for any given school size. For the smallest fifth of schools, the correlation in the change in adjacent years was –0.43, implying that 86 percent of the variance in the changes between any two years is fleeting. For the largest fifth of schools, the correlation was –0.36, implying that 72 percent of the variance in the change was nonpersistent. (pp. 248–249)

Rogosa (2003a) provides detailed analytic results on the deficiencies of the Linn–Haug and Kane–Staiger methodologies and also presents useful data analysis methods for consistency in improvement.

The Linn–Haug stability measure, denoted as r_{LH}, uses four successive yearly measurements to obtain a correlation indicating "stability in the two-year change scores" (Linn & Haug, 2002, p. 33). Similarly, the Kane–Staiger procedure uses three successive years of data to compute a correlational measure indicating "the proportion of the change in test scores that is attributable to nonpersistent factors" (Kane & Staiger, 2002, p. 247). The detailed definitions, using school scores $Y_s(1)$, $Y_s(2)$, $Y_s(3)$, $Y_s(4)$, are $r_{LH} = \text{Correlation}[Y(3) - Y(1), Y(4) - Y(2)]$, and for the Kane–Staiger proportion persistent (i.e., the proportion not nonpersistent for directional convenience) the measure $p_{KS} = 1 + 2r_{KS}$, where $r_{KS} = \text{Correlation}[\, Y(2) - Y(1), Y(3) - Y(2)]$. Technical results from Rogosa (2003a) reveal both stability measures to be functions of the reliability of the year-to-year difference score, and thus the volatility misunderstanding is another confusion between reliability and relevant properties.

Table 2 displays small examples (taken from Rogosa, 2003a) showing year-to-year improvement for a set of five schools, each with four years of test data. (Scores are in the California API scale, yearly scores on a 200 to 1,000 scale, and year-to-year improvement of 50 points is very strong. Alternatively, the reader can divide these numbers by 10 and regard these as improvement in NCLB proportion proficient on a percent scale so that improvement of 5% in percent proficient is strong

TABLE 2

FIVE SCHOOL EXAMPLES, MISUNDERSTANDINGS OF CONSISTENCY IN IMPROVEMENT

		School				
		A	B	C	D	E
I: Extreme volatility?						
Improvement	Year 1 to Year 2	40	40	50	59	45
	Year 2 to Year 3	50	40	40	41	45
	Year 3 to Year 4	50	50	40	49	45
IIa: Up-and-down, Kane–Staiger persistence						
Improvement	Year 1 to Year 2	40	40	50	50	45
	Year 2 to Year 3	−40	−50	−50	−40	−45
IIb: Up-and-down, Linn–Haug stability						
Improvement	Year 1 to Year 2	39	39	49	49	44
	Year 2 to Year 3	7	−3	−3	−1	2
	Year 3 to Year 4	−47	−54	−41	−36	−44

improvement). Two different configurations are shown (Examples I and II). In Example I each school has healthy improvement each year of approximately the same amount. School officials and parents in these schools would cheer. Yet, remarkably, Linn–Haug methods would determine 0% stability, 100% volatility for these school scores (r_{LH} = 0). Kane–Staiger methods, which use the first three years of data, would also determine extreme volatility as p_{KS} = 0.062, indicating 94% of change nonpersistent. An obvious question: If Example I in Table 2 represents "volatile," then can consistent, stable improvement ever be identified?

Example II in Table 2 shows that both Linn–Haug and Kane–Staiger methods can indicate strong stability, but not usefully so. In Example IIa of Table 2 the initial improvements from year 1 to year 2 are erased by the declines of year 2 to year 3, resulting in no overall improvement from year 1 to year 3. Yet Kane–Staiger methods would indicate 0% volatility ($r_{KS} = 0$ and thus $p_{KS} = 1$). In the Example IIb with four years of data, schools initially improve, then flatten out, and then decline, such that the overall improvement over the four years is exactly 0. Yet for these schools $r_{LH} = 0.977$, and thus Linn–Haug methods would determine great stability for these year-to-year improvements in school scores.

Even though the Kane–Staiger and Linn–Haug indices are not useful, the empirical research question of consistency in year-to-year improvement is important. The commonsense data analysis is to ask whether schools (or subgroups) whose scores improve over one year continue to improve (and how much). Demonstrations of consistency in improvement for California schools and disadvantaged subgroups are shown in Rogosa (2003a, 2003b). Here, consider the elementary schools in Los Angeles Unified (LAUSD). For the 418 LAUSD elementary schools in the four-year period 1999–2002, 406 improved their school API in 1999–2000 (median improvement 42 points), and the proportion of those 406 also improving in 2000–2001 is 0.938 (median improvement 37 points). For these 381 schools improving both in 1999–2000 and 2000–2001, the proportion of those also improving in 2001–2002 is 0.955 (median improvement 46 points). Furthermore, for the disadvantaged subgroups in concentrated poverty schools, 341 of the 353 subgroups improved their API in 1999–2000 (median improvement 43 points), and the proportion of those 341 also improving in 2000–2001 is 0.944 (median improvement 43 points). For the 322 disadvantaged subgroups improving both in 1999–2000 and 2000–2001 the proportion of those also improving in 2001–2002 is 0.972 (median improvement

50 points). The amount of year-to-year improvement is substantial, and slightly larger for the disadvantaged subgroups. In California, one aspect of the ongoing debate on school accountability was the contention, put forth by the California Teachers Association and others, that year-to-year improvement in API scores was well described by a "see-saw" metaphor, in that schools with scores that showed strong gains (and achieved awards) in one two-year cycle reversed those gains in the succeeding two-year cycle. The "see-saw" represents a legitimate empirical conjecture about (the lack of) consistency in improvement, similar to empirical conclusions voiced in Linn and Haug (2002), but that is a conjecture that is just not supported by these California data.

Vignette 3. Properties of Scores and Properties of Accountability Decisions

Understanding the accuracy of school or subgroups scores (or more to the point, not misunderstanding the properties) is an important first step, but far from fully informative about the properties of an accountability system. The standard error of a school score has some usefulness as a global indicator of statistical uncertainty. But the properties of scores and properties of an accountability system are (almost) two separate, but not separable, topics. Knowing standard errors does not directly reveal properties of an accountability system; it is better to have more precise scores, but properties can be good even in the face of some statistical uncertainty.

For descriptive purposes Table 3 provides some results for the California API in elementary schools (1999 scores). Results are listed by state decile with the s.e.(API) entry being the median standard error for the roughly 480 schools in each decile (more detail in Rogosa, 2002d), and with the bottom and top of each decile also shown. In addition to the obvious dependence of standard error on school size, plots in Rogosa (2002d) show substantial differences in s.e.(API) for schools of the same size, mainly a result of the additional dependence on the level of school's API score, seen in Table 3 as the largest values

TABLE 3

STANDARD ERROR OF CALIFORNIA ELEMENTARY SCHOOL API BY STATE DECILE

Decile	1	2	3	4	5	6	7	8	9	10
s.e.(API)	10.24	11.99	12.74	13.24	13.55	13.67	13.15	12.40	11.35	8.76
Min(API)	302	449	497	543	587	629	670	715	763	818
Max(API)	448	496	542	586	628	669	714	762	817	958

are in the middle of the score distribution. One lesson from Tables 1 and 3 is that scores with very high reliability (>0.99, see 'Table 1) still may have nontrivial uncertainty. Another important lesson is that accuracy can only be evaluated in terms of the use of the scores—for the California examples statistical uncertainty in the school scores allows solid determination of the statewide decile rank, but relatively poor determination of the similar schools rank. It is not the size of the standard error, it is how you use it.

The statistical approach to the properties of accountability systems follows standard ideas from medical diagnostic and screening tests. The properties are expressed in terms of false positive and false negative events, which are depicted in the chart in Table 4. Commonly accepted medical tests have less-than-perfect accuracy. For example, prostate cancer screening (PSA) produces considerable false positives, and in tuberculosis screening, false negatives (sending an infected patient into the general population) are of considerable concern. Table 4 shows two layered labelings for the rows (observed outcome, success or not) and columns (true state, deserving or not); the top layer pertains to NCLB accountability in which proportion proficient for schools and subgroups are compared to a performance goal (to earn AYP), and the bottom layer pertains to past California accountability in which year-to-year improvement by schools and subgroups was compared to a growth target (to earn awards). The entries are the joint probabilities a, b, c, d. In this education context, false positives describe events where statistical variability alone produces an (undeserved) successful outcome. False negatives describe events for which success is denied due to statistical variability in the scores, despite underlying ("real") performance or improvement. The trade-off between false positives and false negatives is the important policy decision in the formulation of an school accountability award or sanction system. The common derived quantities from Table 4 are *sensitivity*, $a/(a + c)$, which determines the propor-

TABLE 4

2 × 2 DIAGNOSTIC ACCURACY FOR SCHOOL ACCOUNTABILITY: NCLB (AND CALIFORNIA API)

	Good Real Performance (Good Real Improvement)	Poor Real Performance (No Real Improvement)
Meet AYP (Award)	TRUE POSITIVE a	FALSE POSITIVE b
Fail AYP (No award)	FALSE NEGATIVE c	TRUE NEGATIVE d

tion of false negative results, and *specificity*, $d/(b + d)$, which determines the proportion of false positive results.

Inclusion of subgroup criteria in school accountability creates a disconnect between properties of a school score and the properties of decisions from the accountability system. Statistical variability in the school and subgroup scores serves to make the accountability criteria far more formidable than they might appear, because to have high probability that all subgroup scores (each of the subgroups has larger uncertainty than the school index) will meet the criteria requires underlying performance that exceeds (blows through) the often seemingly modest target (see Rogosa, 2003c, for NCLB calculations). One explanation is the "herding cats metaphor": it is unlikely that a set of cats will all move in the same direction (past the performance goal or growth target) by chance, but a strong enough probe (performance or improvement) may persuade all the cats to move in unison.

An illustration of the effect of subgroups and the lack of a strong relation between the properties of the accountability system and the standard error of the school score is provided in Figure 1. The data are California elementary schools all having three significant subgroups (the state modal value) and with API scores located in the middle deciles

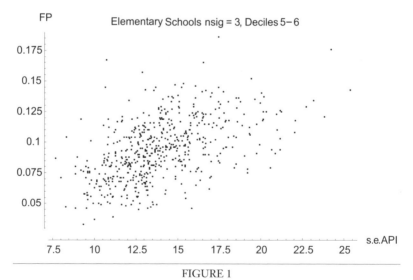

FIGURE 1

Illustration of less-than-perfect relation between false positives (FP) in school accountability and standard error of school score (s.e.API) for California elementary schools scoring in deciles 5 or 6 and having three significant subgroups.

of the statewide API distribution. The false positive (FP) probability is probability of award given no improvement. For schools with standard errors around the median value, the false positive probabilities have a wide range of 0.04 to 0.16, even for this homogeneous grouping. Another property of the accountability system to note is that, if subgroups were not included in the award criteria, the false positive probabilities would be increased by approximately a factor of three.

Vignette 4. False Negatives and the Fallacy of Small School Advantage

Disparities in observed accountability results (i.e., small schools faring better) and flawed statistical analyses have led to many press reports of a "small school advantage" in accountability (e.g., Sharon, Tulley, & Campbell, 2002). In their prescriptions for remediating claimed flaws in accountability systems, Kane and Staiger (2002) in the section "Implications for the Design of Incentive Systems" advise that the effects of school size ("Lesson 1") are so severe as to justify structural changes in accountability systems: "A remedy would be to establish different thresholds for different size schools, such that the marginal net payoff to improving is similar for small and large schools, or offer different payoffs to small and large schools" (p. 257).

The misunderstanding that generates concerns about a small school advantage is in neglecting or ignoring false negatives in considering the properties of the accountability system (e.g., Kane & Staiger, 2002, Figure 7). The one clear fact is that statistical variability (in a school or subgroup score) does decline as the number of students increases. A small school having made no real improvement (or poor real performance) has statistical variability as its friend, in that a false positive result may occur more often than for a large school. But a small school that has made substantial real improvement (or has strong real performance) has statistical uncertainty as its foe, in that a false negative result may occur more often than for a large school.

A useful calculation is to obtain probability of success (award) for different size schools under different levels of underlying real achievement. The numerical illustration here (adapted from Rogosa, 2002b) uses a set of four California elementary schools, where each of these award schools has a 1999 API score in state decile 5 (i.e., slightly below the state median of about 610) with the same three numerically significant subgroups (Socioeconomically Disadvantaged, Hispanic, and White). The contrast in the four schools is the progression of school sizes (specifically number of students included in the school API score)

n = 148, 244, 350, 491 which represent the 5th, 20th, 50th, and 80th percentiles of the elementary school size distribution. The size labels for the four schools in Table 5 are: smaller n (=148), small n (=244), medium n (=350), and large n (=486).

The message of Table 5 is that a small school advantage is only seen if false positives (no real improvement) are considered; any combination of false positives and false negatives appears to erase (if not reverse) such an effect. The leftmost column in Table 5 gives, for reference, the standard error of the school API, which does decrease with school size. The next three columns, true improvement levels 0, 29, 41, reflect incrementation of all student scores to produce an increase in the school API of 0, 29, 41 (see Rogosa, 2002b, for details of the calculations). The entries are the probability that school API and significant subgroups meet or exceed growth targets (the Governor's Performance Award, GPA, criterion, about 10 points year-to-year improvement for these schools and 8 points for the subgroups). The true improvement = 0 column gives the false positive probability, probability that statistical variability alone (i.e., null improvement) will result in school eligibility for GPA, and the false positive probability does decrease in Table 5 as school size triples. On the other hand, when substantial real improvement (set slightly below and above the observed statewide median improvement) is imposed, the probability of award increases with school size. The far right column represents a combination of false positive and true positive probabilities: probability of award averaged over all incrementation, 0 to 50 API points. This probability increases with school size.

A separate group size misunderstanding—determinations of minimum subgroup size in NCLB accountability—provides a segue to the next vignette. Typical guidance (see CCSSO, 2002; Linn, Baker, &

TABLE 5
SMALL SCHOOL ADVANTAGE?

| | | Probability of Award | | | |
| | | True Improvement | | | |
	s.e.(API)	0	29	41	Average
Smaller n	20.2	0.131	0.447	0.596	0.3755
Small n	14.26	0.094	0.620	0.797	0.5244
Medium n	13.7	0.101	0.714	0.890	0.5523
Large n	11.1	0.084	0.822	0.961	0.595

Herman, 2002) has unfortunately focused on the standard error of a single proportion, and such examination of just one component often provides little useful information on the properties of the accountability system. In contrast, Rogosa (2003c) shows "on the margin" calculations for comparing the properties of the accountability system, as constituted, with the properties resulting from setting a smaller (or larger) minimum n.

Vignette 5. How Large Is the "Diversity Penalty"?

No Child Left Behind accountability can be described as "no subgroup left behind," and there are strong policy and political motivations for including the subgroup criteria in AYP. Under NCLB, schools must meet the proportion proficient criteria not only for the school as a whole, but also for numerically significant subgroups defined by race/ethnicity, socioeconomically disadvantaged students, English language learners, and students with disabilities. Legitimate policy research questions are, What is the effect of including subgroup criteria on the properties of the accountability system? What should be the rules for subgroup inclusion and criteria? As previously mentioned, subgroup criteria will reduce false positive probabilities (presumably a good thing). For diversity penalty claims, unlike the school size claims in the previous vignette where false negatives were ignored, for the diversity penalty claims, the focus of accountability critics is on the false negatives. Claims of a large diversity penalty rest on a misunderstanding of the basic distinction between equality of opportunity and equality of results.

A misleading "coin-flip" metaphor that has been picked up in many discussions of the effect of subgroups was introduced by Kane and Staiger (2002): "For a racially integrated school, winning an award is analogous to correctly calling three or four coin tosses in a row, instead of a single toss. As a result, at any given level of overall improvement, a racially integrated school is much less likely to win an award than a racially homogeneous school" (p. 258). The misleading aspect here is the reader's instinct to think in terms of a fair coin (and also to overlook that the number of independent subgroups is often far less than the reported number—for example, a school composed primarily of Hispanics, who are all English learners and almost all disadvantaged are reported as three subgroups). For this coin-flip metaphor to apply in California, NCLB would require nonoverlapping homogeneous subgroups with performance all near the NCLB criteria that are set at less than 0.2 proportion proficient, representing an extreme case given that statewide proportion proficient is around 0.4.

One of the first analyses of the effect of subgroups on the properties of a school accountability system to claim a diversity penalty is the presentation in Kane and Staiger (2002, especially Table 4), using results from the past California API award programs. Kane and Staiger assert as their Lesson 2: "Incentive systems establishing separate thresholds for each racial or ethnic subgroup present a disadvantage to racially integrated schools" (p. 258), and further state in their conclusion: "Rules making any rewards contingent on improvement in each racial group present a great disadvantage to integrated schools and generate a number of perverse incentives that may harm rather than help minority students" (p. 269). The empirical evidence does not support these claims of diversity penalty. Disparity in tabled outcomes (observed number of subgroups crossed with school size or mean achievement) is not credible evidence of "unfairness," as schools differ in many ways other than number of reported (overlapping) subgroups (c.f., Rogosa, 2002b, Section 4 on Kane–Staiger).

More recently, Novak and Fuller (2003) garnered coast-to-coast press attention for their claims (using California NCLB results) that "schools serving diverse students in California are less likely to achieve their growth targets" and "Schools serving middle-class children, for example, are 28 percent more likely to be labeled 'needs improvement' by the feds when serving five student subgroups than schools serving one group" (p. 1). Rogosa (2004) refutes the Novak and Fuller empirical claims and presents simple probability calculations to provide some quantification for questions about the effects of subgroups. These calculations use an "on the margin" logic—what is the effect on probability of award or probability of meeting the NCLB criteria if another subgroup is added? All indications are that such effects are far less than those claimed by the empirical tabulations of disparity in results. One (very basic) result shows that a school that has high probability of meeting the AYP criteria if no subgroups were included has only slightly reduced probability with multiple (representative) subgroups. Table 6 calibrates the effect of additional subgroups in an artificial setting; entries in the table are the probability of meeting both math and English NCLB criteria for a school whose size is proportional to the number of subgroups (n indicates subgroup size). The results show a decrease in AYP probability of about 0.015 for each additional subgroup (i.e., 0.97 for two subgroups decreases to 0.94 for four nonoverlapping subgroups).

TABLE 6
EFFECTS ON PROBABILITY OF MEETING AYP OF ADDITIONAL SUBGROUPS

n	Number of Nonoverlapping Subgroups			
	0/1	2	3	4
50		0.970	0.956	0.941
100	0.985	0.970	0.956	0.941
200	0.985	0.970	0.956	0.941

Another way to calibrate the effects of subgroups (see also Rogosa, 2003c) is through the increase in underlying educational attainment (true proportion proficient) required to maintain the same probability of meeting the NCLB criteria, as the number of subgroups increases (which could be characterized as a slight headwind). In addition, Rogosa (2002b) has some examples and calculations, using the California accountability data, suggesting that since larger schools tend to have more subgroups the effect of additional subgroups to diminish probability of award is approximately balanced by the decreased false negative probability for the larger schools (combining vignettes 4 and 5).

In sum, implementation of subgroup criteria is an important topic for further technical research on the properties of accountability systems, such as the current NCLB. And it may well be possible to develop superior alternatives, especially alternatives more directly focused on the announced aim of NCLB, to reduce (eliminate) achievement gaps.

Vignette 6. The Margin of Error Folly: Blood Pressure Parable

The applications of the *margin of error* in assessment and school accountability can be shown to lead to preposterous results. The uses of a margin of error, typically defined as 1.96 times the standard error of the score, represent a misunderstanding of basic statistical principles, such as the meaning of a confidence interval. One way of expressing margin-of-error logic: If it could be, it is. The succeeding vignettes take up two educational accountability instances of margin of error folly; the blood pressure parable below (adapted from Rogosa, 2005) serves as a lead-in to the school accountability examples.

Blood Pressure Parable

Consider an artificial setting, using diastolic blood pressure (DBP) in hypertension diagnosis; the example uses part of the hypertension standard: DBP, 90 or above. Like educational standards, standards for blood pressure diagnosis are subject to revision (Brody, 2003). For this statistical demonstration consider the distribution of DBP for adult males to be represented as normally distributed with mean 82, standard deviation 11.5, which would indicate about 25% of DPB at or above 90. (Hypertension diagnoses can also be based on elevated systolic pressure, leading to a hypertension rate of 1/3 or more.) Also, for purposes of this example assume DPB has measurement uncertainty indicated by standard error of measurement of 6.12 (due to time of day, patient factors, etc.). Consequently, the margin of error for DPB is taken to be 12.

A patient is measured to have DPB = 101. The margin of error logic indicates that the physician has no idea whether the patient is indeed hypertensive, as by the margin of error interpretation a reading of 101 is not distinguishable from 89. To the contrary, this single DPB measurement does provide information, and the statistical question is: What does a DPB reading of 101 indicate about hypertension status? That is, calculate the conditional probability that true DBP is at least 90 given a DPB measurement of 101. As shown below, this probability is 0.912. That is, the probability is better than 9 out of 10, or odds of 10 to 1, that the true DPB is at least 90. Does the application of the margin of error appear to promote good health (or good educational policy)?

Technical Details for Probability Calculation

The basic statistical facts for what is termed the normal/normal model can be found in Carlin and Louis (2000, Sections 1.5.1 and 3.3.1) and Lehman and Casella (1998, Section 4.2). The likelihood specification is that $Y_i | \theta_i \sim N(\theta_i, V_i)$, a Gaussian distribution with mean θ_i and variance V for units $i = 1, \ldots, k$. Specifying the (prior) distribution of θ over units as $\theta_i | \mu \sim N(\mu, A)$ yields the distribution of the unknown parameter given the data:

$$\theta_i | y_i \sim N(B\mu + (1 - B)y_i, (1 - B)V), \quad \text{where } B = V / (V + A).$$

In the DPB example θ_i is the perfectly measured DBP for individual i, and for the DPB measurement $V = (6.12)^2$. The prior distribution of true DPB in the adult male population has $\mu = 82$, $A = (11.5)^2$. Consequently, $B = 0.221$, and for the DBP observation of 101, the posterior distribution is $N(96.8, 29.21)$ and P{true DPB > 89.5 | DBP = 101} = 0.9117.

Vignette 7. The Margin of Error Folly: California School Accountability

Using margin of error reasoning, the *Orange County Register* (Orange County, California), launched in August 2002 a weeklong series of attack pieces against the state of California school accountability system, in particular criticizing the rewards offered for improvements in the API. The main assertions by the *Register* were: "California's $1 billion school testing system is so riddled with flaws that the state has no idea whether one-third of the schools receiving cash awards actually earned the money" (Sharon et al., 2002) and "the Register's findings, which showed about one-third of the award-winners gains were within the error margin making it impossible to tell if the school really improved" (Sharon & Tully, 2002). Furthermore, these claims have had carryover to NCLB; Gladwell (2003) in a wide-ranging attack on NCLB and school accountability uses the *Register* claims: "But the average margin of error on the A.P.I. is something like twenty points, and for a small school it can be as much as fifty points. In a recent investigation, the *Orange County Register* concluded that, as a result, about a third of the money given out by the state might have been awarded to schools that simply got lucky."

Again, if these claims were true, then school accountability, whether through rewards or sanctions, would not be defensible. Was the California school award program at the mercy of statistical uncertainty? Is this mistake probability, P{no real improvement | award}, really as large as 1/3? (Note in terms of Table 4 quantities the *Register* quantity of interest, P{no real improvement | award} = b/(a + b), which in epidemiology would be termed 1 – predictive value positive.) To the contrary, Rogosa (2002a, 2005) demonstrates that a good estimate of these mistakes is 2% of schools, 1% of money—not 33%. The technical explanation in Rogosa (2005) of this margin of error folly is informative for understanding properties of school accountability decisions. How could the *Register* (and their cited experts, Richard Hill and Thomas Kane) get it so wrong? The prose explanation would be: by piling "could be's" upon "might have's" and counting those as certainties.

To understand the correct calculations, and to see how the *Register* analysis could be wrong by a factor of 20 or more, consider an example of a specific elementary school in Los Angeles that the *Register* counted as "impossible to tell if the school really improved." This average-sized elementary school (CDS code 19647336018253) has two significant

TABLE 7
PROBABILITY CALCULATION FOR API IMPROVEMENT, CDS CODE 19647336018253

	API	n	s.e.(API)	Margin of Error
1999	616	349	14.2	27.8
2000	647	355	13.2	25.9
Improvement	31			34.9

P{true change ≤ 0 | observed data} = 0.00798

subgroups, Socioeconomically Disadvantaged (SD) and Hispanic, and this school received a GPA award of $40,262 for API improvement, 1999 to 2000. The year-to-year improvement of 31 points for this school is 22 points above the growth target of 9 points, but still less than the margin of error for improvement, calculated to be 34.9 points. Thus, according to the *Register* we are to have "no idea" whether this school actually improved, and this school is included in their mistake tally.

From Table 7 (adapted from Rogosa, 2005, Table 1), the probability is 0.992 that the true improvement is greater than 0. In effect, *Register* margin of error methods for determining whether the school "really improved" rounds 0.008 up to 1.0 for the tabulation of "impossible to tell" schools. Moreover, for the school's growth target criterion, P{true change < 9 | observed data} = 0.0386 and thus the odds are 25 to 1 that the true improvement exceeded the year 2000 growth target.

That school example is not atypical; for the 3,585 elementary school GPA award winners in 1999–2000, the median value of P{true change > 0 | observed data} was 0.9988; over 75% of the schools had probabilities above 0.99, over 90% of these schools had probabilities above 0.97, and the expected number of GPA schools showing no real improvement was 35. Thus there is strong empirical evidence that schools receiving awards did have real improvement. Moreover, for these 3,585 elementary school GPA winners in 1999–2000, the median value of P{true change > growth target | observed data} was 0.993; over 90% of these schools had probabilities above 0.91, and the expected number of GPA schools not meeting the growth target was 104.

Vignette 8. The Margin of Error Folly: NCLB Confidence Intervals

Legitimate concerns about the effects of statistical uncertainty on the properties of NCLB accountability and poor understanding of basic statistical principles combine to morph the margin of error folly into NCLB confidence intervals. The important statistical and policy question is, How much benefit of the doubt in AYP criteria should be accorded to schools to offset the effects of statistical uncertainty? And the basic misunderstanding lies in not appreciating the consequences of the confidence interval adjustment (another example of needing to consider the trade-off between false positives and false negatives).

Under the NCLB "confidence intervals" approach adopted by a large majority of states, AYP requirements are adjusted downward, below the AMO (Annual Measurable Objective) established by the state. The amount of adjustment depends on the number of individual student scores contributing to the school or subgroup score so that the adjustment is larger for smaller groups of students. The genesis of these confidence interval procedures appears to be CCSSO (2002) with additional development by the Center for Assessment as seen, for example, in Marion and Gong (2003). Although the confidence interval adjustment is labeled as a "Statistically-Based Approach" (CCSSO, 2002, chapter 3, p. 87 onward), these NCLB confidence intervals (usually implemented via hypothesis tests) should not be confused with good statistical practice.

Rogosa (2003d) quantifies the extreme consequences of these NCLB confidence interval implementations, using calculations based on some of the summary data from Utah testing and on the Utah NCLB procedures (Utah State Office of Education, 2003). Utah employs the 99% confidence interval adjustment typical of many states. The NCLB AYP requires that the school-wide proportion proficient scores meet the AMO in both subjects (in Utah for grades 3–8: language arts, proportion proficient 0.65, and mathematics, proportion proficient 0.57), and also these subject proportion proficient scores meet the AMOs for each of the included subgroups. Table 8 displays the number of proficient students needed to actually meet the stated AMO (the n*AMO column) and the number of proficient students that the Utah procedure would deem as close enough via the 99% confidence interval adjustment (labeled minimum number proficient) for group sizes from 25 to 500 (see Rogosa, 2003d, for computational details). For example, with a group of 25 students, the mathematics AMO of 0.57 would seem to require 15 proficient students out of the 25. But the one-sided hypothesis test described in the Utah NCLB plan would deem only eight proficient students as representing close enough.

In terms of the accountability decisions display in Table 4, the intent of the NCLB confidence interval adjustment is to eliminate (or make very rare) false negatives, statistical uncertainty in the observed proportions proficient creating a failure to meet AYP. But good intentions,

TABLE 8

TABULATIONS OF "CLOSE ENOUGH" FOR UTAH 99% CONFIDENCE

Group Size	Language Arts (AMO = 0.65)		Mathematics (AMO = 0.57)	
	Minimum Number Proficient	n*AMO	Minimum Number Proficient	n*AMO
25	11	17	8	15
75	39	49	33	43
100	54	65	45	57
125	69	82	58	72
300	176	195	151	171
500	300	325	259	285

TABLE 9

PROBABILITY CALCULATION FOR NCLB 99% CONFIDENCE INTERVAL: SCHOOLS WITH THREE NONOVERLAPPING SUBGROUPS

	School with 125 Students; 75 Caucasian, 25 Hispanic, 25 African-American	School with 500 Students; 300 Caucasian, 100 Hispanic, 100 African-American
English/language arts AMO = 0.65	0.000037 (47, 11, 11)	0.0000196 (192, 54, 54)
Mathematics AMO = 0.57	0.0000068 (42, 8, 8}	0.0000098 (169, 45, 45}

Entries are:
Probability true proficiency meets performance goal (AMO)
(number Caucasian, Hispanic, African-American observed proficient)

such as to ensure (as much as possible) that schools are not falsely labeled as "needs improvement," have consequences. These consequences should be understood (perhaps before these state NCLB plans were approved). Among the many kinds of calculations that can be done, the example here from Rogosa (2003d) serves to illustrate the maximum amount of benefit of doubt that the confidence interval adjustments bestow.

Consider two schools, sizes 125 and 500 students, each composed of 60% Caucasian, and 20% each Hispanic and African-American students. With no 99% confidence interval adjustment, the number of proficient students in the larger school required to meet the math AMO for the three subgroups is (171, 57, 57), and for school total, 285 proficient. Then the simplest probability reasoning would say that, given those observed numbers proficient, the probability that the true proportion proficient met the math AMO for all three subgroups (and therefore school also) is about 1/8. Table 9 displays probability calculations from Rogosa (2003d) that show the consequences of the 99% confidence interval adjustment. Given the data—observed minimum number of proficient students meeting the subgroup and school proficiency criteria—what is the probability that the true (measured without statistical uncertainty) proportion proficient would meet the AMO for all subgroups (and therefore school-wide also)? First consider the calculations for math in the larger school. The number of proficient students in the subgroups that meets the AMO for subgroup and school under the 99% confidence interval adjustment is (169, 45, 45) yielding a posterior probability for the true proportions proficient meeting the AMO of about 1/100,000. That is one way of quantifying the benefit of the doubt. The equivalent calculation for English gives a posterior probability of about 1/50,000 for the true proportions proficient meeting the AMO. As AYP requires satisfying both English and math criteria, the probability for both sets of true proportions proficient meeting the AMO is considerably less than either of these very small probabilities.

Do the NCLB confidence intervals represent reasonable benefit of doubt for the effects of statistical uncertainty? Does the confidence interval scheme really satisfy the NCLB legislation's requirement for "statistically valid and reliable" AYP (see, CCSSO, 2002, p. 21)? (Note the state NCLB Accountability Workbooks require under System Validity and Reliability: "9.1 Accountability system produces reliable decisions. 9.2 Accountability system produces valid decisions" [Utah State Office of Education, 2003].) The press caught on early to this NCLB margin of error folly (e.g., Deffendall, 2003; Lynn, 2003; Rado & Little, 2003); researchers and policymakers should also.

Vignette 9. Demographics Are Far from Determinant

The final vignette takes up a controversial and misunderstood topic: the relation between demographic variables and test scores (for schools and individuals). The misunderstandings arise from most analysts and interested parties not having a good understanding of the correlation coefficient: in particular, not appreciating how far away from the upper bound +1 (perfect linear association) is consequential in the interpretation of a correlation coefficient. Certainly, it is very rare for a school drawing from a student population regarded as highly advantaged to score extremely poorly. Similarly, most often a school drawing from a student population regarded as highly disadvantaged does not obtain a very high score. That is the reality that drives the value of the correlation coefficient, but it is very far from the whole story. Examples below and more extensive descriptive analyses in the citations refute the slogan of the California Teachers Association that "It's all zip codes," their way of indicating that demographic characteristics predominantly determine school performance in testing and accountability.

The school demographic measure used here is the School Characteristics Index (SCI), a composite of demographic measures computed by California Department of Education for each school. (Note: Similar results are obtained using a simpler school demographic measure, proportion of disadvantaged students, Rogosa, 2001.) To examine the relation between demographics (SCI) and student achievement (school API), one common first resort is the school-level correlation coefficients for each school type. Many would regard the correlations below as quite large, and educational researchers would typically conclude a very strong relation between school results and demographic characteristics.

	Elem.	Middle	High
1999 Pearson correlation of SCI and API =	0.924	0.951	0.946
2000 Pearson correlation of SCI and API =	0.923	0.951	0.939
2001 Pearson correlation of SCI and API =	0.920	0.943	0.936

(Equivalent results are obtained from analyses that use multiple regression to predict school scores from an assortment of demographic measures.) A more informative view is provided by the corresponding scatterplots of API versus SCI (see Rogosa, 2003b, Figures 7 through 12). The scatterplots reveal that even a correlation of 0.94 is rather far from 1.0, because even though API scores increase as the SCI index increases, the plots also show considerable range on API (perhaps 250–300 points) for a chosen level of SCI.

Useful Data Analysis for the Relation between API Scores and Demographic Characteristics: Range of Similar School API

In the California API reporting, the SCI is used to identify the "100 other schools with similar demographic characteristics," which are listed as *Similar Schools.* For elementary schools, this list, composed of the 50 schools with closest SCI scores above the school and the 50 with the closest SCI scores below the school, comprises a (reasonably narrow) 2% slice out of the distribution of elementary schools. The data analysis opportunity is to use each school's list of 100 Similar Schools to assess whether the API scores for these similar schools lie in a narrow range. For example, do schools that are similar on measured demo-

TABLE 10
RANGE SIMILAR SCHOOL API: CALIFORNIA ELEMENTARY SCHOOLS 1999–2001

N	Mean	Median	Q1	Q3	Minimum	Maximum
4,849	281.50	277.00	243.00	304.00	154.00	522.00
4,775	268.88	257.00	222.00	308.00	125.00	435.00
4,895	242.22	235.00	203.00	282.00	101.00	384.00

graphic characteristics obtain similar API scores? A quantitative answer is to use the quantity *Range Similar School API*, the range of the corresponding 100 similar school API scores: max(API) – min(API).

Table 10 presents results for Range Similar School API in the years 1999, 2000, and 2001 for California elementary schools (further tables in Rogosa, 2003b, Section B2). The 1999 statewide result says that half the elementary schools show a range of their Similar Schools API scores of at least 277 points, and 75% of elementary schools have a range of their Similar Schools API scores of at least 243 points. A good way to calibrate these numbers is to note that for elementary schools the statewide decile categories typically span 40–45 API points. Thus 243 points represents a span of five to six statewide deciles and the median range 277 represents a span of about six (or more) statewide deciles. Contrast those results with the typical interpretation for an API,SCI correlation of 0.92.

In addition, the tables in Rogosa (2003c) show that indications from the entire state data also hold up when examined for each decile, and the Range Similar School API is even larger for schools in the lower state deciles (i.e., lower scoring). For 1999 there are 490 elementary schools placed in the second state decile. Half of those schools have Range Similar School API of over 300 points, and 75% of those schools have Range Similar School API of over 275 points (a width of six deciles). Are these results consistent with the claim that demographics are determinant?

Discussion

Measuring and Judging Schools

School accountability can be thought of as a process with two main components, measuring schools and judging schools. The measuring question is, What type of number should represent the performance of students in the school? and the judging question is, Was that performance, however quantified, *good enough*? The measuring component presents multiple choices for summarizing the student test scores for a school or subgroup. Among the measuring options are: single cut-point measures (proportion at least Basic, proportion at least Proficient); weighted composite indices (differential weighting for multiple performance levels as in California API); with the availability of matched longitudinal data, the proportion of students improving year-to-year; or reflecting NCLB policy goals a measure of achievement gaps among subgroups in the school. In judging a school, the "good enough" criteria for making a decision about the school can be expressed in terms of yearly status (e.g., meeting a standard) or year-to-year improvement (e.g., meeting a growth target), with the judging mechanism possibly applied to subgroup performance as well as school scores.

In a school accountability system a form of "measuring" is joined with a form of "judging" for making decisions about schools. Designing a useful accountability system requires an understanding of which combinations of measuring and judging best serve the intended policy objectives, while also having defensible statistical properties. The statistical challenge is to make good determinations in the face of some uncertainty in the data (i.e., not lean too hard on the data leading to mistakes about schools). In addition, a main policy issue is that the "good enough" criteria used in judging the schools are educationally meaningful and achievable. An analogy is to medical diagnosis where medical measurements are joined with criteria for a disease decision, and statistical properties such as false positives and false negatives are routinely investigated. In NCLB accountability, the particular choice for measuring schools is the proportion of students proficient (where the proficiency standard is determined by the state), and the choice for judging schools is that the yearly status measure for English and math meet a specified level (AMO) for school and included subgroups. That the particular implementation of measuring and judging does matter can be seen in widely publicized disparities between preexisting state accountability systems (such as Texas and California) and NCLB AYP results.

Issues for NCLB

The vignettes identify educational research misunderstandings of statistical issues important not only to NCLB but also to just about all systems of school accountability. Those issues include: the properties of group summary scores; use and consequences of subgroup criteria; proper evaluation of accountability decisions; and adjustments in accountability criteria for statistical uncertainty in group scores. The summative message from these statistical misunderstandings is that instead of good statistical practice guiding NCLB accountability, these education reform efforts are flying blind. And because state Accountability Workbooks are unfortunately not required to contain any useful information on the statistical properties of NCLB accountability (e.g., false positives, false negatives, or the more advanced false discovery rate indices), researchers, education professionals, and the interested public are left totally in the dark. Perhaps the most important statistical misunderstandings reside in the series of vignettes on the margin of error folly, which demonstrate why states should not be allowed to employ the popular NCLB confidence interval adjustments. By no stretch of probabilistic imagination do the "close enough is good enough" NCLB confidence interval adjustments satisfy the requirements of the NCLB statute for statistically valid and reliable decisions about schools.

Another important disconnect between policy intent and NCLB accountability arises in the often-stated goal of NCLB to close achievement gaps (such as between high- and low-poverty students or between ethnic/racial groups). One of the largest misunderstandings about NCLB is that the AYP criteria have little or nothing to do with the goal of closing achievement gaps. NCLB criteria do place a lower bound on subgroup performance by raising the level of lowest-scoring subgroups. But large-achievement gaps may persist even as the proportion proficient requirement in AYP approaches 1.0. In fact, success under NCLB may be as likely to increase gaps because higher-performing students may benefit even more from improved teaching regimens and curricula aligned with the content of tests than will students who are considered to be at risk of failure. Although the NCLB AYP criteria do not directly address or assess achievement gaps, one can construct accountability-useful measures (perhaps as an alternative to the current NCLB implementation) that credit schools for closing achievement gaps (either change in gaps or gaps in change) and judge schools on that basis, resulting in accountability procedures more closely aligned with the stated policy goal.

Implications of the Vignettes

No Child Left Behind represents a situation in which educational policy is far out front of the existing technical knowledge and statistical expertise, with unfortunate results. At a minimum, constructing good educational policy requires confronting and refuting bad educational research. The refutations of prior work described in the vignettes function in part to bring accountability to bear on educational researchers, which only seems fair given that high-stakes accountability currently impinges on students, teachers, and principals. Educational research and policy would be well served by following the example of medical research, where there exists a strong tradition of research rebuttal and correction in many venues, including academic journals and the popular press.

REFERENCES

Brody, J.E. (2003, August 12). "Normal" blood pressure: Health watchdogs are resetting the risk. *The New York Times*, p. F7.

Campbell, R. (2002, August 11). API's error margin leaves a lot to chance: Mathematical imprecision could lead to inaccurate interpretations. *The Orange County Register*. Retrieved January 5, 2005, from http://www.ocregister.com/features/api/text_version/index.shtml

Carlin, B.P., & Louis, T.A. (2000). *Bayes and empirical Bayes methods for data analysis* (2nd ed.). New York: Chapman & Hall.

Council of Chief State School Officers (CCSSO). (2002). *Making valid and reliable decisions in determining adequate yearly progress*. A paper in the series: Implementing the State Accountability System Requirements under the No Child Left Behind Act of 2001. ASR-CAS Joint Study Group on Adequate Yearly Progress, Scott Marion and Carole White, Co-Chairs. Retrieved December 12, 2004, from http://www.ccsso.org/content/pdfs/AYPpaper.pdf

Deffendall, L. (2003, October 19). No statistics are being left behind. *The Lexington Herald-Leader*.

Gladwell, M. (2003, September 15). Making the grade. *The New Yorker*.

Kane, T.J., & Staiger, D.O. (2002). Volatility in school test scores: Implications for test-based accountability systems. In D. Ravitch (Ed.), *Brookings papers on education policy* (pp. 235–269). Washington, DC: Brookings Institution.

Lehman, E.L., & Casella, G. (1998). *Theory of point estimation* (2nd ed.). New York: Springer-Verlag.

Linn, R.L., Baker, E.L., & Herman, J.L. (2002, Fall). Minimum group size for measuring adequate yearly progress. *The CRESST Line*, *1*, 4–5.

Linn, R.L., & Haug, C. (2002). Stability of school-building accountability scores and gains. *Educational Evaluation and Policy Analysis*, *24*(1), 29–36.

Lynn, R. (2003, December 18). Federal mandate: A complex statistical formula allowed them to meet their targets. *The Salt Lake Tribune*. Retrieved from http://166.70.46.216/2003/dec/12182003/utah/120969.asp

Marion, S., & Gong, B. (2003, September). *Evaluating the validity of state accountability systems*. Paper presented at CCSSO, St. Louis, MO. Retrieved November 12, 2004, from http://www.ccsso.org/content/pdfs/CCSSO_Validity_BGSM03.pdf

No Child Left Behind Act of 2001, Pub. L. No. 107-110, 115 Stat. 1425 (2002).

Novak, J.R., & Fuller, B. (2003, December). *Penalizing diverse schools? Similar test scores, but different students, bring federal sanctions*. PACE Policy Brief 03-4. Retrieved January 3, 2004, from http://pace.berkeley.edu/policy_brief_03-4_Pen.Div.pdf

O'Connell, J. (2004, March 24). *Fight for changes to NCLB*. California Department of Education. Retrieved December 3, 2004, from http://www.cde.ca.gov/eo/ce/sl/nclbfight.asp

Rado, D., & Little, D. (2003, September 28). Schools toying with test results: Some states meet standards with art of statistics. *The Chicago Tribune*, *1*, 22.

Rogosa, D.R. (2001, October). *Year 2000 update: Interpretive notes for the academic performance index*. California Department of Education, Policy and Evaluation Division. Retrieved April 1, 2004, from http://www.cde.ca.gov/ta/ac/ap/researchreports.asp

Rogosa, D.R. (2002a, September). *Commentaries on the* Orange County Register *series: What's the magnitude of false positives in GPA award programs? Application of OCR "margin of error" to API award programs*. California Department of Education, Policy and Evaluation Division. Retrieved April 1, 2004, from http://www.cde.ca.gov/ta/ac/ap/researchreports.asp

Rogosa, D.R. (2002b, October). *Irrelevance of reliability coefficients to accountability systems: Statistical disconnect in Kane–Staiger "Volatility in School Test Scores."* CRESST deliverable. Retrieved December 5, 2004, from http://www-stat.stanford.edu/~rag/api/kscresst.pdf

Rogosa, D.R. (2002c, July). *Plan and preview for API accuracy reports.* California Department of Education, Policy and Evaluation Division. Retrieved April 1, 2004, from http://www.cde.ca.gov/ta/ac/ap/researchreports.asp

Rogosa, D.R. (2002d, December). *Accuracy of API index and school base report elements.* California Department of Education, Policy and Evaluation Division. Retrieved April 1, 2004, from http://www.cde.ca.gov/ta/ac/ap/researchreports.asp

Rogosa, D.R. (2003a, June). *Confusions about consistency in improvement.* CRESST deliverable. Retrieved December 5, 2004, from http://www-stat.stanford.edu/~rag/api/consist.pdf

Rogosa, D.R. (2003b, September). *Four-peat: Data analysis results from uncharacteristic continuity in California student testing programs.* California Department of Education, Policy and Evaluation Division. Retrieved April 1, 2004, from http://www.cde.ca.gov/ta/ac/ap/researchreports.asp

Rogosa, D.R. (2003c, October). *California's AMOs are more formidable than they appear.* California Department of Education, Policy and Evaluation Division. Retrieved April 1, 2004, from http://www.cde.ca.gov/ta/ac/ap/researchreports.asp

Rogosa, D.R. (2003d, November). *The NCLB "99% confidence" scam: Utah-style calculations.* CRESST deliverable. Retrieved December 5, 2004, from http://www-stat.stanford.edu/~rag/nclb/utahNCLB.pdf

Rogosa, D.R. (2004, January). *Assessing the effects of multiple subgroups: A rebuttal to the PACE Policy Brief December 2003 "Penalizing diverse schools? Similar test scores, but different students, bring federal sanctions."* California Department of Education, Policy and Evaluation Division. Rejoinder: Being fair to NCLB. Retrieved December 5, 2004, from http://www.cde.ca.gov/ta/ac/ap/researchreports.asp

Rogosa, D.R. (2005). A school accountability case study: California API awards and the *Orange County Register* margin of error folly. In R.P. Phelps (Ed.), *Defending standardized testing* (pp. 205–226). Mahwah, NJ: Lawrence Erlbaum Associates.

Sharon, K., & Tully, S. (2002, August 16). State testing expert says API margin of error is insignificant: Leader who helped design index calls it as accurate as possible. *The Orange County Register.* Retrieved January 5, 2005, from http://www.ocregister.com/features/api/text_version/index.shtml

Sharon, K., Tully, S., & Campbell, R. (2002, August 11). Test scores unreliable: Error margin means state can't precisely measure how schools are doing, but the cash still flows. *The Orange County Register.* Retrieved December 5, 2004, from http://www.ocregister.com/features/api/text_version/index.shtml

Utah State Office of Education. (2003). *State of Utah consolidated state application accountability workbook.* Plan Approved by U.S. Department of Education, June 10, 2003. Retrieved from http://www.ed.gov/admins/lead/account/stateplans03/index.html

Part Three
ISSUES OF FAIRNESS AND CONSEQUENCES

CHAPTER 8

Issues and Consequences for English Language Learners

JAMAL ABEDI

A fair and valid assessment for every child, as mandated by legislation such as the No Child Left Behind Act (NCLB) of 2001 and the Improving America's School Act of 1994, must consider the complexity inherent in assessments for subgroups of students. Due to the rapid growth of the population of English language learners (ELLs) in the United States, and because of the confounding of language proficiency with content assessments of ELL students, issues concerning the assessment of these students deserve special attention. ELL students, relative to their non-ELL counterparts, are not performing as well academically, which has implications for their future success. However, if assessment results do not provide valid indicators of what these students know and can do, how can such results appropriately guide policy changes and improvement efforts?

Jamal Abedi is the Director of Technical Projects at the UCLA National Center for Research on Evaluation, Standards, and Student Testing (CRESST) and a faculty member at the UCLA Graduate School of Education.

The work reported herein was supported under the Educational Research and Development Centers Program, PR/Award Number R305B960002, as administered by the Institute of Education Sciences (IES) and the U.S. Department of Education. The findings and opinions expressed in this report are those of the author and do not necessarily reflect the positions or policies of the National Center for Education Research, the Institute of Education Sciences (IES), or the U.S. Department of Education.

Invalid assessment outcomes may result in misinformation and unfair consequences for schools, students, and teachers. Unfortunately, assessing the validity of assessment for ELL students is more complex than for other students, since there are additional influential variables that come into play for ELL students. For example, the confounding of language and cultural factors with assessment results makes the interpretation of assessment more complicated for these students.

Considering the rapid and continuing increase in the number and percentage of ELLs, fairness and validity concerns regarding their assessment are becoming a focus of attention of educational policymakers. Between 1990 and 1997, the number of U.S. residents born outside the United States increased by 30%, from 19.8 million to 25.8 million (Hakuta & Beatty, 2000). According to the National Clearinghouse for English Language Acquisition, over 4.5 million Limited English Proficient (LEP) students were enrolled in public schools in 2000–2001, representing nearly 10% of the nation's total public school enrollment for pre-kindergarten through grade 12 (Kindler, 2002). Both federal (e.g., No Child Left Behind Act of 2001) and state legislation requires the inclusion of all students—including ELLs—in large-scale assessments in an effort to assure that schools are accountable for every child in this country (Abedi, Lord, Hofstetter, & Baker, 2000; Mazzeo, Carlson, Voelkl, & Lutkus, 2000). Such inclusion mandates have prompted increased interest in modifying assessments to improve the level of ELLs' participation as well as to enhance the validity and equitability of inferences drawn from the assessments.

There are several major concerns in the design of appropriate accountability systems for ELL students. To provide a fair and valid assessment for a group of students, first and foremost, there must be a clear and correct identification of the group. In the landmark case *Lau v. Nichols* (1974), non-English speaking Chinese students in San Francisco brought a class action suit against their school district for not providing additional instruction. The Supreme Court, basing their ruling on the Civil Rights Act of 1964, granted the district appropriate relief to provide these students with equal educational opportunities. The justices ruled that schools and districts have the responsibility to respond affirmatively by meeting the needs of ELLs. However, in order to meet the needs of ELL students, they must be properly identified.

Unfortunately, existing literature does not provide a clear description of the ELL student population. Research suggests that while the common characteristic of ELL students is their possible lack of English proficiency, English proficiency test scores are not a major determinant of the ELL classification system. For example, Abedi (2004a) found that English language proficiency test scores explain a small amount of variation in the ELL classification code (less than 1% to 10%). Rivera, Stansfield, Scialdone, and Sharkey (2000), in their review of state policies, found that the LEP definition utilized by about half the states differed widely in criteria, yet as Grissom (2004) observed, different criteria may result in different classification decisions. Misidentification of ELL students clearly could have negative implications for their assessment and for accountability efforts.

The differential rate of inclusion/exclusion of ELL students in state and national assessments is another major issue affecting the accountability system for ELL students. Since different states and even different districts and schools within states may use different classification criteria (such as different combinations of home language surveys, language proficiency tests, achievement tests, and/or teacher evaluation), inclusion/exclusion rates may vary widely. Students with a particular level of English proficiency may be included in the regular assessment in some states, but may be excluded in other states, compromising any attempts to compare performance across venues.

As mentioned, the confounding of language factors with the intended assessment target also adds to the complexity of assessments for ELL students. Since assessment tools are constructed mainly for mainstream native English speakers and often are administered in English, the language demands of the assessment may confound performance, and ELLs may not have the opportunity to demonstrate their knowledge, producing results that do not reflect their achievement and are unfair.

To reduce the impact of language factors on the assessment of ELL students, assessment in a student's native language has been proposed. While this seems an attractive idea and many districts and states use this approach, research results do not support its fairness (Abedi, Hofstetter, & Lord, 2004). One major issue here is the alignment between the language of instruction and the language of assessment. If the language of assessment is not the same as the language of instruction, then the assessment outcome may be even less valid, again raising fairness as a serious issue. For example, when a native Spanish speaker learns content terminology in English but is tested in Spanish, the assessment outcome may not be valid due to the student's lack of content terminology knowledge.

Accommodations are meant to "level the playing field" for ELL students by accommodating their potential language limitations in an assessment. Unfortunately, there are major equity issues with many of the accommodations used for ELL students. The practice of using accommodations was first developed for students with disabilities (Rivera et al., 2000) and transferred for use with ELLs. However, some accommodations that are appropriate for students with disabilities may not be relevant for ELL students. For example, using large print may be an effective accommodation for some students with visual impairments, but ELL students specifically need accommodations to address their linguistic needs. Thus, while an accountability system for ELL students may include accommodations, the accommodations may cause a new set of issues contributing to the inequity of the assessment for these students.

The influence of cultural factors on the assessment of ELLs is yet another source of equity issues in the assessments of these students. Assessment tools that are influenced by mainstream cultural factors may not be fair for ELL students. ELL students may perform poorly on assessments not because of their lack of content knowledge but because of their unfamiliarity with mainstream cultural concepts. For example, a math test item could require familiarity with a mainstream Western/Anglo custom in addition to the content knowledge, thereby introducing construct irrelevance.

This chapter is structured around a discussion of factors that potentially have a great impact on the equity and fairness of assessment for the ELL student population. These factors include: (1) the classification of ELL students; (2) inclusion/exclusion criteria; (3) the impact of language factors on the assessment of ELL students; (4) the use of test forms in different languages as an accommodation; (5) the appropriateness, validity, and feasibility of accommodations; and (6) cultural and other factors. These issues can have a significant impact on the authenticity of the accountability system for ELL students. The greater the impact of these factors on ELL student performance, the more the fairness of accountability systems is compromised.

Classification of ELL Students

The first step and the most important requirement in providing a fair assessment and accountability system is to correctly identify ELL students. Unfortunately, research shows inconsistencies in the classification of ELL students across the nation (Abedi, 2004a). Different states and even different districts within states use varying criteria for classifying students as ELL or non-ELL (Abedi, 2004a; Abedi, Lord, & Plummer, 1997). While the main underlying theme and the most logical criterion of ELL classification is students' level of English language proficiency, scores of English language proficiency tests do not show a strong relation with the actual ELL classification code.

Abedi and Leon (2003) found a weak relationship between the students' ELL classification code and English language proficiency and achievement test scores. Using data from several locations nationally, they found that students' scores on the Language Assessment Scales (LAS) explained less than 5% of the variance in their ELL classification code. The effect size for the comparison of LAS scores between ELL and non-ELL students was 0.228, which is considered small (Kirk, 1995, p. 181). The relationship between Stanford Achievement Test, 9th Edition (SAT-9) test scores and ELL classification code was also weak, with correlation coefficients between math concepts and students' ELL code ranging from 0.045 ($n = 35,981$) to 0.168 ($n = 25,336$). The effect sizes ranged from 0.043 to 0.170, which again, based on Kirk (1995), are considered very small. These results suggest that neither students' level of English proficiency nor the students' achievement test scores are the major determinants of ELL classification.

Other factors clearly influence decisions on ELL classifications. Abedi (2004a), Aguirre-Muñoz and Baker (1997), Grissom (2004), and Steele and Aronson (1995) all found that variables such as gender, socioeconomic status (as measured by free/reduced price lunch eligibility), ethnicity, immigrant status, number of years lived in the United States, and parent education are powerful predictors of ELL classification. Since these variables are not directly related to students' language background, they may not be considered valid predictors of ELL classification, but they certainly are confounded with students' language background.

When an ELL student reaches a proficiency level, as defined by the state, he or she may be reclassified as non-ELL. However, even in reclassification decisions, measures of English proficiency may not be a major criterion. Different states use somewhat different criteria in this case. For example, Grissom (2004) indicated that in California, multiple criteria are used for reclassifying from ELL to R-FEP (Reclassified Fluent English Proficient). These criteria, according to Grissom, include: (1) assessment of English language proficiency; (2) teacher evaluation; (3) parent opinion and consultation; and (4) comparison of performance in basic skills. While Grissom provided a more defined set of criteria for ELL classification/reclassification, it is still not quite clear how these criteria are used in practice.

Another issue in the classification of ELL students is the heterogeneity of the ELL subgroup. ELL students are inherently heterogeneous, since they come from different backgrounds and therefore may differ in the language or languages spoken, literacy and fluency in those language(s), and proficiency in English. They may also differ in previous schooling experience, socioeconomic status, and parent level of education, among other background characteristics. Abedi, Leon, and Mirocha (2003) found that achievement outcomes for ELL students varied depending on certain family and cultural background characteristics. For instance, ELL students of parents with less than a high school education had a mean reading score of 25.23 on the SAT-9 (n = 30,091, SD = 14.10), as compared with a mean of 40.35 (n = 1,649, SD = 19.56) for ELL students of parents with a postgraduate education.

Data presented above suggest that the ELL subgroup is not a well-defined, homogeneous group of students, and classifying students as ELL can be challenging. When subjective criteria are used, it leaves room for inconsistencies. This is a major obstacle in providing a fair assessment system for ELL students. When there is no clear understanding of the cognitive and personal background of these students, how can a fair assessment system for these students be designed?

Inclusion/Exclusion of ELL students

Prior to federal legislation, such as NCLB, that mandated the inclusion of ELL students in mainstream assessments, they were traditionally excluded from accountability measures. Both national and state assessments now include ELL students, often by providing testing accommodations. The National Assessment of Educational Progress (NAEP) has modified its criteria to be more inclusive of these students (see Lutkus & Mazzeo, 2003).

Unfortunately, however, the mechanisms for including ELL students in assessments and selecting appropriate testing accommodations for them vary widely and in many instances are inconsistent across the nation. Classification issues, as described earlier, contribute to some of these inconsistencies. Based on NAEP's recent policy on inclusion, all ELL students should be included in the NAEP assessment unless they have received fewer than three years of academic instruction in English *and* are judged to be incapable of participating in the assessment in English (Lutkus & Mazzeo, 2003)—criteria that leave much room for subjective decisions.

Information on the number of years ELL students have received instruction in English may be difficult to obtain, since ELL students tend to be more transient than other students. Data on how the capability of ELL students to participate in the assessment is judged are even more problematic, since it is not clear exactly upon what this decision is based. Is it based on students' level of English proficiency, as measured by some "objective" criteria, or something else, such as teacher evaluation? If decisions are based on English language proficiency test scores, then variables such as the type of tests, the content they measure, the cut-scores, and the all-around reliability and validity of these tests would need to be examined; inconsistencies may mean significant variations in NAEP's inclusion decisions across the nation. Potentially, ELL students who are included in one state may be markedly different in terms of language background and English language proficiency from students included in another state.

Impact of Language Factors on the Assessment of ELL Students

Another major source of inequity in the assessment and accountability system for ELL students is the impact of language factors on assessment outcomes. Research has identified nuisance variables that influence the performance of different subgroups and alter the assumptions underlying classical test theory (Haladyna & Downing, 2004). Nuisance variables are variables that confound assessment results by making it difficult to separate out individual effects from construct-irrelevant sources, such as the effects of cultural biases or unnecessary linguistic complexity of test items. Among the most influential sources of nuisance variables that confound assessment results for ELL students is the unnecessary linguistic complexity of content-based assessments. If it is irrelevant to the content being measured such linguistic complexity may become a source of measurement error, thereby reducing the reliability of the content-based tests for ELL students. Unlike many other variables that may randomly contribute to measurement error, this source may be a systematic source of error of measurement. As a source of construct-irrelevant variance (Messick, 1994), the linguistic complexity of test items may also impact the con-

182   ENGLISH   LANGUAGE   LEARNERS

struct validity of tests, particularly for students with lower levels of English proficiency.

The effect of language factors on students' assessment outcomes may raise concerns over the validity and fairness of assessment for all students. If language interferes with ELL students' understanding of test items, then students may perform poorly on the test not because they lack the targeted content knowledge, but because the questions lack clarity for adequate comprehension.

Study results on the assessment and accommodation of ELL students show a large performance gap between ELL and non-ELL students (see Abedi et al., 2004; Sireci, Li, & Scarpati, 2003). This performance gap can be explained partly by the impact of language factors on the assessment of ELL students. The *Standards for Educational and Psychological Testing* (American Educational Research Association, American Psychological Association, & National Council on Measurement in Education, 1999) elaborated on this issue:

For all test takers, any test that employs language is, in part, a measure of their language skills. This is of particular concern for test takers whose first language is not the language of the test. Test use with individuals who have not sufficiently acquired the language of the test may introduce construct-irrelevant components to the testing process. In such instances, test results may not reflect accurately the qualities and competencies intended to be measured . . . Therefore it is important to consider language background in developing, selecting, and administering tests and in interpreting test performance. (p. 91)

Generally speaking, ELL students perform lower than non-ELL students in all areas. This makes sense, since language skills are required to take tests. However, an examination of this performance gap between ELL and non-ELL students across test items and subject areas reveals the powerful impact of language demand on test items. That is, the higher the level of language demand of test items, the wider the performance gap between ELL and non-ELL students. As a result, the performance gap between ELL and non-ELL students is highest in English language subject areas such as reading/language arts, and smaller in math subject areas, where there is less language demand (see Abedi, 2002; Abedi et al., 2003, for further details).

Although language inherently confounds assessment outcomes (where language is not the subject of assessment), test makers and administrators might consider ways to reduce this confounding so that we may more adequately gauge ELL students' knowledge in specific content areas. One approach to testing ELL students involves rewording test items to minimize construct-irrelevant linguistic complexity. Minor changes in the wording of content-related test items can raise student performance (Abedi & Lord, 2001; Abedi et al., 1997, 2000; Cummins, Kintsch, Reusser, & Weimer, 1988; De Corte, Verschaffel, & DeWin, 1985; Hudson, 1983; Riley, Greeno, & Heller, 1983). For example, rewording a verbal problem can make semantic relations more explicit, without affecting the underlying semantic and mathematical structure; thus the reader is more likely to construct a proper problem representation and to solve the problem correctly. The results of recent studies have shown that reducing the unnecessary linguistic complexity of test items helps improve the performance of ELL students without compromising the validity of the assessment (see Abedi & Lord, 2001; Abedi et al., 2000; Kiplinger, Haug, & Abedi, 2000; Maihoff, 2002).

The reliability and validity of assessments can be improved for ELL students by reducing the level of unnecessary linguistic complexity of test items. An assessment with clearer language involves less measurement error; therefore, it will be more reliable. The less linguistically complex assessment may also be more valid due to a lesser impact of construct-irrelevant variance. Reducing the reliability and validity gap between ELL and non-ELL students makes the assessment fairer for everyone.

To illustrate the effects of language factors on the reliability and validity of content-based achievement tests, we present the results of studies based on the analyses of several data sites nationally. Item-level data were available from four data sites (see Abedi et al., 2003, for more details).

We compared internal consistency coefficients for the SAT-9 test data for ELL and non-ELL students. The internal consistency coefficients (alpha) were computed for math problem solving, math concepts, math estimation, math data interpretation, math computation, and reading. The results indicated that:

- Alpha coefficients for ELL students were generally lower than for non-ELL students.
- The gap between alpha coefficients for ELL/non-ELL students was larger in the higher grade (grade 8) when compared with the lower grade (grade 3).

Lower alpha coefficients mean more measurement error and consequently lower validity. The larger difference in alpha between ELL and non-ELL students in the higher grade makes sense since linguistic structures tend to become more complex in progressively higher grades. Linguistic factors in content-based assessments (such as math and science) may also be considered a source of construct-irrelevant variance, since they are not conceptually related to the content being assessed (Messick, 1994; Sandoval & Duran, 1998).

With respect to the distortion of task performance, some aspects of the task may require skills or other attributes having nothing to do with the focal constructs in question, so that limitations in performing construct-irrelevant skills might prevent some students from demonstrating the focal competencies (Messick, 1994, p.14).

To examine the possible differences in the construct validity of standardized achievement tests between ELLs and non-ELLs, we used a multiple group confirmatory factor analysis model with reading and science test data from one of the four sites. The reading tests for grades 10 and 11, which had 54 items were used to construct five parcels (measured variables) and a reading latent variable (see Abedi et al., 2003). Similarly, four parcels and a science latent variable were constructed from the 40-item science tests. We created multiple-group factor models to test the statistical significance of differences between structural relationships for ELL and non-ELL students' assessment results. We examined the hypotheses of invariance of factor loadings and factor correlations between ELL and non-ELL students. The results showed significant differences between ELL and non-ELL students. There were significant differences between ELL and non-ELL students on the correlations between parcel scores and latent variables. For example, on the reading subscale, the hypothesis of invariance of factor loadings between ELL and non-ELL students on parcels 3 was rejected. There was also a significant difference between ELL and non-ELL students on the correlation between science latent variables.

In summary, the data presented above suggest that assessment results for ELL students do not follow the same pattern of relationship as those for non-ELL students. For example, a lower correlation between parcel scores and the reading latent variable of ELL students suggests a lower internal consistency for ELL students. Since lower reliability (internal consistency) puts a limit on the validity (see, e.g., Allen & Yen, 1979; Linn & Gronlund, 1995; Salvia & Ysseldyke, 1998), it affects the validity of assessment. More importantly, the lower correlation between the content-based latent variables strongly suggests a lower criterion-related validity for ELL students. Since language factors affect performance of ELL students more than other groups, fairness becomes a major issue in this regard.

Using Test Forms in Different Languages as an Accommodation

To make assessments fairer for ELL students, performance gaps due to the impact of nuisance variables (such as the linguistic complexity of items) must be reduced. To reduce such performance gaps, assessment accommodations have been proposed. Among the most commonly used accommodation practices for ELL students is using tests translated into students' native languages. However, when the language of instruction is not in the students' native language, the validity of this form of accommodation becomes questionable. There are at least two areas of concerns: (1) technical issues in translating a test into another language; and (2) issues concerning the alignment of language of instruction and language of assessment.

Translation

The validity of translated assessments is a threat to the fairness of assessment and accountability for ELL students. It is often difficult when translating to find the exact term to convey a concept precisely. Some items representing cultural concepts that are particularly Western/Anglo, for example, may be improperly translated, or the translated version may become easier or harder to understand than the original. Additionally, the length of the translated version may not always be the same as the original version, which may give an unfair advantage or disadvantage if it takes a longer or shorter amount of time to read.

In particular, difficulty in translating idioms may lead to a poor translation. For example, "Out of sight, out of mind" literally translates from English into French as "invisible, insane." Hambleton (2001) noted that it is hard to find equivalents for phrases such as "cold fish" and "bleeding heart" and expressions such as "every cloud has a silver lining." Additionally, some languages have different words that mean the same thing, while other languages may not (see, e.g., Hambleton & Patsula, 1999).

Hambleton (2001) presented a nine-step guide that he felt would maximize the success of test adaptations. These steps include: reviewing the construct equivalence in the language and cultures of interest; choosing well-qualified translators; reviewing the adapted version of the test and making any necessary changes; conducting a small tryout of the adapted version of the test; conducting a validation investigation; choosing and implementing a design for placing scores from the source and target language versions of the test on a common reporting scale and documenting the process; and preparing a manual for the users of the adapted test.

As can be seen from the discussion above, translation is a complex process and leaves room for many sources of threats to the validity and authenticity of the translated assessment. Therefore, when deciding to use translated assessments, special care must be taken in translating the instruments and in interpreting the results of translated assessments.

Alignment of Language of Instruction and Language of Assessment

While proponents of assessment in students' native language believe that such assessments may provide more opportunities for a fair assessment of ELL students, others note that inequities may be aggravated when the language of assessment is not the same as the language of instruction.

Some researchers argue that although students may develop social skills in English fairly quickly, development of cognitive/academic language proficiency or school language proficiency may take five to seven years (Cummins, 1984, 1989; Ramirez, Yuen, Ramey, & Billings, 1991), and that students who are in situations where there is little opportunity to acquire academic English would be expected to score lower on content-based assessments conducted in English than those who are continuously exposed to standard academic English. Thus, test scores may well underestimate students' capability until there has been at least seven years of exposure to English in an academic context (Cummins, 1984). Accordingly, some educational assessment specialists argue that students can and should be tested in their native language until they become proficient in English in an academic context.

However, testing students in their native language leads to the possibility of misalignment of the language of instruction and language of assessment. Results from ELL student assessment studies suggest that translating tests into a student's native language is effective only if the language of instruction was also in a student's native language. To elaborate on this issue, we present a summary of a study that used a translated version of a math test under a randomized field study design.

Abedi, Lord, and Hofstetter (1998) randomly assigned 1,394 eighth-grade students from 49 math classrooms in nine southern California middle schools to three different versions of a math test: (1) Original English; (2) Modified English; and (3) Original Spanish. Math test items were derived from alternate versions of the 1996 NAEP Grade 8 Bilingual Mathematics booklet (M921CG, M9CP, M10CG). All test versions contained the same math items, differing only in their linguistic demands. The mean NAEP math achievement test score for the sample was 12.71 (SD = 6.46, n = 1,394) out of 35 points possible. Results showed the largest difference between math items in Original Spanish and Modified English. Spanish-speaking students taking the Original Spanish version of the test performed the lowest (mean = 9.04, SD = 3.67, n = 242) as compared with students taking the Modified English version (mean = 13.84, SD = 6.92, n = 593) and those taking the standard (Original) English (mean = 13.10, SD = 6.33, n = 559). This difference was significant above and beyond the 0.01 nominal level (F = 28.82; df = 21,388; P = 0.00).

One interpretation of these results is that since nearly all students in the sample received math instruction in English (Sheltered English, English only), it is possible that ELL students perform best on math tests where the language of items matches their language of instruction. This hypothesis was validated in additional subanalyses with ELL students enrolled in math classes where instruction was in Spanish. For these students, their performance was significantly higher on the math test in Original Spanish (mean = 8.74, SD = 3.40, n = 62) than in standard Original English (mean = 3.60, SD = 3.26, n = 11) or in Modified English (mean = 5.29, SD = 2.56, n = 7). Although the numbers of students in this subsample are small, these findings suggest that language of instruction is an important consideration in identifying suitable test accommodations for ELL students.

In summary, the data presented above suggest that students perform better on math tests that are conducted in their language of instruction. A student may be a native speaker of one language, but if he or she has learned math concepts and technical vocabulary through the medium of the English language, then he or she will likely perform better on a math test that uses English. Translating test items from English to other languages thus may not necessarily accommodate ELL students when their language of instruction is English.

Appropriateness, Validity, and Feasibility of Accommodations

The purpose of testing accommodations is to make allowances for certain limitations that a student might have and provide a "level playing field." Accommodations were first developed for students with disabilities, but were later also extended to ELL students (Rivera et al.,

2000). The major concern in using testing accommodations for ELL students is their appropriateness. The effectiveness, validity, and feasibility of accommodations are important considerations in this regard.

Appropriateness

How appropriate are accommodations for ELL students? Since the common characteristic that distinguishes ELL from non-ELL students is the level of English proficiency, it is reasonable to expect that accommodations that help ELL students with their potential language limitations would be the most relevant. However, in many places, the current practice regarding accommodations for ELL students is to use whatever accommodations might be available and/or regarding whatever decision makers find relevant, which may not always result in the most appropriate forms of accommodations for these students. For example, Rivera (2003) presented a list of 73 accommodations that are used nationwide for ELL students. Our analyses of these accommodations revealed that of these 73 accommodations, only 11–15% of them were highly relevant for ELL students in providing assistance with students' language needs (Abedi, 2004b).

The list, for example, included accommodations such as:

- test administered in location with minimal distraction;
- test taker provided preferential seating;
- increased or decreased opportunity for movement;
- adaptive pencils provided;
- person familiar with test taker administers test;
- test taker marks answers in test booklet;
- enlarged answer sheets provided.

Since none of these accommodations address ELL students' language needs, they are not adequate or appropriate for them.

The National Assessment of Educational Progress also uses some accommodations that, at face value, are not very relevant to ELL students' language needs. For example, among the accommodations NAEP used for ELL students in the national sample of the 1998 civics assessment were large print, extended time, reading questions aloud, small group testing, one-on-one testing, and scribe or computer testing (see Abedi & Hejri, 2004). While some of these accommodations may be helpful for some other groups of students (e.g., students with disabilities), they may not be that effective for ELL students.

Studies have found that the provision of accommodations in NAEP increased the *inclusion* rate for these students (Mazzeo, Carlson, Voelkl,

& Lutkus, 2000). However, some studies have shown that accommodations did *not* increase ELL student scores on the NAEP; that is, the performance gap between ELLs and non-ELLs did not narrow. Abedi and Hejri (2004), for example, found no statistically significant differences between the performance of accommodated and nonaccommodated ELL students in the 1998 NAEP main assessments in reading, writing, and civics for students in fourth and eighth grades. Among the most likely explanations for this is the lack of *relevant* accommodations. As indicated earlier, if the accommodations provided to ELL students have no relevance to their cause (mainly English language proficiency), then one would not expect any positive impact of accommodations on the outcome of assessments. Some relevant accommodations, for example, are providing a glossary for noncontent terminology or modifying complex linguistic features. These accommodations directly address ELL students' language needs.

Furthermore, another problem for this comparison was the very small number of ELL students who were accommodated. In the main NAEP assessments, between 7% and 8% of the sampled students were included ELL students, but only a fraction of these students, who had been accommodated by their schools in earlier assessments, received NAEP accommodations. For example, in the main assessment of the 1998 grade 4 reading test, 934 ELL students were included, but only 41 (4%) of the included ELL students were provided with accommodations. In the grade 8 sample, 896 ELL students were included, but only 31 (3.5%) of them were accommodated. Similarly, in the 1998 main assessment in civics, 332 ELL students in grade 4 were included and only 24 (7%) were accommodated. In the same assessment, 493 ELL students were included in grade 8 but only 31 (6%) were accommodated (Abedi & Hejri, 2004).

Validity

Validity is also an important concern when using accommodations for ELL students. If accommodations affect the construct, then the accommodated and nonaccommodated assessments cannot be aggregated. Studies have found that some forms of accommodations may alter the construct being measured (see, e.g., Abedi et al., 2000, 2004a, 2004b). For example, providing a general published dictionary may affect the measurement of the construct, since it may provide content-related information that students can use to answer the questions. Thus, it is likely that the validity of many commonly used accommodations is questionable. However, research on the validity of accommodation is very limited; the validity of only a handful of accommodation strategies used for ELL students have been experimentally examined (see, e.g., Abedi et al., 2004; Sireci et al., 2003).

Feasibility

Feasibility of implementation is yet another issue with accommodation strategies. Accommodation strategies should not become too much of a logistical or financial burden. Computer testing, as one example, could be a burden if a school lacks funding for adequate computers. One-on-one testing may also be logistically challenging in large-scale assessments if there are insufficient personal or financial resources.

The main goal of accommodation is to make assessment more accessible across subgroups of students who otherwise could be affected unfairly by many nuisance variables. The discussion above casts doubt about the ability of current accommodation practices to reach this important goal. There is no firm evidence to suggest that the accommodations used widely by states are effective, feasible, and valid. However, results of some recent studies introduce some accommodation strategies for ELL students that, in addition to being valid, are also effective in reducing the performance gap between ELL and non-ELL students in content area assessments. Below is a brief discussion of research-supported accommodations.

Recommendations for Accommodations

Recent studies at the National Center for Research on Evaluation, Standards and Student Testing (CRESST) have experimentally examined several different forms of accommodation. CRESST and others (see, e.g., Maihoff, 2002; Rivera & Stansfield, 2001) used the linguistic modification approach, and found it to be an effective and valid accommodation in the assessment of ELL students. With this approach, simpler versions of items with language that might be difficult for students were drafted; the task remained the same but noncontent vocabulary and linguistic structures were changed (see Abedi et al., 1997, for further discussion of the nature of and rationale for the modifications). These studies compared student scores on original test items with comparable, linguistically modified items. The following are a few examples of such studies.

Abedi and Lord (2001) examined the effects of linguistic modification of test items as a form of accommodation with 1,031 eighth-grade students in southern California. Test booklets with either Original English versions of the items or Modified English versions of the items were randomly assigned to the students. The results showed significant improvements in the scores of students in low- and average-level mathematics classes who received the booklets with linguistic modifications. Among the linguistic features that appeared to contribute to the differences were low-frequency vocabulary and passive voice verb constructions. English language learners and low-performing students benefited the most from linguistic modification of test items.

In another study, Abedi et al. (1998) examined the impact of linguistic modification on the mathematics performance of English learners and non-English learners. Using items from the 1996 NAEP Grade 8 Bilingual Mathematics booklet, three different test booklets (Original English, Modified English, and Original Spanish) were randomly distributed to a sample of 1,394 eighth-grade students in schools with high enrollments of Spanish speakers. Results showed that modification of the language of items contributed to improved performance on 49% of the items. The students generally scored higher on shorter problem statements.

A third study (Abedi et al., 2000) examined the impact of four different forms of accommodation on a sample of 946 eighth-grade students being tested in mathematics. The accommodations were: (1) Modified English; (2) Extra Time only; (3) Glossary only; and (4) Extra Time plus Glossary. These four accommodation types, along with a standard test condition, were randomly assigned to the sampled students. Findings suggested that some accommodations increased the performance of both English learners and non-English learners, compromising the validity of the assessment. Among the different options, only the Modified English accommodation narrowed the score gap between English learners and other students.

Other studies have also employed the language modification approach. Kiplinger et al. (2000) found linguistic modification of math items helpful in improving the math performance of ELL students. Maihoff (2002) found linguistic modification of content-based test items to be a valid and effective accommodation for ELL students in mathematics testing. Rivera and Stansfield (2001) compared English learner performance on regular and modified fourth- and sixth-grade science items. Although the small sample size did not show significant differences in scores, the study demonstrated that linguistic modification did not affect the scores of English-proficient students, indicating that linguistic modification is not a threat to score comparability.

While the current prevalent trends in accommodations are not supported by research (Solano-Flores & Trumbull, 2003), there is growing evidence that states are paying more attention to research findings on the effectiveness and validity of accommodations. The increasing use of research-supported accommodations for ELL students (such as linguistic modification of items) is encouraging. This trend may result in fairer assessments for ELL students.

Cultural and Other Factors

In addition to language factors, ELL students' ability to succeed on assessments may be affected by cultural factors, since these students come from many different cultural and socioeconomic backgrounds (Hawkins, 2004; Pellegrino, Chudowsky, & Glaser, 2001; Solano-Flores & Trumbull, 2003).

Stiefel, Schwartz, and Conger (2003) found major differences in the performance of ELL students with different cultural/language backgrounds. They found, for example, that Chinese-Dialect and Korean language students score over one standard deviation above average in math (1.036 and 1.028 respectively) as compared with Haitian-Creole speaking students who performed over one-quarter standard deviation below the average (−0.306). They also found that their largest group sampled, students exposed to Spanish at home, tended to perform poorly on tests even when they were proficient in English, suggesting that "lack of English proficiency is only one of several obstacles to English success. [Our] analyses suggest that the performance of students . . . may be related to other characteristics, such as poverty and race/ethnicity" (p. 11). Grissom (2004) found differences between the proportions of ELL students classified across language/cultural lines; for example, Spanish ELL students had a 27% chance of being reclassified as R-FEP, compared with other language ELL students who had a 40% chance of being reclassified as R-FEP.

These results suggest that there might be other factors at play when examining ELL student performance, related to different cultural and socioeconomic factors. These factors include native language literacy and fluency, previous schooling experiences, parent education level, and mental health issues related to mobility, separation from family, and/or trauma (e.g., witnessing civil war). It can be difficult to tally how many years of instruction a mobile student like migrant workers' children or shelter children may have had; it is likely, though, that the number of years of schooling is likely to be significantly different for geographically stable as compared with mobile students. Any and all of these factors can have an impact on students' ability to learn, and it is difficult to separate the many different possible effects.

Discussion

Major issues regarding the equity and validity of assessments for ELL students threaten the authenticity of the accountability system for these students. Unless these issues are resolved, ELL students may be left behind in spite of legislation mandating their inclusion in the educational system and their improvement. Some of these issues need immediate attention.

First, the ELL population must be clearly defined and identified. This must be done before examining the validity and fairness of assessments for them. If the ELL population characteristics are not clearly defined, there will be inconsistency across schools, districts, and states, and consequently, potentially negative implications for their instruction and assessment. Unfortunately, however, the results of studies summarized in this chapter point to legitimate concerns about the current identification system. Thus, the first step in building a valid and fair accountability system for ELL students is to improve the quality of the existing classification system for these students, based on quality research, and then applied through appropriate methodologies.

Inconsistencies in ELL classification may lead to problems in the inclusion of ELL students in the national and state assessments, which is the second major issue for ELL student accountability. Inconsistencies in the inclusion criteria may result in different inclusion rates of ELL students across the nation, which may affect assessment and reporting. While NAEP is suggested as a national benchmark for the NCLB accountability system, the problems in inclusion criteria, as discussed in this chapter, make this role a questionable one for NAEP.

A third major concern for ELL students is the impact of language on the reliability and construct validity of content-based assessments. Unnecessary linguistic complexity in content-based assessments for ELL students may be a source of measurement error, which reduces the reliability of the assessment. More importantly, language factors can be a source of construct-irrelevant variance and may jeopardize the validity of assessments. Thus, if the reliability and validity of standardized achievement tests are suspect for ELL students, the accountability system for these students will be adversely affected. It is therefore imperative to examine assessment systems for ELL students and control for any sources of nuisance variables or construct-irrelevant variance.

The use of accommodations for ELL students is another important consideration when equity issues and for their assessments are discussed. The purpose of accommodations for ELL students is to help them with their linguistic needs without compromising the validity of assessments. However, many of the accommodations used for ELL students originally came from accommodations used for students with disabilities (Abedi, 2004b), which may not be appropriate or adequate for ELL students. On the other hand, all accommodations that are related to students' level of English proficiency are not necessarily valid. For example, test translation has been a questionable form of accommodation, since it is a complex and time-consuming process with the potential for yielding invalid results. As discussed in this chapter, it is therefore essential to examine the effectiveness, validity, and feasibility of all accommodations before they are actually used in the assessment of ELL students. Effective accommodations for ELL students should address their language needs. A useful accommodation would provide them with the help they need to understand assessment questions. For example, reducing unnecessary linguistic complexity may be an example of a relevant accommodation for these students. It is also essential to study the validity of accommodation under experimentally controlled research conditions in which both ELL and non-ELL students are tested under the accommodated and nonaccommodated condition. Research should identify accommodations that, while effective and valid, will also be feasible and can be implemented with minimal effort and resources.

Finally, there are other factors, cultural and socioeconomic, that influence the assessment of ELL students. Large-scale national and state assessments should be sensitive to such factors, though it is clear that there are no easy answers for acknowledging and addressing the obstacles many children face while simultaneously meeting the expectations of state and federal policies mandating adequate yearly progress.

In summary, accountability testing for ELL students may be influenced by many different factors that can be unique to these students. It is imperative to recognize and examine these factors before drawing any implications from test results. The impact of extraneous factors on accountability testing for ELL students may have serious consequences for classification, instruction, and assessment of these students. Before using data for ELL accountability purposes, we must make every effort to try to control these.

REFERENCES

Abedi, J. (2002). Standardized achievement tests and English language learners: Psychometrics issues. *Educational Assessment, 8*(3), 231–257.

Abedi, J. (2004a). *Who is LEP?* Manuscript submitted for publication.

Abedi, J. (2004b). *What is the role of research in accommodation decision-making for English language learner?* Paper presented at the 2004 annual meeting of the American Educational Research Association in San Diego.

Abedi, J., & Hejri, F. (2004). Accommodations in the National Assessment of Educational Progress for students with limited English proficiency. *Applied Measurement in Education, 17*(4), 371–392.

Abedi, J., Hofstetter, C., & Lord, C. (2004). Assessment accommodations for English language learners: Implications for policy-based empirical research. *Review of Educational Research, 74*(1), 1–28.

Abedi, J., & Leon, S. (2003). *LEP classification.* Los Angeles: University of California, Center for the Study of Evaluation/National Center for Research on Evaluation, Standards, and Student Testing.

Abedi, J., Leon, S., & Mirocha, J. (2003). *Impact of student language background on content-based performance: Analyses of extant data* (CSE Technical Report 603). Los Angeles: University of California, National Center for Research on Evaluation, Standards, and Student Testing.

Abedi, J., & Lord, C. (2001). The language factor in mathematics tests. *Applied Measurement in Education, 14*(3), 219–234.

Abedi, J., Lord, C., & Hofstetter, C. (1998). *Impact of selected background variables on students' NAEP math performance* (CSE Technical Report 478). Los Angeles: University of California, National Center for Research on Evaluation, Standards, and Student Testing.

Abedi, J., Lord, C., Hofstetter, C., & Baker, E. (2000). Impact of accommodation strategies on English language learners' test performance. *Educational Measurement: Issues and Practice, 19*(3), 16–26.

Abedi, J., Lord, C., & Plummer, J. (1997). *Language background as a variable in NAEP mathematics performance* (CSE Technical Report 429). Los Angeles: University of California, National Center for Research on Evaluation, Standards, and Student Testing.

Aguirre-Muñoz, Z., & Baker, E.L. (1997). *Improving the equity and validity of assessment-based information systems* (CSE Technical Report 462). Los Angeles: University of California, National Center for Research on Evaluation, Standards, and Student Testing.

Allen, M.J., & Yen, W.M. (1979). *Introduction to measurement theory.* Monterey, CA: Brooks/Cole.

American Educational Research Association, American Psychological Association, & National Council on Measurement in Education. (1999). *Standards for educational and psychological testing.* Washington, DC: American Educational Research Association.

Cummins, J. (1984). *Bilingualism and special education.* San Diego, CA: College Hill Press.

Cummins, J. (1989). *Empowering minority students.* Sacramento: California Association for Bilingual Education.

Cummins, D.D., Kintsch, W., Reusser, K., & Weimer, R. (1988). The role of understanding in solving word problems. *Cognitive Psychology, 20*(4), 405–438.

De Corte, E., Verschaffel, L., & DeWin, L. (1985). Influence of rewording verbal problems on children's problem representations and solutions. *Journal of Educational Psychology, 77*(4), 460–470.

Grissom, J.B. (2004). Reclassification of English language learners. *Education Policy Analysis Archives, 12*(36). Retrieved September 3, 2004, from http://epaa.asu.edu/epaa/v12n36/

Hakuta, K., & Beatty, A. (Eds.) (2000). *Testing English-language learners in U.S. schools.* Washington, DC: National Academies Press.

Haladyna, T.M., & Downing, S.M. (2004). Construct-irrelevant variance in high-stakes testing. *Educational Measurement: Issues and Practice, 23*(1), 17–27.

Hambleton, R.K. (2001). The next generation of the ITC test translation and application guidelines. *European Journal of Psychological Assessment, 17*(3), 164–172.

Hambleton, R.K., & Patsula, L. (1999). Increasing the validity of adapted tests: Myths to be avoided and guidelines for improving test adaptation practices. *Journal of Applied Testing Technology, 1,* 1–12.

Hawkins, M.R. (2004). Researching English language and literacy development in schools. *Educational Researcher, 33*(3), 14–25.

Hudson, T. (1983). Correspondences and numerical differences between disjoint sets. *Child Development, 54,* 84–90.

Improving America's Schools Act of 1994 (IASA), Pub. L. No. 103-382, 108 Stat. 4056 (1994).

Kindler, A.L. (2002). *Survey of the states' limited English proficient students & available educational programs and services, 2000–2001 Summary Report.* Washington, DC: National Clearinghouse for English Language Acquisition and Language Instruction Educational Programs.

Kiplinger, V.L., Haug, C.A., & Abedi, J. (2000, April). *Measuring math—not reading—on a math assessment: A language accommodations study of English language learners and other special populations.* Presented at the annual meeting of the American Educational Research Association, New Orleans, LA.

Kirk, R.E. (1995). *Experimental design, procedures for the behavioral sciences.* Pacific Grove, CA: Brooks/Cole Publishing Company.

Lau v. Nichols. (1974). No. 72-6520, 414 U.S. 56.

Linn, R.L., & Gronlund, N.E. (1995). *Measuring and assessment in teaching* (7th ed.). Englewood Cliffs, NJ: Prentice-Hall.

Lutkus, A.D., & Mazzeo, J. (2003). *Including special-needs students in the NAEP 1998 reading assessment.* Washington, DC: U.S. Department of Education, Institute for Education Sciences, National Center for Education Statistics.

Maihoff, N.A. (2002, June). *Using Delaware data in making decisions regarding the education of LEP students.* Paper presented at the Council of Chief State School Officers 32nd Annual National Conference on Large-Scale Assessment, Palm Desert, CA.

Mazzeo, J., Carlson, J.E., Voelkl, K.E., & Lutkus, A.D. (2000). *Increasing the participation of special needs students in NAEP: A report on 1996 NAEP research activities* (NCES Publication 2000-473). Washington, DC: National Center for Education Statistics.

Messick, S. (1994). The interplay of evidence and consequences in the validation of performance assessments. *Educational Researcher, 23*(2), 13–23.

No Child Left Behind Act of 2001, Pub. L. 107-110, 115 Stat. 1425 (2002).

Pellegrino, J.W., Chudowsky, N., & Glaser, R. (2001). *Knowing what students know: The science and design of educational assessment.* Washington, DC: National Academies Press.

Ramirez, J., Yuen, S., Ramey, D., & Billings, D. (1991). *Final report: Longitudinal study of structured English immersion strategy, early-exit and late-exit bilingual education programs for language minority children* (Vols. 1, 11) (No. 300-87-0156). San Mateo, CA: Aguirre International.

Riley, M.S., Greeno, J.G., & Heller, J.I. (1983). Development of children's problem-solving ability in arithmetic. In H.P. Ginsburg (Ed.), *The development of mathematical thinking* (pp. 153–196). New York: Academic Press.

Rivera, C. (2003, June). *State assessment policies for English language learners.* Paper presented at Council of Chief State School Officers 33rd Annual National Conference on Large-Scale Assessment, San Antonio, TX.

Rivera, C., & Stansfield, C.W. (2001, April). *The effects of linguistic simplification of science test items on performance of limited English proficient and monolingual English-speaking students.* Paper presented at the annual meeting of the American Educational Research Association, Seattle, WA.

Rivera, C., Stansfield, C.W., Scialdone, L., & Sharkey, M. (2000). *An analysis of state policies for the inclusion and accommodation of English language learners in state assessment programs during* 1998–1999. Arlington, VA: The George Washington University, Center for Equity and Excellence in Education.

Salvia, J., & Ysseldyke, J. (1998). *Assessment.* Boston: Houghton Mifflin.

Sandoval, J., & Durán, R.P. (1998). The influence of language: Interpreting tests given to non-native English speakers. In J. Sandoval (Ed.), *Test interpretation and diversity.* Washington, DC: American Pschological Association.

Sireci, S.G., Li, S., & Scarpati, S. (2003). *The effects of test accommodation on test performance: A review of the literature* (Center for Educational Assessment Research Report 485). Amherst: University of Massachusetts.

Solano-Flores, G., & Trumbull, E. (2003). Examining language in context: The need for new research and practice paradigms in the testing of English-language learners. *Educational Researcher, 32*(2), 3–13.

Steele, C.M., & Aronson, J. (1995). Stereotype threat and the intellectual test performance of African Americans. *Journal of Personality and Social Psychology, 69,* 797–811.

Stiefel, L., Schwartz, A.E., & Conger, D. (2003, February). *Language proficiency and home languages of students in New York City elementary and middle schools.* Taub Working Paper. New York: Taub Urban Research Center, New York University. Retrieved from http://www.urban.nyu.edu/education/nyclanguage.pdf

When One Size Does Not Fit All—The Special Challenges of Accountability Testing for Students with Disabilities

DIANA PULLIN

Current national efforts at education reform rely largely on the use of standardized testing, the cornerstone of federal education policy as a result of the No Child Left Behind Act (NCLB) of 2001, with its requirements for regular testing of all students and demonstrations of adequate yearly progress on tests by all schools. The challenges associated with test-driven education reform are considerable. For the population of students with disabilities, their schools and families, and educators, as well as the testing industry, these reforms present even more significant challenges. In a relatively modest period of time, the nation dramatically shifted its social policy goals and educational practices concerning students with disabilities. Since the beginning of compulsory attendance requirements, most students with significant disabilities were excluded from schooling altogether (Pullin, 1999). In the mid-1970s, a choice was made to mandate inclusion of people with disabilities into the mainstream of American life and efforts were made to actively seek out and identify children with disabilities, from mild to the most severe, and to educate these students, utilizing unique legal protections to insure the provision of individually appropriate programs and services. But by the late 1990s, there were growing concerns that students with disabilities continued to fall short in the attainment of educational opportunities sufficient to meet their needs and the nation's aspirations for social, economic, and civic progress. When states and the federal government began to implement high-stakes, test-driven education reform and accountability initiatives, little attention was initially paid to students with disabilities (National Research Council

Diana Pullin is Professor of Education Law and Public Policy and Coordinator of the Dual Degree Program in Law and Education at Boston College.

[NRC], 1997). However, in 1997, Congress made a series of policy choices to require the inclusion of students with disabilities in state and local education reforms and testing programs (Heubert & Hauser, 1999). The challenges associated with this policy commitment have been substantial.

This chapter assesses the impact of accountability testing of students with disabilities and the use of test data concerning these students. The history of educating students with disabilities, the social and educational policy goals for these students, and the legal provisions for these students create a unique set of challenges for accountability testing. These challenges are exacerbated by the limited research available to inform the implementation of these initiatives. And as the stakes and visibility of current testing programs increase, the challenges of teaching and testing students with disabilities become clearer and the uses and misuses of data concerning these students become more significant.

Social Policy and Historical Contexts

In 1971, it was estimated that only about 40% of the nation's children with disabilities were being provided public education services (Weintraub, Abeson, & Braddock, 1972). All but one of the states had compulsory attendance laws that exempted students with disabilities from school attendance requirements (Children's Defense Fund, 1974). The U.S. Congress determined in 1975 that there were 1 million students with disabilities excluded from public education (Education for All disabled Children Act; 20 U.S.C. § 1401(b)(4), 1975).

When the nation's social policies concerning the education of students with disabilities were modified in 1975, the new initiatives embraced several key policy goals: every child with a disability is educable and should be educated; students with disabilities should be educated to the maximum extent appropriate in the same settings and classrooms as their nondisabled peers; all students with disabilities should receive an individually appropriate education as defined in an individualized educational program (IEP); and procedural safeguards should be in place to protect the rights of disabled students (Hehir & Gamm, 1999; Minow, 1990; NRC, 1997; Pullin, 1999; Turnbull, 1993).

Since federal and state special education and disability rights laws were first passed, substantial progress has been made in identifying and serving students with disabilities. The U.S. Department of Education (2000) has now reported to the Congress that the goal of educating all students with disabilities is being met. Although fraught with chal-

lenges, overall, the provision of special education services has improved
(Aleman, 1995; Gartner & Lipsky, 1987; Singer & Butler, 1987). The
number of students with disabilities being served is large: over 6 million.
Almost 9% of the students in the country received special education
services in 2000–2001 under the federal Individuals with Disabilities
Education Act (IDEA) and another smaller group of students with
disabilities who received supportive services but did not need special
education was also served (U.S. Department of Education, 2002). The
nation progressed from the exclusion of most students with disabilities
from schooling 30 years ago to a contemporary expectation that most
students with disabilities would finish high school and perhaps go to
college (Jennings, 2001).

However, concerns still remain that students with disabilities do not
receive the appropriate opportunities to learn to high academic standards and that, aside from individual family reporting through the
annual IEP process, there has been little accountability on the part of
states or local school districts for the sufficiency of the education provided to students with disabilities (NRC, 1997; Thurlow & Wiley,
2004). These factors led to the U.S. Congress' mandate in 1997 that
students with disabilities should be included in state accountability
systems (IDEA; 20 U.S.C. § 1412(a)(17)(A); 34 C.F.R. § 300.138(a)). In
2001, Congress implemented explicit and detailed requirements for the
participation of these students in the state accountability initiatives of
NCLB. And, in 2004, Congress highlighted the problems associated
with setting low expectations for the educational outcomes of students
with disabilities (IDEA, 2004). The federal government recognized that
too often in the past students with disabilities were excluded from
learning opportunities and that high-stakes accountability systems
could play a role in ameliorating this problem (U.S. Department of
Education, 2003b). States also recognized that some students with disabilities were never taught academic skills and concepts, even at very
basic levels (Massachusetts Department of Education, 2002). As a result
of NCLB requirements, states are to include all, or almost all, students
with disabilities in assessments, and to aggregate these students' results
with those of nondisabled students, as well as disaggregating results to
demonstrate specifically how this population is doing.

Many educators and parents believe that participation in large-scale
assessments is a critical component of insuring access to education and
equality of opportunity for students with disabilities (Heubert, 2004;
Heubert & Hauser, 1999; Lehr & Thurlow, 2003; Thurlow, 2004).
Federally funded research at the National Center for Educational Out-

comes (NCEO) on the participation of students with disabilities in accountability testing describes several arguments in support of the movement: to provide an accurate picture of educational achievement by students with disabilities; to allow students with disabilities to benefit from education reforms; to allow accurate comparisons of schools, school districts, or states; to avoid inappropriate grade retention of students with disabilities and to inhibit inappropriate referrals to special education among students who might seek to obtain a high school diploma without having to pass a graduation test; to promote high expectations for students with disabilities; to promote access to the general curriculum and academic content knowledge, rather than functional real-life and socialization skills for students with disabilities; and to meet legal requirements (Quenemoen, Rigney, & Thurlow, 2002; Thurlow, Elliott, & Ysseldyke, 2003).

Others argue that the participation of students with significant or complex disabilities will be unnecessarily traumatizing, demoralizing, or even abusive (Koretz & Barton, 2003–2004; see also Quenemoen et al., 2002) or will result in a loss of the individualization goals of the special education process (Holbrook, 2001). The problem is particularly significant in states or localities where students with disabilities had access in the past to alternate types of diplomas or other credentials, which could have the same value as the general diploma in the workplace or in higher education even though students met standards very different from those in the general education curriculum (Karger & Pullin, 2002).

Putting aside controversies over the desirability of the participation of students with disabilities, there are considerable problems associated with the test data generated by these systems and with how those data are used. To understand fully issues of test data use and misuse for students with disabilities in high-stakes accountability systems, some background information is in order.

Legal Protections for Students with Disabilities

One of the most salient considerations for the education of students with disabilities is their unique set of legal protections. The federal IDEA (1975/2004), in place since 1975 and most recently amended in 2004, and analogous state laws ensure the provision of an appropriate education, defined by each student's IEP. Section 504 of the Rehabilitation Act (1973)[1] and the Americans with Disabilities Act (ADA) (1990) and their implementing regulations bar discrimination on the basis of

disability and require the provision of appropriate education and reasonable accommodations for students with disabilities participating in
testing programs. ADA and its regulations include requirements that
credentialing tests in secondary education be offered "in a place and
manner accessible to persons with disabilities or offer alternative accessible arrangements for such individuals" (42 U.S.C. 12189; 29 C.F.R.
36.309).

There have been a relatively limited number of court cases concerning high-stakes accountability testing. Courts have concurred that federal constitutional law, as first established in *Debra P. v. Turlington* (1979,
1981), bars the deprivation of a high school diploma based on a test
unless government can prove that the students received adequate notice
about the test, that the test was fundamentally fair and valid, and that
the test covered material actually taught in the classroom (Heubert &
Hauser, 1999; Karger & Pullin, 2002).

In cases specifically addressing graduation testing for students with
disabilities, courts have sanctioned requirements that these students
pass a test as a prerequisite for receipt of a diploma (Karger & Pullin,
2002; Pitoniak & Royer, 2001). However, courts have often found that
the general constitutional requirements applying to all students were
expanded by federal special education laws and that students in special
education are entitled to appropriate IEPs to allow them to be prepared
for the tests (Karger & Pullin, 2002). While federal and state courts
have found that, under disability laws, states are required to provide
students with disabilities with reasonable accommodations, states are
not required to provide "substantial modifications" in testing that would
have an impact on the meaning or interpretation of the exam score
(Center on Education Policy, 2004; Karger & Pullin, 2002; Pitoniak &
Royer, 2001).

The IDEA requires the participation of students with disabilities in
state and district-wide assessments, with appropriate accommodations
where necessary (§ 614; 34 C.F.R. § 300.138(a)). Similarly, Title II of
the ADA (42 U.S.C. § 12132; 28 C.F.R. § 35.130(b)(7)) and Section 504
(29 U.S.C. § 794(a); 28 C.F.R. § 41.53) require states and school districts to provide students with disabilities with reasonable accommodations (Karger & Pullin, 2002). The provisions of the most recent
revisions of the IDEA also allow alternate assessment systems and place
responsibility for determining participation in alternate assessments
with the IEP team (Public Law 108-446, § 614). It is this individualized
decision making about the nature and extent of the participation by a
student with disabilities in testing and the power of a local IEP team to

make these decisions (Kyle, Papadopoulou, & McLaughlin, 2004; Minnema, Thurlow, & Warren, 2004) that lead to many of the difficulties associated with the data generated in a high-stakes testing program.

Accommodated Testing

The overwhelming majority of students with disabilities participate in accountability testing right alongside every other student (Heubert & Hauser, 1999; Thurlow & Wiley, 2004). However, some students with disabilities can only participate in accountability testing with provision of appropriate or reasonable accommodations. A test accommodation is any variation in the standardized administration of a large-scale test in response to a student's disability (AERA/APA/NCME, 1999), in an effort to enhance the validity of the information obtained about a student (Elliott, Kratochwill, & McKevitt, 2001; Koenig & Bachman, 2004; Koretz & Barton, 2003–2004; NRC, 1997; Pitoniak & Royer, 2001). The most common types of accommodation are extended time administrations for a timed test, large print versions of tests, and reading items or directions aloud (Koretz & Barton, 2003–2004). The use of test accommodations for students with disabilities should, according to the APA Test Standards, be subject to empirical study to assess the appropriateness of the changes to the test (AERA/APA/ NCME, 1999, Standard 10.3).[2]

There is a policy value addressed by accommodated administrations; it is reported that they make most students, parents, and educators feel as if testing is both fairer and a better indicator of the knowledge and skills of students with disabilities, although some students find accommodations demeaning (Lang, Kumke, Cowell, & Ray, 2003). However, the technical challenges associated with accommodated administrations are considerable. Variations in accommodation practices may be reasonable given the different content or constructs states may be measuring, or they may reflect a lack of clarity about how to make appropriate accommodations decisions. Accommodation determinations must be made both at the macro level, in policy declarations by the testing agency, based on the skills and knowledge the test is designed to measure, and at the micro level, by the family and educators who are members of each IEP team (Pitoniak & Royer, 2001; Thurlow & Wiley, 2004). States vary considerably in their determinations of which accommodations are acceptable, with some states allowing considerable local latitude on these decisions (Center on Education Policy, 2004; Lehr & Thurlow, 2003). Accommodations might vary from the provision of open-ended timing on a timed test to the provision of a reader, or a scribe to write out responses.

Students with disabilities vary enormously in their capabilities and need for accommodations and some students receive multiple accommodations (Elliott et al., 2001; Koretz & Barton, 2003–2004). Even within a particular disability type, there can be considerable variability in both the severity of the disability and in the range of disability characteristics across a spectrum, from almost undetectable to almost totally debilitating, such as occurs in the largest disability category (specific learning disabilities) that range across reading, writing, mathematics, and general information processing capabilities (Fuchs & Fuchs, 1999). However, to the extent there is flexibility to determine which accommodations to use, there is a threat to the validity and reliability of these scores, as well as the validity of inferences from the scores (Koretz & Barton, 2003–2004).

For all accommodations, validity considerations must focus clearly on the content, or constructs, a test seeks to measure (AERA/APA/NCME, 1999; Pitoniak & Royer, 2001). The accommodation of reading a mathematics test aloud might do little to diminish the validity of inferences about a student's mathematics achievement; however, reading aloud a reading test might or might not be an accommodation that diminishes the validity of inferences, depending on whether the test seeks to assess comprehension as opposed to other reading skills (Fuchs & Fuchs, 1999; Koretz & Barton, 2003–2004).

The research on the effects of accommodations is still somewhat limited and is mixed in terms of outcomes (Pitoniak & Royer, 2001). There is considerable difficulty associated with the design of research to assess validity, since there are no clear criteria or sources of evidence for comparison of accommodated test administrations with other assessments of the performance of students with disabilities (Koretz & Barton, 2003–2004; Pitoniak & Royer, 2001).[3] Koretz and Barton argue, based in part on an analysis of the studies of the validity of predictive testing for higher education admissions, that accommodations may be used too extensively and may undermine validity. Some research indicates that there are many instances in which an accommodation has no impact on the validity of inferences that can be made based on a test score (Fuchs & Fuchs, 1999). In one set of experimental studies, accommodations were found to have a moderate to large effect for the vast majority of students with disabilities (Elliott et al., 2001). The same study reported significant positive effects for the scores of students without disabilities as well. For some of the more common accommodations for students with disabilities, like extended time, it is not clear that the problems associated with accommodated testing could not be alleviated substantially simply by making all accountability tests untimed.

Since accommodations and their administration at the local level vary so significantly and since validity evidence regarding accommodated administrations is relatively limited, there must be doubt raised about test data collected from accommodated administrations, particularly when those data are aggregated, as NCLB requires, with data from regular administrations of tests. As a result, the use of data from accommodated tests must be undertaken with some caution, particularly when the data are used for high-stakes accountability purposes (Pitoniak & Royer, 2001).

Alternate Assessments

For the very small proportion of the school population with significant cognitive disabilities, test-driven education reform has come to be embodied in alternate assessments. For students unable to participate in general testing due to significant cognitive disabilities, even with accommodations, these alternate approaches take several possible forms: portfolios of student work or the collection of a body of evidence about success in attainment of standards and goals set out in a student's IEP; performance assessments; checklists; and an approach somewhat resembling more traditional paper and pencil tests, most often filled out by teachers on the basis of one-on-one assessments of students (Lehr & Thurlow, 2003). The most common approach in alternate assessment is the use of a portfolio assessment linked to grade-level expectations, scored with the same achievement level descriptors as the general assessment. Some states use more than one alternate assessment approach (Thompson & Thurlow, 2003). One particularly controversial form of alternate assessment is out-of-level assessment, or assessment based on alternate standards. Most often, this practice entails testing a student at a level below the student's assigned grade level (Thurlow, 2004). The U.S. Department of Education regards out-of-level assessments as a type of alternate assessment for the purposes of calculating adequate yearly progress (AYP) and expects that no more than 9.0% of students with disabilities will participate in assessments based on alternate achievement standards, or failing that, that no more than this proportion will be included in AYP calculations (U.S. Department of Education, 2003a). Despite federal efforts to limit the use of out-of-level testing, it is reportedly utilized more frequently now than it was prior to the federal effort at limitation (VanGetson, Minnema, & Thurlow, 2004). And many states have aggregated out-of-level data in ways that could make it impossible to meaningfully understand (VanGetson et al.).

Alternate assessment approaches were created very quickly over the past decade in response to state and federal accountability mandates in a context in which there has been little experience or research evidence to inform either educators or testing experts on how to proceed with large-scale assessment of students with significant disabilities (Quenemoen, Thompson, & Thurlow, 2003; Thurlow, Quenemoen, Thompson, & Lehr, 2001). In 2004, Congress mandated national studies to examine the use of alternate assessments and their validity, reliability, and effectiveness (IDEA, § 664(c)). Despite the limited body of research evidence, as of 2003 twenty-four states used alternate assessment in determining the award of standard high school diplomas to students with disabilities, with three other states working on implementation of such a system; seven states allowed students with disabilities to obtain a standard diploma without passing the graduation assessment. A small minority of six states makes grade-to-grade promotion determinations on the basis of alternate assessment (Thompson & Thurlow, 2003).

Alternate assessments must adhere to the same standards for technical quality as other assessments, including reliability and validity standards (68 Fed. Reg. 68699; 34 C.F.R. § 200.2(b) and 200.3(a)(1); AERA/APA/NCME, 1999). There are considerable challenges associated with establishing content coverage and appropriate scoring criteria for alternate assessments (Quenemoen et al., 2003). As a result of the data gathering methods utilized, there are considerable problems associated with standard-setting, as well as significant validity and reliability issues associated with alternate assessment (Quenemoen et al., 2002).

Content domains. First, there is the problem of determining the content domains for alternate assessments. In most instances, an effort is made to assess achievement of state academic content standards (in some form) as opposed to the types of purely functional skills previously assessed, in an effort to ensure the exposure of students with disabilities to the general curriculum and to high standards of performance (Lehr & Thurlow, 2003). This is consistent with the reform goals of accountability testing. And, for the particular reform goals associated with educating students with disabilities, the movement has had a noted impact in changing the practice of special educators of students with significant disabilities who, in the past, often were not familiar with standards-based academic curriculum content (*Education Week*, 2004; Quenemoen et al., 2003; Zatta & Pullin, 2004).

Scoring and standard-setting. Scoring and standard-setting present challenges in alternate assessment. Scoring criteria for alternate assessments, in many instances, take into account not only such factors as student performance on a content standard, but also such contextual variables as the extent to which the student can generalize performance in a variety of settings beyond the assessment context (not typically embedded in most general assessments) and the extent to which a student requires the support of others (such as a teacher, an aide, or another student giving cues, prompting a student response, or guiding the hand of a student with a disability) to perform a skill (Quenemoen et al., 2003; Thompson & Thurlow, 2003). The latter would seldom be considered appropriate in most general assessment or testing contexts, except in a limited number of accommodated administrations.

Aggregation of results. Another set of alternate assessment data problems arises when states attempt to aggregate alternate assessment results with those from regular assessments, as NCLB requires. Some states scale the results of their alternate assessment so they have the same or very similar values as those used in the general assessment. Other states scale alternate assessment results so that they are on the lower end of a scale scoring spectrum and general assessment scores occupy the top of that spectrum (with perhaps the possibility of an overlap on the scale for high-performing alternate assessment examinees) (Quenemoen et al., 2002). Massachusetts, for example, referring to the latter approach as "expanded" scaling, has categorized the lowest of the four performance levels on the standard assessment into three subcategories for the alternate assessment. Hence, the general assessment categories of "advanced," "proficient," "needs improvement," and "warning" also include three subcategories within the warning category ("awareness," "emerging," and "progressing") that can, in addition to "needs improvement," be used as score levels on the alternate assessment (Wiener, 2002). As of 2003, only 47 of the 2,000 students with disabilities who participated in Massachusetts' portfolio-based alternate assessment met the minimum proficiency standard and received regular high school diplomas (Schworm, 2004). In the Spring 2004 testing, 5,200 students participated in alternate assessment; 35 were "proficient" and only two 10th graders were "proficient" on both of the 10th-grade tests used to determine the award of a high school diploma (Massachusetts Department of Education, 2004).

Efforts to link scores on two very different kinds of assessments, like the general assessment and the alternate, raise numerous validity and equating problems, particularly when the content coverage differs significantly on the two types of assessments (Koretz & Barton, 2003–2004; Minnema, Thurlow, Moen, & VanGetson, 2004).[4] In the face of the numerous and perhaps irresolvable technical issues associated with attempting to put the results for alternate and general assessments on the same scale, when the assessments are in fact measuring different skills, one commentator suggests that the only solution is a policy choice—one that is perhaps not that difficult given the relatively low number of students with disabilities involved in alternate assessment in most schools (Hill, 2001). Hill argues that if the use of the scores is solely to demonstrate student improvement over time[5] and if there is consistency in both testing conditions and score scaling over time (which is a significant assumption), then placing both alternate and general assessments on the same scale, even if the two assessments are not measuring the same things, is acceptable. Hill's approach places in the hands of policymakers a set of fairness choices regarding how to weight the various types of student gains (a dilemma they confront in any event, as they try to weigh the impact of reading versus mathematics achievement, for example). If, however, a state attempts to assess school gain and school status, as in the case where high-performing schools have different requirements for improvement from low-status schools, then the treatment of alternate assessment participants can have an impact, particularly if a school has considerable power, under a state's procedures, to classify which students should participate in the alternate assessment and how.

All of the variations possible in alternate assessment systems raise real concerns about the reliability of alternate assessment results and considerably complicate validity inquiries about the assessments. Any data resulting from the aggregation of results from alternate and general assessments should be utilized with caution.

Test Data Generated by Including or Excluding Students with Disabilities

The validity challenges associated with accountability testing are considerable for the regular administrations of tests to students who have no disabilities and who participate in the general curriculum. It has been properly asserted that setting content and performance standards and establishing cut scores for general accountability testing involves the complexity of both normative and descriptive components (Haertel & Lorie, 2004) and that, in fact, there may be little real agreement on even such fundamental premises of standards-based testing as the definitions of the knowledge that ought to be tested (Wilson, 2004). The "cultural construction" of knowledge and of validity arguments is fraught with complexity when dealing with the general population of students. The issue of disability, with its own unique weighty cultural biases, adds to this complexity (Minow, 1990). Indeed, there are already suggestions that there has been insufficient attention to issues of item bias for individuals with disabilities (Koretz & Barton, 2003–2004). Layering on the difficulties associated with alternate achievement standards, alternate assessments, and accommodated administrations for students with disabilities compounds the challenges of enhancing the validity of these measures, where content and performance, as well as measurement methodologies, can be quite new and not fully researched. In fact, the matter of ascertaining the validity of test score inferences for students with disabilities may exceed our current scientific capacity.

Given all of these difficulties, what can be said about test data that reflect the inclusion or exclusion of students with disabilities in accountability testing programs? Initial failure rates on most accountability assessments have tended to be quite high and group disparities quite large, particularly for disadvantaged minority, disability, and low-income groups. The rates are even larger when the excluded, those who were "held back" from their age cohort group and dropouts who never participated in the tests, are considered. As of the early part of this decade, the failure rate for students with disabilities was about 30–40% higher than for other students (Heubert, 2004). These high failure rates occur in a context in which the stakes associated with the tests are increasing. Exit exams are used for high school graduation in 20 states and will affect about 70% of all high school students by 2008 (Center on Education Policy, 2004). Exit tests tend to encourage more content coverage, but also tend to correlate with higher dropout rates (Center on Education Policy, 2004) and clearly have an increasing impact on students with disabilities. Fourteen states require special education students to pass high-stakes tests in order to earn regular high school diplomas, while 24 states allow students with disabilities to earn diplomas even if they did not pass the tests (*Education Week*, 2004).

The social policy goals that resulted in the individualization of education for students with disabilities present a challenge in the pursuit of the new social policy goals of seeking educational accountability for all students. Accommodated testing and alternate assessment practices, as well as the participation of individuals with disabilities in general education and testing, lead to a variety of questions about the utility of data generated in high-stakes testing programs. And the present limited body of research means that data on the effects of accommodations and alternate assessments are very limited (Koretz & Barton, 2003–2004; Pitoniak & Royer, 2001).

Inconsistency

There are several additional problems associated with test data concerning students with disabilities. There is a high degree of inconsistency from district to district and state to state in the identification of disabilities, resulting in over- and underidentification and variable classifications depending on location, availability of services, gender, and ethnicity (NRC, 2002). In particular, there is over- and underidentification of students into disability categories on the basis of socioeconomic status, language background, and ethnicity (NRC). This is particularly true for those disabilities based not on a medical diagnosis of eligibility, but instead on a more subjective determination. There is particular variability in the specific learning disabilities category (NRC), probably the largest group of students participating in these assessments and receiving accommodations in testing (Pitoniak & Royer, 2001).

Lack of Data

Next, some of the data necessary to understand more fully the problems associated with test information simply have not been collected. Under NCLB, states have to report participation rates in testing programs for students with disabilities. One study found that in 2002–2003, 19 states and the District of Columbia were unable to calculate the number of students by disability status and grade level who took state tests. Where data were available, the participation rate for students with disabilities in state testing programs ranged from 40% to 100% across the states (*Education Week*, 2004). Further, states can allow students to participate in alternate assessment who should not really be included, can lower standards, and can exclude students from the accountability system (Quenemoen et al., 2002). In compiling data, states take different approaches to the question of how to account for students who do not participate in testing due to truancy, illness, or other factors. Some do not count these students at all, some give these students a zero or failing score, and some states are still trying to determine what to do (Thompson & Thurlow, 2003). One report found 10 states that excluded the results of tests given with accommodations and 18 states automatically giving a zero score or a score below the proficiency level for tests given with nonstandard accommodations or out-of-level assessments (*Education Week*). Small schools, schools with small populations of students with disabilities, and schools with special education centers serving a concentrated population of students with disabilities pose particular data problems (Thompson & Thurlow). Some states and large districts provide limited or no reporting on the performance of students with disabilities in special programs. Clearly, knowing how each state makes each of these decisions is important to an understanding of that state's test data and their appropriate uses or potential misuses.

Given state variability in classifications of students and in assessment approaches, state-to-state comparisons are useless and even some within-state comparisons are meaningless, given the role of local decision making about individual participation. States vary in not only the content standards they use, the tests they employ, and the scoring criteria and proficiency standards they set, but also in the decision rules they utilize to define participation, to compute the AYP data, and to aggregate and disaggregate data for subgroups like disability as required by NCLB.

Educational Settings

When data collection includes students with disabilities, there are many more opportunities for data anomalies due to the higher levels of complexity associated with educating these students. For example, there are a considerable number of students with disabilities placed in private schools, under the IDEA mandates for public schools to provide a free and appropriate education to students with disabilities even if this means sending them to a private school at public expense. Other students with disabilities are in juvenile justice facilities. In total, about 4% of students with disabilities nationwide are not educated in public school settings, and states have insufficient mechanisms for obtaining accountability data for these students and for the programs educating them (Kyle et al., 2004). Massachusetts, which places a high proportion of students with disabilities full time in private schools in order to meet their educational needs, has found that these students are often "lost" in the state testing program, not participating in alternate assessment to the extent that would be predicted, and not included in any AYP calculations (Driscoll, 2004).

Appeals Procedures

In another initiative complicating data collection, some states have undertaken laudable efforts to enhance the fairness of their testing systems by instituting test appeal procedures. In Massachusetts, for example, for the high school graduating classes of 2003 and 2004 participating in the general assessment, about 2% of students were deemed proficient not on the basis of the test, but through one of two "performance appeals processes" using student portfolios or other indicators of student achievement (i.e., evidence from teachers, cohort group performance comparisons) (Center on Education Policy, 2004; Nelhaus, 2004). It is unclear how many of those deemed "proficient" through waivers of their test scores were students with disabilities, but it is clear that students attaining a proficiency determination in this manner are being assessed under a very different, almost qualitative, metric, rather than the quantitative measures used in general assessment.

Corruption

Finally, any system with high-stakes consequences for individual students, educators, or institutions can generate data subject to many sources of corruption, either intended or not (Haney, 2000; Ysseldyke, Dennison, & Nelson, 2004). This is true for data about all students, of course, not just students with disabilities. The factor of disability status only increases the number of moments in the system in which corruption can occur—in initial classification into the special education system; in a sudden classification into a disability status when the prospect of a low test score looms; in the decision of an individual student's IEP team about how a student should participate in testing; and on and on. The consequences, particularly the local-level consequences, of accountability data make a difference in the potential intentional or inadvertent corruption of the system. The greater the consequences associated with testing, the greater the potential for corruption (see Kornhauber, 2004).

Adequate Yearly Progress

Perhaps the two most significant decisions based on test score data from students with disabilities are, first, individual decisions about high school graduation, grade-to-grade promotion, or class placement and, second, the collective accountability determinations required by the NCLB mandates for measures of AYP. For both sets of decisions, there is a clear need to assure the reliability and validity of the test score information being used to make the determinations. And there is a need to follow professional standards and guidelines clearly calling for the use of multiple sources of information in addition to test data to substantiate such critical decisions, particularly when there are associated high-stakes consequences for individuals (AERA/APA/NCME, 1999).

The AYP measures allow for school, district, and state accountability data, and the requirement for disaggregated AYP reporting for students with disabilities, among other particular subgroups, draws attention to the achievement of at-risk students. For students with disabilities, these AYP requirements mark a policy shift from individualized approaches and an accountability to one family for one special child's progress to a broader effort to insure institutional accountability for the educational progress of all special education students. Students with disabilities who participated in accommodated or alternate assessments should, as a matter of good professional practice, be included in accountability data along with students who participated in the general assessment and have the same impact on the accountability index (NRC, 1997). However, the technical challenges associated with this effort have been recognized (Thurlow et al., 2001) and are still largely unresolved.

Consistent with NCLB requirements, the U.S. Department of Education requires that each state must have a coherent assessment plan and a state-defined and federally approved set of assumptions and algorithms for calculating AYP for all students in schools and for calculating AYP for the mandatory subgroups of students (U.S. Department of Education, 2003b). However, in an effort to reduce the burdens on state and local educators, the U.S. Department of Education has recently minimized the impact of test data from students with the most significant cognitive disabilities in AYP calculations by allowing the exclusion of the scores on alternate assessments for up to 1% of the students tested (U.S. Department of Education, 2003b; 68 Fed. Reg. 68699; 34 C.F.R. § 200.13(c)). The Department has also now allowed states to exclude from AYP calculations up to 2.0% of the scores of the total tested school population when those scores are based upon modified academic achievement standards (such as out-of-grade testing of students with learning disabilities) (U. S. Department of Education, 2005).

The most recent test data of students with disabilities show some trends, although these can only be called general trends given the problems associated with the data. There is clearly an achievement gap between students without disabilities and students with disabilities, particularly as students get older, although the gap varies across states and can narrow considerably when students are given chances for retesting (Thurlow & Wiley, 2004). An otherwise high-performing school can be deemed low-performing by missing AYP solely on the basis of the scores of students with disabilities.

Where there are data available, recent reports demonstrate that in a majority of the states, the achievement gap between special and general education students is over 30 percentage points (*Education Week*, 2004). One study reported that most urban school districts, by 2004, had no schools that had achieved AYP for students with disabilities (Nagle & Crawford, 2004). Some suggest that high failure rates on accountability tests are, on their face, evidence of a denial of access to sufficient high-quality instruction, particularly for disadvantaged students like students with disabilities (Heubert, 2004). Insufficient capacity to deliver sufficient opportunity to learn will not be addressed easily or quickly and in many instances, it is not clear what to do or how long it will take (Elmore, 2004). Many special educators do not know how to align their instruction to state accountability content standards (Heubert) and we know that one of the most significant challenges for educating students with disabilities is the severe shortage of qualified special educators (McLaughlin, Artiles, & Pullin, 2001; NCR, 2002).

As the stakes associated with standards-based testing increase for students and for institutions and educators, the uses and misuses of data concerning students with disabilities become more significant. The possibilities for data corruption and for other unintended consequences increase. Some reports are being made that students with disabilities are being exposed to more educational opportunities as a result of the high-stakes, standards-based testing programs (Zatta & Pullin, 2004), while others report that previous educational policy goals of including more students with disabilities in regular classrooms are now being undermined by efforts to optimize test scores by isolating students with disabilities in special classes or schools (Nagle & Crawford, 2004).

Conclusion

When it comes to the use and possible misuses of test data concerning students with disabilities, there is ample room for controversy. There is no small amount of irony associated with the NCLB call for a scientific research base for education programs when there is such a limited research base concerning the accountability testing of students with disabilities (Koretz & Barton, 2003–2004). Our social policy aspirations and our social science capabilities are far apart, as they have been many times previously in our efforts to promote equity for individuals with disabilities (Pullin, 2002).

We have learned a great deal since 1997 when Congress mandated the inclusion of students with disabilities in state testing programs. There is still much more research that needs to be done, particularly on the effects of accommodations and the validity of scores (Koretz & Barton, 2003–2004) and on issues associated with alternate assessments. Some of this research may not be possible within the constraints of traditional quantitative analysis because of the subjective factors associated with classifying students with disabilities and the individualization approaches of educating and assessing students with disabilities.

The ultimate test of the tests will be found in a study of the extent to which the students taking the test do better on other tests and assessments or, most important, in employment or higher education (Kornhauber, 2004). Some evidence has been accumulated, indicating improved instruction and improved performance for students with disabilities (Ysseldyke et al., 2004). Other reports indicate teacher time spent compiling an alternate assessment portfolio is very high (Zatta & Pullin, 2004), which may detract from time spent teaching or may in fact, more desirably, strengthen the academic standards-focus of the teaching.

The validation of test use for high-stakes decisions must, according to the Test Standards, include analysis of empirical evidence of the intended and unintended consequences of test use (AERA/APA/NCME, 1999, Standards 1.23 and 1.24). As one of the intentions of the current accountability testing movement was the enhancement of student learning, then corroborating evidence will have to be gathered to ascertain whether this is in fact the case. In addition, a reasonable empirical evaluation of the unintended negative consequences of high-stakes accountability tests will be needed (Baker & Linn, 2004). Baker and Linn call for more evidence of test validity for children with disabilities and for accommodated and alternate assessments and longitudinal studies undertaken to assess the effects of an accountability system over time. A recent panel at the National Academy of Sciences also calls for further research on testing students with disabilities, particularly to inform such programs as the National Assessment of Educational Progress (Koenig & Bachman, 2004).

Some suggest that the testing industry should adopt concepts of universal design (Johnstone, 2003; Thompson, Johnstone, Thurlow, & Clapper, 2004). This approach, now recommended for all educational programs in the most recent reauthorization of the IDEA, might encourage such efforts as untimed testing. Universal design, once employed solely by the architects who designed curb-cuts and door handles to make sidewalks and entryways accessible for individuals with physical disabilities, resulted in the unintended consequence of making life easier for all sorts of individuals with baby carriages to push or with bags of groceries to carry into an apartment building. If test design could be more universalized, stripping tests to their most fundamental and simple formats, some see a solution to the problems of aggregating and interpreting test score data. If new assessments are developed using a widely representative group of students of all types, posing fewer barriers to students with disabilities, and targeted to the essence of the content knowledge to be assessed, then perhaps some of the problems just discussed could be resolved (Johnstone, 2003). Unfortunately, there are limited data on the validity, reliability, or consequences of such approaches. And, in particular, it is not clear that such approaches could be developed without stripping them of meaningful academic content. However, further consideration of such approaches, as well as alternate assessment techniques like portfolios or teaching rating sheets, could be fruitful for informing our testing practices for all students.

The nation's policy goals of including students with disabilities in education reform and accountability are indisputably important. The quest for closing the gap between our policy goals and our educational and psychometric capabilities has far to go. Our laudable efforts to include students with disabilities in education reform initiatives, however, present clear illustrations of some of the challenges to be confronted in implementing test-based education reform. Until more evidence on the testing of students with disabilities is compiled, there is a need for great caution in making meaningful comparisons among these groups of students and in basing significant decisions for individuals or institutions on the test scores.

NOTES

1. All students in special education are covered by IDEA and by Section 504. For the much smaller population of students with disabilities who do not need special education, Section 504 bars discrimination on the basis of disability status and the provision of an appropriate education and supportive services or accommodations. This chapter primarily addresses issues concerning IDEA. However, many 504 students participate in accommodated testing and this discussion is fully applicable to them.

2. A number of administrative opinions by the Office of Civil Rights (OCR) of the U.S. Department of Education, the federal agency charged with investigating education complaints under Section 504 and the ADA, have concluded that accommodations are

not required when they interfere with the skill being measured and compromise the validity of a test or program (Karger & Pullin, 2002).

3. The same problem exists in some respects for students without disabilities, for whom the use of something like teacher's grades would also be an unacceptable data source to those who argue that the lack of rigor of teacher judgments was what prompted the call for high-stakes accountability tests in the first place.

4. As a result of the settlement of a court case, Oregon considers all accommodations allowed by a state review panel to be valid unless there is evidence to the contrary (*Education Week*, 2004).

5. This is not necessarily what NCLB calls for nor what all state AYP calculations do (Linn, 2003).

REFERENCES

Aleman, S. (1995, March) *Special education: Issues in the state grant program of the Individuals with Disabilities Education Act.* Washington, DC: Congressional Research Service of the Library of Congress.

American Educational Research Association, American Psychological Association, National Council on Measurement in Education (AERA/APA/NCME). (1999). *Standards on educational and psychological testing.* Washington, DC: American Educational Research Association.

Americans with Disabilities Act. Pub. L. No. 101-336, 42 U.S.C. 12101 et seq. (1990).

Baker, E., & Linn, R. (2004). Validity issues for accountability systems. In S. Fuhrman & R. Elmore (Eds.), *Redesigning accountability systems for education* (pp. 47–72). New York: Teachers College Press.

Center on Education Policy. (2004). *State high school exit exams: A maturing reform.* Washington, DC: Author.

Children's Defense Fund. (1974). *Children out of school in America.* Washington, DC: Author.

Debra P. v. Turlington. 474 F. Supp. 244 (M.D. Fla. 1979), *aff'd in part, rev'd in part,* 644 F.2d 397 (5th Cir. 1981), *on remand,* 564 F. Supp. 177 (M.D. Fla. 1983), *aff'd,* 730 F.2d 1405 (11th Cir. 1984).

Driscoll, D. (2004, July 6). *MCAS participation by students with significant disabilities, a memorandum to Directors of Approved Private Special Education Schools.* Retrieved August 13, 2004, from http://www.doe.mass.edu/mcas/alt

Education for All Disabled children Act of 1975, Pub. L. No. 94-142, 89 Stat. 773 (1975).

Education Week. (2004, January 8). *Special education in an era of standards: Count me in.* (Quality Counts 2004 Supp.). Retrieved from http://counts.edweek.org/sreports/qc04/

Elmore, R. (2004). *School reform from the inside out: Policy, practice, and performance.* Cambridge, MA: Harvard Education Press.

Elliott, S.N., Kratochwill, T.R., & McKevitt, B.B. (2001). Experimental analysis of the effects of testing accommodations on the scores of students with and without disabilities. *Journal of School Psychology, 39*(2), 3–24.

Fuchs, L., & Fuchs, D. (1999, November). Fair and unfair testing accommodations. *The School Administrator, 56*(10), 24–30.

Gartner, A., & Lipsky, D. (1987). Beyond special education: Toward a system for all students. *Harvard Educational Review, 57,* 367–395.

Haertel, E., & Lorie, W. (2004). Validating standards-based test score interpretations. *Measurement: Interdisciplinary Research and Perspectives, 2*(20), 61–103.

Haney, W. (2000). The myth of the Texas miracle in education. *Education Policy Analysis Archives, 8*(41). Retrieved January 12, 2005, from http://epaa.asu.edu/epaa/v8n41/

Hehir, T., & Gamm, S. (1999). Special education: From legalism to collaboration. In J. Heubert (Ed.), *Law and school reform: Six strategies for promoting educational equity* (pp. 205–243). New Haven, CT: Yale University Press.

Heubert, J. (2004). High-stakes testing in a changing environment: Disparate impact, opportunity to learn, and current legal protections. In S. Fuhrman & R. Elmore (Eds.), *Redesigning accountability systems for education* (pp. 220–242). New York: Teachers College Press.

Heubert, J., & Hauser, R. (Eds.). (1999). *High stakes: Testing for tracking, promotion, and graduation.* Washington, DC: National Academies Press.

Hill, R. (2001). *The impact of including special education students in accountability systems.* Dover, NH: National Center for the Improvement of Educational Assessment, Inc. Retrieved August 25, 2004, from http://www.nciea.org

Holbrook, P. (2001). When bad things happen to good children: A special educator's views of MCAS. *Phi Delta Kappan, 82*(10), 781–785.

Individuals with Disabilities Education Act (IDEA). 20 U.S.C. 1400 et seq., as amended by Public Law 108-446. (1975/2004).

Jennings, J. (2001). *A timely IDEA: Rethinking federal education programs for children with disabilities.* Washington, DC: Center on Education Policy. Retrieved August, 2004, from http://www.cep-dc.org

Johnstone, C.J. (2003). *Improving validity of large-scale tests: Universal design and student performance* (Technical Report 37). Minneapolis: University of Minnesota, National Center on Educational Outcomes. Retrieved January 1, 2005, from http://education.umn.edu/NCEO/OnlinePubs/Technical37.htm

Karger J., & Pullin, D. (2002, June). *Exit documents and students with disabilities: Legal issues.* College Park: Education Policy Reform Research Institute, The University of Maryland.

Koenig, J.A., & Bachman, L.F. (Eds.). (2004). *Keeping score for all: The effects of inclusion and accommodation policies on large-scale educational assessments.* Washington, DC: National Academies Press.

Koretz, D., & Barton, K. (2003–2004). Assessing students with disabilities: Issues and evidence. *Educational Assessment, 9*(1&2), 29–60.

Kornhauber, M. (2004, January and March). Appropriate and inappropriate forms of testing, assessment, and accountability. *Educational Policy, 18*(1), 45–70.

Kyle, S., Papadopoulou, E., & McLaughlin, M. (2004, September). *Accountability for all: Results from a study on accountability policies affecting students with disabilities educated in special schools and settings.* College Park: Educational Policy Reform Research Institute (EPPRI), Institute for the Study of Exceptional Children, University of Maryland.

Lang, S., Kumke, P., Cowell, E., & Ray, C. (2003, April). *The consequences of using testing accommodations: Student, teacher, and parent reactions to and perceptions of testing accommodations.* Madison: Wisconsin Center for Education Research, University of Wisconsin at Madison. WCER Working Paper 2003-3. Retrieved August 28, 2004, from http://www.wcer.wics.edu/publications

Lehr, C., & Thurlow, M. (2003). *Putting it all together: Including students with disabilities in assessment and accountability systems* (Policy Directions 16). Minneapolis: University of Minnesota, National Center on Educational Outcomes. Retrieved August 20, 2004, from http://education.umn.edu/NCEO/OnlinePubs/Policy16.htm

Linn, R. (2003, Winter). *Requirements for measuring adequate yearly progress.* National Center for Research on Evaluation, Standards, and Student Testing (CRESST). Policy Brief 6. Los Angeles: CRESST.

Massachusetts Department of Education (2002, February). *Massachusetts Comprehensive Assessment System: Concerns and questions about alternate assessment.* Malden, MA: Author.

Massachusetts Department of Education. (2004). *Massachusetts Comprehensive Assessment System: MCAS results, 2004.* Malden, MA: Author.

McLaughlin, M., Artiles, A., & Pullin, D. (2001, November). Challenges for the transformation of special education in the 21st century: Rethinking culture in school reform. *Journal of Special Education Leadership, 14*(2), 51–62.

Minnema, J., Thurlow, M., & Warren, S.H. (2004). *Understanding out-of-level testing in local schools: A first case study of policy implementation and effects* (Out-of-Level Testing Project Report 11). Minneapolis: University of Minnesota, National Center on Educational Outcomes. Retrieved January 1, 2005, from http://education. umn.edu/NCEO/OnlinePubs/OOLT11.html

Minnema, J.E., Thurlow, M.L., Moen, R.E., & VanGetson, G.R. (2004). *States' procedures for ensuring out-of-level test instrument quality* (Out-of-Level Testing Project Report 14). Minneapolis: University of Minnesota, National Center on Educational Outcomes. Retrieved January 1, 2005, from http://education.umn.edu/NCEO/OnlinePubs/OOLT14.html

Minow, M. (1990). *Making all the difference: Inclusion, exclusion, and American law.* Ithaca, NY: Cornell University Press.

Nagle, K., & Crawford, J. (2004, April). *Opportunities and challenges: Perspectives on NCLBA from special education directors in urban school districts.* College Park: Educational Policy Reform Research Institute (EPPRI), Institute for the Study of Exceptional Children and Youth, University of Maryland.

National Research Council (NRC). (1997). *Educating one and all: Students with disabilities and standards-based reform.* L. McDonnell, M. McLaughlin, & P. Morison (Eds.). Committee on Goals 2000 and the Inclusion of Students with Disabilities, National Research Council. Washington, DC: National Academies Press.

National Research Council (NRC). (2002). *Minority students in special and gifted education.* M.S. Donovan & C. Cross (Eds.). Committee on Minority Representation in Special Education, National Research Council. Washington, DC: National Academy of Science.

Nelhaus, J. (2004, June). *One state's approach to holding students to a common standard for high school graduation and addressing the AERA/APA/NCME standards.* Paper presented at the annual Large-Scale Assessment Conference of the Council of Chief State School Officers, Boston, MA.

No Child Left Behind Act of 2001, Pub. L. No. 107-110, 115 Stat. 1425 (2002).

Pitoniak, M.J., & Royer, J.M. (2001, Spring). Testing accommodations for examinees with disabilities: A review of psychometric, legal, social, and policy issues. *Review of Educational Research, 71*(1), 53–104.

Pullin, D. (1999). Whose schools are these and what are they for? The role of the rule of law in defining educational opportunity in American public education. In G.J. Cizek (Ed.), *Handbook of educational policy* (pp. 3–29). San Diego, CA: Academic Press.

Pullin, D. (2002). Testing individuals with disabilities: Reconciling social science and social policy. In Committee on Disabilities, American Psychological Association (Eds.), *Assessing individuals with disabilities in educational, employment, and clinical settings* (pp. 11–31). Washington, DC: American Psychological Association.

Quenemoen, R., Rigney, S., & Thurlow, M. (2002). *Use of alternate assessment results in reporting and accountability systems: Conditions for use based on research and practice* (Synthesis Report 43). Minneapolis: University of Minnesota, National Center on Educational Outcomes. Retrieved August 20, 2004, from http://education.umn.edu/NCEO/OnlinePubs/Synthesis43.html

Quenemoen, R., Thompson, S., & Thurlow, M. (2003). *Measuring academic achievement of students with significant cognitive disabilities: Building understanding of alternate assessment scoring criteria* (Synthesis Report 50). Minneapolis: University of Minnesota, National Center on Educational Outcomes. Retrieved August 20, 2004, from http://education.umn.edu/NCEO/OnlinePubs/Synthesis50.html

Rehabilitation Act. (1973). 20 U.S.C. 794.

Schworm, P. (2004). MCAS detour proves tough. *The Boston Globe,* July 12, pp. B-1, B-4.

Singer, J., & Butler, J. (1987, May). The Education for All Handicapped Children Act: Schools as agents of social reform. *Harvard Educational Review, 57*(2), 125–152.

Thompson, S.J., Johnstone, C.J., Thurlow, M.L., & Clapper, A.T. (2004). *State literacy standards, practice, and testing: Exploring accessibility* (Technical Report 38). Minneapolis: University of Minnesota, National Center on Educational Outcomes. Retrieved January 1, 2005, from http://education.umn.edu/NCEO/OnlinePubs/Technical38.htm

Thompson, S., & Thurlow, M. (2003). *State special education outcomes: Marching on.* Minneapolis: University of Minnesota, National Center on Educational Outcomes. Retrieved January 3, 2005, from http://education.umn.edu/NCEO/OnlinePubs/2003StateReport.htm./

Thurlow, M. (2004). Biting the bullet: Including special-needs students in accountability systems. In S. Fuhrman & R. Elmore (Eds.), *Redesigning accountability systems for education* (pp. 115–137). New York: Teachers College Press.

Thurlow, M., Elliott, J., & Ysseldyke, J. (2003). *Testing students with disabilities: Practical strategies for complying with district and state requirements* (2nd ed.). Thousand Oaks, CA: Corwin Press.

Thurlow, M., Quenemoen, R., Thompson, S., & Lehr, C. (2001). *Principles and characteristics of inclusive assessment and accountability systems* (Synthesis Report 40). Minneapolis: University of Minnesota, National Center on Educational Outcomes. Retrieved August 24, 2004, from http://education.umn.edu/NCEO/OnlinePubs/Synthesis40.html

Thurlow, M.L., & Wiley, H.I. (2004). *Almost there in public reporting of assessment results for students with disabilities* (Technical Report 39). Minneapolis: University of Minnesota, National Center on Educational Outcomes. Retrieved January 1, 2005, from http://education.umn.edu/NCEO/OnlinePubs/Technical39.htm

Turnbull, H. (1993). *Free appropriate public education: The law and children with disabilities* (3rd ed.). Denver, CO: Love Publishing Company.

U.S. Department of Education. (2000). *Twenty-second annual report to the Congress on the implementation of the Individuals with Disabilities Education Act.* Washington, DC: Author.

U.S. Department of Education. (2002). *Twenty-fourth annual report to the Congress on the implementation of the Individuals with Disabilities Education Act.* Washington, DC: Author.

U.S. Department of Education. (2003a). *Title I—Improving the academic achievement of the disadvantaged; Part II; Final rule.* 68 Fed. Reg. 68698 (2003) (codified at 34 CFR Part 200)

U.S. Department of Education. (2003b). *Title I—Improving the academic achievement of the disadvantaged, background.* 68 Fed. Reg. 69698.

U.S. Department of Education. (2004, March 2). *Letter to chief state school officers regarding inclusion of students with disabilities in state accountability systems.* Retrieved January 23, 2005, from http://www.ed.gov/admins/lead/account/csso030204.html

U.S. Department of Education. (2005, April 7). *Raising achievement: Alternate assessment for students with disabilities.* Retrieved April 15, 2005, from http://www.ed.gov/print/policy/elsec/guid/raising/alt-ass-long/htm

VanGetson, G., Minnema, J., & Thurlow, M. (2004). *Rapid changes, repeated challenges: States' out-of-level testing policies for 2003–2004* (Out-of-Level Testing Project Report 13). Minneapolis: University of Minnesota, National Center on Educational Outcomes. Retrieved January 1, 2005, from http://education.umn.edu/NCEO/OnlinePubs/OOLT13.html

Weintraub, F., Abeson, A., & Braddock, D. (1972). *State law and education of handicapped children: Issues and recommendations.* Arlington, VA: Council for Exceptional Children.

Wiener, D. (2002). *Massachusetts: One state's approach to setting performance levels on the alternate assessment* (Synthesis Report 48). Minneapolis: University of Minnesota, National Center on Educational Outcomes. Retrieved January 7, 2005, from http://education.umn.edu/NCEO/OnlinePubs/Synthesis48.html

Wilson, S. (2004). Opening Pandora's Box: The human side of validation. *Measurement: Interdisciplinary Research and Perspectives, 2*(2), 125–128.

Ysseldyke, J., Dennison, A., & Nelson, R. (2004). *Large-scale assessment and accountability systems: Positive consequences for students with disabilities* (Synthesis Report 51). Minneapolis: University of Minnesota, National Center on Educational Outcomes. Retrieved January 1, 2005, from http://education.umn.edu/NCEO/OnlinePubs/Synthesis51.html

Zatta, M., & Pullin, D. (2004, April). Education and alternate assessment for students with significant cognitive disabilities: Implications for educators. *Education Policy Analysis Archives, 12*(16) 1–27.

CHAPTER 10

Is the Glass Half Full or Mostly Empty? Ending Social Promotion in Chicago

MELISSA RODERICK, JENNY NAGAOKA, AND ELAINE ALLENSWORTH

There is perhaps no more controversial policy in education today than the decision to retain students on the basis of standardized tests. There is also most likely no arena in which there is such a wide divide between researchers on the one hand and policymakers on the other. To policymakers, such efforts are popular. They send a strong message. They give focus to reform efforts. They are often popular with teachers who express on surveys that social promotion hurts children (Byrnes, 1989; Jacob, Stone, & Roderick, 2004; Tompchin & Impara, 1992). And they make sense to the public. Students should not be allowed to progress without having the basic skills they need. But national education organizations and research review panels have taken strong stands against "high-stakes testing," arguing that such policies are a misuse of testing and rely on a failed practice, grade retention, as a means of remediating poor performance (American Educational Research Association, 2000; Heubert & Hauser, 1999; National Association of School Psychologists, 2003).

In 1996, Chicago became the epicenter for this debate when it "ended social promotion" in the third, sixth, and eighth grades. While not the first, Chicago's initiative has been the most sustained to date and has produced the clearest evidence of positive as well as negative results. Test scores rose rapidly after the institution of high-stakes testing and the proportion of students with very low test scores fell. Early evidence suggested, however, that those students retained under

Melissa Roderick is an Associate Professor in the School of Social Service Administration at the University of Chicago. Jenny Nagaoka is a Project Director at the School of Social Service Administration at the University of Chicago. Elaine Allensworth is an Associate Director of the Consortium on Chicago School Research in Chicago.

the policy—nearly 1 in 5 third graders and 1 in 10 sixth and eighth graders—were struggling (Roderick, Nagaoka, Bacon, & Easton, 2000). In this chapter, we look more closely at the long-term evidence on the effects of Chicago's initiative based on findings from the Consortium on Chicago School Research's multiyear evaluation. We begin by laying out the theory of action of high-stakes testing and the debate over its impact. After describing the Chicago policy and the evaluation, we then focus on two questions. First, is there evidence from the Chicago study that would support the claims on either side of the debate over how high-stakes testing will shape students', parents', and teachers' response to the policy? Second, what do we know about the effects of the policy on test scores, overall, and on those students who were retained, in particular, and, given the evidence presented, can we make sense of the patterns of these impacts across students and grades?

The Policy Debate Over High-Stakes Testing and Retention

Often in the debate over high-stakes testing it seems that researchers and policymakers are talking about two different sets of initiatives and are seeing quite different policy mechanisms at work. The central premise of high-stakes testing is that promoting students who have not mastered basic skills sets these students up to fail in later grades and that it is critical that students master the basics before they are allowed to progress. The theory of action of such policies is that the threat of retention combined with extra short-term remedial supports will be enough to move students forward. Proponents argue that the policy will motivate students to work harder and encourage parents to carefully monitor their child's progress. It sends strong signals to teachers to focus attention on low-performing students and to stress the development of basic skills. The approach in Chicago and other school districts also relies heavily on after-school and summer-school programs to provide extra instructional time and more focused remedial support. Thus, increased motivation, when combined with increased instructional support and extra time on task, will help students raise their test scores and be promoted. Those students who do not meet the standards, moreover, will get additional instructional time by repeating the grade. Many educators believe strongly that an extra year of instruction can give low-achieving students the extra time they need to raise their skills and that this extra time will lay the foundation for more positive achievement later on (Alexander, Entwistle, & Dauber, 1994; Byrnes, 1989; Jacob et al., 2004; Tompchin & Impara, 1992).

Opponents focus on three central arguments: (1) that the policy will not invoke the intended response from teachers, principals, and students; (2) that even if elements such as summer school do work, the use of retention ultimately makes sacrificial lambs of the most vulnerable students; and (3) that the diagnosis of the problem is wrong and misses the central processes generating low performance in urban schools. First, opponents argue that, rather than improving instruction, high-stakes testing leads teachers to focus too much time on test preparation and on the specific skills students need to pass the test, resulting in a significant narrowing of the curriculum (Koretz, 1999; Linn, 1993; Mehrens, 1998). There is strong evidence for this contention. Research on test-based accountability generally finds that teachers react to accountability programs by altering their content coverage and assessment methods so that they are aligned with the test and by increasing time on test preparation (Darling-Hammond & Wise, 1985; Firestone, Mayrowetz, & Fairman, 1998; Jones, Jones, & Hardin, 1999; Koretz, 1988; Koretz, Barron, Mitchell, & Stecher, 1996; Rosenholtz, 1987; Smith 1991; Urdan & Paris 1994). Advocates of standards argue that with the right test, alignment would be positive and would lead to greater opportunity to learn (Cohen, 1996; Darling-Hammond, 1996; Rowan, 1996). But accountability linked to a basic skills test may hinder instruction if it creates disincentives for teachers to engage in the kind of intellectually challenging instruction that is associated with higher achievement in urban schools (Bryk, 2003; Newmann, Bryk, & Nagaoka, 2001). Rather than improving student motivation, moreover, opponents worry that high-stakes testing will have precisely the opposite effect. Too much time on test preparation and an overly narrow focus on test performance may lead students to see their class work as less engaging and relevant to their lives. And low-achieving students may become more, not less, disengaged in school if they feel that they cannot do well on standardized tests and that promotional standards are out of their reach (Betts & Costrell, 2001; Lee, Smith, Perry, & Smylie, 1999; Wheelock, Bebell, & Haney, 2000).

Second, opponents argue that grade retention hurts children. There is some debate over the short-term effects of retention. Meta-analyses of research results on retention generally conclude that retention is associated with negative short-term effects on achievement, particularly in the upper grades (Holmes, 1989; Holmes & Matthews, 1984; Jackson, 1975; Jimerson, 2001). More recent studies offer varying conclusions about the academic effects of retention in the early grades with several more recent studies finding no to positive effects (Alexander et al. 1994; House, 1998; Jimerson et al., 1997; Peterson, DeGracie, & Ayabe, 1987; Pierson & Connell, 1992) and others finding significant negative effects for all grades or in very early grades (Holmes, 2000; Reynolds, 1992). Studies that have examined the long-term effects of retention, however, find that even when there are short-term positive benefits, they are not sustained over time (Alexander et al., 1994; Holmes 1989; Peterson et al., 1987). And there is strong evidence that students who are overage for grade face an increased risk of dropping out (Allensworth, 2004; Gampert, 1987; Grissom & Shepard, 1989; House, 1998; Reardon, 1996; Roderick, 1994).

And third, critics of high-stakes testing argue that the basic diagnosis of the problem and its proposed remedy—that if students simply worked harder, teachers focused their efforts, and low-achieving students were given extra instructional time that supplemented their current instruction they would raise their test scores—are simply incorrect (Bryk, 2003; Elmore, 2002). Richard Elmore has characterized arguments for high-stakes testing as "fatally" simple approaches that fail to recognize the importance of creating better capacity within schools. Without paying attention to instruction, according to this argument, accountability focused on students will not lead to sustained improvements in test performance. And by missing the problem, high-stakes testing may ultimately work to exacerbate rather than ameliorate differences in performance across students and schools.

In this debate, critics often stand on a stronger research base. There is evidence that expanded learning time is linked to improved student achievement during the regular school hours and that summer programs are effective, at least in the short term (Cooper, Kelly, Valentine, & Muhlenbruck, 2000; Cooper, Nye, Kelly, Lindsay, & Greathouse, 1996; Denham & Lieberman, 1980; Fisher & Berliner, 1985; Levin & Tsang, 1987; Smith, 1998). There is mixed evidence and much debate on the effectiveness of after-school programs focused on instruction and we know little about the potential impact of after-school and summer-school supports under high-stakes regimes (Fashola, 1998; Smith, Degener, & Roderick, 2004). Most importantly, arguments for high-stakes testing rely heavily on the idea that students, teachers, and parents will change their behavior and that this will be enough to raise student performance. There has been little research on whether these effects actually occur. Previous studies of high-stakes testing in the elementary grades focused almost exclusively on the impact on students who did not make the test-score cutoffs and were retained, tracking their achievement following the retention decision (Gampert, 1987;

House, 1998). There has been little investigation of whether high-stakes testing in the elementary grades, particularly when combined with extra resources, increases achievement on standardized tests for all students prior to the promotional gate—both those who are promoted as well as those who may later be retained (Catterall, 1989; Mehrens, 1998; Roderick & Engel, 2001).

The Chicago Policy

Chicago's initiative to end social promotion began in 1995, when the mayor of Chicago gained control over the school system.[1] The new policy was part of an array of initiatives aimed at turning around public perception, expectations, and climate, and ultimately performance in the Chicago public schools (CPS) (Bryk, 2003; Hess, 1999, 2002). What the mayor inherited seemed like a mess. The central office was badly mismanaged, and the school system was in fiscal and physical disarray. Only 26% of elementary school students in grades 3 to 8 had reading test scores that placed them at or above national norms on the Iowa Test of Basic Skills (ITBS). Over 40% of students scored in the bottom quartile on the ITBS. While there was evidence that some schools had improved under the first wave of school reform, by the mid-1990s it was clear that a significant group of schools and students had essentially been left behind (Sebring, Bryk, Roderick, & Camburn, 1996).

The new administration brought fiscal talent and union peace and initiated substantial investments in the physical plant of the CPS. On the education side, the new administration brought a singular focus to bear on achievement, namely test scores on the ITBS, by coupling a strong accountability program for schools with high-stakes testing for students (Bryk, 2003; Hess, 2002). Seventy-one of the city's 475 elementary schools and over half of the high schools were placed on probation because of very low test score performance (Finnigan & O'Day, 2003; Hess, 1999).[2] Usurping the role of local school councils created under Chicago's prior reform, these schools were assigned promotion managers and were mandated to develop corrective action plans for improvement.

The new promotion policy was straightforward. Students in the third, sixth, and eighth grades would face mandatory summer school and ultimately retention if they did not meet minimum test-score cut-offs on the ITBS in reading and mathematics.[3] The initial test score standards were set relatively low—one year below grade level for the third grade, a year and a half below grade level in the sixth grade, and a year and eighth months below grade level in the eighth grade. These cutoffs correspond to roughly the 20th percentile on the national ability distribution. Students in special education and students who were in bilingual education for three years or less were exempted from the policy, meaning that their promotional decisions would not be made solely on the basis of test scores.

The administration invested heavily in after-school and summer-school supports to give students extended instructional time, focused remediation, and extra chances to pass the test. Students who did not meet the test-score cutoffs at the end of the school year were required to participate in Summer Bridge and were given a second chance to meet the standard in August. The program provided six weeks of instruction for three hours a day for third and sixth graders. Eighth graders attended four hours a day for seven weeks. Summer Bridge provided a significant reduction in class size, on average 16, and a highly prescribed and centrally developed curriculum that was aligned with the ITBS (Roderick, Engel, & Nagaoka, 2003). Teachers were provided with daily lesson plans and all instructional materials and monitors visited classrooms to ensure that teachers were following the prescribed program. (Summer Bridge continues to be offered to students who do not meet test-score cutoffs.)

Schools were also provided monies for an after-school program, called Lighthouse. Lighthouse began as a small program in 1996–1997 in 40 low-performing elementary schools but expanded rapidly so that by the 1999–2001 school year, over 356 elementary schools in Chicago provided Lighthouse to over 81,000 students, making it one of the largest after-school programs in the country (Jacob et al., 2004; Smith et al., 2004). The program provided funding for 20 weeks of after-school programming and schools were given wide flexibility in designing their programs and in deciding which grades and which students to serve.[4]

In Summer Bridge, Chicago adopted a prescribed approach to addressing the needs of students. In comparison, the district's approach to retention is quite traditional with one twist—additional chances to pass the test. The primary focus of the retention experience is to help students raise their test scores to the cutoffs. Retained students were held to the policy during their retained year, and if they did not raise their test scores to the cutoffs by the spring, they were required to attend a second Summer Bridge. In the winter of 1998 and 1999, retained students were provided a third chance to meet the promotional test-score cutoffs in January. These "mid-year promotes," along with retained students who passed the promotional requirement at the end of the school year with scores well above the cutoff, were allowed to rejoin their age-appropriate classmates after an intensive double dose of summer school.[5] Other than mandatory retesting, the district gave little structure to the retained year. Decisions about how to group retained students for instruction, whether they would have the same teacher, or whether they would be given extra supports were left to the principal. Initially, schools with high retention rates were provided extra funding but there was little prescription as to how these resources should be used. Stone, Engel, Nagaoka, and Roderick (2005), in a qualitative analysis of the experience of retained students, found that schools differed somewhat in how they structured the retention year, for example, whether students received the same teachers, but a common theme was that students received few extra supports or alternative intervention. Thus, the educational experience of retention amounted to going through the policy a second time.

The magnitude of Chicago's initiative was unprecedented. As seen in Table 1, in the first year, only half of third graders subject to the policy, 65% of sixth graders, and 72% of eighth graders met the promotional cutoffs at the end of the school year, resulting in nearly 27,000 students needing to attend Summer Bridge (Roderick, Bryk, Jacob, Easton, & Allensworth, 1999). By the end of the summer, CPS retained 20% of eligible third graders and approximately 10% of sixth- and eighth-grade students (Roderick et al., 1999). Even with high retention rates, early trends were promising. In 1995, in the year prior to the policy, only 60% of Chicago's sixth graders had reading and mathematics ITBS test scores above 5.3 grade equivalents, the promotional cutoff for that grade. In 1999, fully 74% of sixth graders reached this cutoff by the then end of the school year and fully 85% by the end of the summer. Thus, the Summer Bridge program and the second chance opportunity it afforded seemed particularly effective in allowing more students to be promoted. There also appeared to be consistent improvements in school year passing rates, perhaps reflecting implementation effects as schools adjusted to the policy and the expansion of the Lighthouse after-school program. Given both high retention rates and these trends in passing rates, an important focus of the evaluation of this initiative was to look more carefully at what might be generating these trends and the impact of the various components of the policy on student achievement.

The Ending Social Promotion Study

The Consortium on Chicago School Research's evaluation of the Chicago policy focused on the period from 1996, the first full year in

TABLE 1.

A Summary of Passing, Retention, and Progress Rates among Third, Sixth, and Eighth Graders in the Chicago Public Schools, Prior to and After the Policy

	Third Grade			Sixth Grade			Eighth Grade		
	Prior to Policy	After Policy		Prior to Policy	After Policy		Prior to Policy	After Policy	
	1994–95	1996–97	1998–99	1994–95	1996–97	1998–99	1994–95	1996–97	1998–99
Proportion of students who were able to meet the minimum test-score cutoffs for promotion									
In May (end of school year) or August (end of Summer Bridge)	49%	52% 69%	64% 76%	60%	65% 80%	74% 85%	57%	73% 84%	73% 86%
Proportion retained	1.5% 359	20% 4,644	19% 4,522	1.0% 232	12% 3,047	11% 2,768	1% 232	10% 2,217	8% 1,791

which the policy was implemented, to 2001. The study drew on three sources of data. First, we used longitudinal school records including achievement test files and administrative records from the mid-1990s to the present. These data include test scores from first to eighth grade for both pre- and postpolicy cohorts, information on students' demographics, special education and bilingual education status, age and grade, school attendance, and school outcomes such as school dropout. Second, the study relied heavily on surveys conducted both prior to and after the policy. The Consortium's longitudinal survey project regularly surveyed all CPS teachers, principals, and sixth- and eighth-grade students. Surveys were conducted in 1994, 1997, and, during the study, in 1999 and 2001. Survey data, as we will see later in this chapter, were used to trace trends in students' reports of their experiences in school and teachers' reports of instruction. In 1999 and 2001, surveys included a special supplement that asked teachers and principals about their attitudes toward retention and their assessment of the impact of the promotional policy and its accompanying programs. In the summer of 1999, the study also surveyed sixth and eighth graders and all teachers in Summer Bridge.

Finally, quantitative data were supplemented with a longitudinal qualitative study of students and a qualitative classroom observation study of Summer Bridge. The longitudinal study followed 100 low-achieving African-American and Latino sixth- and eighth-grade students in five elementary schools during the year before they took the test, over the summer, and during the retained or promoted year. We collected teachers' assessments of these students and interviewed teachers regarding their instructional approach toward assisting students in raising their test scores. The Summer Bridge evaluation included an intensive study of Summer Bridge classrooms during the summer of 2000. We observed third-, sixth-, and eighth-grade classrooms in 12 schools four times over the summer for a total sample of 140 observations. The goal of this chapter is to provide a general overview of our findings and the main themes that emerged from the multiple components of our evaluation. We are unable in this short chapter to give detailed descriptions of samples and methods. Further information can be obtained in our published reports and research articles including findings on: (1) pregate achievement effects (Roderick et al., 1999; Roderick et al., 2000; Roderick & Engel, 2001; Roderick, Jacob, & Bryk, 2003; Smith et al., 2004); (2) effects on students' experiences of school, on instruction, and teacher and principal attitudes toward retention and the policy (Jacob et al., 2004); (3) the effects of Summer Bridge

(Roderick et al., 2003a; Roderick, Jacob, & Bryk, 2004); and (4) the effects of retention (Allensworth, 2004; Nagaoka & Roderick, 2004; Roderick & Nagaoka, 2005; Stone et al., 2004).

Results

Evaluating the Claims of Proponents and Opponents: Teachers' and Principals' Evaluation of the Effect of the Policy and Evidence of Changes in Student and Teacher Behavior, Instruction, and Support for Students

The ending social promotion policy was associated with significant improvements in support for low-achieving students from teachers and parents with some evidence of positive motivational effects. Few studies have evaluated the claim that the threat of retention will change the amount of support low-achieving students receive from adults and spur students to take their achievement more seriously (Mehrens, 1998). We looked at evidence for these effects using three sources of information: (1) surveys of teachers and principals in both 1999 and 2001; (2) trends in sixth and eighth graders' reports of their experience in school; and (3) qualitative interviews with students and teachers. Table 2 shows teachers' and principals' responses to a series of questions on the 1999 surveys on their assessment of the impact of the ending social promotion initiative.[6] Teachers and principals generally felt that the policy had a positive impact on increasing teacher and parental support for low-achieving students. Almost 90% of principals and 75% of teachers agreed or strongly agreed that the policy had made parents more concerned about their child's progress, sentiments that were echoed in our teacher interviews (Jacob et al., 2004). Teachers also expressed that the policy had a positive impact on their own behavior. Over 80% of teachers agreed or strongly agreed that the policy made them more sensitive and responsive to students' needs and had worked to focus their instructional efforts.

Educators' assessment that the policy led to improvements in adults' support for low-achieving students was reflected in students' own report of the academic support they received from teachers. Figure 1 presents trends in a key indicator of academic support, "personal support from teachers for school work." We present trends for eighth graders. A similar trend was observed in the sixth grade (Jacob et al., 2004). In each survey year, students were asked to respond to a series of questions about the academic support they received from teachers, such as the extent to which they believed their teacher was willing to give them extra help, believed they could do well in school,

PRINCIPALS' AND TEACHERS' ASSESSMENT OF THE IMPACT OF THE ENDING SOCIAL PROMOTION POLICY IN CHICAGO: CONSORTIUM ON CHICAGO SCHOOL RESEARCH SURVEY RESULTS, 1999

	Elementary School Teachers				Elementary School Principals			
	Strongly Disagree	Disagree	Agree	Strongly Agree	Strongly Disagree	Disagree	Agree	Strongly Agree
How much do you agree with the following statements?								
The threat of retention motivates students to work harder	5%	28%	58%	9%	2%	26%	63%	5%
The policy has made parents more concerned about students' progress	3%	15%	66%	16%	1%	10%	67%	22%
As a result of the CPS promotion policy . . .								
Nearly all teachers feel extra responsibility to help students meet standards	3%	12%	63%	22%	1%	10%	70%	19%
I am more sensitive to individual student needs/problems	2%	16%	69%	13%	1%	18%	67%	14%
The school instructional efforts have been focused in positive ways	1%	15%	71%	13%	2%	11%	72%	15%
How much do you agree with the following statements?								
Summer Bridge has had positive effects on students	2%	13%	68%	17%	2%	7%	75%	16%
Lighthouse has had positive effects on students	4%	12%	68%	16%	1%	5%	70%	24%
I feel supported in helping students at risk for retention	5%	17%	63%	15%	1%	11%	73%	15%
To what extent do you think the CPS promotional policy . . .								
Places too much emphasis on basic skills	14%	63%	19%	4%	6%	65%	24%	5%
Is consistent with my own views about what's best for student learning	3%	20%	65%	12%	6%	26%	58%	10%
Limits my attention to higher-order thinking	10%	59%	26%	5%	5%	60%	30%	5%

Note: In 1999, 7,900 teachers, or approximately 47% of the 16,895 elementary school teachers in the system, responded to the survey, representing approximately 315 of the 450 CPS elementary schools. Of the elementary schools in the system, 80% were represented in the 1999 survey. At the school level, there was no evidence of response bias. The proportion of teachers in low-income, minority, and low-performing schools who responded to the survey was the same as for the school system as a whole. When comparing teacher demographic information reported on teacher surveys with that contained in the CPS personnel files, we found that the 1999 survey had fewer African-American respondents than the system had as a whole (33% in the survey versus 41% systemwide). Survey respondents were also more highly educated than teachers in the system as a whole (54% reported a graduate degree or higher in the survey versus 31% in the system as a whole). There were no differences between the survey respondents and the system with respect to gender. Since our analysis found that African-American and less-educated teachers were in fact more positive about the reform's impact, we would hypothesize that their underrepresentation in this sample leads us to underestimate teachers' positive assessments of the policy.
Source: Jacob, Stone, & Roderick, 2004.

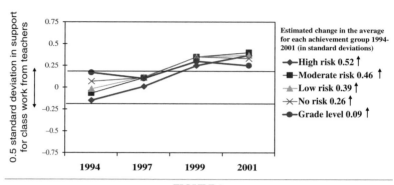

FIGURE 1

Trends in Chicago public school eighth graders' reports of personal support from teachers for class work, 1994–2001. The scale on this graph shows each groups' average measure in standard deviation units from the overall average of 1994. Trends have been adjusted for differences in student characteristics across time (Jacob et al., 2004). A student was considered at high risk of retention if, in any year, their predicted seventh-grade test scores placed them 1.5 years below the 1999 test-score cutoff for promotion or over three years below grade level. Moderate-risk students were those whose test scores placed them 0.5–1.5 years below the cutoff and low-risk students were between 0.5 below to 0.5 above the cutoff. A student was considered at grade level if their entering test scores placed them on or above grade level at national norms. A students' pregate achievement was estimated using a growth curve model that estimated a student's "latent" pregate achievement based on their previous test score trajectory.

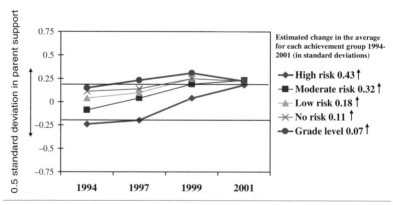

FIGURE 2

Trends in Chicago public school eighth graders reports of parental support for school-work, 1994–2001. The scale on this graph shows each group's average measure in standard deviation units from the overall average of 1994. Trends have been adjusted for differences in student characteristics across time. See footnote on Figure 1 for a description of the risk categories.

or noticed if they had trouble learning something. Students' answers are combined into a summary measure that is "anchored"—placed on a common scale—so that responses can be compared across time (Jacob et al., 2004). Students were grouped into achievement categories based on their estimated risk of retention under the 1999 promotional cutoffs. Thus, even though students in 1994 did not face the promotional gate, grouping students into achievement categories using the 1999 cutoffs allowed us to compare students with similar underlying achievement across time. These trends were further adjusted for changes over time in the racial, ethnic, and demographic characteristics of CPS students.

Trends in our measure of academic support suggest there were significant improvement in low-achieving students' perceptions of their teachers' attention to their academic needs over the postpolicy period. In 1994, eighth graders with the lowest achievement (*high risk*) reported significantly less personal support for their schoolwork from their teachers than students whose test scores placed them close to or above grade level (*no risk* to *grade level*). In 2001, high-risk students reported significantly higher levels of personal support from their teachers (over half a standard deviation higher) than their counterparts in 1994. As a result, by 2001, high- and moderate-risk eighth graders were reporting levels of attention to their schoolwork from their teachers similar to their classmates with skills closer to grade level. These trends were observed in both low- and higher-performing schools (Jacob et al., 2004).

Similar trends were observed in measures of parental support for schoolwork. In each survey year, sixth and eighth graders were asked how often they discussed school activities and things studied in class with their parents, how often their parents encouraged them to work hard in school or praised their work in school, and how often their parents helped with or checked homework and discussed their school performance. Confirming the assessment of teachers and principals, students with the lowest skills also reported much higher levels of parental support and attention to their schoolwork in 2001 than in 1994.

These changes in student motivation and teacher support were also confirmed in our qualitative research. In *The Grasshopper and the Ant*, we examined low-achieving sixth and eighth graders' motivational responses to the promotional test in five low-performing elementary schools (Roderick & Engel, 2001). We found that the majority of low-achieving students in our study responded positively to the motivational incentives created by the policy. Students described increased work effort, reported greater attention to class work and increased support from teachers, and reported participating in after-school programs for help with school work. In most cases, students' reports were confirmed by teachers in their assessment of the student's behavior. Teachers themselves appeared to use the policy as a tool to spur student work effort. As one eighth-grade teacher explained:

> Because the students know, especially in eighth grade you know we need the score or we are coming to (this school) next year . . . Especially since I let them know, I'm not the one failing you, I'm not the one holding you back. And so then the students are much more motivated to do their work, especially as the year progresses. (Jacob et al., 2004, p. 13)

Teachers, principals, and students also responded positively to programmatic supports. While the ending social promotion initiative directed teacher and parental attention to the needs of low-performing students, Summer Bridge and Lighthouse also directed significant resources to these students. Students' reports of participation in after-school programs increased significantly in almost every survey year, with the largest increases being among students at risk of retention and in the lowest-achieving schools (Jacob et al., 2004). As seen in Table 2, teachers and principals appeared to welcome these supports. Teachers and principals felt that the programs had positive impacts and felt supported in their efforts to help students at risk.

Students also seemed to react positively to the environment of Summer Bridge with its small classes and personal attention. Despite concerns that students would not participate in mandatory summer programs, we estimated that between 85% and 90% of students who failed the ITBS in spring attended the program (Roderick, Engel, & Nagaoka, 2003). In surveys, students portrayed Summer Bridge as a positive learning environment in which they were expected to work hard and where teachers supported their efforts. Students who attended Summer Bridge also reported higher levels of academic press and support from their teachers in the summer than these same students did during the school year (Roderick, Nagaoka et al., 2003).

Teachers changed the content of their instruction so that they spent significantly more time on test preparation and on the material covered on the test. If low-achieving students were getting more support and were working harder in school, the critical question is: What were they getting support to do? A central critique of high-stakes testing is that it will result in a narrowing of the curriculum focused on basic skills. Importantly, this focus seemed to align with the general approach of many Chicago educators. In 1999, three-quarters of teachers agreed that the policy was consistent with their own views about what was best for students' learning, while less than a quarter agreed or strongly agreed that the policy placed too much emphasis on basic skills. Teachers' endorsement of a focus on basic skills may have reflected the reality these CPS teachers faced in a school system in which many students were struggling. As one teacher noted, "I think the teachers understand the students are missing basic skills . . . Our kids are missing so many basic skills . . . basics, period, in everything" (Jacob et al., 2004, p. 15). Teachers' endorsement of the focus on basic skills may have also reflected the demographics of Chicago's teaching force, which at the time was predominantly older and less educated. In the 1999 teacher survey, for example, over half (54%) of teachers reported having more than 15 years of teaching experience and 42% reported that they had received only a bachelors degree. Younger teachers and teachers with advanced degrees were significantly less positive about the impact of the policy (Jacob et al., 2004).

What did it mean for teachers to focus on the basics? Most prior research, as discussed above, finds that teachers are highly responsive to accountability programs and align their curriculum to prepare students for the test. We tracked trends in test preparation and content alignment from 1994 to 2001 using teachers' reports of their instructional practices. In each survey year, teachers were asked to report how many hours they had spent that year preparing students for standardized tests. In addition, we examined trends prior to and after the policy in teachers' reports of the extent to which they emphasized specific mathematics skills and reading content that were covered on the ITBS. Because test scores were rising over this period, teachers who have higher-achieving students might teach more advanced content. We used a multivariate analysis to adjust trends for changes over time in students' incoming test scores in each grade and student and teacher demographic characteristics (Jacob et al., 2004).

Not surprisingly, time on test preparation increased substantially after the introduction of accountability and the high-stakes testing program for students. The largest increases occurred in the third and eighth grades and in the lowest-performing elementary schools (see Figure 3). From 1994 to 1999, the estimated percentage of teachers who reported that they spent over 20 hours or more on test preparation each year increased by over 30% in the third and eighth grades and by one-

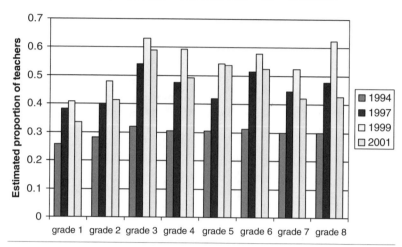

FIGURE 3

Estimated proportion of Chicago public schools teachers reported spending 20 hours or more on test preparation by grade 1994–2001. Estimates shown are from a hierarchical linear model that controls for the demographic characteristics of the teachers responding to the survey. See Jacob et al. (2004) for a complete description of the model. A separate model was estimated for each grade.

quarter in the sixth grade. Using statistical modeling, we estimate that the average number of hours teachers spent on test preparation doubled between 1994 and 1999, from approximately 10.5 hours to over 20 hours a year.

Teachers were also aligning what they taught so that it focused on the skills tested on the ITBS. The most significant changes occurred in the upper elementary grades. Seventh- and eighth-grade teachers in both 1999 and 2001 were significantly more likely to report that they covered mathematics topics that would be considered at grade level on the ITBS and we observed declines in the proportion of time teachers in these grades spent on the most basic mathematics content. Teachers in these grades also reported spending significantly more time teaching reading comprehension versus other language arts activities and specif- ically spending time on those reading comprehension activities, such as analyzing and interpreting literature, differentiating fact from opinion, or drawing inferences, that were tested on the ITBS. The shift to a focus on reading and specifically to reading comprehension occurred across all schools. There was evidence, however, that improvements in teachers' emphasis on grade-level material in mathematics were greatest in the lowest-performing schools.

Few would argue that time on test preparation, in and of itself, is a positive instructional strategy. The effect of content alignment is more debatable. In an influential report using data prior to the 1996 reforms, Julia Smith and her colleagues conducted an analysis of CPS students' opportunities to learn mathematics (Smith, Smith, & Bryk, 1998). Using Consortium survey data, these researchers found that pacing in mathematics slowed down dramatically in the upper elementary grades so that seventh and eighth graders in the CPS were rarely exposed to grade-level material that they were expected to know on the ITBS. This problem was worst in high-poverty and in majority African-American schools. Thus, while a sole focus on test preparation may not lead to significant improvements in student learning, changes in content focus in the upper grades may have improved opportunity to learn. Without classroom observations, we cannot assess the nature of that content alignment. We also cannot assess the extent to which the focus on alignment in the middle grade meant that students were getting little of the science, social studies, and conceptual skills that might lay the basis for high school-level work.

There was little evidence that students experienced increased academic expectations. One of the concerns raised by critics of high-stakes testing is that such programs place too much pressure on students, raising expectations and standards without concomitant increases in support (Lee et al., 1999). Research on effective schools, including research in Chicago, consistently concludes that students learn more in classrooms that provide high levels of personal support while at the same time hold high expectations for student performance, often called *academic press* (Lee et al., 1999). One of the unexpected findings of our evaluation was that we found little evidence that teachers were changing their expectations for performance. As with academic support, our evaluation examined trends in critical measures of student reports of the academic expectations of teachers, academic demands in the form of homework, or in students' report of their engagement in their school work (Jacob et al., 2004). The lowest-achieving eighth graders did show small, but statistically significant, increases in academic engagement, the extent to which they reported working hard and enjoying their class work. These changes were moderate compared with the changes we observed in students' reports of personal support and were not observed in the sixth grade. In addition, higher-achieving students and students in initially higher-performing schools reported lower levels of academic press (i.e., expectations for performance) and academic engagement in the pre-versus postpolicy period. These declines might mean that teachers were paying less attention to the highest-achieving students because they expected them to do well without extra attention, a lowering of the bar effect of ending social promotion. These declines might also reflect, as opponents expressed, the impact of the significant time that teachers spent on test preparation. Thus, contrary to predictions, our findings suggest that students experienced increases in social support without concomitant increases in academic expectations, suggesting that students were getting more support to do the same level of work. These shifts may have appeared to low-achieving students as though they were getting support for a goal that was important to them, but in the context of the research literature on effective schools, may have been selling these students short.

The ending social promotion initiative did little to increase the capacity of teachers and schools. Results of the Summer Bridge evaluation demonstrate that instructional capacity mattered. The picture that emerges from these trends is that Chicago's initiative created strong incentives for teachers to change whom they pay attention to and what they teach. There was, however, little incentive in the policy for teachers and schools to focus on the basic technology of instruction—the "how" they teach. Indeed, one reading of our findings is that ending social promotion offered a solution that did little to challenge teachers. The problem as communicated in the policy and its associated programs was not in the basic nature of what was happening in classrooms. The problem was simply that students were not working hard and were not getting enough time and attention. The solution to low performance then was not to challenge what was happening during the school day other than to ask teachers to focus on basic skills—an approach that may have addressed the central struggle educators were facing in their classroom, but did so in a way that did little to challenge or improve the central technology they were working with to address those problems. It was striking in our interviews how seldom teachers answered that they were doing anything to improve their instructional capacity as a means of helping their at-risk students, either by changing how they taught, how they engaged students in the classroom, or by improving their professional knowledge of how to teach reading and mathematics (Jacob et al., 2004). Why would this matter? As discussed earlier, a central critique of high-stakes testing and accountability is that such programs do not increase the ability of teachers and schools to meet their students' needs and thus in the end will leave behind students in those schools and classrooms with the least capacity. To what extent is there evidence that capacity mattered in how well teachers and schools were able to respond to students' needs? While there are several ways of addressing this question, perhaps the most convincing evidence that instructional capacity mattered came in our evaluation of the Summer Bridge program.

On average, our evaluation concluded that Summer Bridge was effective in producing significant short-term test score increases, particularly in the sixth and eighth grades. Even with its highly structured approach, however, students' learning gains in Summer Bridge varied widely across schools. Higher-achieving elementary schools were able to mount much more effective programs for their students than lower-achieving schools, even after controlling for differences across schools in the achievement and demographic characteristics of students who failed to meet the standard and attended the program. For example, we estimate that the predicted summer reading test score gain for an average third grader would be nearly three times larger (0.10 versus 0.29 grade equivalents) if a student attended Summer Bridge in a school that had high achievement during the school year (over 40% of their students reading at national norms) than if that same student attended Summer Bridge in a low-achieving elementary school (less than 25% of students reading at national norms). We would expect that school effects would be largest in the third grade in reading because this is the grade and subject in which teachers' underlying knowledge of reading instruction would have the greatest impact on the capacity of students to benefit from the curriculum.

The Summer Bridge study similarly found significant variation in classroom effects (Roderick, Engel, & Nagaoka, 2003). Summer Bridge presented an ideal setting to study the effect of quality teaching. The qualitative study observed third-, sixth- and eighth-grade Summer Bridge classrooms in 12 schools. Each class was observed four times and the sample included six matched pairs so that we were able to observe two teachers in two schools in the same neighborhood teaching the same lesson on the same day. Even with its mandatory curriculum, we observed significant differences in the quality of instruction and the resultant learning gains. Students in schools in which the teacher in that grade was coded as having "tailored instruction," meaning that he or she not only delivered the curriculum but had meaningful and constructive interactions with students, taught topics in multiple ways, and individualized instruction, experienced significantly greater learning gains in Summer Bridge than students in schools in which teachers simply followed the curriculum, providing "sufficient instruction." Unfortunately, only about 20% of Summer Bridge classrooms were coded as having high-quality instruction (Roderick, Nagoaka et al., 2003).

Given the strength of our summer-school results, it is not surprising that retention rates were highly concentrated. In 1998, there were 416 schools in Chicago that had more than 20 third-grade students included under the policy. Fifty percent of retained third graders, however, were retained in the 100 Chicago public schools with the highest retention rates, and nearly two-thirds were retained in 150 high-retention schools (Nagaoka & Roderick, 2004). In the 100 schools with the highest retention rates, 42% of third graders were retained, or 11.4 students per class of 27. Eighth grade was even more concentrated, with 61% of retained students in 100 schools.

The ending social promotion initiative fell the most short in its lack of attention to increasing the capacity of teachers and schools to deal with students with the most significant learning problems. The lack of attention to improving teaching capacity became most evident in the one arena where technical solutions were most needed—for those lowest-performing students and for those schools that could not respond to motivational effects or that could simply not raise their test scores with greater work effort. Because high-stakes testing relies so heavily on motivation effects and short-term interventions, such policies have the effect of sorting low-achieving students by their parents', their teachers', and their own capacity to respond. In our qualitative study, we found that those low-achieving students who responded positively to the motivational aspects of the policy did relatively well; they had higher-than-average learning gains and the majority passed the promotional test and were promoted (Roderick & Engel, 2001). But even with the supports provided, approximately one-third of low-achieving students in our qualitative sample did not show increased work effort. These were students who, while expressing the desire not to be retained, faced one or several of three conditions: (1) they were extremely far behind and had major skills gaps; (2) they faced significant home problems or other barriers that precluded consistent participation in school, leading to a lack of adequate attendance and emotional barriers to engagement in the classroom, such as depression; and (3) they faced significant barriers to learning, such as learning disabilities or unaddressed health problems. These students experienced relatively modest learning gains that year and few had positive outcomes under the policy. But there was little in the supports provided to schools to address these needs or to assist teachers in better diagnosing these problems and constructing an effective approach. Teachers struggled with understanding these students' situations and often diagnosed the problems as "lack of motivation" or lack of caring about school (Roderick & Engel, 2001). As one teacher noted: "And the policy, I really agree with it for some children. For others, I think we need to get some expert in to tell us how to handle the others who are not going to respond" (Jacob et al., 2004, p. 21).

Summer Bridge also did little to help students who were the farthest behind. Students with the lowest entering test scores had the lowest Summer Bridge gains, with the exception of the highest-risk third graders in reading (Roderick, Engel, & Nagoaka, 2003). The test score gains these very low-achieving students did make, moreover, were not enough to raise their test scores to the promotional cutoffs because they began so far behind. For example, only 11% of third graders and only one-quarter of those sixth and eighth graders whom we characterized as facing the highest risk of retention were able to meet the promotional cutoffs during the summer, compared with nearly 80% of students with test scores close to the cutoff.

In summation, the prospects for students who were retained under Chicago's policy were not promising. Those students who were retained were those who for various reasons could not raise their test scores during the school year and summer. And these students were concentrated in schools that had demonstrated the least capacity to serve their needs.

Retention was not effective in improving the achievement of third graders and was associated with negative effects on achievement in the sixth grade. Retained students faced significantly increased rates of special education placement and were more likely to drop out. Chicago's approach to retention differed significantly from many subsequent district efforts because it provided little direction to schools as to how to respond to students who were retained. Not surprisingly, retained students struggled their second time through the policy.

Among the first group of retainees, only 39% of third graders and 42% of sixth graders were able to raise their test scores to the promotional cutoffs by the spring of the next school year. Even after a second Summer Bridge, only about half of retained third graders and 57% of retained sixth graders had raised their test scores to the promotional cutoff. And even when retained students in 1999 had an extra chance to meet the test-score cutoffs in January, only slightly more than 65% of retained students were able to meet the cutoff by their second time through the policy. Thus, after two years in a grade, in some cases two summers of Summer Bridge, and multiple attempts at meeting the cutoffs, these students had still not raised their test scores to a year below grade level in third grade and a year and a half below grade level in sixth grade.

Part of the reason for these low passing rates was that high proportions of these students were placed in special education during their retained year and were no longer subject to the promotion policy. Between 8% and 13% of retained third and sixth graders were placed in special education during their second time through the grade. Retained students, particularly those who did not meet the cutoff at the end of their retained year, continued to face high rates of special education placement. Within two years of the gate grade, between 15% and 20% of retained third and sixth graders had been placed in special education. Using comparison groups of low-achieving students both prior to and after the policy, we estimate that retained students were placed in special education at over three times the rate of other low-achieving third graders and over six times the rate of other low-achieving sixth graders.

Why did retained students experience such high rates of placement in special education? One explanation is that this was simply an attempt to get students who were struggling out from under the policy, because special education students were not held to the promotional cutoffs. A second explanation is that after students were retained, teachers did identify undiagnosed learning disabilities. And yet another explanation is that this reflects a mislabeling of students as "learning disabled" because teachers lacked an alternative explanation and strategies and resources to address the difficulties students were presenting. Most likely, the answer is some combination of the above. This is not just a high-stakes testing problem. A National Research Council study (2002) recently concluded that reading difficulties are one of the most frequent reasons that teachers refer students to special education. Retention under high-stakes testing without an alternative intervention, however, clearly highlighted those reading difficulties and increased the likelihood that teachers would look to special education as an answer.

The fact that retained students continued to struggle does not address the question: Did retention ultimately benefit or harm their academic achievement? The district's reliance on a strict cutoff in making promotional decisions provided an important opportunity to study the effects of retention under high-stakes testing. In general, students' test scores vary widely from test to test. Because there is wide variation from test to test in students' performance on the ITBS, a difference in one question, right or wrong, could determine whether the promotional cutoff was met. Thus, students within a narrow range around the test-score cutoff look quite similar in their underlying growth trajectories prior to Summer Bridge and, in the absence of retention, we would expect their postgate achievement growth to also be similar. Our basic approach, then, was to compare the performance of students who attended Summer Bridge and whose test scores fell just below the promotional cutoff (the majority of whom were retained) to their low-achieving counterparts who attended Summer Bridge but just managed to pass the promotional cutoff (the majority of whom were promoted) (Nagaoka & Roderick, 2004; Roderick & Nagaoka, submitted).[7] We limited our analysis to estimating achievement effects in the third and sixth grade because eighth graders who moved to high school took a different test than eighth graders who were retained. Using both growth curve analysis and methods that allowed us to explicitly address selection effects, we found that third graders who were retained experienced slightly higher learning gains than our control group one year after retention with no benefit to their achievement two years later. In the sixth grade, estimates suggest that retained students' achievement gains, both one and two years after retention, were approximately 6% lower than their low-achieving counterparts who were promoted.

In summation, our evaluation found that those low-achieving students who were retained did not benefit educationally during the retained year and, in the sixth grade, experienced lower achievement gains than students with similar test scores who were promoted. But they were now a year older and still lagging behind. Research on retention would suggest that these students would face increased risks of dropping out. It is too early to evaluate the long-term effects of retention in the third and sixth grades. In our recent report, Allensworth (2004) took a rigorous look at the effects of retention in the eighth grade on students' likelihood of dropping out. Using statistical modeling, Allensworth (2004) estimated that retention under the promotion policy increased the probability of dropping out by age 17 for a typical retained eighth grader by 23%. By age 19, estimated dropout rates among students who were retained were 13 percentage points higher than among similar prepolicy, nonretained students. Importantly, eighth graders who had already been retained prior to the promotional gate—who were already overage for grade when they faced the policy for the first time—were very likely to get retained again in eighth grade and were very likely to drop out. By age 19, fully 78% of eighth graders who were already overage for grade and who were then retained under the policy had dropped out of school. Those retained third and sixth graders who are now overage for grade and are still substantially behind their peers face the significant possibility that they will fail again when they reach eighth grade. If these findings among the earlier eighth graders hold true, we might predict that those third and sixth graders retained under the policy will also experience very poor graduation outcomes.

What Happened to Test Scores in Chicago?

Chicago's effort to end social promotion was intended to address persistent low performance in two ways. First, the initiative was aimed at decreasing the numbers of very low-achieving students prior to the retention decision by using a combination of incentives and resources—incentives for students to work harder and for teachers and parents to direct attention to at-risk students and resources through after-school programs and focused intervention during Summer Bridge. In the previous section, we found some evidence for those changes in behavior. But many students did not raise their test scores to the promotional requirements. For these students, Chicago's approach was retention—a second dose of the material they had struggled with and continued incentives to work hard through additional chances to pass the test. From the evidence presented in the previous section, it is clear that retention was not effective in addressing the lowest-achieving students' needs. But did the observed changes in instruction, in teacher and parental support for students, and in the number of students participating in after-school and summer-school programs lead to improvements in test scores?

Achievement Effects in the Gate and Pregate Grades

In *The Impact of High-Stakes Testing in Chicago on Student Achievement in Promotional Gate Grades*, we looked closely at the effects of the policy in shaping achievement gains in the promotion and prepromotional gate grades (Roderick, Jacob, & Bryk, 2003). Using growth curve modeling, we estimated a value-added in the gate grades (test score increases over and above that predicted from a student's prior growth trajectory) for successive cohorts of students and derived policy effects by comparing the size of the value-added in the gate grade prior to and after the policy. By focusing on the value-added in the gate and pregate grades, we were able to examine whether the average gains of students in these grades improved from before to after the policy, controlling for differences across time in general improvements in the school system, in the overall achievement of cohorts, and in changes over time in the racial and demographic characteristics of the population in the CPS. This method may still overestimate the extent to which accountability policies led to improvement in test scores if, for other reasons, achievement gains in these grades in the postpolicy period were improving.[8] Our analysis looked only at the first three postpolicy cohorts.

In the third grade, there was little evidence of positive effects in reading with moderate positive effects in mathematics. We did, however, find significant evidence of policy effects in the sixth and eighth grades, with policy effects being larger in the second and third year of the policy. In the sixth and eighth grades, the average gain in student achievement was approximately one-third to one half of a year's learning gain higher in post- versus prepolicy cohorts. There was some evidence that middle-grade students in low-achieving schools showed the greatest positive effects. The patterns of results, however, differed across subjects and grades. In the sixth and eighth grades, students with the lowest skills and in the lowest-achieving schools demonstrated the largest policy effects in reading achievement. In sixth- and eighth-grade mathematics, perhaps reflecting the positive content alignment in mathematics we discussed earlier, policy effects were largest in low-achieving schools but greater among better-achieving students in those schools. Most disturbing, however, was the finding that not only were policy effects in reading not found in the third grade in the lowest-achieving schools, but that we actually observed declines in the expected learning growth of third graders with better-than-average achievement. To be explicit, we found that the average achievement growth of third graders with entering test scores closer to grade level was actually lower in the postpolicy period among students who attended the lowest-achieving schools in Chicago, suggesting that the policy and the significant stress on test preparation we observed in these grades led to lower-than-expected achievement of students with better skills in the most struggling schools.

The fact that we observe policy effects in the sixth and eighth grades does not tell us what generated these effects. The gate-grade effects could simply reflect that those students take the test more seriously or reflect the effects of the significant rise in test preparation that we observed. Research on the effects of accountability generally find that when a single test is used for accountability, school systems experience increases in scores on that test that are often short lived and are not generalizable to other measures of performance (Amrein & Berliner,

2002; Bryk, 2003; Klein, Hamilton, McCaffrey, & Stecher, 2000; Koretz, 1999; Koretz & Barron, 1998; Linn, 2000). This research would suggest that, even if the changes in student motivation and support for low-achieving students had not happened in the CPS, we would have expected improvement in test scores in the first several years of the policy as teachers and schools began to emphasize the test and students worked harder to demonstrate their achievement.

Systemwide Trends in Eighth-Grade Achievement and Effects on System Dropout Rates

Figure 4 takes a closer look at pre- and postgate trends in eighth-grade achievement for students included and excluded from the pol-

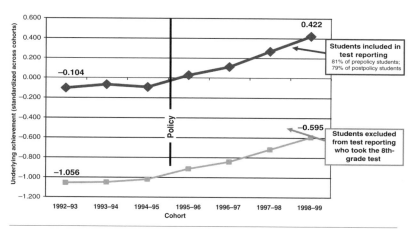

FIGURE 4

Estimated trends in the latent achievement of eighth graders in Chicago public schools based on the trajectory of their performance on the ITBS in reading and mathematics: equated Rasch scale scores, 1992–1993 to 1998–1999. Students excluded from test reporting, because of special education or bilingual exemptions, might take the test and not have their scores included in public reporting statistics, or they might not take the test at all. Students who did not take the test cannot be added into cohort averages. After the policy, many more excluded students took the test than in the prepolicy cohorts. Therefore, a larger percentage of students in special education and bilingual programs are added into the postpolicy averages of students excluded from test reporting. It is surprising that average test scores among students excluded from test reporting improved, since the inclusion of more of the students with bilingual/special education exemptions would have been expected to depress average scores. In addition, about 2% more students were excluded from test reporting after the policy because of higher rates of classification into special education. This may have slightly elevated the postpolicy scores for both included and excluded students, especially in the 1998–99 cohort, by as much as 0.070 standard deviation.
Source: Allensworth, 2004.

icy (Allensworth, 2004). In Figure 4, we present an estimated "latent" achievement score for each cohort that is estimated using a two-level hierarchical linear model of students' achievement growth for reading and mathematics over all of the years that they were enrolled in CPS between grades 3 through 8. We also use ITBS scores that have been converted to Rasch scale scores, in logits, based on equating different forms and levels of the test so that ITBS test scores can be used to measure growth and compared across cohorts. By using information on the entire test trajectory of each cohort, the estimated achievement in each year takes out the particular influence of gate-grade effects—for example, eighth graders showing above-average performance because of testing and motivational effects on the date of the test. By looking at both included and excluded students, moreover, we can check whether the rise in achievement simply reflects changes in whose test scores "count" over the time period. In Figure 4, students' estimated latent scores in reading and mathematics are combined into one measure by averaging the standardized underlying scores.

This analysis suggests that eighth-grade achievement rose substantially after 1996 among both included and excluded students. By the 1998–1999 cohort, eighth-grade achievement was more than one half of a standard deviation higher than it was in prepolicy cohorts among students included in the retention policy. If these test score improvements reflected real changes in achievement, we would expect that they would lay the basis for improved high school performance. And there is some evidence they did. Miller, Allensworth, and Kochanek (2002) concluded that improvements in eighth-grade test scores were associated with concomitant improvements in the percentage of ninth graders who were "on track" freshman year, meaning that they had enough credits to be promoted, and in the percentage of students passing a college course taking sequence. In our more recent study, Allensworth (2004) concluded that improvements in the entering test scores of ninth graders were associated with a reduction in the probability of dropping out among students who were promoted. This reduction in dropout rates that occurred because of the significant rise in eighth-grade test scores more than offset the fact that retained eighth graders were more likely to drop out, leading to a small net decline in dropout rates in the school system.

In summation, it is difficult to explain away all of the improvements in students' performance in the sixth through eighth grades as simply the result of students taking the test more seriously and by changes in whose test scores count.[9] While these overall trends are not causal, the rise in student achievement is consistent with the policy effects anticipated by proponents of high-stakes testing. So in the end, did test scores really increase and were they the result of the policy? This is the question that dominates much of the research literature on accountability and is the domain of many of the contributors to this volume. In Chicago, there is no definitive answer to these questions and they will be the topic of debate and further research for many years to come. Our look at the evidence suggests that the general conclusions are that there were overall positive improvements in the sixth through eighth grade and little evidence of any substantial improvement in the early grades. These test score improvements may not be solely attributed to high-stakes testing policy alone because they occurred simultaneously with school-level accountability. But in general, we would conclude that the 1996 reforms were associated with improvements in performance in the middle grades that carried over into high school.

A Glass Half Full—Making Sense of These Trends

How do we explain the relatively larger impact of the policy in the upper grades? At the beginning of this chapter, we argued that the theory of action of ending social promotion implies that low test scores are being caused by a lack of student motivation, a lack of attention to these students' needs on the part of teachers and parents, and not enough time on task focused on basic skills. Given the evidence presented in this chapter, it would make sense that the greatest impact of the policy happened in the upper grades. First, policies that rely on student motivation may have little effect on younger students. Eighth graders are at a very different point in their development; they have a greater capacity to shape their school performance through their own motivation and effort. In our qualitative interviews, we found that eighth graders demonstrated a greater capacity than even sixth graders to understand the reasons for the policy, its importance to them, and their role in their own learning experience and work effort (Roderick & Engel, 2001). Eighth graders were more likely to connect the importance of achievement not only to the immediate payoff of promotion, but to their own futures in high school and, not surprisingly, were more likely to respond positively to the policy. Third graders may be less sensitive to the threat of retention, less capable of understanding what it means to translate a future desire not to be retained into immediate concrete behaviors, less capable of shaping their own learning through

RODERICK,   NAGAOKA,   AND   ALLENSWORTH   251

effort, and less able to overcome skills barriers with intensive spurts of effort and concentration.

Second, there is also evidence that attention to the needs of low-achieving students was a problem in the middle grades. As seen in Figures 1 and 2, prior to the policy, the lowest-performing sixth and eighth graders were reporting significantly lower levels of academic monitoring and support from both teachers and parents, suggesting that adults were disengaging from the academic progress of the lowest-achieving students. This suggests that getting teachers and parents to pay attention to the academic needs of the lowest-performing sixth and eighth graders might actually improve performance. And finally, there was also evidence in Chicago that teachers were slowing down the pace of their instruction in the upper grades, even when measured on the content knowledge required on a basic skills tests such as ITBS, and that there were improvements in this area after the policy.

But what was the problem in the third grade? Most educators would agree that in the early grades problems in poor performance lie less with student motivation or the distribution of support within class-rooms than with instructional capacity and, more specifically, with the level of available technology in urban schools to teach reading, diagnosis difficult reading problems, and assemble appropriate interventions. But, as we have argued in this chapter, there was little in the Chicago policy to address these technological constraints. Without such direction and support, teachers in the third grade turned to a short-term strategy, test preparation, so that by 2001 the percentage of teachers who reported spending significant time preparing students to take standardized tests was highest in the third grade.

Thus, in the end, our analysis supports both sides of the debate. While our evaluation demonstrates the "best case" scenario under high-stakes testing, the results of our evaluation point out the clear limitations of high-stakes testing strategies. A focus on student and teacher motivation, on short-term programmatic supports, and on test score improvements in basic skills was a strategy that seemed to provide immediate help to low-performing students, spurring improvements in a system with relatively weak human capital and instructional capacity. Teachers and principals felt that help was on the way, students got extra services and supports, and the basic thrust of the policy seemed to address many of the concerns of Chicago educators. In some ways, Chicago's experience with ending social promotion is a test of how much a low-performing urban school system could improve without addressing the basic capacity issues it was facing. In the third grade, the answer was "not much." The lack of improvement in third-grade achievement in the postpolicy period suggests that the quality of reading instruction and the capacity of schools in the early grades to identify students with problems and provide effective instruction and intervention was a binding constraint that could not be solved by simply adding instructional time or focused effort without changing the conditions of and quality of instruction that was delivered. In the sixth and eighth grades, the answer is more complicated because it is in these grades where we saw some benefits, but also the highest cost to students who were retained. And with that reality, Chicago fell into the trap that has befallen previous high-stakes testing efforts. By not taking seriously the problems that retained students would bring into the classroom and the magnitude of the task facing the lowest-achieving students and the teachers that served them, the Chicago initiative fell short.

Conclusion

The goal of this chapter was to review what we have learned from Chicago's significant and long-standing initiative to end social promotion in elementary schools and the potential effects, the promise, and the pitfalls of such an approach. While our evaluation of Chicago's initiative has allowed us to understand better the reaction of students, teachers, and parents to the policy, the impact of the policy on instruction, and the impact of high-stakes testing in shaping achievement both prior to and after the test, ultimately this evaluation is a look at the effect of a particular set of policies in one city. We do not know the extent to which these findings are generalizable to other cities, how they would vary if the policy had been constructed differently, and whether we would have seen the same effects if ending social promotion had not been accompanied in Chicago by a parallel accountability initiative at the school level. In Chicago, policy effects were driven both by the ending social promotion initiative and by the impact of the accountability program aimed at the lowest-achieving elementary schools. Because both initiatives began simultaneously, it is difficult to disentangle the effects of ending social promotion in particular from the effect of the school-based accountability initiative, especially because at-risk students are most likely to attend low-achieving schools that were subject to the probation policy. Throughout our evaluation, we were careful to examine how policy effects may have differed given the kinds of schools students attended. But overall trends reflect the impact of both initiatives and a broader policy environment of greater account-ability for all educators in the system. In this conclusion, we offer two arenas for future research.

First is in the area of retention. Our conclusions about the negative effects of retention under high-stakes testing are based on an evaluation of the approach to retention as implemented in Chicago. The Chicago policy differs from many subsequent district and state efforts to end social promotion in which school districts adopted alternatives to reten-tion or much more prescribed approaches, along with better warning and intervention systems prior to retention. Our evaluation did not evaluate the effect of Chicago's approach versus other approaches. Such evaluations would afford the opportunity to better understand how variation in policy regimes and environments may produce different results. The risks of these comparisons are that different findings across states and districts on the effects of retention may simply spur a "find-ing" war over which study is the "right" study of retention. This would be unfortunate and misguided. As we have emphasized throughout this chapter, understanding the lack of intervention provided to retained students as well as which students ultimately were retained—students who were the farthest behind, who had struggled before and after retention, and who were also concentrated in schools where many children were failing—is critical to understanding the effects of reten-tion in Chicago. In an era of No Child Left Behind, every school system is facing the question of how best to mount effective intervention programs for their weakest students. A useful arena for research is to develop a better understanding of how different approaches to serving the needs of students who are struggling and different uses of identifi-cation and earlier identification may ultimately assist school systems shape the uses and effects of testing.

Second, what is clear from our research and the mounting body of evidence on the effects of accountability is that testing and accountabil-ity are powerful levers. Incentives matter, and teachers and schools are highly responsive to the messages they receive about what is important, which students they should care about, and what to teach. The content of the test matters. In Chicago, the choice of a basic skills test may have been central to the effects of the policy. It created a promotional stan-dard that was within the reach of many low-performing students, and for many Chicago teachers it aligned with their vision for what they should be doing in the classroom. But in the long run, moving urban school systems to higher levels of performance must ultimately involve raising the bar. The research literature is largely unequivocal on this point—higher achievement occurs when teachers hold high expectations for their students and are pushing their own instruction to move students to higher levels of performance and engage them in challenging work. It is clear that this is where the Chicago policy fell short. Again, the key is to move beyond the debates of retention versus social promotion, accountability versus capacity building, to begin to understand how we may better build accountability and incentives systems that combine the best of both worlds: that promotes attention to students, motivates students to achieve, and makes parents, teachers, and students partners in education, while at the same time pushing instruction in positive ways and building strong systems of supports for teachers and schools to mount effective strategies.

NOTES

1. In 1995, the Illinois General Assembly turned control of the CPS over to the mayor, giving the mayor authority to appoint a new Board of Trustees and replace the superintendent with a mayoral-appointed Chief Executive Officer. Under the first wave of reform, in 1988, local schools gained control over their resources and personnel. Elected local school councils appointed their own principals, teachers were hired by principals without concern for seniority, and substantial discretionary resources were made available to schools through the allocation of their Chapter 1 monies. In giving the CEO power to place schools on probation, the legislature essentially allowed the new administration to override the powers of local school councils in low-performing schools.

2. For a more detailed description of Chicago's school accountability program see Finnigan and O'Day (2003) and Hess (1999). Between 1996 and 2000, approximately 23 of the over 70 elementary schools initially placed on probation had raised their test scores to the criteria for getting off, with at least 20% of students scoring at or above national norms in reading. While several high schools underwent reconstitution (temporary shutdown and reopening with new staff and programs), the policy was never invoked for an elementary school.

3. From the 1995–1996 to 2000–2001 school years, the promotion policy relied solely on promotional cutoffs set according to the grade equivalent. The eighth-grade standard, initially set at a 1.8 grade equivalent below grade level, was raised in each subsequent year. In the 2001–2002 school year, the district adopted substantial changes to the policy in response to a civil rights complaint. The changes included using a range around the test-score cutoffs in making promotional decisions and including grades and teacher recommendations in the promotion decision. In the next school year, the district also moved to a new form of the ITBS and began to use scale scores rather than grade equivalents (Nagaoka & Roderick, 2004).

4. For further explanation of the Lighthouse program and evaluation of its effects on achievement, see Smith et al. (2004). The Lighthouse program was discontinued in the 2000–2001 school year and replaced with a program that gave schools even greater flexibility, decoupling the program from the promotional gate grades.

5. Students who passed in January had the opportunity to rejoin their classmates and be promoted mid-year. In addition, some retained students were given the opportunity to be doubly promoted after participating in a double summer school. Schools were given flexibility in deciding whether to immediately move students who had met the standard mid-year or to move them ahead at the end of the school year after summer school. In

1998 and 1999, over a quarter of retained third graders and over 30% of retained sixth graders rejoined their classmates under this policy (Nagaoka & Roderick, 2004).

6. Table 2 shows survey results for 1999. Between 1999 and 2001, there was a slight decline in the proportion of teachers who could be characterized as extremely positive about the impact of the policy overall but these declines were moderate (Jacob et al., 2004).

7. In a related article, Jacob and Lefgren (2002) also used a regression-discontinuity design to estimate the sustainability of summer-school and retention effects. They used a more complex model using multiple pre- and postpolicy cohorts and investigated effects in both reading and mathematics. Our findings are quite similar to those reported by Jacob and Lefgren. These authors, however, excluded students who were placed in special education after the retention decision and thus find slightly less negative effects of grade retention.

8. Anthony Bryk (2003) has argued that there was evidence that under the first wave of school reform, some schools were improving in their productivity (the average learning gains for students in each grade) and that these improvements continued through the postpolicy period. This would have led to improvement in the "value-added" in these grades in the postpolicy period.

9. While Figure 2 shows trends in latent eighth-grade achievement, test scores also rose substantially in the sixth grade in both reading and mathematics after relatively flat trends prior to the policy. For example, between 1993 and 1995, the average ITBS score of 12-year-old in the CPS was approximately 5.7 grade equivalents, about a year below grade level. In 1997, the average ITBS score of 12th graders increased to 6.0 grade equivalents in reading and to 6.2 by 1999. Similarly, while in the years prior to the policy the average 12-year-old had a mathematics test score on the ITBS that placed her seven months below grade level, by 2001 that gap had been cut by more than half, to 0.27 grade equivalent below national norms. In comparison, among nine-year-olds (third grade), test scores improved moderately and quickly leveled off. After relatively flat test score trends prior to 1996, the average mean grade equivalent test score on the ITBS among nine-year-olds rose by approximately 0.25 grade equivalents in the first two years, after which progress slowed (Rosenkranz, 2001).

REFERENCES

Alexander, K.L., Entwisle, D.R., & Dauber, S.L. (1994). *On the success of failure: A reassessment of the effects of retention in the primary grades.* New York: Cambridge University Press.

Allensworth, E. (2004). *Ending social promotion in Chicago: The effects of ending social promotion in the eighth grade on dropout rates.* Chicago: Consortium on Chicago School Research.

American Educational Research Association. (2000). *AERA position statement concerning high-stakes testing in preK-12 education.* Washington, DC: American Educational Research Association.

Amrein, A.L., & Berliner, D.C. (2002, March 28) High-stakes testing, uncertainty and student learning. *Education Policy Analysis Archives, 10(18).* Retrieved November 13, 2004, from http://eepa.asu/eepa/v10n18

Betts, J.R., & Costrell, R. (2001). Incentives and equity under standards-based reform. In D. Ravitch (Ed.), *Brookings Papers on Education Policy* (pp. 9–74). Washington, DC: The Brookings Institution.

Bryk, A.S. (2003). No Child Left Behind, Chicago style. In P.E. Peterson & M.R. West (Eds.), *No Child Left Behind? The politics and practice of school accountability* (pp. 242–268). Washington, DC: Brookings Institution Press.

Byrnes, D. (1989). Attitudes of students, parents and educators toward repeating a grade. In L. Shepard & M. Smith (Eds.), *Flunking grades: Research and policies on retention* (pp. 108–131). London: The Falmer Press.

Catterall, J. (1989). Standards and school dropouts: A national study of tests required for high school graduation. *American Journal of Education, 98*(November), 1–34.

Cohen, D.K. (1996). Rewarding teachers for student performance. In S.H. Fuhrman & J.A. O'Day (Eds.), *Rewards and reform: Creating educational incentives that work* (pp. 60–112). San Francisco: Jossey-Bass.

Cooper, H., Kelly, C., Valentine, J., & Muhlenbruck, L. (2000). *Making the most of summer school: A meta-analysis and narrative review.* Monographs of the Society for Research in Child Development, 65: 260. Malden, MA: Blackwell.

Cooper, H., Nye, B., Kelly, C., Lindsay, J., & Greathouse, S. (1996). The effects of summer vacation on achievement test scores: A narrative and meta-analytic review. *Review of Educational Research, 66*(3): 227–268.

Darling-Hammond, L. (1996). Restructuring schools for high performance. In S. Fuhrman & J.A. O'Day (Eds.), *Rewards and reform: Creating educational incentives that work* (pp. 144–191). San Francisco: Jossey-Bass.

Darling-Hammond, L., & Wise, A. (1985). Beyond standardization: State standards and school improvement. *The Elementary School Journal, 85*(3), 315–336.

Denham, C., & Lieberman, A. (Eds.). (1980). *Time to learn.* Washington, DC: US Department of Education, National Institute of Education.

Elmore, R.F. (2002). Unwarranted intrusion. *Education Next.* Retrieved October 3, 2004, from http://www.educationnext.org/20021/30.html

Fashola, I. (1998). *Review of extended-day and after-school programs and their effectiveness.* Baltimore, MD: Center for Research on the Education of Students Placed at Risk.

Finnigan, K., & O'Day, J. (2003). *External support to schools on probation: Getting a leg up?* Chicago: Consortium on Chicago School Research & University of Pennsylvania: Consortium for Policy Research in Education.

Firestone, W.A., Mayrowetz, D., & Fairman, J. (1998). Performance-based assessment and instructional change: The effects of testing in Maine and Maryland. *Educational Evaluation and Policy Analysis, 20*(2), 95–113.

Fisher, C.W., & Berliner, D.C. (Eds.). (1985). *Perspectives on instructional time.* New York: Longman.

Gampert, R.A.. (1987). *A follow-up study of the 1982–1983 promotional gates students.* New York: New York City Public Schools, Office of Educational Assessment: 1–41.

Grissom, J.B., & Shepard, L.A. (1989). Repeating and dropping out of school. In L. Shepard and M. Smith (Eds.), *Flunking grades: Research and policies on retention* (pp. 34–63). London: Falmer.

Heubert, J.P., & Hauser, R.M. (Eds.). (1999). *High stakes: Testing for tracking, promotion and graduation*. Washington, DC: National Academies Press.

Hess, G.A. (1999). Expectations, opportunity, capacity, and will: The four essential components of Chicago school reform. *Educational Policy, 13*(4), 494–517.

Hess, G.A. (2002). Accountability and support in Chicago: Consequences for students. In D. Ravitch (Ed.), *Brookings Papers on Education Policy* (pp. 339–385). Washington, DC: The Brookings Institution.

Holmes, C.T. (1989). Grade level retention effects: A meta-analysis of research studies. In L. Shepard & M. Smith (Eds.), *Flunking grades: Research and policies on retention* (pp. 16–33). London: Falmer.

Holmes, C.T. (2000). Promoting the end of retention. *Journal of Curriculum and Supervision, 15*(4), 300–314.

Holmes, C.T., & Matthews, K. (1984). The effects of non-promotion on elementary and junior high school pupils: A meta-analysis. *Review of Educational Research, 54*(2), 225–236.

House, E.R. (1998). *The predictable failure of Chicago's student retention program*. Boulder, CO: University of Colorado School of Education.

Jackson, G.B. (1975). The research evidence on the effects of grade retention. *Review of Educational Research, 45*(4), 613–635.

Jacob, B.A., & Lefgren, L. (2002). *Remediation education and student achievement: A regression-discontinuity analysis (NBER Working Paper 8918)*. Cambridge, MA: National Bureau of Economic Research.

Jacob, R.T., Stone, S., & Roderick, M. (2004). *Ending social promotion: The response of teachers, students and parents*. Chicago: Consortium on Chicago School Research.

Jimerson, S.R. (2001). Meta-analysis of grade retention research: Implications for practice in the 21st century. *School Psychology Review, 30*(3), 420–437.

Jimerson, S., Carlson, E., Rotert, M., Egeland, B., & Sroufe, L.A. (1997). A prospective, longitudinal study of the correlates and consequences of early grade retention. *Journal of School Psychology, 35*(1), 3–25.

Jones, M.G., Jones, B.D., & Hardin, B. (1999). The impact of high-stakes testing on teachers and students in North Carolina. *Phi Delta Kappan, 81*(3), 199–203.

Klein, S.P., Hamilton, L.S., McCaffrey, D.F., & Stecher, B.M. (2000). *What do test scores in Texas tell us?* Santa Monica, CA: The RAND Corporation.

Koretz, D.M. (1988). Arriving in Lake Woebegone: Are standardized tests exaggerating achievement and distorting instruction? *American Educator, 12*(2), 8–15, 46–52.

Koretz, D. (1999). *Foggy lenses: Limitations in the use of achievement tests as measures of educators, productivity*. Devising Incentives to Promote Human Capital, Irvine, CA.

Koretz, D.M., & Barron, S.I. (1998). *The validity of gains in scores on the Kentucky instructional results information system (KIRIS)*. Santa Monica, CA: RAND.

Koretz, D.M., Barron, S.I., Mitchell, K.J., & Stecher, B.M. (1996). *Perceived effects of the Kentucky Instructional Information System*. Santa Monica, CA: RAND.

Lee, V., Smith, J.G., Perry, T., & Smylie, M. (1999). *Social support, academic press and student achievement: A view from the middle grades in Chicago*. Chicago: Consortium on Chicago School Research.

Levin, H., & Tsang, M.C. (1987). The economics of student time. *Economics of education review, 6*(4), 357–364.

Linn, R.L. (1993). Educational assessment: Expanded expectations and challenges. *Educational Evaluation and Policy Analysis, 15*(1), 1–16.

Linn, R.L. (2000). Assessments and accountability. *Educational Researcher, 29*(2), 4–16.

Mehrens, W.A.. (1998). Consequences of assessment: What is the evidence? *Educational Policy Analysis Archives, 6(13)*. Retrieved October 4, 2004, from http://epaa.asu.edu/epaa/v6n13.html

Miller, S.R., Allensworth, E.M., & Kochanek, J.R. (2002). *State of Chicago public high schools 1993–2000. Student performance: Course taking, test scores and outcomes*. Chicago: Consortium on Chicago School Research.

Nagaoka, J., & Roderick, M. (2004). *Ending social promotion: The effects of retention*. Chicago: Consortium on Chicago School Research.

Nagaoka, J., & Roderick, M. (2004). *Ending social promotion: The effects of retention*. Chicago: Consortium on Chicago School Research.

National Association of School Psychologists. (2003). *Position statement on student grade retention and social promotion*. Bethesda, MD: National Association of School Psychologists.

National Research Council. (2002). *Minority students in special and gifted education*. Washington, DC: National Academies Press.

Newmann, F., Bryk, A.S., & Nagaoka, J. (2001). *Authentic intellectual work and standardized tests: Conflict or coexistence*. Chicago, IL: Consortium on Chicago School Research.

Peterson, S.E., DeGracie, J., & Ayabe, C. (1987). A longitudinal study of the effects of retention/promotion on academic achievement. *American Educational Research Journal, 24*(1), 107–118.

Pierson, L., & Connell, J.P. (1992). Effect of grade retention on self-system processes, school engagement and academic performance. *Journal of Educational Psychology. 84*(3), 300–307.

Reardon, S. (1996, April). *Eighth grade minimum competency testing and early high school dropout patterns*. Paper presented at the annual meeting of the American Educational Research Association, New York.

Reynolds, A. (1992). Grade retention and school adjustment: An exploratory analysis. *Educational Evaluation and Policy Analysis, 14*(2), 101–121.

Roderick, M. (1994). Grade retention and school dropout: Investigating the association. *American Educational Research Journal, 31*(4), 729–759.

Roderick, M., Bryk, A.S., Jacob, B.A., Easton, J.Q., & Allensworth, E. (1999). *Ending social promotion: Results from the first two years*. Chicago: Consortium on Chicago School Research.

Roderick, M., & Engel, M. (2001). The grasshopper and the ant: Motivational responses of low achieving students to high-stakes testing. *Educational Evaluation and Policy Analysis, 23*(3), 197–227.

Roderick, M., Engel, M., & Nagaoka, J. (2003). *Ending social promotion: Results from Summer Bridge*. Chicago: Consortium on Chicago School Research.

Roderick, M., Jacob, B., & Bryk, A.S. (2003). High stakes testing in Chicago, IL: Effects on achievement in promotional gate grades. *Educational Evaluation and Policy Analysis, 24*, 333–358.

Roderick, M., Jacob, B., & Bryk, A.S. (2004). Summer in the city: Achievement gains in Chicago's Summer Bridge program. In G.D. Borman & M. Boulay (Eds.), *Summer learning: Research, policies and programs* (pp. 73–102). Mahwah, NJ: Lawrence Erlbaum Associates.

Roderick, M., & Nagaoka, J. (2004). *Retention under high stakes testing: Helpful, harmful, or harmless?*

Roderick, M., Nagaoka, J., Bacon, J., & Easton, J.Q. (2000). *Update: Ending social promotion in Chicago: Passing, retention and achievement trends among promoted and retained students*. Chicago: Consortium on Chicago School Research.

Rosenholtz, S.J. (1987). Education reform strategies: Will they increase teacher commitment? *American Journal of Education, 95*, 534–562.

Rosenkranz, T. (2001). *2001 CPS test trend review: Iowa Test of Basic Skills*. Chicago: Consortium on Chicago School Research.

Rowan, B. (1996). Standards as incentives for instructional reform. In S. Fuhrman & J.A. O'Day (Eds.), *Rewards and reform: Creating educational incentives that work* (pp. 195–225). San Francisco: Jossey-Bass.

Sebring, P.B., Bryk, A.S., Roderick, M., & Camburn E. (1996). *Charting reform in Chicago: The students speak.* Chicago: Consortium on Chicago School Research.

Smith, M.L. (1991). Put to the test: The effects of external testing on teachers. *Educational Researcher, 20,* 8–11.

Smith, B.A. (1998). *It's about time: Opportunities to learn in Chicago Public Schools.* Chicago: Consortium on Chicago School Research.

Smith, B.A., Degener, S., & Roderick, M. (2004). Extended learning time and student accountability: Assessing outcomes and options for elementary and middle grades. *Education Administration Quarterly, 41*(2), 195–236.

Smith, J.B., Smith, B.A., & Bryk, A.S. (1998). *Setting the pace: Opportunities to learn in Chicago's elementary schools.* Chicago: Consortium on Chicago School Research.

Stone, S., & Engel, M. (2005). Who gets retained and what happens to them? A qualitative analysis.

Stone, S.I., Engel, M., Nagaoka, J., & Roderick, M. (2005). Getting it the second time around: Student classroom experience in Chicago's Summer Bridge Program. *Teachers College Record, 107*(5), 935–957.

Tompchin, F.M., & Impara, J.C. (1992). Unraveling teachers' beliefs about grade retention. *American Educational Research Journal, 29,* 199–223.

Urdan, T.C., & Paris, S.G. (1994). Teachers' perceptions of standardized achievement tests. *Educational Policy, 8*(2), 137–156.

Wheelock, A., Bebell, D., & Haney, W. (2000). Student self-portraits as test-takers: Variations, contextual differences, and assumptions about motivation. *Teachers College Record.* Retrieved October 10, 2004, from http://www.tcrecord.org

CHAPTER 11

High School Exit Examinations: When Do Learning Effects Generalize?

JOHN BISHOP

High-stakes national examinations, the SAT-I and ACT, have been a rite of passage in America for more than a half a century. These college entrance exams are offered by two private organizations that are independent of the state education departments that set curriculum and fund K-12 education. Competitive pressures to keep unit costs low and attract customers—universities and students—from all 50 states prevent these tests from being comprehensive measures of learning during high school.[1] As Harvard's admissions director put it shortly after the college switched to the SAT-I, "Learning in itself has ceased to be the main factor [in college admissions]. The aptitude of the pupil is now the leading consideration" (Gummere, 1943, p. 5).

Most other nations have a very different approach to measuring academic achievement at the end of high school and signaling that information to universities and other interested parties. In Australia, Denmark, England, Scotland, Finland, France, Ireland, the Netherlands, and many Canadian and German provinces, for example, high school exit examinations are developed by (or under the supervision of) the same Ministry of Education that establishes content standards for each subject, funds K-12 education, and regulates the training and licensing of teachers. Taken over a period of two weeks or more, exams for each academic subject are about three hours long and require students to write essays, describe experiments, and show how they solved multistep problems. All students are typically required to take exams in a few core fields, but students select the rest of their exam subjects. These universal Curriculum-Based External Exit Examination systems

John Bishop is an Associate Professor of Human Resource Studies in the School of Industrial and Labor Relationships at Cornell University.

(universal CBEEES) certify the learning of all students, not just those planning to go to university. The exams signal many different levels of achievement, not just whether a student has exceeded a minimum standard. Doing poorly on these exams typically does not prevent one from graduating from secondary school; one completes high school with a record of *modest* accomplishment. Exam grades influence college admissions decisions just as the ACT and SAT-I do in the United States. They are requested on job applications, appear on resumes, and often influence hiring decisions. The questions used in the exams and the distribution of exam grades for each school are reported and discussed in local and national newspapers. The stakes are high for both students and schools. These examination systems are designed to simultaneously achieve four goals: induce teachers to set high standards, motivate students to learn what is being taught, recognize and reward them when they do, and assist in the sorting of students across different postsecondary programs and employment options. The high stakes generated by the use of grades on these curriculum-based external exit exams in admissions and hiring decisions is what gives the examinations the leverage to achieve the other three goals of the system.

Students from these nations study harder than American students (Loveless, 2001) and did much better on Third International Math and Science Study (TIMSS) mathematics and science assessments at the end of upper-secondary school (Mullis et al., 1998; Takahira, Gonzales, Frase, & Salganik, 1998). The greater effort and achievement of the students in these nations may be due in part to the incentives created by their national exit exam systems. Blue ribbon panels studying American secondary education have frequently called for the introduction of high- or moderate-stakes curriculum-based achievement exams like those found abroad. In 1993, for example, the Competitiveness Policy Council proposed that "external assessments be given to individual students at the secondary level and that the results should be a major but not exclusive factor qualifying for college and better jobs at better wages" (1993, p. 30).

Many states are pursuing a standards-based reform strategy that involves developing content standards for core academic subjects, administering tests assessing this content to *all* students, publishing individual school results, and attempting in a variety of ways to hold schools and students accountable for student achievement. The most popular way of holding students accountable (20 states in 2004–2005) has been to require that they pass a *minimum competency test* (MCT) or a more difficult *standards-based exam* (SBE) to receive a regular high school diploma. This approach focuses pressure for higher standards on schools serving disadvantaged students and on students taking lower track courses.

A small group of states—New York, North Carolina, Virginia, and a few other members of the Southern Regional Education Board—have developed or are developing systems of end-of-course exams that are intended to take over the accountability function currently served by the state's MCT. These systems are structured like the universal CBEEES found abroad. Compared with the European universal CBEEES, however, student stakes tend to be lower because American colleges and employers seldom take exam grades into account when making admissions and hiring decisions.

Another type of high school exit exam system is the voluntary Curriculum-Based External Exit Exam systems (Voluntary CBEEES). Advanced Placement (AP) and International Baccalaureate (IB) exams are growing rapidly and are of increasing importance for admission to top colleges. For the first 125 years of their existence, the New York State Regents (high school) exams were voluntary. Despite their voluntary character, they were crucial in maintaining high standards in an ethnically diverse, rapidly growing high school system.

This chapter reviews empirical evidence on the effects of these three different approaches to assessing and signaling achievement to students, parents, colleges, employers, and the local community. It begins by describing the critical features of these approaches to signaling and accountability and how they contrast with the system of student stakes built around aptitude tests and teacher grades that prevailed during the 1960s and 1970s. The second section explains the theory of action behind the expectation that these new signaling/ accountability systems will raise teacher standards and student effort and achievement above the levels that prevail when diplomas are based on seat time and high-stakes college admission decisions are based largely on teacher grades and three-hour-long multiple-choice format aptitude tests. The third section of the chapter reviews the empirical literature on the effects of voluntary and universal curriculum-based external exit examinations and minimum competency examinations on learning, school attendance, and labor market outcomes. The final section analyzes the impact of changes in state policies regarding signaling and accountability on gains in eighth-grade National Assessment of Educational Progress (NAEP) mathematics achievement since 1990.

Deconstructing Systems for Signaling Achievement and Holding
Students Accountable

Exactly how are domestic student accountability strategies similar
to or different from the universal CBEEES found abroad? We begin
by noting the three features they all have in common. MCTs, SBEs,
universal CBEEES, and voluntary CBEEES all:

1. *Produce signals of achievement that have real consequences for students
   and schools.* MCTs and SBEs are tests that must be passed to get
   a regular high school diploma. For CBEEES the nature and the
   magnitude of the rewards vary. In New York, North Carolina,
   and Canada, CBEEE grades are averaged with teacher assessments to generate final grades for specific courses. In Europe and
   East Asia, exam results influence hiring decisions of employers
   as well as access to popular lines of study in university such as
   law and medicine. CBEEES sometimes make one eligible for a
   more prestigious diploma or scholarship or confer rights to
   enroll in higher-level postsecondary institutions.
2. *Define achievement relative to an external standard, not relative to
   other students in the classroom or the school.* Fair comparisons of
   achievement across schools and across students at different
   schools are now possible.[2]
3. *Are controlled by the education authority that establishes the curriculum for and funds K-12 education.* When a national or provincial
   ministry of education sponsors an external exam, it is more likely
   to be aligned with the national or provincial curriculum and to
   be used for *school* accountability, not just for student accountability. Curriculum reform is easier because changes in instruction
   and exams can be coordinated. The school system as a whole
   needs to accept responsibility for how *all* students do on the
   exams.

The coverage of an exam system is the feature that distinguishes
voluntary CBEEES and college entrance exams such as the SAT-I and
ACT from MCTs, SBEs, and universal CBEEES.

4. *MCTs, SBEs, and universal CBEEES are taken by almost every
   student.* Exams for a set of elite schools, advanced courses, or
   college applicants may raise standards at the top of the vertical
   curriculum, but are unlikely to have much effect on the rest
   of the students. Achievement gaps between high- and low-
   socioeconomic status (SES) students are likely to increase.

Universality makes the school system responsible for how all students do on the exams. A single exam taken by all is not essential. Many nations (e.g., the Netherlands, Germany, Ireland, Scotland, France, and England) allow students to choose which subjects to offer for examination and offer high- and intermediate-level exams in the same subject.

Curriculum-based external exit exam systems are distinguished from MCTs and SBEs by the following additional features. CBEEES:

5. *Assess a major portion of what students should know and be able to do.* Studying to prepare for an exam (whether set by one's own teacher or by a state department of education) should result in the student learning important material and developing valued skills. Some MCTs, SBEs, CBEEES, and teacher exams do a better job of achieving this goal than others. External exams cannot assess every instructional objective, so teacher grades continue to have an important role.

6. *Are collections of end-of-course exams.* End-of-course exams assess the content of specific courses (or sequences of courses). Assessment becomes better aligned with instruction, so teachers become more accountable. This also tends to align the interests of teachers, students, and parents. Grades on end-of-course exams are often a part of the overall course grade, further integrating the external exam into the classroom culture.

7. *Signal multiple levels of achievement in the subject.* If only a pass–fail signal is generated by an exam and passing is necessary to graduate, the standard will almost inevitably be set low enough to allow almost everyone to pass after multiple tries. The bulk of students who can easily pass the test are not induced to work harder (Becker & Rosen, 1992; Betts & Costrell, 2001; Costrell, 1994). CBEEES signal achievement levels, so all students, not just those at the bottom of the class, have an incentive to study hard.[3] Consequently, CBEEES should have a more pervasive effect on classroom culture than MCTs and SBEs.

8. *Assess more difficult material.* Since CBEEES signal the full range of achievement in the subject, they contain more difficult questions and problems. This induces teachers to spend more time on cognitively demanding skills and topics. MCTs (and SBEs to a lesser extent) are designed to identify which students have failed to surpass a minimum standard, so they tend not to ask difficult questions.

America's college admissions tests—the SAT-I and ACT—have some of these features (1, 2, 7, and 8). However, they fail to satisfy four of the criteria defining universal CBEEES. They are not controlled by the state education departments that fund and regulate K-12 education (3), they are voluntary and so a sizable minority of students do not participate (4), they cover only a small part of what students study during high school (5), and they are not tied to specific courses and curricula (6).

Now let's take a closer look at the three types of high school exit exams that have become increasingly important over the last 30 years.

Minimum Competency and Standards-Based Graduation Exams

Twenty-one states required students in the graduating class of 2005 to pass a series of tests before they were awarded a regular high school diploma ("No Small Change," 2005, p. 91). According to a report of the Center on Education Policy (2004), seven states used MCTs focusing on basic skills below the high school level and 11 states used SBEs that were aligned with state standards and generally targeted at the high school level. Half the states set no time limits for the tests. The other states gave students between five and seven hours to complete the test battery. MCTs and SBEs raise standards, but *not* for everyone. The standards set by the teachers of honors classes and AP classes remain the same. Students in these classes pass the MCT/SBE on the first try without special preparation. The higher standards are experienced by the students who are in the school's least challenging courses. School administrators want to avoid high failure rates, so they are expected to focus additional energy and resources on raising standards in the early grades and improving the instruction received by struggling students. There is a danger, however, that teaching to such a test may narrow or "dumb down" the curriculum for the majority of students who are not at risk of failing (Koretz, McCaffrey, & Hamilton, 2001; Linn, 2000, 2003).

Voluntary Curriculum-Based External Exit Examinations

Participation in the College Board's AP program has been growing rapidly. In 2004 a total of 1,101,802 students (about 16% of high school seniors and smaller shares of 10th and 11th graders) took one or more AP examinations (College Board, 2005, p. 43).

The Regents of New York State have been sponsoring end-of-course exams since the 1870s. Panels of local teachers grade the exams using rubrics supplied by the state Board of Regents. Scores on the three-hour exams appear on transcripts and are a final exam mark that is averaged with the teacher's quarterly grades to calculate the final course grade. Taking Regents exams was voluntary until late in the 1990s; nearly half of students took the easier "local" courses intended for noncollege-bound students. Students taking a full schedule of Regents courses took about 10 Regents exams during their high school career.

Universal Curriculum-Based External Exit Examination Systems

In 1994 the New York City Board of Education decided that starting with those entering ninth grade in the fall of 1994, all students would have to take three Regents-level math and three Regents-level science courses before graduating. Two years later the State Board of Regents voted to require all students in the state to take Regents-level courses in English, mathematics, American history, global history, and a science, and to pass the associated Regents exams. Ninth graders in 1996 were the first group to be affected. Ninth graders in 1999 had to pass all five exams. Supporting changes were also made in elementary and middle school curricula and school accountability tests.

North Carolina introduced end-of-course exams for Algebra 1 and 2, Geometry, Biology, Chemistry, Physics, Physical Science, American History, Social Science, and English 1 between 1988 and 1991. Except for a four-year interlude in which some tests were made a local option, all students taking these courses were required to take the state tests. Test scores appear on the student's transcript and most teachers have been incorporating end-of-course exam scores in course grades. Starting in the year 2000, state law required the end-of-course exams to have at least a 25% weight in the final course grade (North Carolina Board of Education, 1999, 2004). A number of other states—Maryland, Mississippi, Oklahoma, Tennessee, Virginia, and others—are developing end-of-course examination systems.

Holding Secondary Schools Accountable

Formal systems for holding schools accountable are also growing in popularity. Forty-nine states publish school report cards and 16 states have a formal mechanism for rewarding schools either for year-to-year gains in achievement test scores or for exceeding student achievement targets. Thirty-six states have special assistance programs to help failing schools turn themselves around. If improvements are not forthcoming, 24 states have the power to close down, take over, or reconstitute failing schools ("Count Me In," 2004, pp. 106–108). Tests typically carry low or no stakes for students but potentially moderate or high stakes for teachers and school administrators. The lack of real consequences is likely to result in many high school students not putting much effort into answering constructed response questions of tests that are not part of a course grade.[4]

Why Are CBEEES and MCTs Hypothesized to Increase True Learning?

The purpose of the educational enterprise is learning. Engagement is essential to achieving this purpose. Students must come to school, pay attention, do homework, engage with the subject, and construct their new knowledge in ways that allow them to retrieve it later. How are students induced to do all this hard work? Teachers try to make their subject interesting, but 61% of American students, nevertheless, say they "often feel bored" (Organization of Economic Cooperation and Development [OECD], 2002, p. 330). Additional motivators—diplomas, grades, exit exams, college admissions, and so on—are therefore essential. We assess each student's learning, we honor it in ceremonies, and we signal (describe) it to parents, employers, and colleges, expecting each to reward the learning in their own way. The prospect of these external rewards strengthens incentives for students to attend school, participate in class, and become engaged in learning. How these rewards manifest themselves also influences the priority that parents, school board members, teachers, and administrators place on hiring better teachers and setting higher standards for students versus keeping school taxes low. Debates about MCTs and CBEEES are, at their root, debates about whether additional motivators for learning are needed and how they should be structured.

The education leaders, politicians, and policy analysts who support MCTs and/or CBEEES typically make the following arguments:

- Technical change and globalization have substantially increased the economic payoff for all types of academic and technical skills, so the current generation of students needs to achieve at higher levels than earlier generations.
- Many of the employers that offer good jobs have lost confidence in the high school diploma as a guarantor of literacy, numeracy, and competence and, as a result, have become reluctant to hire recent high school graduates. States that force schools to set higher graduation standards by making the diploma contingent on passing an MCT will raise achievement

and help graduates get better jobs. This hypothesis is tested in the next section.

- The high stakes attached to the ACT and the old SAT-I—tests that have little relationship to the high school curriculum— undermine incentives for students to develop high-level skills in history, science, foreign language, writing, and English literature (Board of Admissions and Relations with Schools, 2002; Jencks & Crouse, 1982). CBEEES supporters argue that expanding AP and IB courses and introducing universal CBEEES will strengthen incentives to take rigorous courses and to study diligently (Mathews, 2002; Ravitch, 1995).

- Economists who have analyzed learning incentives agree that teacher grades are valuable motivators for students to try hard in class. The incentive effects of external assessments are different but complementary to the incentive effects of teacher grades (Becker & Rosen, 1992; Betts & Costrell, 2001; Costrell, 1994; Powell, 1996). Both forms of evaluation should be used (Board of Admissions and Relations with Schools, 2002; Coleman et al., 1997).

- Teacher assessments contribute a great deal to the valid assessment of student learning. Many important instructional goals can also be assessed externally and these assessments add a new and important perspective to the evaluation of learning (Becker & Rosen, 1992; Betts & Costrell, 2001; Costrell, 1994). Student evaluations that combine continuous and external assessment are more valid measures of learning than assessments based on only one methodology (Board of Admissions and Relations with Schools, 2002).

The proposal is then that universal CBEEES should supplement teacher grades, not replace them. When information from multiple sources is used, learning is measured more validly and high-stakes decisions should become better informed. Incentives for learning should be enhanced; opportunities for students and parents to "game" the system by seeking out easy graders or pressuring teachers to set lower learning standards should diminish (Competitiveness Policy Council, 1993).

Figlio and Lucas (2000) have found that even though students learn substantially more when their teacher is a tough grader, parents do "not perceive tougher teachers to be better teachers" (p. 20). Difficult homework assignments intrude on parents' time and often put the family under stress, so parents complain. This may be one of the reasons why 30% of American teachers feel pressured "to reduce the difficulty and amount of work [assigned]" and "to give higher grades than students' work deserves" (Hart Research Associates, 1995). When the only signal of student achievement is teacher grades, parents seem to prefer high grades, not high standards.

Teachers who work in systems with external exams are aware of their tendency to protect themselves from pressures to lower standards. When a proposal was tabled in Ireland to drop the nation's system of external assessments and have teachers assess students for certification purposes, the union representing Ireland's secondary school teachers reacted as follows:

Major strengths of the Irish educational system have been:
(i) The pastoral contribution of teachers in relation to their pupils
(ii) the perception of the teacher by the pupil as an advocate in terms of nationally certified examinations rather than as a judge.
The introduction of school-based assessment by the pupil's own teacher for certification purposes would undermine those two roles, to the detriment of all concerned . . .
The role of the teacher as judge rather than advocate may lead to legal accountability in terms of marks awarded for certification purposes. This would automatically result in a distancing between the teacher, the pupil and the parent. It also opens the door to possible distortion of the results in response to either parental pressure or to pressure emanating from competition among local schools for pupils. (Association of Secondary Teachers of Ireland, 1990, p. 1)

In the United States locally elected school boards and the administrators they hire make the thousands of decisions that determine academic expectations and program quality. Accountability advocates claim that when external assessment is absent, students and their parents benefit little in the short term from administrative decisions that opt for higher standards, more qualified teachers, or a heavier student workload. The immediate consequences of such decisions are largely negative: higher local property taxes, more homework, having to repeat courses, lower grade point averages (GPAs), complaining parents, and higher risks of not graduating on time (Finn, 1991; Ravitch, 1995). Tests of some of these hypotheses are presented in the third section.

Opponents of external exams argue that focusing student attention on extrinsic rewards for learning will weaken a student's intrinsic motivation to learn. Madaus (1991), for example, hypothesizes that "test scores come to be regarded by parents and students as the main, if not the sole, objective of education" and the result is "undue attention to material that is covered in the examinations, thereby excluding from teaching and learning many worthwhile educational objectives and experiences" (1991, p. 7). Madaus also points out that "preparation for high-stakes tests often emphasizes rote memorization and cramming of students and drill and practice teaching methods" and that "some kinds of teaching to the test permits students to do well in examinations without recourse to higher levels of cognitive activity" (pp. 7–8). Some tests of these hypotheses are presented in the next section.

Advocates of external exams argue to the contrary that the end-of-course examinations developed by committees of experienced teachers are generally better than the teacher-made final exams they replace.[5] Proposed questions are carefully reviewed for ambiguity and bias and then pretested. The exams are published shortly after test day and receive another round of intense public scrutiny. States are trying to push teachers to give students better instruction in writing by adding externally set essay exams to their state testing programs. Well-designed essay questions can also enliven class discussions and induce better teaching.[6]

Steinberg, Brown, and Dornbusch's (1996) study of nine high schools in California and Wisconsin concluded that:

The adolescent peer culture in [middle class] America demeans academic success and scorns students who try to do well in school . . . less than 5 percent of all students are members of a high-achieving crowd that defines itself mainly on the basis of academic excellence . . . Of all the crowds the "brains" were the least happy with who they are—nearly half wished they were in a different crowd. (pp. 145–146)

James S. Coleman explained this phenomenon in the following way: "students who get especially high grades create negative externalities for other students, insofar as the teacher grades on the curve . . . Often a norm arises in this case . . ; students impose a norm that restricts the amount of effort put into schoolwork" (1990, p. 251). External exams may be one way of changing student perceptions. On external exams, everyone in the class can get an A. One is competing with anonymous students in other schools, not one's classmates. Peers should become less supportive of students who joke around in class or try to get the class off track and more supportive of those who cooperate with the teacher. Improved classroom culture should result in students learning more (Coleman et al., 1997).

Do CBEEES and MCT/SBEs Increase True Learning? Evidence from Studies Analyzing Nationally Representative Data Sets

The websites of most of the state education departments implementing high-stakes testing systems report that growing numbers of students are reaching proficiency on the state's MCT and school accountability tests. While flat or declining scores on a new high-stakes test might reasonably lead one to conclude that true achievement has not improved, rising scores do not necessarily imply that true achievement has risen. Numerous authors (Carnoy, Elmore, & Siskin, 2003; Koretz et al., 2001; Linn, 2000) have pointed out that rising test scores might instead reflect teaching to the test—that is, improved alignment of instruction with the topics and question formats found on the state's high-stakes test. Consequently, studies evaluating the effects of high-stakes testing on achievement must track their effects by studying scores on a zero-stakes audit test—for example, TIMSS, the Program for International Student Assessment (PISA), NAEP—that represents a broader domain of knowledge than the content standards that informed the construction of the high-stakes tests.[7] The issue is not whether the positive time trends on the state's high-stakes test are steeper than the trends on the audit test. That is almost guaranteed. The issue is "Do the audit tests respond to the introduction of a CBEEES or MCT?" and if so, "How large is the response?" To assist the reader in judging whether estimated effects are substantively important, I have translated all impact estimates into a common metric: U.S. grade level equivalents (GLE).

Review of Studies Employing Nationally Representative Data Sets

The hypothesis that universal CBEEES improve achievement has been tested by comparing nations and provinces that do and do not have such systems. In most studies of impacts, national mean test scores (for an age group or a grade) were regressed on per capita gross domestic product deflated by a purchasing power parity price index, a dummy for East Asian nations, and a dummy for universal CBEEES. Analyzing 1994–1995 TIMSS data, Bishop (1996, 1997) found that 13-year-old students from countries with medium- and high-stakes universal CBEEE systems outperformed students from other countries at a comparable level of economic development by 1.3 GLE in science and by 1.0 GLE in mathematics. Analysis of data from the 1990 to 2001 International Association for the Evaluation of Educational Achievement's study of the reading literacy of 14-year-olds in 24 countries found that students in countries with universal CBEEES were about 1.0 GLE ahead of students in nations that lacked a universal CBEEES (Bishop, 1999). Analysis of data from both waves of TIMSS data collection also implies that universal CBEEES have highly significant effects (of about 1.5 GLEs) on math and science achievement in eighth grade (Bishop, 2003). Analyses of year 2000 data on 15-year-olds from PISA also yields large statistically significant estimated effects of CBEEES on the reading, mathematics, and science literacy of native-born students (Bishop, 2003). Achievement gaps between high and low-SES students are also significantly lower in nations that have a universal CBEEES (Bishop & Mane, 2004).

Four other studies (Fuchs & Wößmann, 2004; Wößmann, 2000, 2003a, 2003b) have conducted hierarchical analyses of the entire TIMSS and PISA micro data sets and included a comprehensive set of controls for family background, teacher characteristics, school resources, and policies at the individual and school level. Wößmann found that eighth graders in universal CBEEES nations were about 1.1 international grade level equivalents ahead in mathematics and about 0.8 international grade level equivalents ahead in science. He also found that learning gains between seventh and eighth grade were significantly larger in universal CBEEES nations.

Another five studies compare students living in different provinces/states in Germany, Canada, and the United States. German provinces with centralized secondary school exit examinations have significantly higher scores on the TIMSS assessments (Jurges, Schneider, & Buchel, 2003). Students attending school in Canadian provinces with universal CBEEES were a statistically significant one half of a GLE ahead of comparable students living in provinces without universal CBEEES in math and science (Bishop, 1997, 1999a). In 1990 New York State's Regents exam system was the only example of a voluntary curriculum-based external exit exam system in the United States. Graham and Husted's (1993) analysis of 1991 SAT test scores in the 37 states with reasonably large test taking populations found that New York State students did much better than students of the same race and social background from other states. Bishop, Moriarty, and Mane (2000) confirmed Graham and Husted's SAT findings and also found that 1992 NAEP math scores of New York eighth graders were significantly higher than in other demographically similar states. Analyzing National Education Longitudinal Study of 1988 (NELS:88) data Bishop, Mane, Bishop, and Moriarty (2001) found that New York students learned about one half of a GLE more between eighth grade and 12th grade than comparable students in other states. Controlling for ethnicity, social background, and other standards-based reform policies, eighth graders in New York and North Carolina in 1996–1998 were about one half of a GLE ahead of comparable students in other states in reading, math, and science. In these cross-section analyses state MCTs had small (less than 10% of a GLE) nonsignificant effects on achievement (Bishop et al., 2001, Jacobs, 2001).

What was the primary mechanism by which universal CBEEES increased student achievement? The impacts of universal CBEEES on school policies and instructional practices have been studied in the TIMSS data and in the Canadian International Assessment of Educational Progress data. Universal CBEEES were not associated with higher teacher–pupil ratios or greater spending on K-12 education. They were, however, associated with higher minimum standards for entry into the teaching profession, higher teacher salaries, a greater likelihood of having teachers specialize in teaching one subject in middle school, and a greater likelihood of hiring teachers who have majored in the subject they will teach. Teacher satisfaction with their job was significantly lower, possibly because of the increased pressure for accountability that results from the existence of good signals of individual student achievement. Schools in universal CBEEES jurisdictions devote significantly more hours to math and science instruction and build and equip better science labs. For homework time the Canadian and TIMSS studies got contradictory results (Bishop, 1996, 1997, 1999b).

What about the quality of instruction and student attitudes toward the subject? Students in universal CBEEES nations and Canadian provinces were significantly less likely to say that memorization is the way to learn the subject and significantly more likely to do experiments in science classes. Quizzes and tests were significantly more common in Canadian CBEEES provinces, but in other respects these provinces were not significantly different on a variety of indicators of pedagogy. Students were just as likely to enjoy the subject and they were significantly more likely to believe that science is useful in everyday life and more likely to talk with their parents about schoolwork. Students in the TIMSS study were significantly more likely to get tutoring assistance from teachers after school. Madaus's prediction that students would avoid opportunities to learn material that is not likely to be on the exam was not supported. Students in Canadian provinces with CBEEES spent significantly more time reading for fun and watching science documentaries (Bishop, 1996). The study using TIMSS data found no relationship between CBEEES and reading for fun (Bishop, 1999b).

274   HIGH SCHOOL EXIT EXAMINATIONS

Do CBEEES Improve the Functioning of Decentralized Education Systems?

Advocates of external measurement of student achievement with important stakes attached argue that it will improve the functioning of decentralized education systems. Parents will be better able to judge which schools are doing a good job. The information will influence the choice of school and strengthen competitive pressures for excellence. State policymakers and Ministries of Education no longer need to try to improve education quality by rigidly specifying inputs—teacher qualifications, salaries, budget allocations, and textbooks. Instead, teachers and school administrators can be given authority to use their local knowledge about teacher talents and budget circumstances to maximize school quality (Finn, 1991; Hess, 2003; Ravitch, 1995). Publishing data on achievement, it is theorized, creates accountability pressures that induce teachers and administrators to place greater emphasis on improving academic achievement. Tests of these hypotheses have been supportive. Bishop's (1999b) analysis of IAEP data found that controlling for student background, math achievement of students in private schools was higher only in the Canadian provinces that required externally set diploma exams at the end of secondary school. Analyzing TIMSS and PISA data, Wößmann (2000, 2003a) found that school autonomy over salaries and teacher influence over course content, textbooks, and budget allocations had positive effects on student achievement in nations with external exams. In nations without external exams, in contrast, high levels of school and teacher autonomy were associated with lower student achievement. This is a promising line of research. Since changes in school governance and autonomy are commonly proposed as a way to make schools more efficient, it is critical that we understand how the effects of school choice and autonomy are influenced by the measurement and signaling of student achievement.

Does Better Signaling of Achievement Influence School Attendance and Labor Market Success?

What effects do high-stakes curriculum-based external exit exam systems have on high school enrollment rates and college attendance? Many believe a tradeoff exists between the standards and quality of an educational system and the number of students who can or will stay in school into their late teens and twenties. Bishop and Mane (2004) recently evaluated the effects of universal CBEEES on school enrollment rates of 15- to 19-year-olds and of 20- to 24-year-olds, upper-secondary graduation rates, and years spent in school using Organization of Economic Cooperation and Development data. Universal CBEEES had no significant effect on any of these indicators. The statistically significant predictors were per capita GDP and the share of upper-secondary students in prevocational and career-technical educational programs.

Well-controlled cross-section studies of aggregate state-level data have concluded that enrollment rates and graduation rates are negatively related to the total number Carnegie units required to graduate. These studies (Bishop & Mane, 2000; Dee, 2003; Jacobs, 2001; Lillard & DeCicca, 2001) found no tendency for aggregate completion rates to be significantly lower in states with MCTs or SBEs. When, however, the analysis is conducted separately for schools in low-income neighborhoods, for disadvantaged students, or for low-achieving eighth-grade students, a number of studies have found that high school enrollment and completion rates are lower in MCT/SBE states (Bishop & Mane, 2004; Bishop et al., 2001; Reardon, 1996). The longitudinal NELS:88 data set allows a more refined look at the distributional effects of voluntary CBEEEs and MCT/SBEs on high school completion. Students with low or average GPAs in eighth grade were significantly more likely to get their diploma late or to get a Graduate Equivalency Diploma (GED) when they were from New York or a state with an MCT/SBE. Eighth graders with average or above-average GPAs were no less likely to get some kind of diploma (either a GED or regular diploma) when they lived in MCT states. Low-GPA students, however, were significantly less likely to get a regular diploma or GED when they lived in MCT states (Bishop et al., 2001). As in Europe, fast paced instruction and high standards for getting an academic diploma results in some students taking longer to get the diploma and other students switching over to less demanding programs of study.

Critics of high-stakes testing argue that teaching to exit exams diminish the time spent on more important skills that would help students in college and in jobs (Lee, Smith, & Croninger, 1995; Resnick, 1987). If this were the case, we would expect students in states with graduation tests to be less likely to go to and stay in college and to be less likely to get good jobs. When this was tested, however, eighth graders in states with high school exit exams were found to be *more* likely to go to college and equally likely to graduate from college (Bishop & Mane, 2004; Bishop et al., 2001).

Economic theory predicts that raising graduation standards will improve the average quality of high school graduates and raise their mean wage and earnings (Betts & Costrell, 2001). Analysis of High School and Beyond NELS:88 data supports this prediction and contradicts claims to the contrary. Controlling for high school completion, college attendance, and local labor market characteristics, students from states with MCTs earned significantly more—9% more in the calendar year following graduation—than students from states without an MCT. The MCTs also helped recent graduates get jobs that offered better opportunities for training and advancement (Bishop et al., 2001). As a result, eight years after graduating from high school, those growing up in MCT states earned between $1,100 and $2,000 per year more than those who had attended high school in states without graduation exams (Bishop & Mane, 2004). Diplomas that reflect both teacher judgments and external exams appear to be worth more in the labor market than diplomas awarded mainly for seat time or GED certificates based solely on test scores.

Effects of Introducing High School Exit Exams on Achievement Gains since 1990

Another way to assess the effects of exit exams is to compare achievement gains in states that have recently introduced exit exams to gains in states that have not. The first such study was by Fredericksen (1994), who found that states introducing "high-stakes" testing systems (MCTs for graduation for the most part) achieved larger gains on NAEP mathematics questions between 1978 and 1986.

Subsequent studies have all examined data from the 1990s, a period during which many states were introducing standards-based reform strategies holding schools accountable for improving student achievement. The indexes of high-stakes testing used in these studies largely reflect the growth of school accountability testing systems, not high school exit examinations. Carnoy and Loeb (2003) found that fourth- and eighth-grade math achievement gains from 1996 to 2000 were significantly larger in states with strong test-based accountability. Effects were particularly strong for Blacks and Hispanics and remained large when adjustments were made for changes in exclusion rates. Hanushek and Raymond (2003a, 2005) also report that states introducing test-based accountability tended to have larger test score gains from fourth to eighth grade, and conclude as well that special education placement rates did not rise any more rapidly in states introducing test-based accountability. Rosenshine (2003) excluded states with big increases in exclusion rates and then compared four-year NAEP test score gains of the remaining high-stakes states with the gains in states with no stakes. He concluded that "students in the clear high-stakes states were, indeed, learning mathematics and reading that was beyond the specific content of the statewide tests" (p. 3). Braun's (2004) study of gains between 1992 and 2000 concluded: "For each grade, when we examine the relative gains of states over the period, we find that the comparisons strongly favor the high-stakes testing states. Moreover, the results cannot be accounted for by differences between the two groups of states with respect to changes in the percent of students excluded from NAEP over the same period" (p. 2).

Figure 1 plots the relationship between gains on eighth-grade NAEP math tests from 1992 to 2003 and *Education Week*'s (January 2003) overall rating of the quality of each state's standards and school accountability system. The figure tells the same story as the studies discussed above. School accountability systems were not well developed in 1992, so the positive relationship visible in Figure 1 suggests that the introduction and continuing development of school accountability sys-

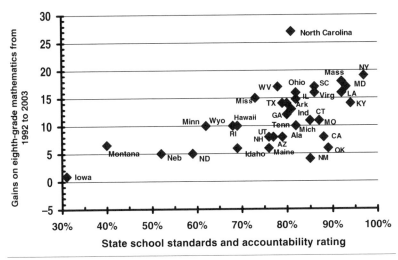

FIGURE 1

Relationship between state standards and accountability rating and gains on NAEP eighth-grade math: 1992–2003.
For the 1992–2003 analysis, the states introducing an MCT between 1993 and 2003 graduating classes—Indiana, Massachusetts, Minnesota, Ohio, and Virginia—are coded as "1" on this variable. Hawaii ended a minimum competency exam during the period, so it is coded "–1." For the 1990–2003 model Louisiana, which first applied their MCT graduation requirement to the class of 1991, is also coded as a 1. States that did not introduce an MCT prior to 2003 or had an MCT prior to the time period analyzed and retained it are coded as a zero.
Source: ("The Teacher Gap," 2003).

tems during the 1990s may have had positive effects on NAEP math scores. Some of these states, however, were also introducing new student accountability systems during this period. During this period Hawaii ended its MCT, five states introduced new MCTs, and two introduced a universal CBEEES. Previous studies of impacts have either not distinguished between student and school stakes or analyzed one without controlling for the other. What effects did the new exit exams have and how do the impacts of student accountability compare with the impacts of school accountability?

Plans for new high school graduation tests and school accountability systems are announced many years in advance of actual implementation. These announcements start a change process that affects elementary as well as secondary school teachers. Consequently, it will typically be "half a generation" (Center on Education Policy, 2004, p. 26) before students exhibit the full effects of a new MCT, SBE, or universal CBEEES.[8] This implies that statistical power is maximized by measuring change over a long period—one that runs at least from the announcement date to many years after the new graduation requirements are imposed.

Multivariate regressions were run to assess the effects of introducing school accountability and various types of student accountability on test score gains from 1992 to 2003 and from 1990 to 2003. Increases in the exclusion of students from testing tend to generate spurious increases in mean test scores that may bias efforts to evaluate high-stakes testing. To avoid such a bias and to adjust for allowing testing accommodations in 2003, changes in the exclusion of students from NAEP testing were included in the regressions. Results are presented in Table 1. The coefficients on the exclusion variables imply that an increase in exclusion rates removes from the NAEP sample students who tend to score about 68 points (5.6 GLEs) below the statewide average. This is a high but not implausible estimate of the size of the bias that results. When this variable is dropped (compare row 2 with row 3 or row 6 with row 7), coefficients on the school and student accountability variables hardly change at all. Carnoy and Loeb (2003) and Braun (2004) came to similar conclusions about the lack of an effect of changing exclusion rates on estimates of the effect of high-stakes testing for school accountability.

The Quality Counts school accountability index is a significant predictor of the growth of mathematics achievement. In models with no controls for student accountability, a two standard deviation (22 points) increase in the 1996–2003 School Accountability Index led to a 5-point gain in math achievement. The estimated effects of a two

TABLE 1

EFFECTS OF INTRODUCING STUDENT AND SCHOOL ACCOUNTABILITY SYSTEMS ON NAEP MATHEMATICS ACHIEVEMENT IN EIGHTH GRADE

	Quality Counts Index of Standards and Accountability	Universal Curriculum-Based Exit Exam	New High School Minimum Competency Graduation Test	Test Score in 1992 or 1990	Change in Exclusions from 1990–92 to 2003	Adjusted R^2 (No. of observations)
Achievement growth 1992→2003						
Eighth grade	0.232*** (0.055)				0.722** (0.285)	0.377 (41)
Eighth grade	0.187*** (0.052)	7.44*** (2.50)	2.22+ (1.43)			0.418 (41)
Eighth grade	0.189*** (0.057)	7.10*** (2.32)	2.19* (1.32)		0.677** (0.256)	0.499 (41)
Eighth grade	0.081* (0.047)	7.23*** (2.84)	4.06*** (1.16)	−0.238*** (0.055)	0.679*** (0.209)	0.666 (41)
Achievement growth 1990→2003						
Eighth grade	0.236*** (0.059)				0.876*** (0.319)	0.406 (37)
Eighth grade	0.177*** (0.050)	10.54*** (2.59)	3.08** (1.64)			0.530 (37)
Eighth grade	0.183*** (0.048)	9.60*** (2.46)	2.44* (1.41)		0.641** (0.274)	0.586 (37)
Eighth grade	0.090+ (0.055)	9.01*** (2.27)	3.00** (1.31)	−0.199** (0.075)	0.689*** (0.252)	0.652 (37)
Independent variables						
Mean	80.63	0.045	0.091	267	2.90	
Std. Dev.	11.11	0.211	0.362	8.95	2.38	

+ $p < .05$ on a one-tail test, ** $p < .025$ on a one-tail test, *** $p < .005$ on a one-tail test.
Author's analysis of state NAEP data (Braswell, Daane, & Grigg, 2004, Table 2). The dependent variable is the 2003 test score with accommodations allowed minus the 1992 or 1990 test score without accommodations. Data on 1992 were not available for Alaska, Illinois, Kansas, Montana, Nevada, South Dakota, Vermont, and Washington, so they are not included in the estimations. New York and North Carolina introduced universal curriculum-based external exit exams during the 1990s. The Quality Counts Index of standards and accountability is the mean of the 2003 overall rating and an average of 1996 and 1997 standards and accountability ratings. (Henry Braun at Educational Testing Service kindly provided the data on exclusion rates.)

standard deviation increase in the index drops to 4.2 points when student accountability variables are included and drops to 1.8 points when 1992 test scores are also included in the model.

The five states—Indiana, Massachusetts, Minnesota, Ohio, and Virginia—that shifted from a no-student stakes environment to an MCT or SBE between 1992 and 2003 had significantly bigger gains in eighth-grade mathematics than other states with similar Quality Counts school accountability ratings and changes in exclusion rates. On the NAEP mathematics test 12 points is roughly a GLE, so the predicted effect of introducing an MCT or SBE is between 18% and 34% of a GLE.

During the period from 1992 to 2003, the two states that added a universal CBEEE system to an existing MCT system, North Carolina and New York, improved their math achievement by three-fifths of a GLE more than other states with similar Quality Counts school accountability ratings and changes in rates of exclusion. For the 13-year period from 1990 to 2003, the estimated effect of the universal CBEEES is about three-quarters of a GLE.[9] The predicted effect of a state shifting from no student accountability to a universal CBEEES is the sum of the MCT/SBE and the universal CBEEES coefficients, or between 0.8 and 1.1 GLE.

Summary

This chapter has reviewed international and domestic evidence on the effects of three types of high school exit exam systems: voluntary curriculum-based external exit exams, universal CBEEES, and MCTs that must be passed to receive a regular high school diploma.

Voluntary CBEEES like AP, IB, and California's Golden State Exams are particularly difficult to evaluate because they are taken by self-selected groups of students. Participation in New York's Regents exams was over 50% in the early 1990s, so the high achievement of New York students compared with similarly disadvantaged student populations in the early 1990s is suggestive evidence that voluntary CBEEES have positive effects. However, there might be other reasons for the outstanding achievement of New York students, so more research on voluntary CBEEES is needed before conclusions can be drawn.

Universal curriculum-based external exit exam systems are found all over the world, so many studies of their impacts have been conducted. The nations and provinces that use universal CBEEES (and typically teacher grades as well) to signal student achievement have significantly

higher achievement levels and smaller differentials by family background than otherwise comparable jurisdictions that base high-stakes
decisions on voluntary college admissions tests and/or teacher grades.
The introduction of universal CBEEES in New York and North
Carolina during the 1990s was associated with large increases in math
achievement on NAEP tests.

Research on MCTs and high school accountability tests is less con-
clusive because these systems are new and have only been implemented
in one country. Cross-section studies using a comprehensive set of
controls for family background have not found that students in MCT
states score higher on audit tests like the NAEP that carry no stakes for
the test taker. The analysis reported in Table 1 tells us that the five states
that introduced MCTs during the 1990s had significantly larger
improvements on NAEP tests than states that made no change in their
student accountability regime. The gains, however, are smaller than for
the states introducing universal CBEEES, New York and North
Carolina. The most positive finding about MCTs is that students in
MCT states earn significantly more during the first eight years after
graduation than comparable students in other states. This suggests that
MCTs may be improving employer perceptions of the quality of the
recent graduates of local high schools.

Minimum competency tests delay a significant number of gradua-
tions and reduce the number of standard high school diplomas awarded.
They also increase the number of GEDs and Certificates of Attendance
awarded. Rates of school attendance and college completion remain
essentially the same. European universal CBEEES, in contrast, do not
seem to depress school attendance rates or upper-secondary completion
rates.

Probably the most important finding presented in the chapter is the
remarkable ability of European style universal CBEEES to substantially
increase academic achievement without decreasing school enrollment
and graduation rates. Minimum competency graduation requirements,
in contrast, clearly have much smaller (possibly no) effects on achievement and also reduce the number of students getting a regular high
school diploma.

Why are European universal CBEEES so much more successful?
First, they signal the full range of student achievement to universities
and to employers, so all students get increased rewards—better jobs and
access to preferred university programs—if they study harder. An MCT,
in contrast, focuses all of its high-stakes incentive effects on a few low-
achieving students who were already at high risk of dropping out. Most

282   HIGH SCHOOL EXIT EXAMINATIONS

students pass the MCT on the first try. Once they pass, the stimulus to studying and paying attention in class generated by the MCT goes away. Only in the minority of very troubled schools where the majority of students are at risk of failing the MCT is student culture likely to be changed by the high-stakes test.

Second, doing poorly on a European universal CBEEE means you graduate with a record of *modest* accomplishment. It does not prevent you from graduating altogether. Employers and universities take that record into account when they make their decisions. Students with poor exam grades enter less prestigious forms of postsecondary education.

Third, end-of-course exams pressure individual teachers to improve their teaching. Their colleagues will know how their students do on the exam. Since the stakes for the students are high, parents and school administrators are likely to encourage teachers to set high standards. MCTs, in contrast, typically cover material studied in many different courses taught by different teachers. Sometimes they are administered in the fall. Under these circumstances, individual teachers are not considered responsible for how students taking their class this term do on the MCT test. *When everyone is responsible for student performance, no one is responsible.*

Fourth, the component exams of these universal CBEEES are more challenging and higher in quality than the MCT and SBE exams that dominate student accountability in the United States. The challenge and quality of an exam depend on the level and complexity of the tasks students are required to perform, not the percent correct pass–fail cut score. The primary goal of any high- or moderate-stakes exam should be improving teaching and learning. Teachers should be proud to be preparing their students to take it. The long-term political viability of standards-based reform depends on our ability to improve the quality and credibility of the exams used to measure student achievement.

NOTES

1. Most of the skills and knowledge—literature, economics, civics, foreign languages, and writing—that high school students are expected to learn is not assessed by these tests. The ACT's science and history subtests are very short and are not linked to specific curricula. The SAT-I does not assess history and science. Recently, the College Board added a 25-minute computer-graded essay and 35 minutes of multiple-choice questions on grammar and usage to the SAT-I. SAT-II exams assess individual subjects but fewer than 60 colleges require applicants to submit three or more SAT-II scores and few students take them. In 1982–83, for example, only 6% of SAT-I test takers took a science SAT-II and only 3–4% took one in history or a foreign language.

2. Costrell's (1994) analysis of the optimal setting of educational standards concluded that more centralized standard setting (state or national achievement exams) with a local option to set even higher standards results in higher standards, higher achievement, and

higher social welfare than decentralized standard setting (i.e., teacher grading or schools setting their own graduation requirements).

3. Costrell's analysis of optimal standard setting concluded: "The case for perfect information [making scores on external examinations available rather than just whether the individual passed or failed] would appear to be strong, if not airtight: for most plausible degrees of heterogeneity, egalitarianism, and pooling under decentralization, perfect information not only raises GDP, but also social welfare" (1994, p. 970).

4. This observation is based on interviews with the directors of the testing and accountability divisions in Manitoba and New Brunswick, Canada, and on the large increases in student performance that occurred in New Brunswick, Massachusetts, Michigan, and other states when no-stakes tests become moderate- or high-stakes tests. Experimental studies confirm the observation. In Candace Brooks-Cooper master's thesis (1993), a test containing complex and cognitively demanding items from the NAEP history and literature tests and the adult literacy test was given to high school students recruited to stay after school by the promise of a $10.00 payment for taking the test. Students were randomly assigned to rooms and one group was promised a payment of $1.00 for every correct answer greater than 65% correct. This group did significantly better than the students in the other test-taking conditions, one of which was the standard "try your best" condition.

5. Fleming and Chambers's study of tests developed by high school teachers found that "over all grades, 80% of the items on teachers' tests were constructed to tap the lowest of [Bloom's] taxonomic categories, knowledge (of terms, facts or principles)" (Fleming & Chambers, 1983, cited in Thomas, 1991, p. 14). Rowher and Thomas (1987) found that only 18% of history test items developed by junior high teachers and 14% of items developed by senior high teachers required the integration of ideas. College instructors, in contrast, required such integration in 99% of their test items.

6. Judge for yourself. New York's English Regents exam asks students to write four essays over a six-hour period. One of the prompts always has the following "critical lens" format:

> Write a critical essay in which you discuss two works of literature you have read from the perspective of the statement that is provided to you in the "Critical Lens." In your essay, provide a valid interpretation of the statement as you have interpreted it, agree or disagree with the statement as you have interpreted it and support your opinion using specific references to appropriate literary elements from the two works. Guidelines . . .

- Use the criteria suggested by the critical lens to analyze the works you have chosen
- Avoid plot summary. Instead use specific references to appropriate literary elements (e.g., theme, characterization, setting, point of view) to develop your analysis . . .
- Follow the conventions of standard written English.

In June 1999 the "critical lens" was: *In literature, evil often triumphs but never conquers.* In June 2000 it was: *It is not what an author says, but what he or she whispers that is important.*

7. For a more extensive discussion of methodological issues surrounding estimating the effects of external examination systems see Bishop, 1996; Hanushek & Raymond, 2003b; Jacobs, 2001; Linn, 2000; Koretz et al., 2001.

8. This is one of the reasons why Amerein and Berliner's (2002) interrupted time series approach to measuring the effects of high-stakes tests is flawed. The other weaknesses of the study are errors in dating the introduction of high-stakes tests in many states, the use of national average scores as a comparison rather than states that did not

implement high-stakes testing, and the arbitrary way of handling changing rates of exclusion. For a detailed critique see Hanushek and Raymond (2003b).

9. Virginia had an MCT in the early 1980s but dropped it in favor of a sixth-grade high school admission test introduced in 1990. The Standards of Learning were phased in at the end of the 1990s and became a universal CBEEES with the graduating class of 2004. If Virginia is reclassified as a new universal CBEEES, the coefficient on universal CBEEES falls by about 20% and the coefficient on MCT/SBE is unchanged.

REFERENCES

Amerein, A.L., & Berliner, D.C. (2002). *The impact of high-stakes tests on student academic performance.* Educational Policy Studies Laboratory, Arizona State University. Retrieved from http://asu.edu/educ/epsl/EPRU/documents/EPSL-0211-125-EPRU.pdf

Association of Secondary Teachers of Ireland. (1990). Information sheet opposing changes in Examination Systems, 1990.

Becker, W., & Rosen, S. (1992). The learning effect of assessment and evaluation in high school. *Economics of Education Review, 11*(2), 107–118.

Betts, J., & Costrell, R. (2001). Incentives and equity under standards-based reform. In D. Ravitch (Ed.), *Brookings papers on education policy, 2001* (pp. 9–74). Washington, DC: The Brookings Institution.

Bishop, J.H. (1996). The impact of curriculum-based external examinations on school priorities and student learning. *International Journal of Education Research, 23*(8), 653–752.

Bishop, J.H. (1997). The effect of national standards and curriculum-based external exams on student achievement. *American Economic Review, 87*(2), 260–264.

Bishop, J.H. (1999a). Are national exit examinations important for educational efficiency? *Swedish Economic Policy Review, 6*(2), 349–401.

Bishop, J.H. (1999b). Nerd harassment, incentives, school priorities and learning. In S. Mayer & P. Peterson (Eds.), *Earning and learning* (pp. 231–280). Washington, DC: Brookings Institution Press.

Bishop, J.H. (2003). What is the appropriate role of student achievement standards? In Y. Kodrzycki (Ed.), *Education in the 21st century: Meeting the challenge of a changing world* (pp. 250–278). Boston: Federal Reserve Bank of Boston.

Bishop, J.H., & Mane, F. (2001). The impacts of minimum competency exam graduation requirements on high school graduation, college attendance and early labor market success. *Labour Economics, 8*(2), 203–222.

Bishop, J.H., & Mane, F. (2004, September). *Educational reform and disadvantaged students: Are they better off or worse off?* Paper presented at CES-IFO conference in Munich, Germany.

Bishop, J.H., Mane, F., Bishop, M., & Moriarty, J. (2001). The role of end-of-course exams and minimum competency tests in standards-based reforms. In D. Ravitch (Ed.), *Brookings papers on education policy, 2001* (pp. 267–346). Washington, DC: The Brookings Institution.

Bishop, J.H., Moriarty, J., & Mane, F. (2000). Diplomas for learning, not seat time. *Economics of Education Review, 19*(3), 333–349.

Board of Admissions and Relations with Schools. (2002). *The use of admissions tests by the University of California.* University of California office of the president. Retrieved October 10, 2004, from http://www.ucop.edu/news/sat/boars.pdf

Braswell, J.S., Daane, M.C., & Grigg, W.S. (2004). *The nation's report card: Mathematics highlights 2003.* Report No. NCES 2004-451. Washington, DC: National Center for Education Statistics, U.S. Department of Education.

Braun, H. (2004, January 5). Reconsidering the impact of high-stakes testing, *Education Policy Analysis Archives, 12*(1). Retrieved November 12, 2004, from http://epaa.asu.edu/epaa/v12n1/

Brooks-Cooper, C. (1993). *The effect of financial incentives on the standardized test performance of high school students.* Master's Thesis, Cornell University.

Carnoy, M., Elmore, R., & Siskin, L.S. (2003). *The new accountability.* New York: Routledge Falmer.

Carnoy, M., & Loeb, S. (2003). Does external accountability affect student outcomes? *Educational Evaluation and Policy Analysis, 24*(4), 305–331.

Center on Education Policy (Gayler, K., Chudowsky, N., Hamilton, M., Kober, N., & Yeager, M.) (2004). *State high school exit exams: A maturing reform.* Washington, DC: Center on Education Policy.

286 HIGH SCHOOL EXIT EXAMINATIONS

Coleman, J.S. (1990). *Foundations of social theory.* Cambridge, MA: Harvard University Press.

Coleman, J., Schneider, B., Plank, S., Schiller, K., Shouse, R., & Wang, H. (1997). *Redesigning American education.* Boulder, CO: Westview Press.

College Board. (2005). *Advanced Placement report to the nation 2005.* Retrieved January 4, 2005, from http://www.collegeboard.com/prod_downloads/about/news_info/ap/2005/ap-report-nation.pdf

Competitiveness Policy Council. (1993, March). *Reports of the subcouncils.* Washington, DC: Competitiveness Policy Council.

Costrell, R. (1994). A simple model of educational standards. *American Economic Review, 84*(4), 956–971.

Count me in. (2004, January 8). Quality counts 2004. *Education Week, 23*(17), 7.

Dee, T. (2003). The "first wave " of accountability. In M. West & P. Peterson (Eds.), *No Child Left Behind? The politics and practice of school accountability* (pp. 292–323). Washington, DC: Brookings Institution Press.

Figlio, D., & Lucas, M. (2000, October). *Do high grading standards affect student performance?* NBER Working Paper 7985. University of Florida and National Bureau of Economic Research.

Finn, C.E. (1991). *We must take charge: Our schools and our future.* New York: The Free Press.

Fleming, M., & Chambers, B. (1983). *Teacher-made tests: Windows on the classroom.* San Francisco: Jossey-Bass.

Fredericksen, N. (1994). *The influence of minimum competency tests on teaching and learning.* Princeton, NJ: Educational Testing Service.

Fuchs, T., & Wößmann, L. (2004). *What accounts for international differences in student performance? A re-examination using PISA data.* CESifo Working Paper 1235. Munich, Germany: CESifo.

Graham, A., & Husted, T. (1995).Understanding state variation in SAT scores. *Economics of Education Review, 12*(3), 197–202.

Gummere, R. (1943). The independent school and the post war world. *Independent School Bulletin, 4*(April).

Hanushek, E.A., & Raymond, M. (2003a). Improving educational quality: How best to evaluate our schools? In Y. Kodrzycki (Ed.), *Education in the 21st century: Meeting the challenge of a changing world* (pp. 193–224). Boston: Federal Reserve Bank of Boston.

Hanushek, E.A., & Raymond, M. (2003b). Shopping for evidence against school accountability. *Education Next, 3*(3), 1–13.

Hanushek, E.A., & Raymond, M. (2005). Does school accountability lead to improved student performance? *Journal of Policy Analysis and Management, 24*(2), 297–327.

Hart Research Associates. (1995). *Valuable views: A public opinion research report on the views of AFT teachers on professional issues.* Washington, DC: American Federation of Teachers.

Hess, F. (2003). Breaking the mold: Charter schools, contract schools and voucher plans. In W.L. Boyd & D. Miretzky (Eds.), *American educational governance on trail: Change and challenges. The 102nd Yearbook of the National Society for the Study of Education* (pp. 114–135). Chicago: The National Society for the Study of Education.

Jacobs, B.A. (2001). Getting tough? The impact of high school graduation exams. *Educational Evaluation and Policy Analysis, 23*(2), 99–122.

Jencks, C., & Crouse, J. (1982). Aptitude versus achievement: Should we replace the SAT? *The Public Interest, 67,* 21–35.

Jurges, H., Schneider, K., & Buchel, F. (2003). *The effect of central examinations on student achievement: Quasi-experimental evidence from TIMSS.* Munich, Germany: CESifo Working Paper 939.

Koretz, D., McCaffrey, D., & Hamilton, L. (2001). *Toward a framework for validating gains under high-stakes conditions.* CSE Technical Report 551. Los Angeles: National Center for Research on Evaluation, Standards, and Student Testing.

Lee, V.E., Smith, J.B., & Croninger, R.G. (1995, Fall). *Another look at high school restructuring. Issues in restructuring schools.* Madison: University of Wisconsin-Madison, Center on Organization and Restructuring of Schools.

Lillard, D., & DeCicca, P. (2001). Higher standards, more dropouts? Evidence within and across time. *Economics of Education Review, 20*(5), 459–473.

Linn, R. (2000). Assessments and accountability. *Educational Researcher, 29*(2), 4–16.

Linn, R.L. (2003). Accountability: Responsibility and responsible expectations. *Educational Researcher, 32*(7), 3–13.

Loveless, T. (2001). *The 2001 Brown Center report on American education: How well are American students learning?* Washington, DC: The Brookings Institution.

Madaus, G. (1991, June). *The effects of important tests on students: Implications for a national examination or system of examinations.* Paper presented at the American Educational Research Association Invitational Conference on Accountability as a State Reform Instrument, Washington, DC.

Mathews, J. (2002, August 6). AP, IB to be the next SATs? *The Washington Post.*

Mullis, I.V.S., Martin, M.O., Beaton, A.E., Gonzalez, E.J., Kelly, D.L., & Smith, T.A. (1998). *Mathematics and science achievement in the final years of secondary school: IEA's third international mathematics and science report.* Retrieved October 4, 2004, from http://isc.bc.edu/timss1995i/MathScienceC.html

No small change. (2005, January 5). Quality Counts 2005. *Education Week, 24*(17).

North Carolina Board of Education. (1999, fall). Understanding the North Carolina end-of-course tests. *Assessment Brief, 6*(5), 1–4.

North Carolina Board of Education. (2004, May). Understanding the North Carolina end-of-course tests. *Assessment Brief, 9*(4), 1–2.

Organization of Economic Cooperation and Development (OECD). (2002). *Education at a glance.* Paris: OECD.

Powell, A. (1996). Motivating students to learn: An American dilemma. In S. Fuhrman & J. O'Day (Eds.), *Rewards and reform* (pp. 1–59). San Francisco: Jossey-Bass.

Ravitch, D. (1995). *National standards in American education: A citizen's guide.* Washington, DC: The Brookings Institution.

Reardon, S. (1996). *Eighth grade minimum competency testing and early high school drop out patterns.* Paper presented at the American Educational Research Association conference, New York.

Resnick, L. (1987). *Education and learning to think.* Washington, DC: National Academies Press.

Rohwer, W.D., & Thomas, J.W. (1987). Domain specific knowledge, cognitive strategies, and impediments to educational reform. In M. Pressley (Ed.), *Cognitive strategy research.* New York: Springer-Verlag.

Rosenshine, B. (2003, August 4). High-stakes testing: Another analysis. *Education Policy Analysis Archives, 11*(24). Retrieved November 13, 2004, from http://epaa.asu.edu/epaa/v11n24/

Steinberg, L., Brown, B., & Dornbusch, S. (1996). *Beyond the classroom.* New York: Simon and Schuster.

Takahira, S., Gonzales, P., Frase, M., & Salganik, L.H. (1998). *Pursuing excellence: A study of U.S. twelfth-grade mathematics and science achievement in international context* (NCES 98-049). Washington, DC: National Center for Education Statistics.

The teacher gap. (2003, January 8). Quality Counts 2003. *Education Week, 22*(16), 10.

Thomas, J.W. (1991). *Expectations and effort: Course demands, students study practices and academic achievement.* Paper presented at the Office of Educational Research and Improvement Conference on Student Motivation, Washington, DC.

Wößmann, L. (2000). *Schooling resources, educational institutions, and student performance: The international evidence.* Kiel Working Paper 983. Kiel Institute of World Economics, Germany. Retrieved February 19, 2005, from http://www.uni-kiel.de/ifw/pub/kap/2000/kap983.htm

Wößmann, L. (2003a). Central exit exams and student achievement: International evidence. In M. West & P. Peterson (Eds.), *No Child Left Behind? The politics and practice of school accountability* (pp. 292–323). Washington, DC: Brookings Institution Press.
Wößmann, L. (2003b). Central exams as the "currency of school systems": International evidence on the complementarity of school autonomy and central exams. *Journal for Institutional Comparisons*, *1*(4), 46–56.

CHAPTER 12

The Consequences of Student Testing for Teaching and Teacher Quality

LINDA DARLING-HAMMOND AND ELLE RUSTIQUE-FORRESTER

The centerpiece of state educational reforms over the last decade has been the development of educational standards to guide school practices and investments. Increasingly, standards-based reform has centered on test-based accountability, an emphasis reinforced by the passage of the No Child Left Behind Act in 2002. The central assumption of this major federal bill and of many state accountability schemes is that by holding students, teachers, schools, and districts responsible for results on standardized achievement tests, expectations for students will rise, teaching will improve, and learning will increase. While some proponents of testing rest their hopes for stronger learning on the expectation that tests alone will motivate students to work harder, most posit that better learning will result primarily from better teaching— due to curriculum changes, greater attention to student needs, stronger teacher motivation, or focused investments in professional development, the hiring and retention of more expert teachers, and other school resources.

What kinds of actions result from the use of student testing as a policy lever is an empirical question, as is the consequence of such actions for what teachers know and do and for who enters and remains in teaching in different schools. This chapter examines the consequences of student accountability testing for: (1) the nature and quality of teaching, including the curriculum emphases and teaching strategies adopted in the classroom; and (2) the teaching workforce, including the quality of teachers who are recruited and retained in teaching in different schools and districts.

Linda Darling-Hammond is the Charles E. Ducommun Professor of Education at Stanford University. Elle Rustique-Forrester is a Postdoctoral Scholar and Associate Director of Assessment and Accountability for the School Redesign Network at Stanford University.

In examining these questions it is critical to recognize that, despite the homogenizing influence of the extensive federal testing rules required by No Child Left Behind, states still use a wide variety of approaches to assessment, from the portfolios and local performance tasks that characterize the assessment systems of states like Maine, Nebraska, and Vermont to the largely external multiple-choice tests that characterize many other states. A number of systems include both state and local components and both highly constrained items and richer performance tasks. In addition, states vary in the ways in which they use tests for decision making, ranging from states that have used test results to determine student promotion and graduation as well as teacher pay and school sanctions, like North Carolina and South Carolina, to states that, by law, preclude the use of test results as the sole basis for decisions about student placements or graduation, like Connecticut and Rhode Island. Although these differences can strongly affect the outcomes of testing, there has been relatively little policy discussion or analysis that sorts out the ways in which the results of different approaches to testing may be distinct.

Our review of the evidence on the consequences of various systems and approaches to accountability finds that the use of student assessment as a strategy for improving education has, in some contexts, had positive influences on teaching and teacher quality; however, unintended negative consequences have also been found in systems that use limited measures and that emphasize sanctions without attention to improving school and teaching quality. We describe this evidence in relation to the characteristics of specific systems in what follows.

We examine the various rationales for using students' tests to shape teaching and the teacher workforce, and we discuss recent research that has examined both the positive and negative consequences of using different approaches to using student testing. We evaluate these findings with attention to the nature of tests, the use of tests, and the stakes that are attached to test results. We conclude with a discussion of policy recommendations for the design and use of assessment systems that are likely to enhance rather than to undermine the quality of teaching.

The Influences of Testing on Teaching

There are several rationales for the use of tests to shape and (as proponents hope) to improve teaching. The first is a curricular rationale, stemming from the recognition that assessment, especially when it is used for decision-making purposes, can exert powerful influences on curriculum and instruction. A long line of research has shown that tests can "drive" instruction in ways that mimic not only the content, but also the format and cognitive demands of tests (e.g., Madaus, West, Harmond, Lomax, & Vator, 1992). If this influence focuses teachers on useful content and supports more purposeful teaching, it could presumably improve the quality of education students receive.

A related rationale stems from management objectives—to enable tighter control of teaching for purposes of curricular coherence, greater standardization of what is taught across classrooms, and teacher accountability for covering expected content and, hopefully, producing intended results. Some expect that management around assessment data will stimulate alignment between standards, instruction, and materials and will direct investments for professional development and other needed resources. From a management perspective, traditional standardized tests can be especially appealing. They are relatively inexpensive and fairly efficient for schools to administer; they can be mandated with comparative ease and implemented quickly; and they can produce visible and measurable results, at least, in the short term, on item types that become well known (Linn, 2000).

However, school-based performance assessments that are evaluated by teachers and used to inform curricular and teaching changes are also used as management tools in some communities. These can influence instruction when they are incorporated throughout the curriculum, evaluated and discussed collectively by teachers, and used for planning curriculum and instructional improvements. The immediate availability of results, the rich information they provide about students' thinking and reasoning, and the authenticity of the tasks are elements that make these kinds of assessments valuable from teachers' perspectives in guiding their teaching (Darling-Hammond, Ancess, & Falk, 1995).

A third rationale—which is both pedagogical and organizational in origin—focuses on the need for information about student learning to guide ongoing teaching decisions and school improvement processes. From this perspective, assessment data are the necessary grist for daily, weekly, and yearly analyses of how things are going and of teacher responses to students' needs. By making assessment an integral part of the planning and teaching process, teaching improves because it can take into account what students know, believe, and bring to the classroom, as well as what they need to learn. At the school level, an understanding of the aggregate funds of knowledge (Moll, Amanti, Neff, & Gonzalez, 1992) and the needs of students can guide broader decisions about curriculum and program design.

Finally, from an equity perspective, tests are viewed as a vehicle for monitoring access and equality of educational opportunity, in part because test results can reveal inequities in achievement and point out inadequacies in different students' access and opportunities to learn (Education Trust, 2004; Public Education Network, 2002). In addition, some see tests as a lever for standardizing students' school experiences to make sure students get the same kinds of content, while others point out that test data can allow teachers and schools to better focus on meeting students' individual needs. The American Psychological Association (2004) contends that in many instances, without tests, low-performing students and schools could remain invisible and therefore not get the extra resources or remedial help that they need. Both of these are equity rationales, even if they appear to point toward two very different kinds of strategies.

Clearly, the extent to which any of these goals is actualized depends a great deal on what kinds of tests are used and in what context. For example, the kinds of assessments used—the extent to which they focus on valuable content and highlight generative skills that enable transfer of what is learned to new problems and settings—matter a great deal for whether tests that "drive" teaching actually improve what is taught and learned. Also, teachers' abilities to learn from the information assessments can provide—as well as their overall teaching abilities—make a difference for whether assessment results translate into more adaptive teaching or simply result in failure and stigma for struggling students. While tests might be levers for greater equity, they have long been used to keep students separate and to exclude students from educational curricula, programs, and opportunities (Watson, 1996). And whether schools and systems have the capacity, will, and knowledge to respond to test information by investing productively in the learning opportunities of students who score poorly has everything to do with whether testing will improve those opportunities. Finally, the incentives that may operate for the use of scores to allocate rewards and sanctions can determine whether schools are induced to assign more expertise and resources to the education of certain students or, alternatively, to keep or push them out of the testing pool or even the school itself.

Influences of State Assessment Systems on Teaching Quality and Access

Research on the impact of state accountability systems has identified some of the hoped-for influences of testing on teaching, including greater awareness of state standards and increased focus on the standards on the part of school leaders and teachers (DeBard & Kubow, 2002; Ladd & Zelli, 2002; Woody, Buttles, Kafka, Park, & Russell, 2004); greater attention for students who need support and intervention to improve their performance (Ladd & Zelli, 2002); and incentives for principals to provide teachers with opportunities and resources for more professional development (Ladd & Zelli, 2002). Indeed, tests can signal what is important to teach and learn by providing specific goals and feedback on how students are doing, thus enabling a diagnosis of curriculum strengths and weaknesses (Herman, Brown, & Baker, 2000; see also reviews by Linn, 2000; Shepard, 2000).

The extent to which these potential benefits of assessments are realized seems to depend on the nature of both the incentive structures in which tests are embedded and the capacity building that accompanies them. We look first at how these factors appear to influence the general quality of teaching and then at how they influence student access to improved teaching.

Positive Influences of Testing on the General Quality of Teaching

Research suggests that thoughtfully structured assessments can support improvements in the quality of teaching. For example, in the 1990s, when performance assessments were launched in a number of states, studies found that teachers assigned more writing and mathematical problem solving of the kinds demanded on these new assessments in states such as California (Chapman, 1991; Herman, Klein, Heath, & Wakai, 1995), Kentucky (Koretz, Mitchell, Barron, & Keith, 1996; Stecher, Barron, Kaganoff, & Goodwin, 1998), Maine (Firestone, Mayrowetz, & Fairman, 1998), Maryland (Lane, Stone, Parke, Hansen, & Cerrillo, 2000), Vermont (Koretz, Stecher, & Deibert, 1992), and Washington (Stecher, Baron, Chun, & Ross, 2000).

The extent to which these benefits for instruction were apparent in these states, however, seemed to depend in part on how principals and teachers approached the challenge of incorporating new standards—whether they sought to deepen instruction, for example, rather than merely attaching test-like items to lessons—and how much teaching expertise was available in particular schools, as well as investment in teacher professional development (Borko, Elliott, & Uchiyama, 1999; Borko & Stecher, 2001; Wolf, Borko, McIver, & Elliott, 1999). Some studies have also found that teachers who were involved in scoring performance assessments and discussing student work with colleagues felt that these experiences helped them change their practice to become more problem-oriented and more diagnostic (e.g., Darling-Hammond

& Ancess, 1994; Falk & Ort, 1997; Goldberg & Rosewell, 2000; Murnane & Levy, 1996).

A number of studies have found concurrent increases in performance on both traditional standardized tests and performance measures for students in classrooms offering a problem-oriented curriculum that regularly utilized performance assessment. For example, in a study of more than 2,000 students within 23 restructured schools, Newmann, Marks, and Gamoran (1995) found much higher levels of achievement on complex performance tasks for students who experienced what these researchers termed "authentic pedagogy"—instruction focused on active learning in real-world contexts calling for higher-order thinking, consideration of alternatives, extended writing, and an audience for student work. A recent analysis of National Education Longitudinal Study (NELS) data found that students in restructured schools where "authentic instruction" was widespread experienced greater achievement gains on conventional tests (Lee, Smith, & Croninger, 1995).

In some states that have used low- to medium-stakes assessments as part of a comprehensive reform, such as Connecticut, Kentucky, and Vermont, studies have documented improvements in teaching practice and student performance stemming from the combination of performance-based assessments, investments in teacher professional development, and equalization of school resources. We briefly describe these three systems here to illustrate how the design of assessment systems and professional development systems, combined with the availability of resources for improved teaching, has influenced teaching quality in these cases.

Connecticut. The Connecticut Assessment Program includes open-ended performance tasks featuring extended writing and problem solving (e.g., evaluating solutions, developing models, designing and analyzing mini-experiments) (Mitchell, 1992). Teachers are involved in task development and scoring. In addition to public reporting of data, the state education department provides disaggregated data about performance to districts and schools and devotes considerable effort to helping districts use the data to diagnose curricular and professional development needs. The state also provides intellectual and material resources to meet these needs. By law, the scores may *not* be used to allocate rewards or sanctions to individual students or schools. Categorical aid is provided to low-achieving districts to support professional development and school redesign, and investments in teacher quality have been a major thrust of state policy since 1986.

Over the course of the 1990s, Connecticut became one of the top-ranked states in the nation on National Assessment of Educational Progress tests in reading, writing, mathematics, and science, demonstrating steep improvements in its urban areas, even while its populations of minority, low-income, and limited English-speaking students grew. Studies attributed these trends to the state's investments in well-qualified teachers through high and equalized salaries, rigorous teacher education and licensing standards, and extensive professional development around a set of thoughtful standards and assessments that were designed to provide rich information about learning (Baron, 1999; Wilson, Darling-Hammond, & Berry, 2001).

Kentucky. The Kentucky assessments were developed as part of the Kentucky Education Reform Act, which began as a school funding reform that infused new resources into a more equalized system and provided extensive opportunities for teacher professional development. The assessment system featured a combination of short and long extended tasks and portfolios in writing and mathematics. Several evaluations found that the assessments influenced instruction in positive ways, especially in encouraging much more extensive and higher quality student writing (Appalachia Educational Laboratory, 1996; Whitford & Jones, 2000). Although a high-stakes accountability index (later repealed because of its dysfunctional side-effects) eventually caused more emphasis to be placed on short-answer measures than on the portfolios, the performance-oriented assessments were noted as contributors to improved practices for teachers and learning outcomes for students (Appalachia Educational Laboratory, 1996; Stecher, Barron, Kaganoff, & Goodwin, 1998).

Vermont. Vermont's state assessments include both portfolios and "on-demand" performance tasks that are used throughout the school year, so that teachers and students can learn from the results of the assessments and continually improve their work. The writing and mathematics portfolios, developed by teachers across the state, include both "uniform tests" that involve all students in responding to common tasks as well as locally selected work samples that reflect particular kinds of work to be represented in the portfolios. Teachers convene to assess these portfolios in moderated scoring sessions that teach them how to evaluate the work in comparable ways. Although early evaluations found that the initial, nonstandardized portfolios were not scored very reliably, revisions that brought common structures to the portfolios and performance assessments resulted in much higher levels of reliability (Koretz et al., 1992).

Teachers have reported that the process of building portfolios promotes classroom dialogue about standards for good work and helps students as well as teachers learn to evaluate work and revise it until it reaches high standards. Teachers learn how to develop and evaluate assessments and how to teach toward the new standards through teacher-to-teacher support networks that sponsor professional development sessions and summer institutes in which teachers from different schools convene to score assessment tasks together. As one account describes the conversations of teachers who gather in the summer to evaluate portfolios:

> Often heated, the discussions focused on what constitutes good communication and problem-solving skills, how first-rate work differs from less adequate work, and what types of problems elicit the best student work. (Murnane & Levy, 1996, p. 263)

When the Vermont system was initially designed, then-Commissioner Richard Mills rejected the idea of attaching high-stakes sanctions to the assessment results, suggesting that it "would alienate teachers and jeopardize the most important goal, improving teaching in Vermont's public schools" (Murnane & Levy, 1996, pp. 184–185). Nonetheless, the assessments count. They are important because they are widely reported and because they are credible to teachers, parents, and community members who believe they measure important abilities. The "medium stakes" environment has proved productive. Evidence suggests that the assessments, along with the professional development opportunities associated with them, have stimulated instructional improvement (Koretz et al., 1992; Murnane & Levy, 1996).

In all of these contexts, researchers have found that assessment systems in which teachers look at student work with other teachers and discuss standards in explicit ways appear to help schools develop shared definitions of quality. Evaluating work collaboratively rather than grading students in isolation helps teachers make their standards explicit, gain multiple perspectives on learning, and think about how they can teach to produce the kinds of student work they want to see. Where teachers do this, studies find that changes in teaching and schooling practices tend to occur, especially for students who are not as often successful at schoolwork (Darling-Hammond et al., 1995; Kornhaber & Gardner, 1993).

By engaging teachers in collaboratively developing and scoring assessments, using student work from performance assessments to examine learning and its implications for curriculum and teaching, and designing professional development based on the results of assessments, these states have built teaching capacity while leveraging attention to assessments through medium-stakes policies that reported data and flagged schools for additional assistance. (None of these states applied high-stakes sanctions to students or teachers, and only Kentucky applied sanctions to low-performing schools.) All three of these states made investments in the teaching force through reforms of teacher education and licensing as well as statewide professional development around reform curriculum, so that teachers were helped to learn how to deepen and expand their practice, especially in districts serving high-need students.

While studies of these systems illustrate the potential positive influences of student assessments on teaching, research has also found unintended, negative consequences of accountability systems that attach high stakes to tests that are much more limited in scope.

Negative Influences of Testing on Teaching Quality

The assessments described above were found to improve instruction in part because they offered ambitious, open-ended tasks for teachers to study and students to strive for, and used these to organize professional learning. However, as Herman (2002) notes, many of the performance-based assessment initiatives of the 1990s have either been scaled back or abandoned. In 2001, *Education Week's Quality Counts* found only eight states using extended response items outside of English or writing tests. Since the passage of No Child Left Behind in 2002, some additional states have scaled back performance components and added multiple-choice elements to their testing systems in order to comply with federal requirements for annual testing at relatively low cost (Darling-Hammond, 2004).

Curriculum and teaching effects. Research identifying negative effects of tests on teaching quality has noted narrowing of the curriculum to subjects and modes of performance that are tested, loss of instructional time to test preparation, and less instruction focused on complex reasoning and performance (Klein, Hamilton, McCaffrey, & Stetcher, 2000; Koretz & Barron, 1998; Koretz et al., 1996; Koretz, Linn, Dunbar, & Shepard, 1991; Linn, 2000; Linn, Graue, & Sanders, 1990; Stecher et al., 2000). Studies in high-stakes testing states that use limited measures, such as Arizona, Florida, North Carolina, and Texas, have found that, under pressure to show improved performance, teachers often prepare students by spending substantial instructional time on exercises that look just like the test items, reducing time on untested subjects or topics, and reverting to instructional practices such as recall and recitation that they feel will prepare students for standardized tests. In the process, instructional strategies such as projects, research papers, extended writing, and computer use are de-emphasized (Brown, 1992; Haney, 2000; Jones & Egley, 2004; Jones, Jones, Hardin, Chapman, & Yarbrough, 1999; Popham, 1999; Smith, 1991).

National data indicate that, historically, when high-stakes test-oriented accountability measures have been emphasized in American schools, the use of methods focused on the teaching of complex reasoning and problem solving has tended to decrease. When minimum competency tests were introduced between 1972 and 1980, for example, public schools showed a decline in the use of such methods as student-centered discussions, research projects, experiments, and laboratory work (National Center for Education Statistics [NCES], 1982). In a study conducted by the RAND Corporation around this time, teachers described why such narrowing of pedagogy and the curriculum occurred. Where student scores were linked to decisions about curriculum, student promotions, and teacher evaluations, teachers reported that the tasks of preparing for tests, administering tests, and keeping records took time away from what they called "real teaching." Under the heading of real teaching, teachers included the teaching of non-tested subjects, such as science and social studies, and of such nontested modes of thinking and performance as reading books, discussing ideas, engaging in creating activities and projects requiring research, invention, and problem solving (Darling-Hammond & Wise, 1985).

Teachers describe other ways in which the press for coverage to address tested topics can undermine instruction, especially for students who are struggling in school. For example, Plitt (2002, p. 745) describes the dilemma of "providing opportunities for at-risk students to participate in critical thinking in an already tight schedule while still adhering to the state mandated curriculum" that is evaluated by California's Standardized Testing and Reporting (STAR) tests. He notes that the issue of finding time for inquiry and critical thinking is layered onto the fundamental problem of preparing students who "see school as a place where they fail" (p. 745) without driving them away altogether.

A recent national survey of teachers found that teachers in high-stakes testing states were more likely than those in other states to report that the curriculum is distorted by tests and that they feel pressured to use test formats in their instruction and to teach in ways that contradict their ideas of sound instructional practice. For example, teachers in high-stakes states more often said they could not use computers to teach writing because the state test is handwritten (Pedulla et al., 2003). The fact that fewer students are gaining access to computers for writing as a result of paper-based state tests, especially in urban schools, suggests that the format of these tests can impede the acquisition of both writing skills and computer skills (Russell & Abrams, 2004). Teaching to the test also appears to occur more intensely in grade levels where stakes are attached to the test results (Stecher & Barron, 1999) and where students are generally lower-performing, and hence in danger of not passing the tests (Herman & Golan, 1993).

An *Education Week* (2001) survey of more than 1,000 public school teachers reported that two-thirds felt their states had become too focused on state tests, and 85% reported that their school gives less attention to subjects that are not on the state test. One Texas teacher noted, "At our school, third- and fourth-grade teachers are told not to teach social studies and science until March" (Hoffman, Assaf, & Paris, 2001). Teachers often feel that their responses to tests are not educationally appropriate. As two Florida teachers observed:

Before FCAT I was a better teacher. I was exposing my children to a wide range of science and social studies experiences. I taught using themes that really immersed the children into learning about a topic using their reading, writing, math, and technology skills. Now I'm basically afraid to *not* teach to the test. I know that the way I was teaching was building a better foundation for my kids as well as a love of learning. Now each year I can't wait until March is over so I can spend the last two and a half months of school teaching the way I want to teach, the way I know students will be excited about.

I believe that the FCAT is pushing students and teachers to rush through curriculum much too quickly. Rather than focusing on getting students to understand a concept fully in math, we must rush through all the subjects so we are prepared to take the test in March. This creates a surface knowledge or many times very little knowledge in a lot of areas. I would rather spend a month on one concept and see my students studying in an in-depth manner. (Southeast Center for Teaching Quality, 2004, p. 15)

Interestingly, international assessments have shown that higher-scoring countries in mathematics and science teach *fewer* concepts each year but teach them more deeply than tends to be true in the United

States, so that students have a stronger foundation to support higher-order learning in the upper grades (McNight et al., 1987). Ironically, states that test large numbers of topics in a grade level may encourage superficial coverage that leads to less solid learning.

Jones and Egley's (2004) survey of Florida teachers found that 80% believed the testing program was not taking schools in the right direction. They cited negative effects on the curriculum, on the teaching and learning process, and on student and teacher motivation. Most felt that the tests were used improperly, that one-time test scores were not an accurate assessment of students' learning, and that the tests should not be used to retain students or to grade schools. In this study and others, researchers found that teachers were not opposed to accountability, but perceived problems with specific policies and how they were being implemented (see also, Pedulla et al., 2003; Woody et al., 2004). A study in six southern states by the Southeast Center for Teacher Quality (2004) concluded that, "Teachers want accountability systems in place, but they want ones that can help them improve instruction and student learning" (p. 1).

Change without improvement. Echoing teachers' worries are concerns raised in several studies that gains in high-stakes tests may be a function of narrow test preparation rather than the acquisition of more generalizable knowledge (Amrein & Berliner, 2002; Koretz & Barron, 1998; Klein et al., 2000; Neill & Gayler, 2001). As one Texas teacher noted in a survey:

I have seen more students who can pass the TAAS but cannot apply those skills to anything if it's not in the TAAS format. I have students who can do the test but can't look up words in a dictionary and understand the different meanings . . . As for higher quality teaching, I'm not sure I would call it that. Because of the pressure for passing scores, more and more time is spent practicing the test and putting everything in TAAS format. (Haney, 2000, Part 6, p. 10)

Teachers elsewhere have also attributed test-score gains to test preparation rather than to improved learning (Koretz et al., 1996; Stecher et al., 1998). For example, in Washington state, where tests are increasingly used to monitor school quality, one survey found that three-quarters of fourth-grade teachers and the majority of principals believed that better test preparation, rather than increased student knowledge, was responsible for most of the gains in test scores (Neill, 2003). Nationally, 40% of teachers report that teachers in their school can raise test scores without improving learning, and 75% believe that scores and school rankings do not accurately portray the quality of education (Pedulla et al., 2003).

The possibility that test score increases may not reflect general improvements in teaching and learning is consistent with evidence emerging in the literature that while tests often induce adaptations from teachers, especially in emphasizing the content and format of the tests in the tasks they give to students, they do not as often generate substantial improvements in instructional strategies (Corbett & Wilson, 1991; Firestone & Mayrowetz, 2000) or improvements in the quality of teaching available to specific students, especially those who are lowest-performing (Anagnostopoulos, 2003). To a great extent, this appears to be a function of teacher knowledge and other resources. Teachers may know that some students are doing poorly but may not have the expertise to meet their needs or the curricular or other resources to do so.

As Jennifer O'Day (2002) notes in a discussion of different approaches to accountability:

(N)ot all information leads to learning and change . . . (F)or information to be useful, members of the system must first have access to it, through interaction with other members or the environment. Moreover, if they are to incorporate the information into their cognitive maps or repertoire of strategies, they must attend to it and must have sufficient knowledge and stability to interpret it. Action does not necessarily follow, even once learning occurs, as this step often requires motivation and resources beyond those necessary for the learning itself . . . (T)hese elements—access, attention, knowledge, motivation, and resources—are all essential. A breakdown in any one of them may disrupt the connection between information and change. (p. 5)

O'Day contrasts the accountability systems in Chicago and Baltimore, arguing that Chicago's bureaucratic accountability system, which focuses almost exclusively on testing, is much less productive than Baltimore's professional accountability strategy, which uses achievement targets for schools as the basis for identifying problems and for allocating resources in the form of intensive supports for improved teaching, including professional development, instructional assistance, and improved hiring and retention of teachers. These factors have a great deal to do with whether testing policies improve the quality of education for underserved students or, as studies of Chicago's system have found, increase grade retentions and dropouts without improving achievement for the most vulnerable students (Roderick & Engel, 2001).

302   TESTING   AND   TEACHER   QUALITY

Influences of Testing on Student Access to Quality Teaching

Students' access to higher quality teaching depends on the extent to which tests trigger changes that create better educational experiences for them rather than excluding them from strong programs or from school altogether. Although some studies have found that tests can increase attention to struggling students, others have found that high-stakes testing can result in students being placed in lower tracks (offering lower quality teaching) or being encouraged to leave school. The possibility that testing policies may decrease students' access to education is particularly worrying as nearly half of states now use state tests to determine whether students graduate from high school or are promoted to the next grade (Center on Education Policy [CEP], 2004).

Incentives for student exclusion. A study by Schiller and Muller (2000) seems to confirm both of these influences—greater attention to students *and* greater likelihood of dropout or pushout—under different incentive structures. The authors found that more frequent testing increased the odds of graduating when tests carried consequences for *students* and teachers used scores to identify at-risk students, presumably for greater attention. They also found, however, that test-based consequences for *schools* increased the odds of students dropping out; when schools stood to be sanctioned for low scores, teachers' identifications of at-risk students increased the odds of dropping out. This finding is consistent with other studies that suggest that when schools are rewarded or punished for students' average scores, there are substantial incentives for low-scoring students to be retained in grade (Allington & McGill-Franzen, 1992), which increases their odds of dropping out, or pushed out of school so that schools' average scores will look better (Advocates for Children, 2002; Haney, 2002; Smith, 1986).

A few analysts using state-level data have argued that state graduation rates have not declined as a result of high school exit exams (Carnoy & Loeb, 2002; Greene & Winters, 2004). However, other studies using less aggregated data have found higher rates of retention and dropping out in states and cities that have instituted tougher graduation requirements (Clarke, Madaus, Pedulla, & Shore, 2000; Lilliard & DeCicca, 2001; Orfield & Ashkinaze, 1991; Roderick, Bryk, Jacob, Easton, & Allensworth, 1999; Wheelock, 2003), as well as a widening gap in graduation rates between white and minority students (Orfield et al., 2004).

Using individual-level data from the National Educational Longitudinal Survey, Jacob (2001) found that graduation tests increased the probability of dropping out among the lowest-ability students. Similarly, the Chicago Consortium for School Research found that, although some students' scores improved in response to a high-stakes testing policy tied to grade promotion, the scores of low-scoring students who were retained declined relative to similar achieving students who had been promoted, and their dropout rates increased (Roderick et al., 1999). Summarizing several decades of research, the National Research Council concluded that low-performing students who are held back do less well academically and socially, and are far more likely to drop out than comparable students who are promoted (Heubert & Hauser, 1999). One study, for example, found that retention can increase the odds of dropping out by as much as 250% above those of similar students who were not retained (Rumberger & Larson, 1998).

Concerns about student exclusions from school have emerged in states that have test-based graduation requirements for students and test-based accountability for schools. In Massachusetts, which began requiring a high school exit exam for graduation in 2002, graduation rates decreased from 76% in 2002 to 72% in 2003. Meanwhile some of the steepest increases in test scores occurred in schools with the highest grade retention and dropout rates. For example, high schools receiving state awards for gains in 10th-grade pass rates on the Massachusetts test showed substantial increases in prior year 9th-grade retention rates and in the percentage of "missing" 10th graders (Wheelock, 2003).

In New York City, evidence suggests that many of the city's high schools may be trying to improve their test scores by pushing out weaker students who are unlikely to pass the state's high school graduation tests, first imposed in 1999. By 2000–2001, more than 55,000 high school students were "discharged" without graduating, a number far larger than the 34,000 seniors who actually graduated from high school (Advocates for Children, 2002), and the number of school-age students in General Education Diploma (GED) programs run by the city schools increased by more than 50% as the tests were phased in, from 25,500 to more than 37,000 (Arenson, 2004).

Issues of school capacity. Evidence from England points to similar trends. A study of England's high-stakes accountability system (Rustique-Forrester, 2005) found that it led to a dramatic increase in the expulsion rate of students, while negatively affecting teachers' morale and instructional decision making. Many teachers reported that the pressures from school rankings and increased testing, combined with the dynamics of school choice and a prescriptive curriculum, helped to marginalize low-performing students and increase national exclusion rates.

The extent to which high-stakes tests may lead to "gaming" actions or student exclusions rather than efforts to improve teaching may also depend on school capacity, including whether or not a school has a stable cadre of skilled teachers who can develop strategies that will better meet the needs of struggling students. In many states, schools serving the highest-need students are also those with the highest turnover, greatest numbers of untrained and inexperienced teachers, fewest monetary and curricular resources, and least knowledgeable administrators and senior staff (National Commission on Teaching and America's Future, 1996, 2003). In these contexts, designations that a school is "failing" may be less likely to result in improvements than in actions to improve average test scores by removing the most difficult or lowest-performing students. Indeed, Rustique-Forrester (2005) found that schools with lower rates of exclusion had stronger, more expert staffs with more engagement in decision making and greater investments in professional development, whereas those with high rates of exclusion had large numbers of inexperienced, untrained, and substitute teachers and few resources devoted to improving the knowledge and skills of staff to better meet students' needs.

Similarly, Diamond and Spillane (2002) found that under high-stakes accountability policies focused on school scores, high-performing schools increased academic press, worked to discover and adopt more effective instructional strategies, and created interventions for students who were lower-performing, whereas low-performing schools on probation—schools with more needy students and less school capacity—drilled students on test format and narrowed rather than expanded their instructional strategies; they also focused on their higher-performing students in hopes of getting some to raise their scores and gave up on their lower-performing students.

DeBray, Parson, and Woodworth (2001) also documented the "compliance-without capacity" responses of low-performing schools to accountability systems in Vermont and New York. Whereas higher-performing schools used the policies to create greater internal accountability around the construction of shared goals, curriculum changes, professional development, and teacher evaluation, the low-performing schools lacked the capacity to mobilize themselves for productive change. In these schools, superficial compliance (i.e., getting students into Regents classes in New York and teacher focus on the tests in

Vermont) was not always accompanied by school-wide curriculum reform, initiatives to improve instruction, or efforts to create a sense of collective accountability for student learning.

Similarly, Mintrop's (2003) study of 11 low-performing schools placed on probation in Maryland and Kentucky found that most of these schools did not know how to improve. Most of the schools had high levels of teacher turnover and little teacher expertise. In these schools, teachers did not know how better to teach the students and often blamed them for the low performance; administrators tended to respond with control strategies that rigidified teaching rather than instituting dialogue or teacher learning processes. The few schools able to improve were those that had more skilled teachers and a principal who created a collegial learning process that could tap this expertise and infuse other kinds of knowledge for teaching.

In sum, it appears that testing policies can mobilize *some* schools to improve teaching for *some* students, but also that, absent significant investments in increased school and teacher capacity, these policies can cause the most difficult-to-educate students to be even more poorly educated. This occurs when schools' responses to these students, by policy or by default, are to hold them back, a strategy that does not tend to improve achievement and increases dropout rates, or to exclude them from school altogether, a solution that makes schools look more successful on aggregated measures without actually improving their quality. This is a particularly dangerous response in a society in which education is more important than ever for access to the labor market, and in which dropping out is increasingly highly correlated with unemployment, welfare, and incarceration.

The Influences of Testing on the Quality of Teachers

In tandem with efforts to use testing to shape classroom teaching and schooling, some have also promoted testing as a vehicle for shaping the quality of the teacher workforce, through the use of student test information in teacher evaluation processes, in decisions about individual or group professional development needs, and as a tool for individual merit pay or personnel actions as well as school-level rewards and sanctions. Whether the outcomes of testing use for personnel management are positive or negative depends on what is evaluated, how testing data are used, and whether supports are available to help teachers and schools improve.

Testing and Teacher Evaluation

Research is spotty on the consequences of using test results for personnel-related decisions, such as allocating merit pay or targeting teachers for intensive assistance or possible dismissal. The history of merit pay in elementary and secondary education has been a tortuous one: Merit pay policies were introduced in the 1920s, 1950s, and 1980s, and in each era, the many state and local systems instituted had all failed within a decade, falling prey to problems with the evaluation process, employee competitiveness, and low morale that undermined organizational needs for cooperation, and funding problems (Darling-Hammond & Berry, 1988; Murnane & Cohen, 1986).

While the literature includes many descriptions of efforts to incorporate student achievement data into teacher evaluation systems, we could find no studies that have evaluated the outcomes of such attempts, either for the quality of teaching or for the retention of effective teachers. Along with articles advocating the inclusion of student achievement data in teacher evaluation, the literature includes many cautions about the problems of basing teacher evaluations on student test scores. In addition to the fact that curriculum-specific tests that would allow gain score analyses are not typically available in many teaching areas, other concerns include the possibility of overemphasis on teaching to the test at the expense of other kinds of learning; disincentives for teachers to serve students with high levels of needs, accompanied by the potential reinforcement of the current paradigm in which inexperienced teachers are disproportionately assigned to the neediest students; and problems of attributing student gains to specific teachers.

Both the student diversity problem and the attribution problem are especially knotty, since students are not randomly assigned to teachers. For a variety of reasons, some teachers are assigned to teach more students with exceptional needs (of varying severity), students with home and attendance problems, English language learners, or students with poor prior education. These differences can affect not only overall test scores but also the individual and aggregate gains that are possible on particular tests. Attributing student gains to particular teachers is also problematic. Not only can the effects of particularly good or poor teachers become visible in students' achievement gains in later years, but the efforts of teachers who emphasize higher-order thinking skills in the early elementary grades, for example, are often not evaluated on standardized tests until later years.

Furthermore, students learn skills in multiple contexts, so, for example, students' gains in writing may actually be produced by the social studies teacher who assigns regular research papers and requires revisions, or by an after-school tutoring program, while students' gains in an algebra class might be a function of a strong science teacher who uses mathematics in contexts that encourage deeper understanding. Without looking at practice, inferences about what teachers are doing cannot be made accurately from test scores (Darling-Hammond, 1997a).

While research evidence is sparse regarding the consequences of using student achievement data to evaluate teachers, some studies have found that evaluations of practice based on teaching standards are positively associated with teacher effectiveness. These are cases in which assessments of teachers are based on well-articulated standards of practice and evaluated through evidence including observations of teaching along with artifacts such as lesson plans, assignments, and samples of student work, sometimes assembled into a teaching portfolio. In a study of three districts using standards-based evaluation systems, researchers found positive correlations between teachers' ratings and their students' gain scores on standardized tests (Milanowski, Kimball, & White, 2004). In addition, several recent studies of teachers who have achieved National Board Certification have found that these teachers, whose work has been similarly evaluated through a standards-based assessment system, are more effective with students as evaluated by gains in their students' learning (Cavalluzzo, 2004; Goldhaber & Anthony, 2004; Vandevoort, Amrein-Beardsley, & Berliner, 2004). These kinds of results led Hassell (2002) to conclude in his review of teacher pay systems that tying teachers' pay to their knowledge and skills, as these systems do, is a better approach than evaluation based on student test scores.

These studies suggest that the more teachers' classroom activities and behaviors reflect professional standards of practice, the more effective they are in supporting student learning—a finding that would appear to suggest the desirability of focusing on such professional standards in the preparation, professional development, and evaluation of teachers. Whether the same kinds of benefits would accrue from emphasizing student test scores in teacher evaluation is not known, but it would seem reasonable from these studies to suggest that a move to incorporate student achievement data should not be accomplished at the expense of information drawn from direct evaluation of practice in light of professional expectations for teaching.

Testing and School Incentives

The consequences of using aggregated student test scores to evaluate schools are beginning to be researched. We earlier described state accountability systems that allocate rewards to schools with increasing scores and sanctions to those whose scores do not improve, including labeling schools as "low-performing" or "failing," placing these schools in intervention programs, and sometimes reconstituting them if they do not improve. Although these strategies are intended to stimulate improvement, they can also undermine teacher quality if they discourage qualified teachers from teaching in schools that are subject to test-based sanctions or stigma. This effect was reported as an early outcome of Florida's use of average test scores for school rewards and sanctions. Press reports noted that qualified teachers were leaving the schools rated D or F "in droves" (DeVise, 1999), to be replaced by teachers without experience and often without training. As one principal queried, "Is anybody going to want to dedicate their lives to a school that has already been labeled a failure?" (p. 1B).

A more systematic study of the effects of the North Carolina accountability system found that it negatively affected schools serving low-performing students by impairing their ability to retain teachers (Clotfelter, Ladd, Vigdor, & Diaz, 2004). The North Carolina system uses annual changes in test scores against targets for "expected growth" to allocate financial rewards, to designate the school as "no recognition" or, if students also fail to meet a specific performance standard, as "low-performing." An analysis of the workings of the system found that there is a strong positive correlation between school gains and average performance and a negative correlation between school gains and student poverty (Ladd & Walsh, 2002), which means that schools serving low-income children are most likely to be designated as "low-performing."

Using a discrete time-duration model to examine changes in school attrition patterns for different subsets of schools at the introduction of the policy, the study found that the accountability system exacerbated the movement of teachers out of schools with lower levels of achievement, with an even stronger effect for those that had been labeled as "low-performing" by the state. By stimulating greater turnover, the accountability system also increased the probability that low-performing schools would need to hire more teachers, which tended disproportionately to be novice teachers. Because the state was simultaneously undertaking efforts to improve the quality of teachers (upgrading salaries, preparation, and certification requirements), the overall quality of the teacher workforce was improving; however, because of the countervailing pressures on teachers' choices, this helped high-performing schools more than low-performing ones. Relative to the trends in teacher quality in the state as a whole during these years, the introduction of the accountability system increased the share of lower-quality teachers, novices, and those from nonselective colleges in low-performing schools. The authors note:

(S)imply increasing the pressure on the personnel in low-performing schools to do better may not be the best way to improve the performance of low-performing students. Given our finding that accountability systems make it harder for schools serving low-performing students to retain quality teachers, a more systemic approach is needed to assure that low-performing students have access to effective teachers and a stable teaching environment. (Clotfelter et al., 2004, p. 272)

Testing and Teacher Morale

The North Carolina study also found that the accountability system made teaching, on average, a less attractive job, even for teachers in higher-performing schools, a finding that has been echoed in some other studies. A survey of Texas teachers found that 85% said that some of the best teachers were leaving the profession because of test-related teaching constraints and stresses (Hoffman et al., 2001). A survey of Florida teachers found that, in addition to teachers leaving lower-ranked schools, even teachers in schools given an "A" grade were often demoralized by the pressures created by tests. One teacher in an "A" rated school noted, "The pressure of the scores leading to school grades takes a lot of the joy out of teaching"; another remarked, "The morale in our school is the lowest I have ever seen in my 25 years of teaching" (Jones & Egley, 2004, p. 20).

At the beginning of the minimum competency testing era, a study by Darling-Hammond and Wise (1985) found that, when asked if any policy would make them leave teaching, the single most common response of teachers in districts that had introduced test-based accountability systems was the further tightening of district controls over the process of teaching, which they felt impeded their ability to teach effectively. For example (Darling-Hammond, 1997b, pp. 91–92):

If they started tightening up any more as far as more testing and meeting more requirements . . . If it got any more standardized and routinized, if they told me

310   TESTING   AND   TEACHER   QUALITY

that I couldn't do some of the things that I do in the way of interacting on a human level in the classroom, I would leave in a minute.

I think that any more controls in this school system would just about tilt it for me.

A lot of the really good teachers have been frustrated (by the tests) and they're dropping out of the profession . . . The motivational level for the teachers is low.

In an analysis of teacher survey results in California, a key component of a factor that strongly predicted school-wide teacher turnover problems was "the quality and appropriateness of tests you are required to administer"—which was the most negatively rated of the working conditions teachers were asked to evaluate (Loeb, Darling-Hammond, & Luczak, in press). These studies are reminiscent of Sykes's (1983) observation some years ago that test-based accountability systems accompanied by highly prescribed curriculum can undermine teaching both directly—through effects on instruction—and indirectly—through effects on the quality of the teaching force:

Administratively mandated systems of instruction not only hinder teachers' responsiveness to students but over time discourage teachers from learning to be responsive, from developing sensitivity to individual differences, and from broadening their repertoire of approaches. Ultimately such systems become self-fulfilling prophecies: routinized instruction, and the attendant loss of autonomy, makes teaching unpalatable for bright, independent-minded college graduates and fails to stimulate the pursuit of excellence among those who do enter. Over the long run, then, the routinization of instruction tends to depro-fessionalize teaching and to further discourage capable people from entering the field. (p. 120)

Although test-based instructional systems that tightly constrain teacher decision making appear to be problematic, the use of thoughtful assessment data to inform teacher evaluation and professional development can produce more positive outcomes. As we noted earlier, Connecticut, Kentucky, and Vermont supported teacher quality by coupling performance assessment initiatives with investments in preparation, standards-based teacher assessment, and professional development. In these cases and others (see, e.g., Darling-Hammond, 2004, for descriptions of urban school districts using similar strategies), there have been efforts to use performance assessment data in collegial professional development settings to help teachers become more knowledgeable about student learning, more diagnostic in their approach to planning, and, by sharing knowledge about practice, more skillful in using a range of strategies. Teachers became more committed to teaching, and attrition rates declined, because they felt more efficacious as they became more skilled and were treated more professionally. The local assessment components of the state systems (portfolios and performance tasks) encouraged teachers to learn and use formative assessment strategies, which have been shown to offer a particularly powerful means of improving student learning, especially for previously low-performing students (Black & Wiliam, 1998).

Conclusion

Given wide variations in how states have designed their assessment and accountability systems, it is not surprising that research on accountability has produced mixed results. In general, studies suggest that in states and districts that have invested in performance-based assessments along with improved teacher quality and school capacity, student achievement has increased on multiple measures, even without the application of high-stakes rewards and sanctions. In settings where narrow measures are used with high stakes attached, schools and teachers experience strong temptations to reduce the curriculum to what is tested and the way it is tested, often undermining the quality of teaching, especially in schools where students struggle to pass the tests. Where states have not invested in equalizing school resources and improving teacher capacity, low-performing schools seem unable to substantially improve the quality of education they provide to students, and tend to respond by "gaming" the system, holding students back, or encouraging vulnerable students to drop out.

Among the factors that appear to influence the outcomes of testing are the nature of tests (what kinds of things are assessed and how); the uses of tests (what kinds of decisions are made based on test scores); the capacity for improvement represented by teacher knowledge and skills; and the context for school improvement at the state, district, and school levels, including resource levels and professional development opportunities.

Given current pressures to apply higher stakes to student test results, there is a need for more attention to understanding how these increased pressures may influence the practices of schools and teachers and what the long-term consequences may be for teaching and teacher quality. One set of questions pertains to how teachers may respond, in both positive and negative ways, to the increased pressures and demands to raise student achievement. More needs to be known about how teachers are responding to the demands of increased accountability, and the ways in which their beliefs, expectations, and perceptions of their students may be changing along with the policy climate. In addition, research needs to explore the consequences of student accountability testing for the recruitment and retention of highly qualified teachers in low-performing schools, which raises concerns for students' equitable access to quality teaching and teachers.

If accountability is to ensure better education for students, rather than merely producing test scores that can be used to rank schools and allocate blame, we should evaluate policy strategies on the basis of whether they encourage high-quality learning and teaching for all students. Based on what research has revealed thus far, it seems there are several strategies that could encourage more productive outcomes from testing systems, especially for the most vulnerable students. We would include at least the following:

1. Broader *use of performance assessments* that provide "tests worth teaching to" (Resnick, 1987)—assessments that encourage the kinds of higher-order thinking and performance skills students will need to use in the world outside of school. If the goal is stronger education, then investments in more productive assessments are not just testing costs; they are part of the core costs of instruction and professional development. And where teachers are involved in developing and scoring these assessments, their learning is part of the capacity building that is essential if tests are to improve rather than restrict student learning opportunities.

2. Systems for states, like those in Vermont, Connecticut, Kentucky, Maine, Nebraska, and Rhode Island, that *combine large-scale and classroom assessments* (using, e.g., portfolio assessments or performance tasks), so that teachers are encouraged to engage in formative assessment, strengthen their knowledge about student learning, and increase their capacity to shape instruction to students' needs. As Herman (2002) notes:

   To truly understand why student performance is as it is and to get to the root of whatever teaching and learning issues may exist, schools and teachers really need to move to a more detailed level of assessment and analysis than annual state tests afford . . . (S)uch local assessments are also necessary to provide teachers with essential, ongoing information to gauge student progress and adjust teaching and learning opportunities accordingly. (p. 22)

3. Systematic *investments in teacher knowledge and school capacity*, including, in addition to standards-based professional development and scoring opportunities associated with performance assessments, systemic investments in teachers' and principals' pre-service and in-service education to provide a strong foundation of understanding about learning and about development, curriculum, effective teaching strategies, and formative assessment. These investments need to be made in the education of all teachers, especially those who will teach the least advantaged students—students who currently encounter a large number of untrained, inexperienced, and undersupported teachers who lack the knowledge to respond productively to test information showing that these students are failing.

4. *Standards-based evaluation of teaching practice* as part of accountability systems for licensing, certification, and ongoing evaluation. Evaluation of practice based on professional standards can help develop teacher knowledge and professional accountability, as well as increasingly effective and more widely shared teaching practice, while reducing incentives to teach only to tests or to push out difficult-to-teach students (Herman, 2002, p. 24).

5. *Incentives that support organizational learning* rather than gaming. Lower stakes that are focused on the provision of information and assistance for school improvement will be more productive than emphasizing rewards and sanctions that can distort curriculum, undermine teaching quality, and encourage schools to keep out or push out the neediest students.

Ultimately, raising standards for students so that they learn what they need to know requires raising standards for the system, so that it provides the kinds of teaching and school settings students need in order to learn, guided by rich information about learning, supported by strong teaching expertise, and shaped by appropriate and reasonable incentives. Genuine accountability rests not only, or even primarily, on tests, but on the comprehensive set of supports needed to ensure school, teacher, and student learning.

AUTHORS' NOTE

The authors gratefully acknowledge the assistance of Alethea Andree, who provided valuable research assistance.

REFERENCES

Advocates for Children. (2002). *Pushing out at-risk students: An analysis of high school discharge figures—A joint report by AFC and the Public Advocate.* Retrieved April 4, 2005, from http://www.advocatesforchildren.org/pubs/pushout-11-20-02.html

Allington, R.L., & McGill-Franzen, A. (1992).Unintended effects of educational reform in New York. *Educational Policy, 6*(4), 397–414.

American Psychological Association. (2004). *Appropriate use of high-stakes testing in our nation's schools: How should student learning and achievement be measured?* Retrieved November 22, 2004, from http://www.apa.org/pubinfo/testing.html

Amrein, A., & Berliner, D. (2002). High-stakes testing, uncertainty, and student learning. *Educational Policy and Analysis Archives, 10*(8). Retrieved November 21, 2003, from http://www.epaa.asu.edu/epaa/v10n18

Anagnostopoulos, D. (2003). The new accountability, student failure, and teachers' work in urban high schools. *Educational Policy, 17*(3), 291–316.

Appalachia Educational Laboratory. (1996, February). Five years of reform in rural Kentucky. *Notes from the field: Educational reform in rural Kentucky,* Vol. 5, No. 1. Charleston, WV: Author.

Arenson, K.W. (2004, May 15). More youths opt for G.E.D., skirting high-school hurdle. *The New York Times,* p. A14.

Baron, J.B. (1999). *Exploring high and improving reading achievement in Connecticut.* Washington, DC: National Educational Goals Panel.

Black, P., & Wiliam, D. (1998). Inside the black box: Raising standards through classroom assessment. *Phi Delta Kappan, 80*(2), 139–148.

Borko, H., Elliott, R., & Uchiyama, K. (1999). *Professional development: A key to Kentucky's reform effort.* Los Angeles: University of California at Los Angeles National Center for Research on Evaluation, Standards, and Student Testing.

Borko, H., & Stetcher, B.M. (2001, April). *Looking at reform through different methodological lenses: Survey and case studies of the Washington state education reform.* Paper presented at the annual meeting of the American Educational Research Association, Seattle, WA.

Brown, D.F. (1992, April). *Altering curricula through state-mandated testing: Perceptions of teachers and principals.* Paper presented at the annual meeting of the American Educational Research Association, San Francisco, CA.

Carnoy, M., & Loeb, S. (2002). Does external accountability affect student outcomes? A cross-state analysis. *Education and Evaluation and Policy Analysis, 24*(4), 305–332.

Cavalluzzo, L. (2004).*Online education: District, state, or charter school?* Retrieved November 18, 2004, from http://www.the-atec.org/docDownload.asp?docID=48

Center on Education Policy (CEP). (2004). *State high school exit exams: A maturing reform.* Washington, DC: Center on Education Policy.

Chapman, C. (1991, June). *What have we learned from writing assessment that can be applied to performance assessment?* Presentation at ECS/CDE Alternative Assessment Conference, Breckenbridge, CO.

Clarke, M., Madaus, G., Pedulla, J., & Shore, A. (2000, January). *Statements: An agenda for research on educational testing.* Boston: National Board on Educational Testing and Public Policy.

Clotfelter, C.T., Ladd, H.F., Vigdor, J.L., & Diaz, R.A. (2004). Do school accountability systems make it more difficult for low performing schools to attract and retain high quality teachers? *Journal of Policy and Management, 23*(2), 251–272.

Corbett, H., & Wilson, B. (1991). The central office role in instructional improvement. *School Effectiveness and School Improvement, 3*(1), 45–68.

Darling-Hammond, L. (1997a). Toward what end? The evaluation of student learning for the improvement of teaching. In J. Millman (Ed.), *Grading teachers, grading schools:*

Is student achievement a valid evaluation measure? (pp. 248–263). Thousand Oaks, CA: Corwin Press.

Darling-Hammond, L. (1997b). *The right to learn: A blueprint for creating schools that work.* San Francisco: Jossey-Bass.

Darling-Hammond, L. (2004). From "separate but equal" to "No Child Left Behind": The collision of new standards and old inequalities. In D. Meier & G. Wood (Eds.), *Many children left behind.* New York: Beacon Press.

Darling-Hammond, L., & Ancess, J. (1994). *Authentic assessment and school development.* New York: National Center for Restructuring Education, Schools, and Teaching, Teachers College, Columbia University.

Darling-Hammond, L., Ancess, J., & Falk, B. (1995). *Authentic assessment in action.* New York: Teachers College Press.

Darling-Hammond, L., & Berry, B. (1988). *The evolution of teacher policy.* Santa Monica, CA: RAND Corporation.

Darling-Hammond, L., & Wise, A.E. (1985). Beyond standardization: State standards and school improvement. *The Elementary School Journal, 85*(3), 315–336.

DeBard, R., & Kubow, P.K. (2002). From compliance to commitment: The need for constituent discourse in implementing testing policy. *Education Policy, 16*(3), 387–405.

DeBray, E., Parson, G., & Woodworth, K. (2001). Patterns of response in four high schools under state accountability policies in Vermont and New York. In S. Fuhrman (Ed.), *From the capitol to the classroom: Standards-based reform in the states. The one hundredth yearbook of the National Society for the Study of Education,* Part II (pp. 170–192). Chicago: National Society for the Study of Education.

DeVise, D. (1999, November 5). A+ plan prompts teacher exodus in Broward County. *The Miami Herald,* p. 1B.

Diamond, J., & Spillane, J. (2002). *High stakes accountability in urban elementary schools: Challenging or reproducing inequality?* Institute for Policy Research Working Paper. Evanston, IL: Northwestern University Institute for Policy Research.

Education Trust. (2004). *Measured progress achievement rises and gaps narrow, but too slowly.* Retrieved November 23, 2004, from http://www2.edtrust.org/NR/rdonlyres/F1C402F7-AB53-49ED-A9DC-27A41AA6E7E5/0/MeasuredProgressSumma99F.pdf

Education Week. (2001, January 11) *Quality Counts 2001: A better balance.* Bethesda, MD: Editorial Projects in Education.

Falk, B., & Ort, S. (1997, April). *Sitting down to score: Teacher learning through assessment.* Presentation at the annual meeting of the American Educational Research Association, Chicago, IL.

Firestone, W., & Mayrowetz, D. (2000). Rethinking "high stakes": Lessons from the United States and England and Wales. *Teachers College Record, 102*(4), 724–749.

Firestone, W.A., Mayrowetz, D., & Fairman, J. (1998, Summer). Performance-based assessment and instructional change: The effects of testing in Maine and Maryland. *Educational Evaluation and Policy Analysis, 20*(2), 95–113.

Goldberg, G.L., & Rosewell, B.S. (2000). From perception to practice: The impact of teachers' scoring experience on the performance based instruction and classroom practice. *Educational Assessment, 6*(4), 257–290.

Goldhaber, D., & Anthony, E. (2004). *Can teacher quality be effectively assessed?* Retrieved November 16, 2004, from http://www.urban.org/url.cfm?ID=410958

Greene, J., & Winters, M. (2004). *Pushed out or pulled up? Exit exams and dropout rates in public high schools.* New York: Manhattan Institute for Policy Research.

Haney, W. (2000). The myth of the Texas miracle in education. *Education Policy Analysis Archives, 8*(41), Retrieved February 19, 2005, from http://epaa.asu.edu/epaa/v8n41/

Haney, W. (2002). Lake Wobegauranteed: Misuse of test scores in Massachusetts, part 1. *Education Policy Analysis Archives, 10*(24). Retrieved September 3, 2004, from http://epaa.asu.edu/epaa/v10n24/

Hassell, B.C. (2002). *Better pay for better teaching: Making teacher compensation pay off in the age of accountability.* Progressive Policy Institute 21st Century Schools Project. Retrieved November 18, 2004, from http://www.broadfoundation.org/investments/education-net.shtml

Herman, J.L. (2002). *Black-white-other test score gap: Academic achievement among mixed race adolescents.* Institute for Policy Research Working Paper. Evanston, IL: Northwestern University Institute for Policy Research.

Herman, J.L., Brown, R.S., & Baker, E.L. (2000). *Student assessment and student achievement in the California public school system.* Retrieved November 18, 2004, from http://cresst96.cse.ucla.edu/CRESST/Reports/TECH519.pdf

Herman, J.L., & Golan, S. (1993). Effects of standardized testing on teaching and schools. *Educational Measurement: Issues and Practice, 12*(4), 20–25, 41–42.

Herman, J.L., Klein, D.C.D., Heath, T.M., & Wakai, S.T. (1995). *A first look: Are claims for alternative assessment holding up?* CSE Technical Report. Los Angeles: UCLA National Center for Research on Evaluation, Standards, and Student Testing.

Heubert, J., & Hauser, R. (Eds.). (1999). *High stakes: Testing for tracking, promotion, and graduation.* A report of the National Research Council. Washington, DC: National Academies Press.

Hoffman, J.V., Assaf, L.C., & Paris, S.G. (2001). High stakes testing in reading: Today in Texas, tomorrow? *The Reading Teacher, 54*(5), 482–492.

Jacob, B.A. (2001). Getting tough? The impact of high school graduation exams. *Education and Evaluation and Policy Analysis, 23*(2), 99–122.

Jones, B.D., & Egley, R.J. (2004). Voices from the frontlines: Teachers' perceptions of high-stakes testing. *Education Policy Analysis Archives, 12*(39). Retrieved August 10, 2004, from http://epaa.asu.edu/epaa/v12n39/

Jones, M.G., Jones, B.D., Hardin, B., Chapman, L., & Yarbrough, T.M. (1999). The impact of high-stakes testing on teachers and students in North Carolina. *Phi Delta Kappan, 81*(3), 199–203.

Klein, S.P., Hamilton, L.S., McCaffrey, D.F., & Stetcher, B.M. (2000). *What do test scores in Texas tell us?* Santa Monica, CA: The RAND Corporation.

Koretz, D., & Barron, S.I. (1998). *The validity of gains on the Kentucky Instructional Results Information System (KIRIS).* Santa Monica, CA: RAND, MR-1014-EDU.

Koretz, D., Linn, R.L., Dunbar, S.B., & Shepard, L.A. (1991, April). The effects of high-stakes testing: Preliminary evidence about generalization across tests. In R.L. Linn (Chair) (Ed.),*The effects of high stakes testing.* Symposium presented at the annual meeting of the American Educational Research Association and the National Council on Measurement in Education, Chicago.

Koretz, D., Mitchell, K.J., Barron, S.I., & Keith, S. (1996). *Final report: Perceived effects of the Maryland school performance assessment program.* CSE Technical Report. Los Angeles: UCLA National Center for Research on Evaluation, Standards, and Student Testing.

Koretz, D., Stetcher, B., & Deibert, E. (1992). *The Vermont portfolio program: Interim report on implementation and impact, 1991–1992 school year.* Santa Monica, CA: The RAND Corporation.

Kornhaber, M., & Gardner, H.(1993). *Varieties of student excellence.* New York: National Center for Restructuring Education, Schools, and Teaching (NCREST), Teachers College, Columbia University.

Ladd, H.F., & Walsh, R. (2002, February). Implementing value-added measures of school effectiveness: Getting the incentives right. *Economics of Education Review, 21*(1), 1–17.

Ladd, H.F., & Zelli, A. (2002). School-based accountability in North Carolina: The responses of school principals. *Educational Administration Quarterly, 38*(4), 494–529.

Lane, S., Stone, C.A., Parke, C.S., Hansen, M.A., & Cerrillo, T.L. (2000, April). *Consequential evidence for MSPAP from the teacher, principal and student perspective.* Paper presented at the annual meeting of the National Council on Measurement in Education, New Orleans, LA.

Lee, V.F., Smith, J.B., & Croninger, R.G. (1995, Fall). *Another look at high school restructuring. Issues in Restructuring Schools.* Madison: University of Wisconsin-Madison, Center on Organization and Restructuring of Schools.

Lilliard, D., & DeCicca, P. (2001). Higher standards, more dropouts? Evidence within and across time. *Economics of Education Review, 20*(5), 459–473.

Linn, R.L. (2000). Assessments and accountability. *Educational Researcher, 29*(2), 4–16.

Linn, R.L., Graue, M.E., & Sanders, N.M. (1990). Comparing state and district test results to national norms: The validity of claims that "everyone is above average." *Educational Measurement: Issues and Practice, 9*(3), 5–14.

Loeb, S., Darling-Hammond, L., & Luczak, J. (in press). *Teacher turnover: The role of working conditions and salaries in recruiting and retaining teachers.* Stanford: Stanford University School of Education.

Madaus, G., West, M.M., Harmond, M.C., Lomax, R.G., & Vator, K.A. (1992). *The influence of testing on teaching math and science in grades 4–12.* Chestnut Hill, MA: Center of Study of Testing, Evaluation, and Educational Policy, Boston College.

McNight, C., Crosswhite, F.J., Dossey, J.A., Kifer, E., Swafford, J.O., Travers, K.J., & Conney, T.J. (1987). *Underachieving curriculum: Assessing U.S. school mathematics from an international perspective.* Champaign, IL: Stipes Publishing.

Milanowski, A.T., Kimball, S.M., & White, B. (2004). *The relationship between standards-based teacher evaluation scores and student achievement: Replication and extensions at three sites.* University of Wisconsin: Consortium for Policy Research in Education.

Mintrop, H. (2003, January 15). The limits of sanctions in low-performing schools: A study of Maryland and Kentucky schools on probation. *Education Policy Analysis Archives, 11*(3). Retrieved November 15, 2004, from http://epaa.asu.edu/epaa/v11n3.html

Mitchell, R. (1992). *Testing for learning.* New York: Free Press.

Moll, L.C., Amanti, C., Neff, D., & Gonzalez, N. (1992). Funds of knowledge for teaching: Using a qualitative approach to connect homes and classrooms. *Theory into Practice, 31*(1), 132–141.

Murnane, R., & Cohen, D. (1986). Merit pay and the evaluation problem: Why do most merit pay plans fail and a few survive? *Harvard Educational Review, 56*(1), 1–17.

Murnane, R., & Levy, F. (1996). *Teaching the new basic skills.* New York: The Free Press.

National Center for Education Statistics (NCES). (1982). *The condition of education—1982.* Washington, DC: U.S. Department of Education.

National Commission on Teaching and America's Future (NCTAF). (1996). *What matters most: Teaching for America's future.* New York: Author.

National Commission on Teaching and America's Future (NCTAF). (2003). *No dream denied: A pledge to America's children.* Washington, DC: Author.

National Research Council. (2000). *How people learn.* New York: Houghton Mifflin Company.

Neill, M. (2003). Leaving children behind: How No Child Left Behind will fail our children. *Phi Delta Kappan, 85*(3), 225–228.

Neill, M., & Gayler, K. (2001). Do high-stakes graduation tests improve learning outcomes? Using state-level NAEP data to evaluate the effects of mandatory graduation tests. In G. Orfield & M. Kornhaber (Eds.), *Raising standards or raising barriers?: Inequality and high stakes testing in public education* (pp. 107–125). New York: Century Foundation Press.

Newmann, F.M., Marks, H.M., & Gomoran, A. (1995). *Authentic pedagogy: Standards that boost student performance.* Issue Report No. 8. Madison, WI: Center on Organization and Restructuring of Schools.

318   TESTING AND TEACHER QUALITY

No Child Left Behind Act of 2001, Pub. L. No. 107-110, 115 Stat. 1425 (2002).

O'Day, J.A. (2002). Complexity, accountability, and school improvement. *Harvard Educational Review*, 72(3), 293–329.

Orfield, G., & Ashkinaze C. (1991). *The closing door: Conservative policy and black opportunity*. Chicago: University of Chicago Press.

Orfield, G., Losen, D., Wald, J., & Swanson, C.B. (2004). *Losing our future: How minority youth are being left behind by the graduation rate crisis*. Retrieved April 4, 2005, from http://www.urban.org/url.cfm?ID=410936

Pedulla, J.J., Abrams, L.M., Madaus, G.F., Russell, M.K., Ramos, M.A., & Miao, J. (2003). *Perceived effects of state-mandated testing programs on teaching and learning: Findings from a national survey of teachers*. Boston: National Board on Testing and Public Policy, Boston College.

Plitt, B. (2002). Teacher dilemmas in a time of standards and testing. *Phi Delta Kappan*, 85(10), 745–748.

Popham, W.J. (1999). Why standardized test scores don't measure educational quality. *Educational Leadership*, 56(6), 8–15.

Public Education Network. (2002). *Using NCLB to improve student achievement: An action guide to community and parent leaders*. Retrieved November 21, 2004, from http://www.publiceducation.org/pdf/NCLBBook.pdf

Resnick, L. (1987). *Education and learning to think*. Washington, DC: National Academies Press.

Roderick, M., Bryk, A.S., Jacob, B.A., Easton, J.Q., & Allensworth, E. (1999). *Ending social promotion: Results from the first two years*. Chicago: Consortium on Chicago School Research.

Roderick, M., & Engel, M. (2001). The grasshopper and the ant: Motivational responses of low-achieving students to high-stakes testing. *Educational Evaluation and Policy Analysis*, 23(3), 197–227.

Rumberger, R., & Larson, K. (1998). Student mobility and the increased risk of high school dropout. *American Journal of Education*, 107(1), 1–35.

Russell, M., & Abrams, L. (2004). Instructional uses of computers for writing: The impact of state testing programs. *Teachers College Record*, 106(6), 1332–1357.

Rustique-Forrester, E. (2005). Accountability and the pressures to exclude: A cautionary tale from England. *Education Policy Analysis Archives*, 13(26). Retrieved April 18, 2005, from http://epaa.asu.edu/epaa/v13n26/

Schiller, K., & Muller, C. (2000). External examinations and accountability, educational expectations, and high school graduation. *American Journal of Education*, 108(2), 73–102.

Shepard, L.A. (2000). The role of assessment in a learning culture. *Educational Researcher*, 29(7), 4–14.

Smith, M.L. (1991). Put to the test: The effects of external testing on teachers. *Educational Researcher*, 20(5), 8–11.

Smith, F. (1986). *High school admission and the improvement of schooling*. New York: New York City Board of Education.

Southeast Center for Teaching Quality. (2004). High-stakes accountability in California: A view from the teacher's desk. *Teaching Quality RESEARCH MATTERS*, 12, 1–2. Retrieved September 2, 2004, from http://www.teachingquality.org/ResearchMatters/issues/2004/issue12-Aug2004.pdf

Stecher, B., & Barron, S. (1999). *Quadrennial milepost accountability testing in Kentucky*. CSE Technical Report. Los Angeles: UCLA National Center for Research on Evaluation, Standards, and Student Testing.

Stecher, B., Barron, S., Chun, T., & Ross, K. (2000). *The effects of the Washington state education reform on schools and classroom*. CSE Technical Report. Los Angeles: UCLA National Center for Research on Evaluation, Standards, and Student Testing.

Stecher, B.M., Barron, S., Kaganoff, T., & Goodwin, J. (1998). *The effects of standards-based assessment on classroom practices: Results of the 1996–1997 RAND survey of Kentucky teachers of mathematics and writing.* CSE Technical Report. Los Angeles: UCLA National Center for Research on Evaluation, Standards, and Student Testing.

Sykes, G. (1983). Public policy and the problem of teacher quality. In L.S. Shulman & G. Sykes (Eds.), *Handbook of teaching and policy* (pp. 97–125). New York: Longman.

Vandevoort, L.G., Amrein-Beardsley, A., & Berliner, D. (2004). National board certified teachers and their students' achievement. *Education Policy Analysis Archives, 12*(46), Retrieved October 10, 2004, from http://epaa.asu.edu/epaa/v12n46/

Watson, B.C. (1996). *Testing: Its origins, use, and misuse.* New York: National Urban League.

Wheelock, A. (2003). *School awards programs and accountability in Massachusetts: Misusing MCAS scores to assess school quality.* Retrieved March 3, 2005, from http://www.fairtest.org/arn/Alert%20June02/Alert%20Full%20Report.html

Whitford, B.L., & Jones, K. (2000). Kentucky lesson: How high stakes accountability undermines a performance-based curriculum vision. In B.L. Whitford & K. Jones (Eds.) *Accountability, assessment, and teacher commitment: Lessons from Kentucky's reform efforts* (pp. 9–24). Albany: State University of New York Press.

Wilson, S., Darling-Hammond, L., & Berry, B. (2001). *A case of successful teaching policy: Connecticut's long-term efforts to improve teaching and learning.* Seattle: Center for the Study of Teaching and Policy, University of Washington.

Wolf, S., Borko, H., McIver, M., & Elliott, R. (1999). "*No excuses*": School reform efforts in exemplary schools of Kentucky.* Los Angeles: University of California at Los Angeles National Center for Research on Evaluation, Standards, and Student Testing.

Woody, E.L., Buttles, M., Kafka, J., Park, S., & Russell, J. (2004, February). *Voices from the field: Educators respond to accountability.* Berkeley. Policy Analysis for California Education. Retrieved November 19, 2004, from http://pace.berkeley.edu/ERAP_Report-WEB.pdf

Part Four
MOVING TO BETTER PRACTICE

CHAPTER 13

Data Use and School Improvement: Challenges and Prospects

MARGARET HERITAGE AND RAYMOND YEAGLEY

In 1922 Edward Thorndike wrote, "The task of education is to make changes in human beings. For mastery in this task, we need definite and exact knowledge of what changes are made and what ought to be made" (p. 2). Seventy-nine years after he wrote these words, the 2001 No Child Left Behind (NCLB) legislation stated, "Schools must have clear, measurable goals focused on basic skills and essential knowledge. Annual testing in every grade gives teachers, parents and policy makers the information they need to ensure that every child will reach academic success" (p. 7). While the language of the two may be different, the message is the same: schools need accurate and actionable information about what students know and can do so that they can plan effectively for student learning.

Margaret Heritage is the Assistant Director for Professional Development at the UCLA National Center for Research Evaluation, Standards, and Student Testing (CRESST). Raymond Yeagley is the superintendent of the Rochester School Department in Rochester, New York.

The work reported herein was supported under the Educational Research and Development Centers Program, PR/Award Number R305B960002, as administered by the Institute of Education Sciences (IES), and the U.S. Department of Education. The findings and opinions expressed in this report are those of the authors and do not necessarily reflect the positions or policies of the National Center for Education Research, the Institute of Education Sciences (IES), or the U.S. Department of Education.

However, there is a real difference in the context in which each of these two statements was made. In 1922, the measurement movement in education was in its infancy. Thorndike noted, "The first steps to establish units of education products and to devise instruments to measure them with reasonable precision were taken about a dozen years ago" (Thorndike, 1922, p. 3). The years since have brought both a significant expansion in educational measurement and an associated demand for accountability. To ensure that all students meet the standards that have been set for them, federal, state, and district accountability mandates require schools to measure student performance against established standards, with sanctions for schools that do not make adequate progress to close the gap between low- and high-performing students. These sanctions mean that high stakes are now attached to educational measures, and it has become imperative for educational practitioners to understand measures of achievement and to take action to improve student learning based on what the achievement data tell them.

However, despite the contemporary prominence of achievement data as vehicles to school improvement and research evidence showing that data use is a characteristic of effective schools and districts (Cawelti & Protheroe, 2001; Doolittle, Herlily, & Snipes, 2002; Teddlie & Reynolds, 2000; Tognieri & Anderson, 2003), there remain substantial challenges to the meaningful integration of data use into the everyday practices of schools. This chapter will examine characteristics of effective data use, outline challenges in the implementation of school-based data analysis, and offer perspectives as to how best practice in data use can become a widespread reality in schools.

District and School Inquiry

The starting point for any form of data analysis by education practitioners is to decide what questions they want the data to answer. Herman and Gribbons (2001, p. 5) identified three basic questions that are foundational to district and school inquiry:

- How are we doing?
- Are we well serving all students?
- What are our relative strengths and weaknesses?

And these questions can lead in a more action-oriented direction:

- Why are things the way they are?
- How can we make them better?

These questions are not, of course, confined to schools and districts: classroom teachers will need to answer the very same questions about their students to make plans for student learning. Finding answers to these questions will depend on the degree to which practitioners, at each level of the system, from classroom to district, have a set of useful data to query.

Essential Characteristics of Data to Guide School Improvement

There are essential features that achievement data must have if practitioners are to use these data to make decisions about school improvement. In brief, achievement data must be: (1) aligned; (2) valid and reliable; and (3) sensitive to differences.

Alignment

Alignment is the match between the expectations for students and the assessments used to measure whether or not students are meeting the expectations (Herman, Webb, & Zuniga, 2003; Webb, 1997). As accountability demands increase, the alignment between assessments and state standards for learning remains essential (Webb, 1997). Without strongly aligned assessments and standards, educators will be "chasing the wrong goal and policy makers will not have a good gauge of whether schools are producing the desired results" (American Educational Research Association [AERA], 2003, p. 1). The closer the alignment between standards and assessments, the greater the likelihood that teachers will focus on the desired content and that students will have a fair chance to demonstrate what they know (AERA, 2003). Recent studies have demonstrated that there is a significant need to improve the alignment between standards and assessment (Porter, 2002; Rothman, Slattery, Vranek, & Resnick, 2002; Webb, 1999).

Assessment Quality

Accurate conclusions from assessment results that can be used as the basis for sound decision making about student achievement depend on assessment quality. There are two key concepts to determining assessment quality: validity and reliability. Validity is the extent to which a test measures the underlying quality it is intended to measure. It is evaluated by considering the degree to which accumulated evidence and theory support specific interpretations of test scores entailed by the proposed use of the test. Reliability is the degree to which test scores for a group of test takers are consistent over repeated applications of a measurement procedure. Simply put, the validity of an assessment is dependent on the purpose for which it is being used, while reliability refers to the consistency of scores over time and across raters. For example, an assessment that focuses on multiplication may give highly consistent results but remains an invalid measure of students' math problem-solving skills (Herman, Aschbacher, & Winters, 1992).

Sensitivity to Differences

If administrators and teachers are going to make sound decisions about improving learning, they need accurate information about the performance of *all* their students. However, there are challenges associated with deriving accurate information from outcome data for certain populations. Historically, English language learners (ELLs) perform lower than other students (Abedi & Dietel, 2004). Research shows that the language demands of tests negatively influence the accurate measurement of ELL students (see Abedi, chapter 8, this volume). Rather than an accurate measure of content knowledge, tests become measures of both achievement and language ability (Bailey & Butler, 2004). One way to address the issue of accurate measurement of ELL student achievement is to reduce unnecessary linguistic complexity, simplifying the language of the test without diminishing the rigor of the test (Abedi & Lord, 2001). Providing extra time or dictionaries for ELL students are further test accommodations that can be made for more accurate assessment results. Another way to improve the accuracy of assessments for ELL students on content tests is to ensure that their English proficiency is of a type and level to handle the complexity of language used on the content tests by developing academic English assessments (Bailey & Butler, 2004). Similar issues arise for students with disabilities (see Pullin, chapter 9, this volume).

Types of Data for School Improvement

What kinds of achievement data are potentially available to districts, schools, and teachers to guide school improvement? We will address four main types of data, presenting at very different levels of granularity and detail in the system.

Large-Scale Achievement Tests

Current accountability systems rely on large-scale achievement tests as a lever in standards-based reform. Test results are expected to inform educators about student performance with regard to state standards and on how to improve student academic achievement. Large-scale assessments can provide general information on student achievement and comparative data for stakeholders to make judgments about the quality and effectiveness of programs, schools, and districts. Whatever the value of these tests in providing a framework for macro-level decision making, their value in providing the kind of real-time guidance necessary for curriculum or pedagogic adjustment that is the fulcrum of school improvement is quite limited (Baker, 2001; Herman & Gribbons, 2001; Shepard, 2004). In particular, the infrequency with which these tests are administered and the large period of instruction they cover significantly limit their effectiveness. Practitioners need timely, accurate, detailed, and comprehensive information to provide guidance for ongoing teaching and learning and to steer school improvement efforts. The time lag between the administration of the tests and the publication of their results vitiates their value to teachers and school administrators as far as the cohort of tested students is concerned. Moreover, as is widely recognized, the range of curriculum and instructional practices embraced by this form of testing is large. Hence, these tests unavoidably yield results reflecting aspects of learning at a coarse-grained level, and do not give information about the detailed nature of student learning needed by school administrators and teachers to provide a positive direction for improvement. For this reason, educational policy researchers increasingly advocate multiple probes as an adjunct to annual assessment (see, e.g., Baker, Linn, Herman, & Koretz, 2002). Indeed, the NCLB legislation itself makes provision for the use of multiple forms of assessment, including assessments that are diagnostically useful.

Moreover, it is well recognized that, in the realm of educational measurement, "One assessment does not fit all" (National Research Council [NRC], 2001, p. 220), and that the validity of inferences drawn from a measure depends on the purpose for which that measure is intended (AERA, 2000; AERA, APA, & NCME, 1999). To draw valid inferences about overall school and individual performance, and to provide a sufficiently detailed picture of student achievement to make decisions about school improvement, it is essential for educational practitioners to use evidence from a range of measures. Finally, while assessment data give information about the *level* of student performance, data from other sources can be used to examine the factors that *contribute* to student performance. Understanding the context of student achievement can be just as central to school improvement as knowing the parameters of test performance (Baker et al., 2002).

Benchmark Assessments

In an effort to give principals and teachers more timely and detailed assessment information, many districts are now providing administrators and teachers with benchmark assessment data. Benchmark assessments provide multiple occasions of measurement throughout the year and the results are intended to guide instruction and to identify areas of improvement. For example, in Rochester School District NH, teachers administer benchmark assessments that are aligned to the state standards up to four times each year. The superintendent (one of the authors of this chapter) reports that some teachers in the district are beginning to take advantage of the multiple administration option for instructional guidance, as well as to identify students about whom they need more diagnostic information. At the district level these data are being used as a predictive measure for the state test. Recent studies have highlighted the potential benefits of benchmark assessments when they are used by teachers and principals who have received training in interpreting these data (Snipes, Doolittle, & Herlihy, 2002).

Benchmark assessment has the potential to provide achievement data at a level that is intermediate between large-scale and classroom-based assessment. Most benchmark assessment is intended to be aligned with state standards and can, in principle, provide practitioners with feedback about student performance and prospective achievement, together with some guidance to adjust curriculum and instruction. For these reasons, it is likely that benchmark assessment will be a context in which data use will expand in the next several years. This expansion, however, will require a significant investment in training practitioners to interpret results and to use those results to effect improvement.

Formative Assessment

Black and Wiliam (1998, 2004) stress the importance of formative assessment above other kinds of assessments as sources of information for teaching and learning. An assessment is formative "when the evidence is used to adapt the teaching work to meet the learning needs" (Black, Harrison, Lee, Marshall, & Wiliam, 2003, p. 2). In their landmark meta-analysis of formative assessment, Black and Wiliam (1998) established a very strong body of evidence that improving formative assessment can raise the standards of student performance. Moreover, scholars are increasingly advocating the inclusion of classroom-based formative assessments in accountability systems (Wilson, 2004). However, the use of classroom-based formative assessment as a tool for school improvement is not widespread.

A central problem in the use of classroom-based assessments for accountability and for instructional decision making is that most available classroom assessments will likely not have met the same standards of validity and reliability as external assessments used for accountability purposes (Salinger, 2001; Shepard, 2000). One of the reasons for this is that a considerable imbalance exists between the amount of funding given to the development of classroom-based measures and the resources channeled into large-scale assessment (NRC, 2001; Stiggins, 2002). This imbalance is indicative of the traditional emphasis on large-scale assessment in the educational system. A redress in this imbalance could result in more classroom-based assessments, linked to the instructional goals of teachers, which could be integrated with information from the annual tests to provide a fuller and more detailed picture of student achievement. Indeed, Stiggins (2002) proposes that every dollar invested in large-scale assessments should be matched with another dollar devoted to the development of classroom assessments.

Grading

Grades are without question the most common measure of student achievement in schools. However, Cross and Frary (1999) note that classroom grading has been a source of controversy since the beginning of the 19th century. The basis of all the controversy lies primarily in three areas: teachers use nonachievement factors like behavior and attendance when they factor grades; they weight assessments differently; and they use a single score to represent student performance on a range of skills and abilities. The result of these grading practices is a system that is unreliable and potentially invalid as a measure of achievement (Marzano, 2000). Teacher grades as they are presently conceived do not provide particularly useful data on which to make decisions about school improvement.

However, teachers are the ones who have the most direct knowledge of students and they make judgments about students' learning every day. If current grading practices are an unreliable means of including teachers' judgments in school improvement efforts, how could the system be improved to make use of teacher knowledge? One approach is to situate teacher knowledge in a community of judgment—an interpretive system that connects teacher judgments to student work through a process of moderation (Wilson, 2004). A system of moderation involves two components: *assessment moderation* and *verification*. Assessment moderation concentrates on judging student work. Teachers meet regularly to rate student responses using scoring guidelines and apply consistent and fair grading practices in the assessments. Verification of teachers' ratings is the second part of the moderation system; rated student work is either sampled and rerated by external experts, or a technique of statistical moderation is used (for a full discussion of this technique, see Wilson, 2004). Such a system of moderation would enable teacher knowledge of their students to play a significant role in school improvement efforts and would serve, additionally, as an instrument of professional development.

Going beyond Assessment Data

While assessment data give information about the *level* of student performance, data from other sources can be used to examine the factors that *contribute* to student performance.

In addition to achievement data, Bernhardt (1998) has identified three domains of data that can provide contextual information: (1) demographic data (e.g., grade level, ethnicity, language spoken at home); (2) perception data, which can reveal student, teacher, and parent attitudes about learning, teaching, and school programs—usually obtained through surveys of stakeholders; and (3) school processes, which include information about curriculum, teaching strategies, student discipline, parent communication, teacher qualifications, professional development, and any other aspect of school operation that can have an impact on student learning.

All these data can be integrated to deepen practitioners' knowledge base and provide a broader understanding of what is, and what is not, working in their schools. For example, a Los Angeles high school was concerned about the math performance of Latino students, which was considerably lower than all other student groups, including other minorities. Further inquiry determined that a subgroup of Latino students and a subgroup of African-American students, in particular, were struggling. Both groups, as it turned out, were being bussed from the same distant neighborhood as part of the district's mandated desegregation plan. Parents indicated that their children were too tired after a full day, including two long bus rides, to spend sufficient time on homework. After-school programs, successful for other students, were unavailable because of the immediate bus departure. The decision was made to place a tutor on the bus to help students complete their homework during the bus ride home. While this single intervention did not resolve all of the academic challenges for these students, there was a meaningful improvement in performance from both groups, and the program was considered a success. The program was a result of combining assessment data and academic marks with demographic data that went beyond simply racial classification. This was further supplemented with perception data from a parent survey, and resulted in a change in school processes that was subsequently found to be effective (D. Mitchell, personal communication, August 15, 2004).

To reap the benefits of using data in this way requires practitioners to "think outside the box." NCLB requirements have led to a greater focus on data but in the authors' experience, many practitioners are currently stuck on analyzing student characteristics in relation to achievement data. They may know whether certain ethnic groups are performing better than others on achievement tests, but they do not know *what* to measure to search for the reasons for the differential performance levels. They may want to move beyond this level of analysis but do not understand the possibilities for creating data elements and indicators. It is our belief that the more practitioners are exposed to examples of *combined* data use that encourage unique solutions to problems, the more they will be able to collect and use other types of data in conjunction with achievement data for school improvement.

Integrating Data Use into School Practices

Integrated Assessment System

Earlier we highlighted the imbalance that currently exists between the amount of funding allocated to large-scale versus intermediate and classroom-based assessments. However, increasing funding for classroom assessments to strike a better balance will not necessarily result in a system that satisfies the needs of both policymakers and practitioners. In *Knowing What Students Know* (NRC, 2001), a committee of the National Research Council laid out an ambitious vision for a coordinated system for assessment. The committee outlined three characteristics of such a system:

- *Comprehensiveness.* A system that includes a range of measurement approaches to provide the evidence for educational decision making
- *Coherence.* A system that combines large-scale and classroom-based assessments built on the same underlying model of learning with consistent constructs for both levels of assessments
- *Continuity.* A system that includes measures of students' progress over time to provide a continuous stream of evidence about performance

The committee advocated that these properties would be aligned along three dimensions: vertically across levels of the education system; horizontally across assessment, curriculum, and instruction; and temporally, across the course of a student's education. These proposals highlight the undesirability of a disorganized and unplanned aggregation of ad hoc assessments. In the current context of high-stakes achievement tests, teachers tend to allocate more time to teaching what is on the test at the expense of the broader content of the subject (Stecher & Barron, 2002). The result is a narrowing of the curriculum and an increased focus on the less demanding aspects of the standards (Rothman et al., 2002; Stecher & Hamilton, 2002). The benefits of a coordinated system of assessment are clear: policymakers and the public will have access to the information they need for monitoring and accountability, while practitioners all the way down to the classroom level will be able to take full advantage of assessment information, which embraces the breadth and depth of curricula content, for educational decision making.

Interpreting Assessment Information

Traditionally, neither administrators nor teachers have received formal training in how to assess students or how to make use of assessment information. As Stiggins (2002, p. 5) notes, U.S. educators remain "a national faculty unschooled in the principles of sound assessment." A primary consideration for pre-service and in-service training is that practitioners need to have the skills to gather relevant information and to interpret it to maximize achievement.

Without knowledge of assessment principles, many practitioners will likely not be able to judge the degree to which standards and assessment are aligned, nor to evaluate the validity and reliability of assessments. For example, even if teachers are using a math assessment that is closely aligned to standards and covers the content taught, they may not realize that it is an invalid measure of math achievement for *all* students if it includes vocabulary and a text level that is beyond some.

In an effort to increase assessment literacy across the country, Stiggins (2002) advocates a number of actions. These include establishing a comprehensive program at the national, state, and local levels to foster literacy in classroom assessments, together with a similar program in effective large-scale and classroom assessment use for state, district, and building administrators. Also, he advocates changes in the licensing requirements of all educators to include an expectation of competence in assessment. These are important steps that need to be taken, because without them, even if the integrated assessment system described earlier existed, practitioners will not have the competence to interpret strengths and weaknesses in student performance or to design appropriate interventions.

Data Tools

School data often exist in disparate forms and locations, making it difficult to organize efficiently and to retrieve quickly (Thorn, 2001). This situation prevents educators from easily storing and retrieving data to use for school improvement. Data tools provide a solution to this problem and can permit easy access to a wide range of data.

Most schools use an electronic student information system (SIS) that assists in creation of the master schedule and organizes individual student attendance, discipline, and academic records. However, for effective data use in school improvement, schools and districts need a data warehouse and data analysis tools beyond their SIS. A June 2004 survey revealed that only 20% of New Hampshire school districts were using any recognized data warehouse and analysis tool. An interesting finding from the survey was that several districts believed that they *were* using such a tool, citing only their SIS and/or spreadsheet as the tools used for this crucial function. Current SIS products will not track student achievement from year to year for analysis purposes and do not have any strong analysis capabilities.

Increasingly, there are data tools that allow administrators and teachers significantly enhanced access to data. Although the features of data storage and analysis tools vary considerably, currently available tools permit educators to store, access, and analyze data effectively (Wayman, Stringfield, & Yakimowski, 2004). These tools can be categorized not so much by their data management and analysis capacity as by the way educators access them and the level of outside support available to the school or district.

At the highest level of support are tools in which the vendor acts as the technical arm of the school or district by providing assistance in: (1) identifying data elements and indicators; (2) cleaning, importing, and storing data; (3) developing pertinent questions for analysis; (4) conducting the analysis and generating reports; and (5) assisting the school, if desired, in interpreting the results.

In a more common model, the vendor will serve as an application service provider, working with the school initially to identify data elements and to custom design the data map and preformatted reports.

These vendors may assist in data cleaning and import, and usually will provide further customization as the school's data needs and sophistication increase. But generally, these vendors will not be deeply involved in ongoing training of school personnel as regards question design and interpretation of reports.

A third model provides a tool housed on a local server, with technical training in using and operating the software, training for users in research design and data use, and ongoing technical support for the database. School and district personnel are responsible for their inquiry and analysis to inform educational decisions.

A fourth model, which is now emerging, is an add-on to the student information system that permits some analysis and maintenance of data elements not historically stored in the SIS.

Most of these tools now have reporting capabilities specific to NCLB, and all permit a variety of analyses that can meet some of the demands of accountability while informing instructional planning and school improvement. (For more details on these models, see Wayman et al., 2004.)

Whatever the model adopted and whatever the level of support available, several tasks remain before practitioners can begin data inquiry. School data can exist in many different places, from a main district data store to excel spreadsheets to loose papers in files. One task is to take an inventory to identify data sources and locations and from this inventory determine which data will be useful for analysis and will be imported into the data tool (Wayman et al., 2004). Another task is to make sure that the data are "clean." Inaccurate and incomplete data will present problems for data analysis, and so educators will need to assess the quality of the existing data and take the necessary steps to ensure clean data. Finally, it will be important to identify the resources for any data cleaning and for importing data into the system. Initially, this can represent a considerable time commitment and not all schools and districts will be able to afford to have vendors or dedicated personnel for this task. A study undertaken at the National Center for Research on Evaluation, Standards, and Student Testing (CRESST) at the University of California at Los Angeles (UCLA) on the implementation of a data analysis tool, the Quality School Portfolio (QSP), revealed a possible solution to the personnel problem. Several district consortia pooled resources and were able to dedicate personnel to data cleaning and importing, making data analysis possible for all their schools (Chen, Heritage, La Torre, & Lee, 2005).

Data Analysis Practices

The availability of data analysis tools represents a step forward in using data for school improvement. However, educators frequently lack the skills for making effective use of data (Baker, 2003; Choppin, 2002; Cizek, 2000; Cromey, 2000). In the CRESST study of QSP implementation, a majority of administrators, most with advanced degrees, reported that they were not experienced in data analysis (Chen, Heritage, Danish, Choi, & Lee, 2003). Engaging in a systematic process that involves the skills of defining questions, making meaning from the data, taking action, and evaluating the action can provide the framework necessary for effective data use.

Defining Questions

A frequently asked question in schools might be, "Is the new standards-based math program more effective than our previous math program?" This question certainly identifies something of value for a school or district to know, but it provides little focus for data collection and inquiry. Asking such an overly broad question is a common error made by untrained K-12 practitioners. Unfocused and incomplete questions of this kind will leave practitioners scratching their heads about how to identify and analyze the necessary data, and about where the questions will ultimately lead. CRESST has developed a structure for questions that helps to focus analytical efforts and drive more productive inquiry. The structure involves six components useful in focusing questions for local data-based inquiry: (1) What is the purpose of the investigation? (2) What will be measured? (3) How will it be measured? (4) When will it be measured? (5) Who will be assessed? (6) How will the results be interpreted? (Heritage, 2003).

Consequently, a more effective question to examine and compare the results from the standards-based and the traditional math programs, structured with the CRESST model, might be: What is the magnitude and direction of the difference in Rasch Unit score growth from fall to spring 2004–2005 on the Northwest Evaluation Association math assessment for fourth-grade students in classes piloting a standards-based math program and students in fourth-grade classes using the district's previously adopted math program?

Deepening the Inquiry

The use of descriptive data has become a national mandate through NCLB, which requires description of academic performance accountability test data by race/ethnicity, gender, English proficiency, migrant status, economic disadvantage, and disability. While these categories are useful for highlighting if some subgroups are achieving less well than others, to be truly effective, disaggregation needs to go deeper than a single characteristic like race or gender. Deeper levels of disaggregation are essential for determining the effectiveness of school practices and the equity of services for different populations within a school and district, and educators should look at subgroups within the major categories. For example, academic achievement over time may be better for ELLs who have received English language instruction in one program than for those in another. Further, the program may be more effective for students whose native language is Spanish than for those whose native language is Chinese. Disaggregation of subgroups within the major categories could be used to examine whether the introduction of a new math curriculum is effective in closing the achievement gap and increasing the participation of underrepresented groups in algebra and higher-level math courses.

Descriptive data alone will have limitations as tools of school improvement. If practitioners only examine test scores and student characteristics, they are unlikely to discover the reasons for differences among groups. Deeper understandings mean developing analytical skills that go beyond simple bivariate relationships. Techniques that involve multivariate analysis can be used to examine the relative effectiveness of programs, instructional techniques, staff and resource allocation, and other factors that may have an impact on student learning.

While data are valuable for informing decisions in schools, relying on data alone, without the wisdom of experience and the caution of thoughtfulness, can lead to disaster. In a recent meeting attended by one of the authors, a state official cited research correlating mothers' educational attainment with their children's relative success in school, and pointing to poorly educated mothers as a major cause of poorly performing schools, suggested that getting more future mothers into college would solve most of the problems! Misinterpreting data or relying on a single, often unreliable, data point to make crucial decisions may be even more detrimental to a school and its students than having no data at all.

Every data-based conclusion that will have a major impact on educational decisions needs to be viewed through the microscope of common sense and reasonableness. Data can inform human judgment but should not replace it (Jamentz, 2001; Secada, 2001). Is the sample of students large enough to support a solid evidence-based conclusion?

Does a strong correlation between two variables really suggest causation, or are both being driven by a third factor not measured? Will an apparently obvious solution have unforeseen public support ramifications that may ultimately be detrimental to the school? Should local data that vary substantially from known national results be trusted or retested? To make intelligent use of data, it is important to know how to differentiate between useful and useless data, gold and garbage.

Taking Action and Evaluating Results

Once an analysis of the data is completed, the next step is to decide what action to take for school improvement. This requires practitioners to identify priorities, establish goals, set targets to achieve the goal, and determine strategies to reach the targets. As important as data analysis skills are, any possibilities for school improvement will be thwarted if practitioners do not have the necessary skills to translate analysis into action. Furthermore, practitioners will need to recognize that data use for school improvement is a continuous process. Any change in curriculum, instruction, and organization, and any program interventions designed to improve student achievement, require monitoring and evaluation. This involves determining what data will be collected for evaluation purposes, the frequency with which these data will be gathered, and the kind of analysis that will be undertaken to determine the effectiveness of the interventions.

Data Culture

Although data analysis tools and skills are essential elements of increased data capacity in schools, they will remain largely ineffective if teachers and administrators are unwilling or unable to use them. For practitioners to develop a commitment to data use, district and school cultures that trust data and support high-quality data use must be nurtured.

The culture of a school consists of the expectations, beliefs, and behaviors that constitute the norm for the school and the district (DuFour & Eaker, 1998). A culture that supports data use incorporates an expectation that judicious use of evidence should drive the day-to-day practices of administrators and teachers, as well as the collective decision making in the school (Jamentz, 2001). Stakeholders believe that data should inform human judgment and that planned and targeted data use can provide the necessary indicators to improving student learning. A data culture is one in which teachers and administrators work together in a community of practice—trusting data, focusing on results, and engaging in using data for systematic reflection and planning. Simply put, in a culture that supports data use educators will say, "Using data is the way we do things around here."

In this era of high-stakes accountability educators can harbor suspicions of data, lacking trust in its validity and suspecting that data will be used against them. Rather than viewing data as a vehicle for school improvement, they can see data as penalizing and punitive (Cromey, 2000). Counteracting this view and instilling trust in data involve building a school culture that is supportive of data use and that makes data use transparent, open, and inclusive, enabling the educators to have confidence in the value of data use for improving student achievement (Katz, Sutherland, & Earl, 2002).

Leadership is essential to develop a culture that supports data use (Herman & Gribbons, 2001; Jandris, 2002; Mason, 2001). Marshalling the school's community to a collective sense of purpose about improving student learning, accepting that data use can and will improve learning, aligning data use to school planning and decision-making processes, and creating time for data analysis are key elements of leadership in creating a culture for data use. While school administrators will be pivotal in shaping the culture, leadership does not reside solely with them. Schools can increase leadership capacity by developing the data use expertise of teachers who can provide readily available and site-specific assistance to their colleagues (Feiler, Heritage, & Gallimore, 2000).

Conclusion

No reader of this chapter can fail to be impressed by the magnitude of the task before us if education is truly to become an evidence-based discipline. It is clear that if schools and districts are to make effective use of data a number of far-reaching changes involving a considerable investment of economic and human capital will have to be made.

First, and perhaps least challenging, is the investment in hardware, software, and "pump-priming" data input that will be required before any form of integrated data-driven analysis can get underway. Second, and considerably more challenging, is the investment in human capital required to develop the assessment literacy and data analysis skills that will, ideally, reach from district to classroom level. There can be no question that this is a long-term project that will require considerable changes in in-service and, most importantly, pre-service education. Academic educators have a significant role to play in adjusting the practitioner training curriculum and culture to favor a data literate profession. Policymakers, test developers, and practitioners have an important obligation in the NCLB context, to devise, test, and implement an integrated system of assessment while also ensuring that such a system does not generate perverse incentives to focus instruction on "teaching to the test." The objective of assessment is to provide structure, rather than stricture, for professional practice. Finally, leadership is essential at every level of the system to develop a culture of evidence-based school improvement that will eventually become second nature to all practitioners, regardless of the scope of their responsibilities. Creating the conditions for effective data use is a necessary precursor to the widespread reality of data use as an engine of school improvement.

REFERENCES

Abedi, J., & Dietel, R. (2004, Winter). *Challenges in the No Child Left Behind Act for English language learners* (CRESST Policy Brief 7). Los Angeles: University of California, National Center for Research on Evaluation, Standards, and Student Testing.

Abedi, J., & Lord, C. (2001). The language factor in mathematics tests. *Applied Measurement in Education, 14,* 219–234.

American Educational Research Association (AERA). (2000, July). *AERA position statement concerning high-stakes testing in PreK-12 Education.* Retrieved August 18, 2004, from http://www.aera.net/about/policy/stakes.htm

American Educational Research Association (AERA). (2003, Spring). Standards and tests: Keeping them aligned. *Research Points, 1*(1). Retrieved from http://aera.net/uploadedfiles/Journals_and_Publications/Research_Points/RP_Spring03.pdf

American Educational Research Association, American Psychological Association, & National Council on Measurement in Education (AERA, APA, & NCME). (1999). *Standards for educational and psychological testing.* Washington, DC: American Educational Research Association.

Bailey, A.L., & Butler, F.A. (2004). Ethical considerations in the assessment of the language and content knowledge of U.S. school-age English learners. *Language Assessment Quarterly, 1*(2&3), 177–193.

Baker, E.L. (2001). Testing and assessment: A progress report. *Educational Assessment, 7*(1), 1–12.

Baker, E.L. (2003). *From usable to useful assessment knowledge: A design problem* (CSE Technical Report 612). Los Angeles: University of California, National Center for Research on Evaluation, Standards, and Student Testing.

Baker, E.L., Linn, R.L., Herman, J.L., & Koretz, D. (2002, Winter). *Standards for educational accountability systems* (CRESST Policy Brief 5). Los Angeles: University of California, National Center for Research on Evaluation, Standards, and Student Testing.

Bernhardt, V.L. (1998). *Data analysis for comprehensive schoolwide improvement.* Larchmont, NY: Eye on Education.

Black, P., Harrison, C., Lee, C., Marshall, B., & Wiliam, D. (2003). *Assessment for learning: Putting it into practice.* New York: Open University Press.

Black, P., & Wiliam, D. (1998). Assessment and classroom learning. *Assessment in Education: Principles, Policy and Practice, 5*(1), 7–73.

Black, P., & Wiliam, D. (2004). The formative purpose: Assessment must first promote learning. In M. Wilson (Ed.), *Towards coherence between classroom assessment and accountability. 103rd yearbook of the National Society for the Study of Education,* Part II (pp. 20–50). Chicago: The National Society for the Study of Education.

Cawelti, G., & Protheroe, N. (2001). *High student achievement: How six school districts changed into high-performance systems.* Arlington, VA: Educational Research Service.

Chen, E., Heritage, M., Danish, J., Choi, S., & Lee, J. (2003, August). *Evaluating the web-based quality school portfolio: Year two research report* (CSE deliverable). Los Angeles: University of California, National Center for Research on Evaluation, Standards, and Student Testing.

Chen, E., Heritage, M., La Torre, D., & Lee, J. (2005, January). *Evaluating the web-based quality school portfolio: Final Report* (CSE deliverable). Los Angeles: University of California, National Center for Research on Evaluation, Standards, and Student Testing.

Choppin, J. (2002, April). *Data use in practice: Examples from the school level.* Paper presented at the annual meeting of the American Educational Research Association, New Orleans, LA. Retrieved April 22, 2002, from http://www.wcer.wisc.edu/mps/AERA2002/data_use_in_practice.html

Cizek, G.J. (2000). Pockets of resistance in the assessment revolution. *Educational Measurement: Issues and Practices, 19*(2), 16–23.

338   DATA   USE   AND   SCHOOL   IMPROVEMENT

Cromey, A. (2000). Using student assessment data: What can we learn from schools? *Policy Issues, Issue 6.* (ERIC Document Reproduction Service ED452593).

Cross, L.H., & Frary, R.B. (1999). Hodgepodge grading: Endorsed by students and teachers alike. *Applied Measurement in Education, 12*(1), 53–72.

Doolittle, F., Herlily, F., & Snipes, J. (2002). *Foundations for success: How urban school systems improve student achievement.* New York: MDRC.

DuFour, R., & Eaker, R. (1998). *Professional learning communities at work: Best practices for enhancing student achievement.* Bloomington, IN: National Education Service.

Feiler, R., Heritage, M., & Gallimore, R. (2000, April). Teachers leading teachers. *Educational Leadership, 57*(7), 66–69.

Heritage, H.M. (2003). *Web-based training for the Quality School Portfolio: Module 3.* Los Angeles: University of California, National Center for Research on Evaluation, Standards, and Student Testing (CRESST).

Herman, J.L., Aschbacher, P.R., & Winters, L. (1992). *A practical guide to alternative assessment.* Alexandria, VA: Association for Supervision and Curriculum Development (ASCD).

Herman, J., & Gribbons, B. (2001). *Lessons learned in using data to support school inquiry and continuous improvement: Final report to the Stuart Foundation* (CSE Technical Report 535). Los Angeles: University of California, National Center for Research on Evaluation, Standards, and Student Testing.

Herman, J.L., Webb, N., & Zuniga, S. (2003). *Alignment and college admissions: The match of expectations, assessments, and educator perspectives* (CSE Technical Report 593). Los Angeles: University of California, National Center for Research on Evaluation, Standards, and Student Testing.

Jamentz, K. (2001). Beyond data-mania. *Leadership Magazine, 31*(2). Retrieved August 24, 2004, from http://www.acsa.org/publications/pub_detail.cfm?leadershipPubID=1023

Jandris, T.P. (2002). *Data-based decision-making: Essentials for principals.* Alexandria, VA: National Association of Elementary School Principals.

Katz, S., Sutherland, S., & Earl, L. (2002). Developing an evaluation habit of mind. *The Canadian Journal of Program Evaluation, 17*(2), 103–119.

Marzano, R.J. (2000). *Transforming classroom grading.* Alexandria, VA: Association for Supervision and Curriculum Development (ASCD).

Mason, S.A. (2001, Spring). Turning data into knowledge: Lessons from six Milwaukee public schools. *Using Data for Educational Decision-Making, 6*(1), 3–6.

National Research Council (NRC). (2001). *Knowing what students know: The science and design of educational assessment.* Washington, DC: National Academies Press.

No Child Left Behind Act of 2001, Pub. L. No. 107-110, 115 Stat. 1425 (2002).

No Child Left Behind. Archived information. (n.d.) Retrieved August 10, 2004, from http://www.ed.gov/nclb/overview/intro/presidentplan/proposal.pdf

Porter, A.C. (2002). Measuring the content of instruction: Uses in research and practice. *Educational Researcher, 31*(7), 3–14.

Rothman, R., Slattery, J.B., Vranek, J.L., & Resnick, L.B. (2002, May). *Benchmarking and alignment of standards and testing* (CSE Technical Report 566). Los Angeles: University of California, National Center for Research on Evaluation, Standards, and Student Testing.

Salinger, T. (2001). Assessing the literacy of young children: The case for multiple forms of evidence. In S.B. Neuman & D.K. Dickinson (Eds.), *Handbook of early literacy research* (pp. 390–418). New York: Guilford Press.

Secada, W.G. (2001, Spring). From the director: Data/decision making. *Using Data for Educational Decision-Making, 6*(1), 1–2.

Shepard, L.A. (2000). The role of assessment in a learning culture. *Educational Researcher, 29*(7), 4–14.

Shepard, L.A. (2004). Curricular coherence in assessment design. In M. Wilson (Ed.), *Towards coherence between classroom assessment and accountability. 103rd yearbook of the*

National Society for the Study of Education, Part II (pp. 239–249). Chicago: National Society for the Study of Education.

Snipes, J., Doolittle, F., & Herlihy, C. (2002). *Foundations for success: Case studies of how urban school systems improve student achievement.* Washington, DC: Council of the Great City Schools. Retrieved January 18, 2005, from http://www.cgcs.org/pdfs/Foundations.pdf

Stecher, B.M., & Barron, S. (2002). Unintended consequences of test-based accountability when testing in "milepost" grades. *Educational Assessment, 7*(4), 259–282.

Stecher, B.M., & Hamilton, L.S. (2002). Putting theory to the test: Systems of "educational accountability" should be held accountable. *RAND Review, 26*(1), 17–23.

Stiggins, R.J. (2002, June). Assessment crisis: The absence of assessment for learning. *Phi Delta Kappan, 83*(10), 758–765. Retrieved August 25, 2004, from http://www.pdkintl.org/kappan/k0206sti.htm

Teddlie, C., & Reynolds, D. (2000). *The international handbook of school effectiveness research.* London: Falmer.

Thorn, C.A. (2001, November 19). Knowledge management for educational information systems: What is the state of the field? *Education Policy Analysis Archives, 9*(47). Retrieved August 25, 2004, from http://epaa.asu.edu/epaa/v9n47/

Thorndike, E.L. (1922). *Intelligence tests and their use: The nature, history, and general principles of intelligence testing. The twenty-first yearbook of the National Society for the Study of Education*, Part I (pp. 1–9). Bloomington, IL: Public School Publishing Company.

Tognieri, W., & Anderson, S.E. (2003). *Beyond islands of excellence: What districts can do to improve instruction and achievement in all schools.* Washington, DC: Learning First Alliance. Retrieved from http://www.learningfirst.org/publications/districts/

Wayman, J.C., Stringfield, S., & Yakimowski, M. (2004). *Software enabling school improvement through analysis of student data* (Report 67). Baltimore, MD: Johns Hopkins University, Center for Research on the Education of Students Placed at Risk (CRESPAR).

Webb, N.L. (1997). Determining alignment of expectations and assessments in mathematics and science education. *NISE Brief, 1*(2). Retrieved from http://www.wcer.wisc.edu/nise/Publications/Briefs/Vol_1_No_2/

Webb, N.L. (1999). *Alignment of science and mathematics standards and assessments in four states.* (Research Monograph 18). Madison: University of Wisconsin-Madison, National Institute for Science Education.

Wilson, M. (Ed.) (2004). *Towards coherence between classroom assessment and accountability: 103rd yearbook of the National Society for the Study of Education*, Part II (pp. 1–19). Chicago: National Society for the Study of Education.

CHAPTER 14

Getting Things Right at the Classroom Level

JEROME M. SHAW

The titular focus of this volume is accountability testing. In addressing this topic, many chapters focus on standardized tests of student achievement and macro-level issues such as policy statements and large-scale assessment systems. In this chapter, I approach the theme from a more micro level and offer a response to the question, "What can be done to get assessment right at the classroom level?" My answer refers back to accountability issues by considering that class of assessments most commonly used for such a purpose, herein referred to as external assessments. Whether labeled as large-scale or high-stakes, external assessments enter the classroom most often during annual "testing windows" that temporarily disrupt the flow of instruction. In contrast, curriculum-specific or classroom-based assessments—which I refer to as internal assessments—are part and parcel of, and in some cases indistinguishable from, everyday instruction, which they often inform and guide. Both internal and external assessments play significant roles in the teaching and learning that happens in classrooms.

My purpose for this chapter is to advocate for complementary roles for internal and external assessments. I begin this discussion by presenting two guiding principles that I consider essential to the idea of "getting it right at the classroom level." Next, I briefly present an organizing framework for looking at various components of the assessment process. I then apply that framework to a focused set of assessment practices, discussing contributions from internal and external assessment practices in relation to the guiding principles. To close the chapter, I summarize my remarks vis-à-vis the guiding principles and point to areas in need of future development.

Jerome M. Shaw is Assistant Professor of Education at the University of California, Santa Cruz.

Guiding Principles

Two fundamental principles guide my discussion of assessment: assessment for learning and assessment for equity. As might be inferred from the phrasing, the former has to do with achieving subject matter outcomes while the latter relates to issues of fairness. The first principle invites the question, "To what extent does assessment contribute to and not impede *student learning in individual classrooms*?" The second principle asks, "To what extent does assessment contribute to and not impede *learning for all individual students*?" I discuss each of these principles more fully in the next two sections.

Assessment for Learning

I assess [students] to understand how they see the material we are covering, where my teaching has fallen slack, to understand their own pathways to mastering the material, identify common misconceptions and where these arise in the teaching/inquiry process to improve curriculum.
— Middle school teacher, 2004

The above statement was written by a teacher on a survey for an in-progress research project of mine. Her words express the guiding principle of assessment for learning, which asserts that the central and overriding purpose of assessment is to inform instruction and improve learning. This is consistent with Wolf, Bixby, Glenn, and Gardner's (1991) view of assessment as "an episode in which students and teachers might learn, through reflection and debate, about the standards of good work and the rules of evidence" (p. 52).

Stated simply, "assessments *for* learning serve to help students learn more" (Stiggins, 2002, p. 761, emphasis his). This notion resonates strongly with educational practitioners. Evidence of its widespread popularity can be found in the *Principles of Assessment for Learning* adopted by the International Confederation of Principals (Grobe & McCall, 2004). The 10 principles on the list address elements from teacher knowledge and skills to student motivation, and reflect the organization's position that assessment is at the heart of promoting children's learning.

Assessment *for* learning stands in contrast to assessment *of* learning. The latter concept is described by Stiggins (2002) as "provid[ing] evidence of achievement for public reporting" (p. 761). Given this distinction, it is tempting to characterize external assessments as assessment of learning and internal assessments as assessment for learning. In reality, this is not necessarily the case (Black & Wiliam, 2004a). How results are used is critical to assessment for learning. As Black and Wiliam (2004b) explain in their depiction of formative assessment, assessment only promotes learning when the information "is actually used to adapt the teaching work to meet learning needs" (p. 22). An essential feature of this process is providing students with feedback that clarifies discrepancies between the observed and the desired level of performance, and that offers concrete suggestions for bridging the gap. This can be done with data from both internal and external assessment, time lags in receipt of student scores notwithstanding.

Of similar importance to assessment for learning is the active participation of the student in the assessment process (Shepard, 2000; Stiggins, 2004). Such activity can take many forms, such as student-developed prompts or scoring criteria and peer- or self-assessment. As Black and Wiliam (2004b) note, "learning cannot be done *for* the student; it must be done *by* the student" (p. 34, emphasis theirs).

Assessment for Equity

This test may qualify as a [performance assessment] for native English speakers but not for [Limited English Proficient] students. This particular [performance assessment] emphasizes the ability of the students to read and follow directions in English.

—High school teacher (Shaw, 1997, p. 73)

My second guiding principle relates to the diversity inherent in the student population in the United States and the inequities within the nation's educational enterprise as a whole. Students who are nonwhite, nonnative speakers of English, female, and/or poor typically have fewer educational opportunities and less access to quality resources, and fare poorly on measures of achievement (Hodgkinson, 1985, 1999; Kozol, 1991; Lee, 2004; Oakes, 1990; Sandholtz, Ogawa, & Scribner, 2004; Spencer, Porche, & Tolman, 2003). As conveyed in the above quotation, assessments themselves have been implicated as a factor contributing to such inequities (García & Pearson, 1994; Haney, 1993; Hilliard, 2002; O'Connor, 1989; Shaw, 1997; Valdés & Figueroa, 1994).

In recognition of such realities, the principle of assessment for equity stresses the responsibility of those who design and implement assessments to rectify flaws in the process as it now exists and to take steps to avoid assessment having a role in engendering future inequities. In this regard, I draw on the work of Ladson-Billings (1994) and her notion of culturally relevant teaching, which she describes as "a peda-

SHAW343

gogy that empowers students intellectually, socially, emotionally, and politically by using cultural referents to impart knowledge, skills, and attitudes" (p. 17). As Darling-Hammond (1994, p. 17) proclaims, "if assessment is to be used to open up as many opportunities to as many students as possible, it must address a wide range of talents, a variety of life experiences, and multiple ways of knowing." Indeed, as the Committee on the Foundations of Assessment (National Research Council, 2001) recently declared,

> To improve the fairness of assessment, it must be recognized that cultural practices equip students differently to participate in the discourse structures that are often unique to testing contexts. It is all too easy to conclude that some cultural groups are deficient in academic competence, when the differences can instead be attributable to cultural variations in the ways students interpret the meaning, information demands, and activity of taking tests. (p. 32)

One response to these concerns is an approach known as culturally relevant assessment. The goal of this process is to ensure that "the assessment measures used with culturally diverse students reflect and incorporate their cultural orientations, preferences, and styles of demonstrating mastery" (Gay, 1997, p. xiv). This can be achieved, she explains, by varying assessment techniques to match the communication, presentation, and performance styles of diverse learners. Care must be taken to avoid inappropriate use of this approach, such as instances where proficiency with a particular communication style is central to the learning and, by extension, to the assessment.

The practice of culturally relevant assessment is applicable to both internal and external assessment. The inherent flexibility of internal assessment affords greater leeway to incorporate diverse cultural orientations. To do so poses a challenge for external assessments that are held to stricter standards of consistency and reliability. However, it is conceivable to think of external assessments having multiple forms that exhibit distinct cultural orientations. While not insurmountable, hurdles such as development costs and implementation logistics diminish the probability of such prospects.

In sum, assessment for learning and assessment for equity are two complementary principles, both of which are essential for getting assessment right at the classroom level. The former empowers students to increase their own learning; the latter calls for educators to ensure that assessment supports learning for all students. Such inclusive, interrelated ideals require the privileging of diverse approaches and perspectives as well as synergy across assessment practices, be they external or internal. I next present a broad framework within which to continue that discussion.

Organizing Framework

As a vehicle for navigating the maze of assessment concepts and terminology, I use a "Three-D Framework": design, delivery, and decisions. As described below, these dimensions refer to typical elements in the assessment process, such as developing an assessment and scoring student responses. While the dimensions are presented in what may be presumed to be chronological order, their actual instantiation is more fluid and iterative than linear.

Design

Included within this dimension are elements dealing with assessment development. Key questions to be addressed with respect to design include: Why are we assessing—for what purpose? What are we assessing—knowledge, skills, aptitude? How are we assessing—what method or techniques are we using and why? Decisions made during the design process may also relate to how student responses will be scored.

Delivery

This dimension includes considerations related to administering an assessment. In other words, what actually happens when the assessment as designed is put into use? Important delivery questions include: How are instructions/directions given to students—orally, in writing? What logistics need to be arranged—spacing of students or vertical blinds? What resource restrictions are there—are students allowed access to texts and notes; are there time limits?

Decisions

This dimension includes concerns ranging from deciding what score to assign student responses to determining how those scores will be shared. Included as well is the issue of what relationship the results from a particular assessment will have to other instructional decisions such as assigning grades. Key questions include: How will student responses be scored—analytically or holistically? How will scores be reported—as a single rating for a broad dimension or as a set of ratings for multiple categories? How do the scores relate to an evaluation of performance—are there cutoffs for passing or failing?

Getting It Right: Internal Meets External

In this section I use the above-described framework as an organizing structure within which to continue the discussion of getting assessment right at the classroom level. Taking them in turn, I focus my comments on a key issue within each of the framework's dimensions: standards for design, standardization for delivery, and scoring for decisions. Exploring these issues helps illustrate how internal and external assessments can complement each other in the interest of both assessment for learning and assessment for equity.

Design Considerations

Fundamentally, internal and external assessments can address assessment for learning and assessment for equity by emphasizing the same purpose: to promote learning for *all* students. A previous volume of this yearbook presents insightful and promising approaches to linking internal and external assessments around this common goal (see, e.g., Suter, 2004). As Shepard (2004) argues in that same volume, a shared curriculum is a requirement for coherence between the two assessment types.

Shepard's shared curriculum speaks to the question of "What are we assessing?" As those conversant in the parlance of current educational reform may be inclined to respond, the answer is "standards." These statements of what students should know and be able to do are not neutral; they reflect deep and nuanced philosophical and political beliefs about a given discipline, its curriculum, and instruction (Valencia & Wixson, 2001). Thus, from an assessment for learning perspective, those standards worth assessing must reflect and support current theories of learning, such as Shepard's (2000) "social-constructivist conceptual framework" (p. 65). Standards that do so stress "development of inquiry skills as well as conceptual understanding of core ideas" (Shepard, p. 42). Examples of such standards include the current constellation of national standards in the areas of mathematics (National Council of Teachers of Mathematics, 2000), science (National Research Council, 1996), and social studies (National Council for the Social Studies, 1994).

The assessment for equity principle calls for a broadening of this shared curriculum beyond the typical content standards. In keeping with a standards-based reform mindset, a logical strategy is to identify and assess opportunity to learn standards (see, e.g., Fritzberg, 2001). While acknowledging the value of such an approach I choose to further the discussion by focusing in a similar direction, but on another type of standard.

"*Cultural standards.*" Another avenue for enhancing the shared curriculum is to consider standards that refer to students' cultural realities. One such example is the *Alaska Standards for Culturally Responsive Schools* (Assembly of Alaska Native Educators [AANE], 1998). These "cultural standards" were developed to complement the state's content standards and to "provide a way for schools and communities to examine the extent to which they are attending to the educational and cultural well-being of the students in their care" (AANE, 1998, p. 1). The original set of Alaska Cultural Standards included five categories: students, educators, schools, curriculum, and communities. Subsequent documents provide related guidelines for teacher preparation and school boards (AANE, 1999, 2002).

The cultural standards for students portray "culturally knowledgeable" students as those who are well grounded in the cultural heritage and traditions of their community and who are able to build on the knowledge and skills of the local cultural community, actively participate in various cultural events, engage effectively in learning activities that are based on traditional ways of knowing and learning, and demonstrate an awareness and appreciation of the relationships and processes of interaction of all elements in the world around them (AANE, 1998). As with all of the Alaska Cultural Standards, the student standards are based on the belief that local culture should serve as the foundation for all education for a specific culture (AANE, 1998). Furthermore, the developers of these standards envision their being used in ways that suit local contexts. Speaking to the complete set of cultural standards, they state "each school, community and related organization should consider which of these standards are appropriate and which are not, and when necessary, develop additional cultural standards to accommodate local circumstances" (AANE, 1998, p. 3). Such context-specific application is distinct from use expectations for content standards, all of which are expected to be learned by all students.

Taking the "what" of assessment for learning and assessment for equity as a combination of content and cultural standards begs the question of "How do we assess them?" In general, both principles call for the use of multiple methods of assessment that tap into the variety of learning outcomes and provide access for diverse learning and communication styles. More specifically, a model that integrates both content and cultural standards is presented in the *Handbook for Culturally Responsive Science Curriculum* (Stephens, 2000), a complementary document to the Alaska Cultural Standards. This handbook includes guidelines and specific examples of how cultural standards can be incorporated into content-area instruction. It sets forth the criterion that units of instruction include assessments that "tap deeper cultural, scientific and mathematical understanding, reasoning and skill development tied to the standards" (Stephens, p. A-2).

An example of such an assessment is a mathematics task that was developed by teachers on the Navajo reservation in Arizona. The assessment involves designing a pattern for hand weaving a rug (Farr & Trumbull, 1997, p. 3). In this task students must demonstrate understanding of geometric patterns using a context that is familiar and culturally relevant. In actuality, this task is a revision of one from an external assessment in which the context was designing a floor plan using ceramic tiles. Citing the lack of tile floors in the homes of his students, one of the teachers involved in the task modification explains:

What we're trying to do is, we want to put their knowledge from home into math, to do their design with the rug instead of what they don't really have at home . . . things like that that they have seen would probably be their grandma and their mother weaving rugs.
—Elementary school teacher (Far West Laboratory, 1995)

This example illustrates the relative advantage internal assessment has over external assessment in terms of incorporating both content and cultural standards. Such locally driven variation runs counter to the demands placed on external assessments to be uniform across contexts, a point I take up in the next section. Regardless, careful consideration of content and cultural standards in assessment design is highly germane to both assessment for learning and assessment for equity.

Delivery Considerations

As with design, there is a plethora of issues to consider pertaining to delivering or administering assessments. Some basic considerations that address assessment for learning and assessment for equity include making evaluation criteria explicit to students prior to the assessment and using a variety of configurations (e.g., individual, pair, small group) during the assessment process.

My focus here is on the topic of standardization, which simply can be referred to as the practice of holding certain features constant when conducting an assessment. From a traditional psychometric perspective, the primary reason for standardization is to safeguard the quality of the data gathered during the assessment process. As Meisels, Dorfman, and Steele (1995) explain: "The quest for standardization in measurement is motivated in part by the desire to administer the same test, under the same conditions, to all examinees, in order thereby to make reliable comparisons between the responses of different students" (p. 250). Especially with respect to high-stakes assessment, issues such as legal defensibility bring concerns with standardization to the forefront (Hamilton, 2004).

Historically, standardization is closely associated with external assessments. The fact that such assessments are commonly referred to as "standardized tests" is an indication of this high degree of conceptual overlap. This association with standardization is cited as a factor contributing to the negative track record of external assessments with diverse students (García & Pearson, 1994; O'Connor, 1989). As Hilliard (2002, p. 98) explains, "The results of standardized testing favor children who speak common American English simply because these children are able to respond to questions that are couched in a familiar language based upon familiar experiences."

While many standardization practices also can be observed with internal assessments, teachers have great leeway to vary the delivery of an assessment. Such adjustments are often made in response to struggles students are experiencing with the assessment methodology as opposed to the content. Consider the scenario described by Haertel (1990, p. 16): for the classroom teacher, "standardization matters to the extent that all students should be treated equitably, but, if in the course of [a final] examination, it appeared that a question was unclear, there would be no reason not to write a clarification on the chalkboard for the benefit of the whole entire class."

As the above example shows, when the reality of student needs confronts the desire for standardization, concessions are made in the interest of fairness and accuracy of information. Such breaches of the standardization code need not interrupt an entire class; teachers may choose to respond to students who are experiencing problems on an individual basis. Such adjustments may occur during the administration of both internal and external assessments. In the latter instance, they are officially referred to as accommodations, modifications, and adaptations (Goh, 2004). While such practices are discussed in more detail elsewhere in this volume (see Abedi, chapter 8, and Pullin, chapter 9, this volume), I will provide some relevant background here.

In general, accommodations are changes made to the manner in which an assessment is given that would ordinarily be held constant for all participants. Technically speaking, testing accommodations are defined as "any action taken in response to a determination that an individual's disability requires a departure from established testing protocol" (AERA, APA, & NCME, 1999, p. 101). While this and other definitions refer to presumed student deficiencies, I prefer to consider accommodations as rational responses to student diversity without ascribing a deficit value to certain characteristics, such as level of proficiency in English.

More specifically, accommodations may effect an assessment's environment, content, or format (Goh, 2004). Typical accommodations include those that modify an assessment's setting (e.g., testing in an alternative location or using a bilingual test administrator), presentation format (e.g., providing a test in Braille or reading it orally), response format (e.g., pointing to instead of marking an intended response or writing answers in a non-English language), or timing and scheduling (e.g., allowing additional time or changing the time of day). Extending time allotments and clarifying the meaning of assessment directions and prompts represent modifications called for by students and teachers alike (Shaw, 1997).

The basic idea behind the use of accommodations is that of leveling the playing field so that all students have an equal opportunity to perform well (Tindal & Fuchs, 1999). This principle applies to assessment as well as instruction (e.g., provisions listed on individual education plans for special education students placed in mainstream classrooms). Care must be taken in the use of accommodations to keep this fairness across the board. Accommodations should reduce the gap between those students receiving the accommodation and those who do not, without providing an unfair advantage to the recipients. Researchers have documented such equitable outcomes, with specific accommodations such as linguistic modification of test questions for English language learners (see, e.g., Abedi, Lord, Hofstetter, & Baker, 2000).

While the majority of research on accommodations has been undertaken with respect to external assessment, there are some findings based on assessment practices of classroom teachers. Surveys have found that both special education and general education teachers have limited knowledge of the range of available accommodations, and report limiting their practice to those accommodations they consider easy to use, such as reading written instructions aloud to individual students (Gajria, Salend, & Hemrick, 1994; Putnam, 1992; Siskind, 1993). Furthermore, some teachers express reluctance to make use of accommodations, citing difficulty of implementation, possible threats to the academic integrity of their assessments, and fairness to other students as reasons for such omissions (Gajria, Salend, & Hemrick, 1994; Jayanthi, Epstein, Polloway, & Bursuck, 1996; Siskind, 1993).

Teacher perceptions notwithstanding, it is likewise important to consider the opinions of those most directly affected by accommodations, namely students. In comparison with teachers, there is an even greater paucity of research on students and accommodations. One survey of elementary, middle, and high school special education students found an overall preference for teachers who made use of accommodations during assessment and instruction (Vaughn, Schumm, & Kouzekanani, 1993). However, one subgroup, those students labeled as "learning disabled," viewed being treated the same as other students as preferable to receiving accommodations. This preference was expressed by middle and high school students more than elementary students.

In contrast, my own research has shown a strong preference for accommodations among high school students who are English language learners. One Vietnamese sophomore expressed her frustration with comprehending an assessment's prompts by writing, "Sometimes I don't understand what did the test want to talk?" (Shaw, 1997, p. 731). Savvy teachers understand this need and respond accordingly:

It's difficult even when I'm teaching. They don't seem sometimes to concentrate and just read it, and, if they don't understand, going back and read it. They always come to me like "I don't know." I say, "Well, it's here," and they go "Ohhh!" But, I don't know if it's, you know, it's the insecurity that you get when you're learning a second language, that you just have to ask.
—High school teacher (Shaw, 1997, p. 735)

Mainstream students are also eligible for accommodations. Take for example a left-handed student who breaks his left arm the day before a high-stakes external writing assessment. Depending on local policy and resources, he may be granted a postponement or allowed to dictate his response to a trained scriber (i.e., someone skilled at recording the student's words without unduly influencing his thinking process).

Much of the confusion and controversy over use of accommodations can be mitigated by the application of the concept of "universal design" (Johnstone, 2003; Thompson, Johnstone, & Thurlow, 2002). In contrast to the retrofitting nature of accommodations, this approach takes the diversity of the student population into consideration up front. As Thompson, Johnstone, and Thurlow explain, universally designed assessments "are designed and developed from the beginning to allow participation of the widest possible range of students, and to result in valid inferences about performance for all students who participate in the assessment. Universally designed assessments add a dimension of fairness to the testing process" (p. 5).

Thompson, Johnstone, and Thurlow's (2002) model of universal assessment design includes seven elements: inclusive assessment population; precisely defined constructs; accessible, nonbiased items; amenability to accommodations; simple, clear, and intuitive instructions and procedures; maximum readability and comprehensibility; and maximum legibility. While the fourth element, amenability to accommodations, may appear contradictory, it is a recognition of the fact that no single assessment can be designed to meet the needs of all students. Thus, the standard form of an assessment will still need to be converted to Braille for blind students. The standard form is "amenable" to conversion to Braille if, for example, keys and legends are not placed at the left or bottom of an item where they are more difficult to locate in Braille formats (Johnstone, 2003). An assessment is also considered amenable to accommodations if it has built-in accommodations that benefit all students, such as the removal of time limits.

This discussion shows that, whether as an afterthought or as an up front consideration, assessments can be delivered in ways that reflect equity and, due to increased validity of the results, support learning. Taken together, accommodations and universal design can do much in the way of alleviating educators' concerns with standardization and the delivery of assessments. Research and development efforts on these issues with external assessment can contribute to the improvement of internal assessment.

Decisions Considerations

We have been assessed in these last several decades by standardized tests, and those tests are very narrow and very confining and reduces [sic] the human being to those little numbers. Those numbers can be okay if everyone understands what they are and if in fact those numbers kind of take in a rich picture of what's happening, but people don't really understand when you get a CTBS score what that means, and it leaves out so much . . . Never have those scores ever helped me ever know my kids and what they knew and why they need to know.
—Third-grade teacher Charlotte Higuchi (North Central Regional
Educational Laboratory, 1992)

Higuchi's comments hearken back to the previously discussed concern regarding standardization. From a decision perspective, her comments raise the issues of the meaning and value of student scores. Such concerns are the focus of this section. Assuming that sufficient care has been taken with respect to design and delivery, significant issues remain regarding the interpretation of assessment data. It is perhaps this aspect of my three-D framework that deals most squarely with this yearbook's theme of use and misuse of assessment data.

In the age of No Child Left Behind, student scores on external assessments are a primary determinant of a school's status as warranting sanctions or rewards. These scores are largely from tests consisting of multiple-choice items with single correct responses. Feasibility issues such as cost and complexity often preclude the use of more inclusive formats such as performance assessment in large-scale testing, thus limiting their ability to contribute to assessment for learning.

Given the ambiguity of Higuchi's "little numbers," steps must be taken to help classroom teachers understand and make use of the information such scores do provide. As discussed elsewhere in this volume, numerous efforts are underway that engage classroom teachers in the process of "data-driven decision making" to improve student achievement (see Heritage & Yeagley, chapter 13, this volume). Such approaches specifically deal with making sense of scores from standardized tests and highlight equity issues by disaggregating data to determine achievement gaps between subgroups (see, e.g., Johnson, 2002; Love, 2001).

Internal assessments more readily encompass a wide variety of assessment methods and formats, such as oral questioning, long-term projects, and cumulative portfolios. Considering final scores in the company of detailed rubrics and anchor papers can provide both teachers and students with more detailed information on performance as well as indicate specific areas for improvement. Involving students in the process of developing and applying rubrics is a powerful way of bringing assessment for learning into practice (Stiggins, 2004).

In moving beyond machine-scorable, right/wrong assessment responses, both internal and external assessment systems are faced with the task of evaluating complex student responses. These decisions can and must be informed by knowledge of the nature of responses by diverse students, such as typical spelling patterns that may lead a rater to misinterpret or undervalue a student's writing (see, e.g., Fashola, Drum, Mayer, & Kang, 1996). Raters also need knowledge of diverse students' multiple ways of knowing and styles of demonstrating mastery (Darling-Hammond, 1994; Gay, 1997). As teachers of English language learners have recommended, to accurately score such students' responses, raters must be familiar with either students' native languages or transitional expressions of English literacy or both (Shaw, 1997).

Such knowledge has been applied to assessment in documents such as Kopriva and Sexton's (1999) *Guide to Scoring LEP [Limited English*

Proficient] Student Responses to Open-Ended Science Items. A similar guide exists for mathematics (Kopriva & Saez, 1997). These documents orient raters to the effects of cultural and linguistic influences on student responses accompanied by sample responses by students from multiple backgrounds. For example, some English language learners often substitute "becows" for "because" due to the influence of sounds in their native language (Kopriva & Sexton, 1999, p. 5). Confusion may arise in number writing due to the use of periods instead of commas to designate place value in some countries. Thus, "3.001" could alternatively be read as "three thousand and one" instead of "three and one thousandth" (Kopriva & Sexton, 1999, p. 23).

For assessment results to support both assessment for learning and assessment for equity, educators and assessors have the responsibility to be aware of such variations to avoid under- or overestimating student achievement. The publication of such guides represents an effort to bring this information to a wider audience. Although developed for use in training raters of external assessments, these guides can be readily applied to internal assessments. Classroom teachers with whom I work have found the information in the science guide to be powerful and appreciate it as a source of validation for what they know or have learned from direct experience.

Concluding Remarks

In this chapter I have used the classroom level as a frame of reference for exploring the interplay of assessments internal and external to that context. Both orientations to assessment bring different strengths to the table. Our task as educators and assessors is to draw upon their respective advantages so that all students learn more and are recognized for their divergent approaches to acquiring knowledge and representing understanding.

Such ideals are embodied in the principles of assessment for learning and assessment for equity. At the classroom level, these principles can be addressed by integrating content and cultural standards into assessment design, by judiciously using accommodations during the delivery of assessments, and by basing scoring decisions on knowledge of diverse students' culture and language. Such actions are not panaceas, nor do they address the full range of concerns with assessment practices. Furthermore, they require careful application to individual contexts.

Application of these and other approaches requires time and patience. Ongoing research and professional development can contribute to our knowledge base and support the translation of such information into practice. Stressing the dichotomy between external and internal assessment may be counterproductive. Apart from the locus of the assessment, as Black and Wiliam (2004a) point out, issues of authority, resources, interactivity, and scoring warrant serious attention. My experience with classroom teachers in assessment and professional development venues points to a more personal level. To paraphrase Hilliard (2002, p. 101), there is little need to teach teachers specific techniques for assessing particular subgroups of students. Teachers must be taught so that their total orientation toward assessment, learning, and equity represents the best that we know about those subjects. It is not the "bag of tricks" but the general attitude of a teacher that is important. This is the crux of "getting things right at the classroom level."

REFERENCES

Abedi, J., Lord, C., Hofstetter, C., & Baker, F. (2000). Impact of accommodation strategies on English language learners. *Educational Measurement: Issues and Practice*, 19(3), 16–26.

American Educational Research Association, American Psychological Association, & National Council on Measurement in Education (AERA, APA, & NCME). (1999). *Standards for educational and psychological testing*. Washington, DC: American Educational Research Association.

Assembly of Alaska Native Educators (AANE). (1998). *Alaska standards for culturally-responsive schools*. Anchorage: Alaska Native Knowledge Network.

Assembly of Alaska Native Educators (AANE). (1999). *Guidelines for preparing culturally responsive teachers for Alaska's schools*. Anchorage: Alaska Native Knowledge Network.

Assembly of Alaska Native Educators (AANE). (2002). *Guidelines for culturally-responsive school boards*. Anchorage: Alaska Native Knowledge Network.

Black, P.J., & Wiliam, D. (2004a). Classroom assessment is not (necessarily) formative assessment (and vice versa). In M. Wilson (Ed.), *Towards coherence between classroom assessment and accountability. The 103rd yearbook of the National Society for the Study of Education*, Part II (pp. 183–188). Chicago: National Society for the Study of Education.

Black, P.J., & Wiliam, D. (2004b). The formative purpose: Assessment must first promote learning. In M. Wilson (Ed.), *Towards coherence between classroom assessment and accountability. The 103rd yearbook of the National Society for the Study of Education*, Part II (pp. 20–50). Chicago: National Society for the Study of Education.

Darling-Hammond, L. (1994). Performance-based assessment and educational equity. *Harvard Educational Review*, 64(1), 5–30.

Far West Laboratory [now WestEd]. (1995). *Effective assessments: Making use of local context* (videotape). San Francisco: Author.

Farr, B.P., & Trumbull, E. (1997). *Assessment alternatives for diverse classrooms*. Norwood, MA: Christopher-Gordon.

Fashola, O.S., Drum, P.A., Mayer, R.E., & Kang, S. (1996). A cognitive theory of orthographic transitioning: Predictable errors in how Spanish-speaking children spell English words. *American Educational Research Journal*, 33(4), 825–843.

Fritzberg, G.J. (2001). From rhetoric to reality: Opportunity-to-learn standards and the integrity of American public school reform. *Teacher Education Quarterly*, 28(1), 169–188.

Gajria, M., Salend, S.J., & Hemrick, M.A. (1994). Teacher acceptability of testing modifications for mainstream students. *Learning Disabilities Research and Practice*, 9, 236–243.

García, G.E., & Pearson, P.D. (1994). Assessment and diversity. In L. Darling-Hammond (Ed.), *Review of research in education* (pp. 337–391). Washington, DC: American Educational Research Association.

Gay, G. (1997). Forward. In B.P. Farr & E. Trumbull (Eds.), *Assessment alternatives for diverse classrooms* (pp. xiii–xix). Norwood, MA: Christopher-Gordon.

Goh, D.S. (2004). *Assessment accommodations for diverse learners*. San Francisco: Allyn and Bacon.

Grobe, W.J., & McCall, D. (2004). Valid uses of student testing as part of authentic and comprehensive student assessment, school reports, and school system accountability. *California Journal of Science Education*, 5(1), 53–69.

Haertel, E.H. (1990). Form and function in assessing science education. In A.B. Champagne, B.E. Lovitts, & B.J. Calinger (Eds.), *This year in school science 1990: Assessment in the service of instruction* (pp. 15–28). Washington, DC: American Association for the Advancement of Science.

356 GETTING THINGS RIGHT: LEARNING AND EQUITY

Hamilton, L. (2004). Assessment as a policy tool. In R.E. Floden (Ed.), *Review of research in education* (pp. 69–108). Washington, DC: American Educational Research Association.

Haney, W. (1993). Testing and minorities. In L. Weiss & M. Fine (Eds.), *Beyond silenced voices: Class, race, and gender in United States schools* (pp. 45–74). Albany: State University of New York Press.

Hilliard, A.G. (2002). Language, culture, and the assessment of African American children. In L. Delpit & J.K. Dowdy (Eds.), *The skin that we speak* (pp. 87–106). New York: The New Press.

Hodgkinson, H. (1985). *All one system: Demographics of education, kindergarten through graduate school*. Washington, DC: Institute for Educational Leadership.

Hodgkinson, H. (1999). *All one system: A second look*. Washington, DC: Institute for Educational Leadership and the National Center for Public Policy and Higher Education.

Jayanthi, M., Epstein, M.H., Polloway, E.A., & Bursuck, W.D. (1996). A national survey of general education teachers' perceptions of testing adaptations. *Journal of Research of Special Education, 30*(1), 99–115.

Johnson, R. (2002). *Using data to close the achievement gap: How to measure equity in our schools*. Thousand Oaks, CA: Corwin.

Johnstone, C.J. (2003). *Improving validity of large-scale tests: Universal design and student performance* (Technical Report 37). Minneapolis, MN: National Center on Educational Outcomes. Retrieved September 15, 2004, from http://education.umn.edu/NCEO/OnlinePubs/Technical37.htm

Kopriva, R., & Saez, S. (1997). *Guide to scoring LEP student responses to open-ended mathematics items*. Washington, DC: Council of Chief State School Officers.

Kopriva, R., & Sexton, U. (1999). *Guide to scoring LEP student responses to open-ended science items*. Washington, DC: Council of Chief State School Officers.

Kozol, J. (1991). *Savage inequalities: Children in America's schools*. New York: Harper Perennial.

Ladson-Billings, G. (1994). *The dreamkeepers: Successful teachers of African American children*. San Francisco: Jossey-Bass.

Lee, J. (2004). Multiple facets of inequity in racial and ethnic achievement gaps. *Peabody Journal of Education, 79*(2), 51–73.

Love, N. (2001). *Using data/getting results: A practical guide for school improvement in mathematics and science*. Norwood, MA: Christopher-Gordon.

Meisels, S.J., Dorfman, A., & Steele, D. (1995). Equity and excellence in group-administered and performance-based assessments. In M.T. Nettles & A.L. Nettles (Eds.), *Equity and excellence in educational testing and assessment* (pp. 243–261). Boston: Kluwer Academic.

National Council for the Social Studies. (1994). *Curriculum standards for social studies*. Washington, DC: Author.

National Council of Teachers of Mathematics. (2000). *Principles and standards for school mathematics*. Reston, VA: Author.

National Research Council. (1996). *National science education standards*. Washington, DC: National Academies of Sciences.

National Research Council. (2001). *Knowing what students know: The science and design of educational assessment*. Washington, DC: National Academies Press.

North Central Regional Educational Laboratory. (1992). Interview with Charlotte Higuchi. Excerpted from *Schools that work: The research advantage*, videoconference 4. Alternatives for measuring performance. Oak Brook, IL: Author. Retrieved September 15, 2004, from http://www.ncrel.org/sdrs/areas/issues/methods/assment/as8higuc.htm

Oakes, J. (1990). *Multiplying inequalities: The effects of race, social class, and tracking on opportunities to learn math and science*. Santa Monica, CA: RAND.

O'Connor, M.C. (1989). Aspects of differential performance by minorities on standardized tests: Linguistic and sociocultural factors. In B. Gifford (Ed.), *Test policy and test performance: Education, language, and culture* (pp. 129–182). Boston: Kluwer Academic.

Putnam, M.L. (1992). The testing practices of mainstream secondary classroom teachers. *Remedial and Special Education, 13*(5), 11–21.

Sandholtz, J.H., Ogawa, R.T., & Scribner, S.P. (2004). Standards gaps: Unintended consequences of local standards-based reform. *Teachers College Record, 106*(6), 1177–1202.

Shaw, J.M. (1997). Threats to the validity of performance assessments for English language learners. *Journal of Research in Science Teaching, 34*(7), 721–743.

Shepard, L.A. (2000). *The role of classroom assessment in teaching and learning* (Technical Report 517). Los Angeles: Center for the Study of Evaluation, University of California.

Shepard, L.A. (2004). Curricular coherence in assessment design. In M. Wilson (Ed.), *Towards coherence between classroom assessment and accountability. The 103rd yearbook of the National Society for the Study of Education*, Part II (pp. 239–249). Chicago: National Society for the Study of Education.

Siskind, T.G. (1993). Teachers' knowledge about test modifications for students with disabilities. *Diagnostique, 18*(2), 145–157.

Spencer, R., Porche, M.V., & Tolman, D.L. (2003). We've come a long way—maybe: New challenges for gender equity in education. *Teachers College Record, 105*(9), 1174–1807.

Stephens, S. (2000). *Handbook for culturally responsive science curriculum*. Fairbanks: Alaska Science Consortium and the Alaska Rural Systemic Initiative.

Stiggins, R.J. (2002). Assessment crisis: The absence of assessment FOR learning. *Phi Delta Kappan*, June, 758–765.

Stiggins, R.J. (2004). *Student-involved assessment FOR learning*. Columbus, OH: Pearson Prentice Hall.

Suter, L.E. (2004). Tools for two masters: Classroom assessment and school system assessment. In M. Wilson (Ed.), *Towards coherence between classroom assessment and accountability. The 103rd yearbook of the National Society for the Study of Education*, Part II (pp. 169–182). Chicago: National Society for the Study of Education.

Thompson, S.J., Johnstone, C.J., & Thurlow, M.L. (2002). *Universal design applied to large scale assessments* (Synthesis Report 44). Minneapolis, MN: National Center on Educational Outcomes.

Tindal, G., & Fuchs, L.S. (1999). *A summary of research on test changes: An empirical basis for defining accommodations*. Lexington: University of Kentucky, Mid-South Regional Center.

Valdés, G., & Figueroa, R.A. (1994). *Bilingualism and testing: A special case of bias*. Norwood, NJ: Ablex.

Valencia, S.W., & Wixson, K.K. (2001). Inside English/language arts standards: What's in a grade? *Reading Research Quarterly, 36*, 202–217.

Vaughn, S., Schumm, J.S., & Kouzekanani, K. (1993). What do students with learning disabilities think when their general teachers make adaptations? *Journal of Learning Disabilities, 26*(8), 545–555.

Wolf, D., Bixby, J., Glenn, J., & Gardner, H. (1991). To use their minds well: Investigating new forms of student assessment. In G. Grant (Ed.), *Review of research in education* (pp. 31–74). Washington, DC: American Educational Research Association.

CHAPTER 15

Technology and Effective Assessment Systems

EVA L. BAKER

Over the last 20 years, writing about technology (and more recently about its use in assessment systems) has been a joyful experience, in part because I was usually right about how fast and how unexpected technology progress would be made. A novelty-seeker and early-adopter, I was conducting formative evaluation using mainframe systems in the 1960s (see a museum for a reference) well before the first timeshare (not a condo), mini, micro, desktop, laptop, handheld, or wearable computer interface emerged. Since we have all come to expect and adapt (to a greater or lesser extent) to rapid technological change, my technology discussion will be neither privileged nor exceptionally advanced, eliciting a far less "gee-whiz" reaction for the average reader. But it is time for rethinking assessment systems from design perspectives and the ways in which technology can improve their quality.

New technologies are, of course, pervasive in aspects of work and leisure. In many sectors they have been adopted as a means to improve performance and productivity. In education, productivity and performance have garnered significant attention, but the use of technology, especially in testing and assessment, remains marginal. This chapter will address the design of educational assessment systems as well as the potential of new technologies. Despite widespread policy enthusiasm for testing and accountability, the reader should detect no commenda-

Eva L. Baker is a Professor at the University of California, Los Angeles, Director of the UCLA Center for the Study of Evaluation, and a Co-director of the National Center for Research on Evaluation, Standards, and Student Testing (CRESST).

The work reported herein was supported under the Educational Research and Development Centers Program, PR/Award Number R305B960002, as administered by the Institute of Education Sciences (IES) and the U.S. Department of Education. The findings and opinions expressed in this report are those of the author and do not necessarily reflect the positions or policies of the National Center for Education Research, the Institute of Education Sciences (IES), or the U.S. Department of Education.

tion of testing systems as magical tools to improve education. Nor is technology promoted as a general solution to shortfalls in educational reform. Assessments, whether technological, paper-based, or people-based, may work in the short or long run, or not at all. The significant goals of educational accountability and improvement—of long-range, sustained growth of student performance—depend on a host of very specific plans, conditions, capacities, and warrants, the absence of which will not be much ameliorated by technology. To the extent possible, the ideal assessment system must be conjointly based on scientific precepts, empirical findings, and practical features. In other words, an "ideal" system should connote neither perfection nor fantasy, but rather a dependence on relevant knowledge as its foundation. Discussions of technology, on the other hand, must be in part speculative. Technology will be considered from two perspectives: (1) as it promotes efficiency; and (2) as it expands validity and improves quality. So, to the extent possible let's try to ground the formulation of assessment systems and their supporting technologies in research and considered experience.

System Design for Technology and Assessment

"Design" is a definitional part of the creation of a system; for example, user-focused design emphasizes the way in which the processes or products will be employed by target participants (Norman, 1988). Other design imperatives are esthetics, cost, and longevity. Systems design often includes identifying goals and constraints, arranging components needed to reach goals, and minimizing negative impact (Baker, 1974). In many fields, systems design always refers to a deductive, or top-down, process beginning with an assessment of need and ending with results compared with performance criteria. Such designs are usually rendered in a blueprint or other schematic, sometimes with a verbal set of specifications. These plans are intended to guide development processes, and form the basis of judging system effectiveness. An alternative approach to design, one that is inductive or bottom-up, begins not with a blueprint of desired outcomes but with the engineering of the specific example itself. The contrast is relevant to assessment design. Bottom-up design processes, then, move from the specific intervention to the more general requirement. In fact, they may produce only a single instance or product. If the developer wishes to expand the system or to create additional examples for a different audience, he or she must either induce the features that were responsible for perceived or documented efficacy, or begin anew. Whereas both versions of design processes may rely on successive trials in the field, top-down approaches feature prespecified goals and measures.

Most—but not all—applications of educational technology evolve from bottom-up design perspectives, particularly those employing advanced technology, such as tutors, exploratory learning environments, virtual reality systems, and educational games. A persuasive bottom-up design argument hinges on serendipity: With new technologies we do not know what benefits will accrue or what kinds of strategies will be invented by users. Thus, it is better not to constrain design to meet a set of preordained objectives, for the risk is missing the true benefit of the innovation. As a result, it has been generally difficult to evaluate a technology-based intervention and generalize it to a class of similar examples, since none may share common goals or R&D strategies (Baker & Herman, 2003; Clark, 1994).

Both design perspectives have their benefits. The top-down view provides potentially generalizable, principled design; once in place and vetted, it permits the creation of additional examples (e.g., in different subject matters or for different learners) at lower cost. Each intervention does not start from zero. The initial costs of such a system are higher, involving the revision of the interventions as well as the specifications. A central assumption of this analysis is that the technology platform used for design and delivery will have a sufficiently long life span so that multiple instances of it will be possible. This assumption may be entirely erroneous because of the rapid speed of innovation in technology products. Tailored to specific needs, bottom-up design may be achieved at a lower initial cost, but the approach is thought to be more costly because there are fewer reusable elements and transfer to other settings is restricted. It should be clear that assessments directed to the measurement of standards or domains of achievement are likely to be better suited to elements of top-down design (i.e., the creation of content and skill specifications and the notion of sampling from a domain illustrate top-down processes). However, in the end, both kinds of design processes will have their uses in assessment systems.

An Assessment System for Sustained Learning

Consider the assessment system in three views: its structure—that is, its features and types of information; its functions—who will use what information for what purposes; and its use of technology.

System Structure

Discussions of educational indicator systems typically array their structures in terms of context, inputs, processes, and outputs, with feedback loops intended to communicate successive revision and improvement. Assessment systems focus on the structure of information particularly related to goals and outcomes. Thus, the structure would include the elements represented in Figure 1.

This simplified system hinges on three major assumptions: that the measures will systematically connect to the standards (or goals); that the measures at the outset, during, and at the conclusion of instruction have known relationships to one another; and that the performance targets or goal states can be reached by cycles of assessment and improvement during instruction. The representation also assumes, but does not display, longitudinal coherence among grade levels in a subject field; that is, the standards from grade 3 to grade 4 increase in complexity or shift topics so that progress over time can also be measured.

System Function

To make a trustworthy determination of an individual's status with regard to a skill set or knowledge domain, three questions need to be answered: (1) What is the knowledge or content domain of the standards? (2) How will learners demonstrate their proficiency? (3) Against what standards will that proficiency be judged? First, the domain needs to be articulated so we know what inferences are to be drawn from performance. Approaches to the description of the domain to be measured have occupied researchers for a number of years. One approach, which grew from the psychology of ability testing, involved the idea that a construct along which individual performance might be arrayed

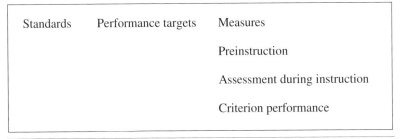

FIGURE 1
Structural elements of educational assessment systems.

existed (Cronbach & Meehl, 1955). Constructs have been described as broad (quantitative ability) or narrow, defined by rules (e.g., multiplication of three-digit numbers) or by examples (e.g., analysis of lyric poems of the complexity of Keats's "Ode on a Grecian Urn," or Emily Dickinson's " 'Hope' is the thing with feathers"). In constructs and domains (early defined by Hively, Patterson, & Page, 1968), both the content intended to be learned and the cognitive tasks intended to be mastered need to be clarified. Other ways of describing the target content of learning have been provided in descriptions of general or content objectives or standards (the current bureaucratic description; National Council on Education Standards and Testing, 1992); specific behavioral objectives (Popham, 1967); prescribed skill sets (writing essays with defined characteristics and omitting identified errors); and unique but essential skills or procedural knowledge (performing a successful laparoscopic appendectomy). Note that for every example of what should be learned and somehow measured, there is an implicit expectation that doing what is asked for (e.g., analysis of a particular ode) will prepare the student to perform subsequent tasks (analyze other examples of lyric poetry), perhaps not at the exact level of proficiency taught and measured formally, but presumably much better than if no instruction and assessment are given. Prediction, then, is often implicit in assessment performance.

The second component of measurement is how students demonstrate their achievement. For the most part, the public, teachers, and policymakers describe the ways students are measured in terms of the observable formats that students encounter. Those with preferences tout or deride multiple-choice or open-ended examinations. Of course, the range of formats is much more extensive than those examples, especially when technology options are considered. But more important, the surface characteristics of much of school learning should not be a main focus of systems. Rather it is the types of thinking skills, cognition, use of memory, and schema that are key (Chi, Feltovich, & Glaser, 1981; Chi, Glaser, & Farr, 1988; Ericsson, 2003; Marshall, 1995). We will argue, as have our predecessors (Bloom et al., 1956; Gagné & Medsker, 1996; Glaser & Klaus, 1962; Merrill & Tennyson, 1977), that the behavioral format of the response is not of prime interest (with one exception to be noted), but rather that we are concerned with the cognitive demands required by the task in relation to the content to be learned. For example, more than 50 years ago, Bloom and associates created what they called the taxonomy of educational objectives (Bloom et al., 1956), which was used to classify and develop test items to reflect increasing levels of cognitive challenge, from recall and recognition at the "knowledge" level through comprehension, analysis, synthesis, and evaluation. Gagné and Medsker (1996) provided another model. A recent update (Anderson & Krathwohl, 2001) of Bloom's work addresses knowledge types to be learned, such as declarative, procedural, and strategic knowledge. Other ways students can display their learning involve performances (e.g., sports or arts, in simulation or demonstration) that differ usually in length, steps, and knowledge, may involve physical skills (e.g., diving), and almost always are recorded and scored by other individuals or technologies (e.g., the electronic stop watch).

At the Center for Research on Evaluation, Standards, and Student Testing (CRESST), a team of researchers working over the last 15 years (Baker, 1997, 2003; Baker, Freeman, & Clayton, 1991; Niemi, 1996, 1997) have evolved a different category system to describe the what and how of performance. The model-based assessment system divides the cognitive demands likely to be encountered in educational tasks into five general families (problem solving, knowledge understanding, communication, teamwork, and metacognition; see Figure 2). Each of these families may be assessed using more than one template (a pattern that describes the testing stimulus and response situation) and ultimately through the use of smaller, reusable components called objects. For instance, mathematical problem solving might focus on the task of problem identification and require an open-ended response. Or it might involve a series of steps that culminate in selecting the correct answer to a complex problem. Thus, the CRESST models do not explicitly require exclusively open or choice responses.

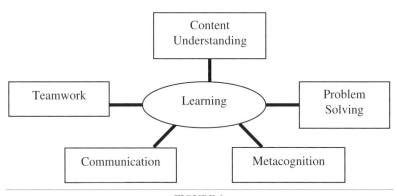

FIGURE 2
Cognitive families of model-based assessment.

The central contribution of model-based assessment is that learning, rather than aspects of measurement, is at the core of the design. The labels within each box in Figure 2 stand for the accumulated research knowledge about how students learn and exhibit performance in each of the cognitive families—communication, metacognition, problem solving, understanding content, or teamwork. Research findings for each are consolidated into principles that are intended to guide assessment practices at every point (before instruction, during instruction, after instruction; Baker, 2003). These principles, embedded in subject matter content specific to one or more standards, specify what intellectual skills and domain-specific strategies are to be used. For example, if identifying the problem is regarded as a key aspect of a problem-solving standard in mathematics or social studies, the level of complexity and task characteristics would be described (resolving conflicts in the situation, avoid surface distractions, etc.). Thus it would be these elements of cognition that connect assessments at different points in the system, in addition to the topical content identified in the standards (e.g., microecology of forests). Far less important would be the particular format in which the measurement occurs, although some tasks invariably call for open-ended or student-constructed answers. We will return to CRESST models at a later point. It is key to note that the models work to help define the standards to be measured, to guide instructional practice, and to create an additional level of relationship among standards and measures and the measures themselves. There is no claim, however, that the same exact assessment should be used to measure performance at different points in the system.

The third component of the "what" of assessment involves how the performance is valued or determined to be good enough. This stage has also been reduced to various types of classifications. One way to interpret someone's results is to compare them with the responses of other students and find the individual student's place in a distribution, described by statistical intervals (e.g., standard scores). In contrast to this normative approach, students' responses can be compared with a criterion—that is, the extent to which a student has satisfied one or more levels of performance deemed to correspond to degrees of described or enacted proficiency (e.g., novice, advanced; Glaser, 1973). Three subtle points may be understood before adopting the habit of discussing norm- versus criterion-referenced valuing of performance. The first is that individual responses, either to a particular multiple-choice question or to an essay, first need to be judged. The characteristics of distractors or wrong answers, for instance, in a multiple-choice test vastly affect the degree to which the test measures learning that has ensued from instruction, or learning and ability developed outside of school in a happenstance manner. For instance, the criteria used to judge students' essays in part must reflect the kinds of skills and content intended to be taught by the school or exemplified in the CRESST models (otherwise how could such data be used to evaluate the performance of the educational system). For an outlandish example, imagine that students were judged in their essays by their sidebar illustrations and by their use of unusual polysyllabic words, without either instruction or cueing in the test to these criteria.

A Functional Description of an Assessment System

Figure 3 displays a functional representation of an assessment system. Its components include instances of external monitoring (ovals), teacher-made measures (rounded squares), pretest decision (diamond), district-managed measures (rectangles), and the success decision (diamond, with linked reports). In addition, the system provides feedback, information to be used by teachers and administrators for the formative assessment of students, the formative evaluation of instruction, the interim evaluation of the system, and the predicted system consequences. The key to the system is that information is available to users

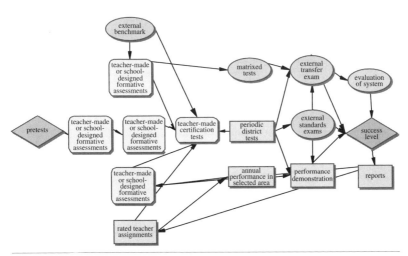

FIGURE 3
An assessment model for sustained learning.

to help them assure the general linkage of their efforts with the content and cognitive demands of the assessment system components.

The system symbolically represents the multiple instances at which teachers may assess students' growth during instruction (five blocks is an arbitrary number). The system also depicts a single instance of external monitoring during instruction (the external benchmark oval), which may be a feature of particular curricula or commercial systems. The proposed assessment model represents fundamental questions of what is assessed and for what purposes. Although it includes many of the same features of extant assessment systems, it displays clear differences. For instance, the system explicitly calls for the use of transfer exams (a student's ability to apply learned skills and content to new situations). This requirement speaks to the robustness of learning. The system also calls for matrix-sampled examinations of content not covered by the external standards examination. This element is intended as protection against unintended narrowing of the instruction to meet the format and limited content of particular tests. Matrix testing of a wide variety of content is a design feature intended to more fully represent attributes of the standards. The system also includes measures of student progress, paired with a measure of teacher action (the assignments given) to assess system alignment. Teacher assignments to students should fall within the domain of the standards and of the cognitive demands as represented in the CRESST model. The system includes student performance demonstrations to display integration of learning. Throughout the system there are feedback mechanisms for improvement. Finally, information is available for users to assess the impact of the reform or the assessment system itself on teacher and administrator capacity development, organizational learning, and attitudes.

For this system to work, it is clear that the number of standards must be limited to fewer than is usually required for any grade level or subject matter. Because all tests are flawed—that is, they are imperfect measures—we can expect some difficulty in mapping obtained performance to intentions. But when the intentions are extraordinarily ambitious and broad, as are most state standards in their scope and sometimes in their language, and testing efficiency is required, there are great gaps between the communicated goals and standards and what actually appears on the test. There are a number of ways to reduce the chasm between curriculum policy and what is measured: (1) by reducing the number and type of standards to a *significant* few that can actually be measured (see Commission on Instructionally Supportive Assessment, 2001); (2) by expanding the testing to represent the range of goals expected (a task that, if taken seriously, could not be accomplished even with multiples of the present budget and time); (3) by using articulated cognitive frameworks to bring common expectations across assessment providers (e.g., commercial and teachers); (4) by designing detailed representations of content to be sampled; or (5) by permitting assessments conducted by teachers to "count" in the overall values used for accountability. We recommend all options but the second, and to work, all need some technological support. As minimal criteria to select fewer standards for system attention, the following suggestions are offered: high cognitive demands, high transfer value (i.e., not only limited to academic use), and challenging and powerful goals that include a set of subgoals or enabling performances for use in instruction and diagnosis.

A second, yet unrepresented feature is the vertical look at the system, for the diagram shows only a cross section. Vertical coherence requires a theory or developmental model that orders learning in the face of no other credible sequence. When the subject matter has sequences for traditional reasons (e.g., chronology in history, complexity in mathematics), particular theories of developmental expertise may be used as an adjunct to situate problems and instruction (Ball & Bass, 2001; Case, 1996).

Let's address the requirement of formative assessment, based on formal teacher-made tests or less formal inquiry. Such tests are used for multiple purposes (Airasian & Jones, 1993) including grades, progress monitoring, and diagnosis. Classroom grades are usually given for assignments, including tests and projects, and summed up by the teacher at mid-term and end of year to signify student accomplishment. Grades and feedback on assignments are intended to help both teacher and student (with parental oversight) monitor progress. The assignments and tests should provide formative or diagnostic insight on the gaps or misconceptions in students' learning that need specific attention and feedback, and there is evidence that the giving of grades rather than elaborated feedback may not be effective (Black & Wiliam, 1998; Nyquist, 2003). One question is whether teacher judgments can be used regularly in accountability systems. This possibility raises the question of whether grades and external judgments inferred from mandated examinations should be congruent. If teachers' judgments are to count in an accountability system, certain requirements need to be met.

The first of these is the quality of teacher assessments, in particular, the degree to which their assessments adequately address cognitive demands and content in standards and the evidence that their estimates and scoring of student work are competent. Second, from the policy perspective, do teachers have a persistent conflict of interest such that their own views ought not to be employed in a system that has consequences for their workplace or remuneration? Third, can their assessments still function to provide instructional guidance for immediate action with students? Fourth, can teachers combine their own measures and those externally given in order to revise instruction in subsequent cycles? Competing with an approach that credits teacher assessment is one that focuses attention on the precise range of content and skills measured by the state assessment (rather than the standards). Instructionally embedded examinations are targeted to assist students to perform better only on the accountability test itself. This closed-system approach focuses on preparation for the test by giving students the opportunity to practice the types of test formats they will encounter on the external test, and by administering to students periodic, sometimes commercially or externally generated examinations in order to identify performance gaps and make predictions. At first, and perhaps second, glance, these approaches have a clear logic. Distributed practice, with feedback, is known to improve performance. Externally provided periodic examinations, sometimes termed "benchmark tests," are usually developed by the same vendor as the external test and are intended to supplement, or even to supplant, teachers' own assessments. Thus, over time, students' performance on benchmark examinations should influence the grade they receive in the course, and that grade should be more tightly reflected in the test score. This approach is well known in training the learning of specific procedures. All that remains is to assure the public that: (1) what is measured on the test is a reasonable and predictive subset of the intended standard(s); (2) test scores are subject to improvement by legitimate instructional means; (3) the system supports the performance of all students (those at the high, middle, and low parts of the performance continuum); and (4) there is compelling evidence that students can transfer their knowledge to test formats, situations, and conditions other than those exactly matching the external examination, or in other words, that students have learned and can apply and generalize their knowledge beyond the test itself. So far there is almost no evidence of this level of effectiveness.

The system, then, while acknowledging the accountability frame, directs significant attention to three areas: (1) the formative assessment or within-course assessment procedures (Shepard, 2001); (2) the identification and focus on cognitive requirements, as well as on content, as the means of developing deeper, more efficient learning (Newell, 1990; Norman, 1981); and (3) a focus on transfer of learning and generalization across conditions as the real criterion for improvement (Bassok & Holyoak, 1989; Kalyuga & Sweller, 2004).

Technology Support for Assessment Design, Development, and Use

To realize the three major features of the assessment system described above, technologies are available to reduce time and cost and to expand the quality of measured performance. In particular, certain technologies support the development of capacity of teachers and others to create assessments. Let's consider the options in sequence.

Deciding on What to Teach and Measure

Without an explicit curriculum detailing goals, subtasks, content, and sequence—a deficiency in many school districts—there is considerable difficulty in identifying the domain of content and cognitive demands, so that they can be *adequately sampled* by the components of the system. Technologies, called ontologies (Gruber, 1995), provide software that supports procedures to elicit, connect, and represent the content and cognitive demands of a domain (or set of standards). These representations can be practically vetted by content experts, teachers, and assessment designers by zooming in or out and allowing explicit estimates of proportions of content covered by particular tests, instruction, and the like—in other words, alignment. Such analyses should be conducted at the state level and used to guide the specifications of assessments to be developed by teachers or commercial partners. They are best used to select among standards and then to operationalize skills and content.

Assessment Design

After goals are selected and analyzed, the next task is assessment design. A second set of emerging technologies is intended to help assessment professionals, including teachers, to prepare good assessments. Computer-supported "authoring" systems such as principled assessment designs for inquiry (PADI) (Mislevy et al., 2002) and assessment design and delivery system (ADDS) (Baker & Niemi, 2001) can help create comparable examinations from a domain that has been made explicit in an ontology (Niemi, Chung, & Bewley, in press; Niemi, Vendlinski, & Wang, 2004; Vendlinski, Niemi, & Wang, 2005) using templates (i.e., preidentified assessment formats, such as visual stimuli or common scoring schemes). Especially if there is a desire to upgrade the quality of teacher-made tests, authoring systems offer a partial solution by providing either rules or default conditions (what happens automatically when the user exhibits no preference on a task) or by providing item pools that have been documented to match the assessment domain (a nontrivial problem). In any assessment development (creating multiple items or tasks for the same domain), one of the common bottlenecks is the difficulty in finding good examples of content or questions to use in the assessments. Browsers and other search engines are beginning to help by searching large amounts of text and other data to find examples that may be candidates for use in the task. The use of such browsers can make the development of examples for assessments (as well as the backup lessons) more tractable for a developer or teacher (see Google, Yahoo, and Amazon URLs). Assessment development can benefit from analysis based on a model of misconceptions and partial learning (Minstrell, 2000; VanLehn, 1996; VanLehn & Martin, 1998). Such analyses can help teachers figure out instruction based on individual student errors. Finally, databases can store and retrieve assessment items, searching by particular terms in order to find out what items have similar properties.

Administration of Assessments

Computers can be used to administer examinations and to expand the complexity and quality of tasks. Computers can present visual displays, including graphic and symbolic stimuli that can assist in both teaching and learning by integrating text and pictures and allowing students to convert representations to different forms (Mayer, 2005). Computers can also administer and score multiple-choice tests. Simulations of real environments for assessment supply fidelity for complex tasks. Here computers may support performance assessments (displayed in the assessment system design) by guiding students through their tasks and by recording responses in a convenient way. Simulation "authoring" systems allow individuals to design simulations and other multistep tasks, for instance, where realism is important. For example, simulations have been developed through an authoring system to measure procedural knowledge and problem solving (Munro, 2004; Munro, Johnson, Pizzini, Surmon, & Wogulis, n.d.). Students can collaborate to solve problems, and their performance as well as their teamwork roles can be monitored (O'Neil, Wang, Chung, & Herl, 2000). Student responses can be automatically tracked to determine time and attention devoted to tasks, and frequency and search patterns can be reviewed on computer- and browser-connected assessment systems using sensors that record certain predetermined or preinstrumented actions (Chen et al.,

2002). Such monitoring allows feedback to be given rapidly and accurately directly to the student or to a teacher or other monitor using a computer or handheld device (PDA or cell phone).

Scoring Performance

All assessments have to be scored, or otherwise judged, to determine the student's level of performance. Here technology is making significant inroads. Aside from simple but effective approaches, such as automated multiple-choice scoring or matching key words to short answers, software is available to judge or rate the quality of more complex behaviors, giving some potential relief for the more costly and burdensome parts of assessment practice. For example, analytical systems can estimate the relationships in real time for the distance between level of student answer and desired outcomes (Anderson, 1983; Chung, Delacruz, Dionne, & Bewley, 2003; Corbett & Anderson, 1992; Jensen, 2001; Koedinger & Anderson, 1998; Koedinger & Nathan, 2004; Mislevy, Almond, & Steinberg, 1998). Neural nets and other database approaches provide another approach to scoring and can reliably and validly classify student responses to open-ended, complex problems (Vendlinski & Stevens, 2000, 2001). In such systems, the software "learns" how to score responses from an analysis of data from a number of students. A variety of essay scoring systems are available using variations or combinations of empirical data from human raters, syntactic parsers, word analysis, and logic (Shermis & Burstein, 2003). At a minimum, students' written or oral responses can be reliably recorded and distributed for live scoring, if needed. To aid in fairness, computer systems can be developed to understand nonstandard English speech and make judgments about adequacy of performance (Hasegawa-Johnson & Alwan, 2002). Whatever the scoring approach, sophisticated statistical programs are available to project learning trajectories for different types of learners (Boscardin, 2001; Muthén, Khoo, Francis, & Boscardin, 2003). This means that these systems can identify one or more different patterns of learning over time that ultimately result in desired performance. This information can be used by teachers or by system developers.

Revising Instruction

Going in chronological order in the assessment system processes, the next task is to implement revised instruction based on the diagnosis of students' needs. While instruction is not a major topic of this chapter, its shadow is everpresent. Unfortunately, the rules for implementing effective instruction are few and far between, but technology offers a reliable way to ensure that certain tasks and content are available for interaction. Numerous systems are available that intend to offer support to teachers for improvement. Many are based on an analysis of best practices, that is, identifying schools that do far better than their cohort on state or other external assessments, and inferring differences in procedures or instructional strategy thought to account for such differences. These analyses, whether conducted at a distance or based on visits or conversations, provide hypotheses or good guesses about what will work, rather than confirmed, scientific information. However, for teachers who are in need of new ideas, such web-based resources may be helpful. In addition, networks of teachers have been developed in particular subjects or for given student groups that allow conversation, sharing of lesson plans, and other professional interaction among teachers. These networks may be a useful part of educational reform, for even if the lesson or strategy shared is not of great effectiveness, the networks offer teachers a remission from isolation and an opportunity to discuss and examine other teachers' ideas.

A Final Task, Although Repeated Throughout the Course of the System, Is Reporting the Results of Assessments

The formality of reporting varies by audience and intended use. Online software permits the collection of longitudinal student information for background, qualitative performance results, and test scores for review by students, parents, and teachers (Baker, 1999; Heritage & Lee, 2004). Group data can be disaggregated, individual students' progress across or within subjects can be examined, and teachers may amend system information with their own "grade book" and examples of student work. In particular, databases of student performance can be interrogated, arrayed, and summarized by a wide variety of variables including student background, instructional experiences, performance in allied areas, attendance, and so on. These systems require unique identification codes for students. The reports they generate may be dynamic, and available online using a variety of devices (computers, PDAs, or phones), static and printed, or distributed in e-mail or other format instantly.

Evaluating the Impact of Assessment Systems

Although we, and others, have advocated the evaluation of assessment and accountability systems (Baker & Linn, 2004; Baker, Linn, Herman, & Koretz, 2002), they are rarely assessed in a systematic way.

Rather, systems, or components thereof, are discarded because of political ideology, impatience with vendors (or the idea that vendors should rotate), technical errors, or the big new thing, for instance, the portfolio assessment wave of the late 1980s. Instead of happenstance, or more accurately, along with it, we propose measuring assessment systems themselves (Baker, 2000). Criteria for their success, in addition to feasibility, would include the following set.

Observed Increases in the Sophistication of Teacher-Made Measures

Over a period of time, one would expect teacher assessments to improve in quality and more effectively connect to standards and inform teachers about needed performance. Such studies are strategically easy to formulate but may be tactically hard to implement. One design would randomly assign assessments developed at different points in time to raters without identifying when they had been developed. Raters would judge the features of the assessments with respect to the standards (cognitive demands and content relationships or alignment). Evidence of improvement would require that raters evaluate the more recent exemplars as superior. A similar design could be applied to determine, when looking at student work, the agreed diagnostic inference to be drawn (again using raters, a rubric, and randomized blind comparisons).

Teachers' Ability to Identify and Assist Students in Acquisition and Application of Skills and Knowledge

In a similar experimental vein, teachers at different points (years) of implementation would be given the same types of student work, with designed-in errors. Teachers would identify errors and supply their suggestions for instructional follow-up. Expert raters in subject matter and pedagogy would judge the quality of the responses, again with the expectation that longer involvement in the system would result in improved instructional acuity.

Students' Acquisition of Knowledge and Skill at Faster Rates

This study simply requires comparisons by grade and subject matter of growth trajectories at different points of system implementation on both the target state assessment and a parallel measure.

Students' Ability to Transfer Learning (Standards) in Situations Other Than the Agreed-upon State Test

In our ideal assessment system, transfer examinations are a built-in component. If systems do not adopt such a recommendation, then they can examine the type and degree of transfer and generalization of performance in particular subject matters or for particular sets of standards. The procedure would be to use extant or specially designed assessments that varied item formats, setting, conditions, and particular topic emphases to determine whether the students were making appropriate inferences and applying sets of knowledge. The feasibility of this task depends on the instructional use of emerging knowledge of learning and schema acquisition.

Summary

Were there resources and intent at this point, we could provide every teacher and every student technology support to dramatically increase capacity and monitor their learning trajectories. The hard part of technology use is to avoid the fool's gold, the apparent magical properties that are the wizard behind the curtain, and to focus on what technology can do to improve sustained learning and transfer. To that end, technology investment in education is best applied to design issues (identifying problems, organizing content and cognitive requirements) and display issues (avoiding pop-ups, unneeded graphics, etc.; Mayer, 2005) and using the logical, search, and display power that technology affords. As far as monitoring and inferring understanding from every move, keystroke, or eye blink, privacy and ethical issues take precedence. Technology-managed data collection of social processes, such as beliefs and values, is also possible, but rich with potential conflict.

In the face of acknowledged difficulties, this chapter attempted to summarize key issues in the present use of and the ideal design and technology support for assessment systems. It did not discuss at length questions of validity and reliability, trusting that the reader understood their preeminence. The chapter emphasized how technologies could help with assessment design and implementation, support capacity of teachers, and improve reports. Finally, the chapter addressed how the impact of the proposed (or any) assessment system might be evaluated.

REFERENCES

Airasian, P.W., & Jones, A.M. (1993). The teacher as applied measurer: Realities of classroom measurement and assessment. *Applied Measurement in Education, 6*, 241–254.

Anderson, J. (1983). *The architecture of cognition.* Cambridge, MA: Harvard University Press.

Anderson, L.W., & Krathwohl, D.R. (Eds.) With (Airasian, P.W., Cruikshank, K.A., Mayer, R.E., Pintrich, P.R., Raths, J., & Wittrock, M.C.). (2001). *A taxonomy for learning, teaching, and assessing: A revision of Bloom's taxonomy of educational objectives.* New York: Addison Wesley Longman.

Baker, E.L. (1974). Formative evaluation of instruction. In W.J. Popham (Ed.), *Evaluation in education: Current applications* (pp. 531–585). Berkeley, CA: McCutchan. (ERIC Document Reproduction Service ED 123 239.)

Baker, E.L. (1997). Model-based performance assessment. *Theory into Practice, 36*(4), 247–254.

Baker, E.L. (1999, Summer). *Technology: Something's coming—Something good.* CRESST Policy Brief 2. Los Angeles: University of California, National Center for Research on Evaluation, Standards, and Student Testing.

Baker, E.L. (2000, May). *Watching the watchers: Standards for accountability systems congressional briefing.* Presentation at the Consortium for Policy Research in Education Congressional Briefing, Washington, DC.

Baker, E.L. (2003, Summer). Multiple measures: Toward tiered systems. *Educational Measurement: Issues & Practice, 22*(2), 13–17.

Baker, E.L., Freeman, M., & Clayton, S. (1991). Cognitive assessment of history for large-scale testing. In M.C. Wittrock & E.L. Baker (Eds.), *Testing and cognition* (pp. 131–153). Englewood Cliffs, NJ: Prentice-Hall.

Baker, E.L., & Herman, J.L. (2003). A distributed evaluation model. In G. Haertel & B. Means (Eds.), *Evaluating educational technology: Effective research designs for improving learning* (pp. 95–119). New York: Teachers College Press.

Baker, E.L., & Linn, R.L. (2004). Validity issues for accountability systems. In S. Fuhrman & R. Elmore (Eds.), *Redesigning accountability systems for education* (pp. 47–72). New York: Teachers College Press.

Baker, E.L., Linn, R.L., Herman, J.L., & Koretz, D. (2002, Winter). *Standards for educational accountability systems.* CRESST Policy Brief 5. Los Angeles: University of California, National Center for Research on Evaluation, Standards, and Student Testing.

Baker, E.L., & Niemi, D. (2001). *Assessments to support the transition to complex learning in science (Proposal to the National Science Foundation Interagency Education Research Initiative).* Los Angeles: University of California, National Center for Research on Evaluation, Standards, and Student Testing (CRESST).

Ball, D.L., & Bass, H. (2001). What mathematical knowledge is entailed in teaching children to reason mathematically? In National Research Council, *Knowing and learning mathematics for teaching: Proceedings of a workshop* (pp. 26–34). Washington, DC: National Academies Press. Retrieved October 3, 2004, from http://books.nap.edu/catalog/10050.html

Bassok, M., & Holyoak, K.J. (1989). Transfer of domain-specific problem solving procedures. *Journal of Experimental Psychology: Learning, Memory, and Cognition, 16*, 522–533.

Black, P., & Wiliam, D. (1998). Assessment and classroom learning. *Assessment in Education: Principles, Policy, and Practice, 5*(1), 7–74.

Bloom, B.S. (Ed.) With (Engelhart, M.D., Furst, E.J., Hill, W.H., & Krathwohl, D.R.). (1956). *Taxonomy of educational objectives: The classification of education goals. Handbook 1: Cognitive domain.* New York: David Mckay.

Boscardin, C.K. (2001). *Strategies for early identification of students with reading difficulties using growth mixture models.* Unpublished doctoral dissertation, University of California, Los Angeles.

Case, R. (1996). Reconceptualizing the nature of children's conceptual structures and their development in middle childhood. In R. Case & Y. Okamoto (Eds.), *The role of central conceptual structures in the development of children's thought. Monographs of the Society for Research in Child Development, Serial 246, 61*(1–2), 1–26.

Chen, A., Muntz, R.R., Yuen, S., Locher, I., Park, S.I., & Srivastava, M.B. (2002, April–June). A support infrastructure for the Smart Kindergarten. *IEEE Pervasive Computing, 1*(2), 49–57.

Chi, M.T.H., Feltovich, P., & Glaser, R. (1981). Categorization and representation of physics problems by experts and novices. *Cognitive Science, 5,* 121–152.

Chi, M.T.H., Glaser, R., & Farr, M. (Eds.). (1988). *The nature of expertise.* Hillsdale, NJ: Erlbaum.

Chung, G.K.W.K., Delacruz, G.C., Dionne, G.B., & Bewley, W.L. (2003). Linking assessment and instruction using ontologies. *Proceedings of the I/ITSEC, 25,* 1811–1822.

Clark, R.E. (1994). Assessment of distance learning technology. In E.L. Baker & H.F. O'Neil, Jr. (Eds.), *Technology assessment in education and training* (pp. 63–78). Hillsdale, NJ: Erlbaum.

Commission on Instructionally Supportive Assessment. (2001, October). *Building tests to support instruction and accountability: A guide for policymakers.* Retrieved November 3, 2004, from http://www.ioxassessment.com/catalog/pdfdownloads/BuildingTestsTo-Support.pdf

Corbett, A.T., & Anderson, J.R. (1992). LISP intelligent tutoring system: Research in skill acquisition. In J.H. Larkin & R.W. Chabay (Eds.), *Computer assisted instruction and intelligent tutoring systems: Shared goals and complementary approaches* (pp. 73–109). Hillsdale, NJ: Erlbaum.

Cronbach, L.J., & Meehl, P.E. (1955). Construct validity in psychological tests. *Psychological Bulletin, 52,* 281–302.

Ericsson, K.A. (2003). The search for general abilities and basic capacities: Theoretical implications from the modifiability and complexity of mechanisms mediating expert performance. In R.J. Sternberg & E.L. Grigorenko (Eds.), *Perspectives on the psychology of abilities, competencies, and expertise* (pp. 93–125). Cambridge: Cambridge University Press.

Gagné, R.M., & Medsker, K.L. (1996). *The conditions of learning. Training applications.* Fort Worth, TX: Harcourt Brace College Publishers.

Glaser, R. (1973). Educational psychology and education. *American Psychologist, 23*(7), 557–566.

Glaser, R., & Klaus, D.J. (1962). Proficiency measurement: Assessing human performance. In R.M. Gagne (Ed.), *Psychological principles in system development* (pp. 419–474). New York: Holt, Rinehart & Winston.

Gruber, T.R. (1995). Toward principles for the design of ontologies used for knowledge sharing. *International Journal of Human-Computer Studies, 43,* 907–928.

Hasegawa-Johnson, M., & Alwan, A. (2002). Speech coding: Fundamentals and applications. In J. Proakis (Ed.), *Wiley encyclopedia of telecommunications* (Vol. 5, pp. 2340–2359). New York: Wiley & Sons.

Heritage, H.M., & Lee, J.J. (2004, March). *The Quality School Portfolio: A new web-based system to support data informed decisions.* Presentation at the Secretary's (U.S. Department of Education) No Child Left Behind Leadership Summit, St. Louis, MO.

Hively, W., Patterson, H.L., & Page, S.H. (1968). A "universe-defined" system of arithmetic achievement tests. *Journal of Educational Measurement, 5,* 275–290.

Jensen, F.V. (2001). *Bayesian networks and decision graphs.* New York: Springer-Verlag.

Kalyuga, S., & Sweller, J. (2004). Measuring knowledge to optimize cognitive load factors during instruction. *Journal of Educational Psychology, 96,* 558–568.

Koedinger, K.R., & Anderson, J.R. (1998). Illustrating principled design: The early evolution of a cognitive tutor for algebra symbolization. *Interactive Learning Environments, 5,* 161–180.

Koedinger, K.R., & Nathan, M.J. (2004). The real story behind story problems: Effects of representations on quantitative reasoning. *Journal of Learning Sciences, 13*(2), 129–164.

Marshall, S.P. (1995). *Schemas in problem solving.* Cambridge, MA: Cambridge University Press.

Mayer, R.E. (2005). Multimedia strategies. In H.F. O'Neil (Ed.), *What works in distance learning: Guidelines* (pp. 7–23). Greenwich, CT: Information Age Publishing Inc.

Merrill, M.D., & Tennyson, R.D. (1977). *Teaching concepts: An instructional design guide.* Englewood Cliffs, NJ: Educational Technology Publications.

Minstrell, J. (2000). Student thinking and related assessment: Creating a facet-based learning environment. In Committee on the Evaluation of National and State Assessments of Educational Progress, N.S. Raju, J.W. Pellegrino, M.W. Bertenthal, K.J. Mitchell, & L.R. Jones (Eds.), *Commission on Behavioral and Social Sciences and Education, Grading the nation's report card: Research from the evaluation of NAEP* (pp. 44–73). Washington, DC: National Academies Press.

Mislevy, R.J., Almond, R.G., & Steinberg, L. (1998). *A note on knowledge-based model construction in educational assessment.* CSE Technical Report 480. Los Angeles: University of California, National Center for Research on Evaluation, Standards, and Student Testing (CRESST).

Mislevy, R.J., Chudowsky, N., Draney, K., Fried, R., Gaffney, T., Haertel, G., Hafter, A., Hamel, L., Kennedy, C., Long, K., Morrison, A.L., Murphy, R., Pena, P., Quellmalz, E., Rosenquist, A., Songer, N.B., Schank, P., Wenk, A., & Wilson, M. (2003). *Design patterns for assessing science inquiry. PADI. Principled Assessment Designs for Inquiry (PADI Tech. Rep. 1).* Menlo Park, CA: SRI International. Retrieved July 8, 2003, from http://padi.sri.com/downloads/TR1_Design_Patterns.pdf

Munro, A. (2004). *Learning by doing in the context of distance learning about complex decisions.* Presentation in the Technology Research Symposium Beyond Web Pages: Advanced Distributed Learning for Complex Training Environments at the annual meeting of the American Educational Research Association, San Diego.

Munro, A., Johnson, M., Pizzini, Q., Surmon, D., & Wogulis, J. (n.d.). *A tool for building simulation-based learning environments.* Retrieved January 6, 2005, from http://btl.usc.edu/rides/shortPapers/bldsim.html

Muthén, B., Khoo, S.T., Francis, D.J., & Boscardin, C.K. (2003). Analysis of reading skills development from kindergarten through first grade: An application of growth mixture modeling to sequential processes. In S.P. Reise & N. Duan (Eds.), *Multilevel modeling: Methodological advances, issues and applications* (pp. 71–89). Mahwah, NJ: Erlbaum.

National Council on Education Standards and Testing. (1992). *Raising standards for American education. A report to Congress, the Secretary of Education, the National Education Goals Panel, and the American people.* Washington, DC: U.S. Government Printing Office.

Newell, A. (1990). *Unified theories of cognition.* Cambridge, MA: Harvard University Press.

Niemi, D. (1996). Assessing conceptual understanding in mathematics: Representations, problem solutions, justifications, and explanations. *Journal of Educational Research, 89*, 351–363.

Niemi, D. (1997). Cognitive science, expert-novice research, and performance assessment. *Theory into Practice, 36*(4), 239–246.

Niemi, D., Chung, G.K.W.K., & Bewley, W.L. (in press). Assessment design using ontologies: Linking assessment, content, and cognitive demands. *Educational Assessment.*

Niemi, D., Vendlinski, T., & Wang, J. (2004, November) *Computer guided assessment design: Assessing students' higher order thinking.* Paper presented at the California Educational Research Association (CERA) 86th Annual Conference, Pasadena, CA.

Norman, D.A. (1981). Twelve issues for cognitive science. In D.A. Norman (Ed.), *Perspectives on cognitive science* (pp. 265–295). Norwood, NJ: Ablex.

Norman, D.A. (1988). *The design of everyday things*. New York: Doubleday.

Nyquist, J.B. (2003, December). *The benefits of reconstructing feedback as a larger system of formative assessment: A meta-analysis.* Unpublished master's thesis, Vanderbilt University, Nashville, TN.

O'Neil, H.F., Jr., Wang, S.L., Chung, G.K.W.K., & Herl, H.E. (2000). Assessment of teamwork skills using computer-based teamwork simulations. In H.F. O'Neil, Jr. & D.H. Andrews (Eds.), *Aircrew training and assessment* (pp. 245–276). Mahwah, NJ: Erlbaum.

Popham, W.J. (1967). *Development of a performance test of teaching proficiency.* Los Angeles: University of California.

Shepard, L.A. (2001). The role of classroom assessment in teaching and learning. In V. Richardson (Ed.), *Handbook of research on teaching* (4th ed., pp. 1066–1101). Washington, DC: AERA.

Shermis, M.D., & Burstein, J. (2003). *Automated essay scoring: A cross-disciplinary perspective.* Hillsdale, NJ: Erlbaum.

VanLehn, K. (1996). Cognitive skill acquisition. In J. Spence, J. Darly, & D.J. Foss (Eds.), *Annual review of psychology* (Vol. 47, pp. 513–539). Palo Alto, CA: Annual Reviews.

VanLehn, K., & Martin, J. (1998). Evaluation of an assessment system based on Bayesian student modeling. *International Journal of Artificial Intelligence in Education, 8*, 179–221.

Vendlinski, T., Niemi, D., & Wang, J. (2005). *Learning assessment by designing assessments: An on-line formative assessment design tool.* Paper presented at the Society for Information Technology and Teacher Education (SITE) 16th International Conference, Phoenix, AZ.

Vendlinski, T., & Stevens, R. (2000). The use of artificial neural nets (ANN) to help evaluate student problem solving strategies. In B. Fishman & S. O'Conner-Divelbliss (Eds.), *Proceedings of the fourth international conference of the learning sciences* (pp. 108–114). Mahwah, NJ: Erlbaum.

Vendlinski, T., & Stevens, R. (2001). Assessing student problem-solving skills with complex computer-based tasks. *The Journal of Technology, Learning and Assessment, 1*(3). Retrieved from http://www.jtla.org

Name Index

Note: This index includes names associated with a theory, concept, program, experiment or other work with a substantive description. It does not include names given in examples or passing references.

Subject Index